THE CLASSICAL WORLD
BIBLIOGRAPHY OF
VERGIL ·

Garland Reference Library
of the Humanities

Volume 96

THE CLASSICAL WORLD
BIBLIOGRAPHIES

Greek Drama and Poetry

Greek and Roman History

Philosophy, Religion, and Rhetoric

Vergil

Roman Drama and Poetry and Ancient Fiction

THE CLASSICAL WORLD BIBLIOGRAPHY OF VERGIL

with a new Introduction by
Walter Donlan

GARLAND PUBLISHING, INC.
New York · London
1978

Library of Congress Cataloging in Publication Data
Main entry under title:
The Classical world bibliography of Vergil.

(Garland reference library of the humanities; v. 96)
1. Vergilius Maro, Publius—Bibliography.
Z8932.C58   1978   [PA6825]   016.873'01   76-52514
ISBN 0-8240-9877-3

Printed in the United States of America

CONTENTS

INTRODUCTION

In an "Editorial Announcement" by the late E. A. Robinson at the close of his first year as Editor of *The Classical Weekly*, the inauguration of a "Survey series" was announced. That same issue (May 1953) saw the first of these "enterprises," E. H. Haight's brief "Notes on Recent Publications About the Ancient Novel."

The surveys proved to be an immediate and lasting success; since that modest beginning CW has published sixty-six bibliographical surveys, the bulk of which appear in this series, collected for the first time. The very success of the CW bibliographies (and the dislocations of time) have made them scarce; offprints, especially of the earlier surveys, are now rare items.

Professor Robinson's initial announcement is worth quoting at some length:

> In the Survey series, we plan to review as comprehensively as possible and—to this extent modifying certain assumptions underlying some European undertakings of a similar nature—with conscious attention to present day conditions of teaching and research in our own schools, colleges, and universities the recent literature on the principal classical authors and fields, the status of classical study in this country and Canada, and recent developments in the teaching of our subject. On the scholarly side, the need for a regular service of this kind has been obvious since the demise of Bursian and the *Year's Work*; on the practical and pedagogical side, nothing, we believe, has been undertaken on this scale since the Classical Investigation nearly thirty years ago; the attempt to integrate the efforts of workers in many different fields is perhaps original.

Of the many contributions made by Robinson as Editor of CW, none has been of such lasting value to the classical profession, especially in the English-speaking world. At the time CW began to commission the surveys, two valuable series of critical bibliographies had just ceased publication—Bursian's *Jahresbericht* (1873-1945) and *Year's Work in Classical Studies* (1907-1947). New European publications such as *Anzeiger* and *Lustrum* helped to fill the vacuum, but at a time when American graduate schools were beginning to expand their programs and to graduate a new postwar generation of classicists and the first rumblings of the publication explosion had started, no current English-language bibliographical survey-series existed. What was needed, and envisioned, was a critical series, in English, by distinguished North American scholars, directed towards the particular requirements of research and pedagogy in the United States and Canada.

As books and articles began to proliferate, and as undergraduate as well as graduate programs in the Classics swelled in number, teachers found their way through the treacherous scholarly swamps eased. The surveys could be used to plan new courses, to select texts and commentaries, to become familiar with the scholarship on authors or genres often being taught for the first time; students could be provided easily accessible and readable bibliographies never available before. Predictably, by the time Robinson retired from the editorship in 1968, the CW surveys had become indispensable research and teaching tools, not only here but abroad.

With the printing of the second offering, G. M. Kirkwood's "A Survey of Recent Publications Concerning Classical Greek Lyric Poetry," in CW 47 (1953), a standard was set which has marked the series ever since: a comprehensive, though not exhaustive, listing, summary, and analysis of major books and articles covering a discrete period of time. In volume 56 (1962-63) a "second series" was begun; it updated the earlier reports, ensuring chronological continuity. As time went on, and as teachers and students became accustomed to turning automatically to the surveys, the articles became longer and more comprehensive, the format became more uniform, and new types of surveys, reflecting recent developments in scholarly perspectives, came into being. By 1960 the increasing complexities of commissioning, refereeing, editing, and checking required the services of Survey Editors—first W. M. Calder III and later (and currently) A. G. McKay.

The collection in reprint of more than two decades of CW bibliographical surveys affords students and researchers a historical retrospective of classical scholarship going back to the thirties and forties. Since they are arranged topically, each of the five volumes gives a continuing overview of modern research in the principal areas of classical studies. If the compilation of such a collection required a justification, one need only glance at the ever-fattening volumes of *L'Année Philologique* to realize the need for systematic and expert guidance to the classical scholarship of the recent past.

No Roman author has inspired more critical evaluation than Vergil; from the moment of his death to today, legions of writers, captured or confounded by his charm and power, have sought to explicate the complexities of the man, the poet, and the thinker, whose rich legacy is still one of the glories of the artistic achievement of Western man. To comprehend even in outline the movements and shifts of scholarly opinion on Vergil is an arduous task for students of Vergil; to venture into the jungle itself of Vergilian studies is to risk losing one's way, to become confused by the huge and exotic mass of the rich (or rank) *flora* of books, monographs, articles, reviews, notes, or to sink into the quagmires of this or that Vergilian "problem."

Readers of CW and consulters of this volume are fortunate in their steady and trustworthy guides to Vergilian scholarship in the three surveys reprinted here, which span thirty-four years of modern work on Vergil (1940 through 1973).

For his 1958 survey G. E. Duckworth chose 1940 as the *terminus a quo*, since that was the publication date of G. Mambelli's massive two-volume bibliography of Vergilian scholarship in the twentieth century, as well as the most recent of Duckworth's own lists in

Vergilius. Duckworth noted that in the seventeen years covered by this survey approximately 1,300 books and articles on Vergil had been published, hence "only the most significant of these can be discussed in the space available." (Among the items omitted by Duckworth are most school editions, many of which are treated in the bibliographical handlist included in this volume.) Duckworth lists bibliographical items under thirteen main headings and twenty subheadings—a scheme that he retained in his second survey and which A. G. McKay followed essentially in his 1974 article. Users of this volume will thus be able to check the items of three surveys following a single plan. Unfortunately, Duckworth's initial survey did not have a table of contents, and readers are advised to refer to his second article for the topical outline, which treats all aspects of the poet's life and work in systematic order. Sections on bibliography and editions and translations in general are followed by coverage of the corpus: *Appendix Vergiliana, Eclogues, Georgics, Aeneid*, with appropriate subheadings devoted to individual poems, books of the *Aeneid*, and special topics. Specific aspects of Vergil's life and works are treated next (e.g., religion and philosophy, Rome and Augustus), succeeded by coverage of style, language, meter, interpretation and textual criticism, earlier writers, ancient authors after Vergil, manuscripts, *Nachleben*. There is a useful final section on Vergil societies.

Within these major and minor headings, Duckworth, in his two surveys (1940-1956, 1957-1963), lists individual studies, with brief summaries and evaluations; copious footnotes are appended, in which, among other things, reviews of books are noted.

With equal ease A. G. McKay guides researchers through the welter of modern Vergilian scholarship. His 1974 survey of a decade of Vergil studies (1964 through 1973) is a model of scholarly surveys in terms of clarity, readability, and ease of consultation. McKay, the current Surveys Editor for *The Classical World*, lists all items under topical headings and follows with a narrative summary and assessment of individually numbered books and articles, an arrangement which permits frequent cross-reference. Some 1,344 books, monographs, and articles are listed, and reviews are noted in the citations; the categories are those established by Duckworth. Two minor deviations from these, which serve to illustrate changes in scholarly fashion, are the elimination by McKay of a special subsection on the Fourth Eclogue and the addition of a section on computer studies.

The three surveys on current scholarly work on Vergil are complemented by a fourth, prepared by J. E. Heffner (with M. Hammond and M.C.J. Putnam), which lists works useful to teachers and students in secondary schools. This bibliographical handlist has "the aim of broadening the study of the *Aeneid* in the high school Latin curriculum . . . by suggesting both collateral reading for students in high school and works of reference helpful to teachers. . . ." The handlist offers titles of books up to 1966 under a variety of headings; a table of contents and an Index of Books Discussed make reference easy. Teachers of Vergil at the college level will also find this survey useful, especially since it lists school texts and editions omitted in the surveys of Duckworth and McKay.

Walter Donlan

Recent Work
on Vergil
(1940-1956)

George E. Duckworth

from Volume 51, pp. 89-92, 116-117, 123-128, 151-159, 185-193, 228-235

RECENT WORK ON VERGIL (1940-1956)

1. Preliminary Remarks. Bibliography

The appropriate *terminus a quo* for a survey of the more important books and articles on Vergil is 1940, as that year saw the publication of Mambelli's bibliography on twentieth century Vergilian scholarship.[1] Much attention has been devoted to Vergil since 1939 by scholars both here and abroad. All phases of Vergilian studies have been treated, from the *Appendix* to Vergil's *Fortleben*, with particular emphasis on the *Eclogues* (especially the Fourth) and the *Aeneid*, its structure, the symbolism of the work, and its significance as a poem of Augustan Rome. In 1955 appeared the monumental Pauly-Wissowa article (VIIIA, cols. 1021ff.) on Vergil by K. Büchner, also published separately under the title *P. Vergilius Maro, Der Dichter der Römer* (Stuttgart 1956).[2] This work of 471 closely-packed columns will, in spite of many omissions, long remain the standard source of information on modern Vergilian scholarship.

The total number of books and articles in the seventeen-year period under consideration is approximately 1300, and only the most significant of these can be discussed in the space available. I regret that many books and articles will be passed over with a brief mention and that numerous others must be omitted entirely.[3] It is hoped, however, that the survey will be helpful to all teachers of Vergil and will furnish Vergilian scholars with a useful summary of important new work as a foundation for further investigation.

Several useful bibliographical articles have appeared in recent years; see K. Büchner—J. B. Hofmann, *Lateinische Literatur und Sprache in der Forschung seit 1937* (Bern 1951; = *Wissenschaftliche Forschungsberichte*, Bd. 6) 110-126; H. Fuchs, "Rückschau und Ausblick im Arbeitsbereich der lateinischen Philologie," *MH* 4 (1947) 181, 183; V. Pöschl, "Forschungsbericht über Vergil," *AAHG* 3 (1950) 69-80, 6 (1953) 1-14; W. F. J. Knight, "New Principles in Vergilian Commentary," *Humanitas* 3 (1950-51) 161-174; F. Eggerding, "Ueber das Virgilbild im heutigen Frankreich," *Gymnasium* 61 (1954) 555-568; G. Radke, "Fachbericht: Vergil (Auswahl)," *Gymnasium* 64 (1957) 161-192.

The new edition of *J. A. Nairn's Classical Hand-List*, ed. B. H. Blackwell, Ltd. (3d ed., Oxford 1953) 69-71, names several books on Vergil since 1939, but omits others; T. E. Wright's chapter on the Augustan poets in M. Platnauer (ed.), *Fifty Years of Classical Scholarship* (Oxford 1954) is in general unsatisfactory and contains almost nothing about work on Vergil since 1939 (cf. B. Otis, *CW* 49 [1955-56] 154f.); likewise, the bibliography appended to C. Bailey's article on "Virgil" in the *Oxford Classical Dictionary* (1949) contains only one item after 1939: Rose's *The Eclogues of Vergil* (1942).

2. Editions and Translations[4]

Of the many new editions of the works of Vergil which have appeared since 1939, the majority by far has been published with notes for use in schools, especially in Italy and Great Britain. A few are of a more scholarly nature.

Editions of the *Eclogues* include those by O. Tescari, *Virgilio, Le Bucoliche* (Milano 1947), F. Giancotti, *Il libro delle Bucoliche* (Roma 1952), E. de Saint-Denis, *Virgile, Bucoliques* (2d ed., Paris 1949),[5] and L. Herrmann, *Virgile, Bucoliques* (Bruxelles 1952); all four have, in addition to the text, an introduction, a brief critical apparatus, and a translation.[6]

The editions by L. Castiglioni and R. Sabbadini (see note 6 ad fin.), J. Mehler, *Bucolica et Georgica* (Leiden 1950), and J. Goette, *Vergil, Landleben* (*Bucolica, Georgica, Catalepton*) (München 1949; 2d ed. 1953), contain the *Georgics* as well as the *Eclogues*. For the *Georgics* we have also a critical edition by A. Colonna, *P. Vergili Maronis Georgica* (Torino 1946), with a preface on the MSS and selected notes from Servius and other commentators, and an edition of *Georgics* 1-2 with notes by E. Paratore, *Virgilio, Le Georgiche, libri I-II* (Milano 1946, 3d ed. 1952). The new Budé edition, replacing the 1926 edition of H. Goelzer, is by E. de Saint-Denis, *Virgile, Géorgiques* (Paris 1956); both introduction and notes contain numerous references to recent literature.

New editions of the *Aeneid* are few. The *Aeneid* is published with a critical apparatus by L. Castiglioni, *P. Vergilius Maro, Aeneidos libri XII* (Torino 1945), the text being that of the well-known 1930 edition by R. Sabbadini.[7] The *Aeneid* as a whole is edited also by M. J. Pattist, *Aeneis* (Amsterdam 1941), and Books 1-6 are edited both by G. P. Landmann, *Aeneis I-VI* (Zurich 1952) and by G. Vitale, *Aeneis I-VI* (Milano 1946). Landmann relegates to the bottom of the page a few verses, chiefly those bracketed by Hirtzel (O.C.T.) and Janell (Teubner), but this edition contains neither notes nor critical apparatus; Vitale has two sets of notes, one on problems of text and interpretation of details, the second on matters of esthetic interpretation.

Editions of individual books of the *Aeneid* are numerous, but mostly elementary Italian and British school editions.[8] The edition of *Aeneid* 2 by V. Ussani, Jr., *Virgilio, Eneide II* (Roma 1952), is praised by A. Grisart in *Latomus* 12 (1953) 325 as indispensable. *Aeneid* 4 continues to fascinate scholars. Two editions have appeared, one by E. Paratore, *Virgilio, Eneide, libro quarto* (Roma 1947), the other by R. G. Austin, *P. Vergili Maronis Aeneidos Liber Quartus* (Oxford 1955); both commentaries are less ambitious than those of Buscaroli (1932) and Pease (1935) but contain much of value; both stress Aeneas' love for Dido (see Paratore on 4.395; Austin on 331-361, 360f., 393).

The edition of Book 6 by Sir Frank Fletcher, *Virgil, Aeneid VI* (Oxford 1941), is likewise for more mature students; both the introduction and the commentary are planned to give to the reader "understanding and appreciation and enjoyment."

The period since 1940 has been rich in English translations of all major classical authors — translations of high quality in both prose and verse —, and Vergil's works are well represented in this group.

. E. V. Rieu, *Virgil, The Pastoral Poems* (Penguin ed. 1949), translates the *Eclogues* into prose, and R. C. Trevelyan, *Virgil, The Eclogues and the Georgics* (Cambridge 1944), has poetic versions of the *Eclogues* and the *Georgics*. Three other verse translations of the *Georgics* have appeared in recent years, those by L. A. S. Jermyn, *The Singing Farmer: A Translation of Virgil's Georgics* (Oxford 1947), C. Day Lewis, *The Georgics of Vergil* (New York 1947), and S. P. Bovie, *Virgil's Georgics: A Modern English Verse Translation* (Chicago 1956). Of these four verse translations, that by Lewis seems preferable to those by Trevelyan and Jermyn, and Bovie's is recommended as the best of all; it is accurate, readable, and poetic.

For the *Aeneid* we also have four new translations, two in prose, by K. Guinagh, *The Aeneid of Vergil* (New York 1953), and W. F. Jackson Knight, *Virgil, The Aeneid* (Penguin ed. 1956); two in verse, by R. Humphries, *The Aeneid of Virgil* (New York 1951), and C. Day Lewis, *The Aeneid of Virgil* (New York 1952). To make a decision between good translations is difficult; the two poetic versions seem more readable. Lewis is uneven at times, especially when he strives to be colloquial, and my own preference is for Humphries' version, which maintains a high level of excellence. Each of the translations cited above has an introduction: those by Bovie on the *Georgics* and by Guinagh on the *Aeneid* seem particularly well suited to the general reader. In addition to his introduction, Rieu has a valuable short essay on each of the ten *Eclogues*.[9]

3. *Appendix Vergiliana*

Before turning to the authentic works of Vergil, I wish to discuss briefly the relatively few editions. books, and articles which deal with the *Appendix Vergiliana*. It seems appropriate to treat this material

first, since some of the poems are probably early efforts of Vergil and since it is possible that the longer poems (*Culex, Ciris*), if not by Vergil, at least reflect the poetic climate of Vergil's early years. Although there is still little agreement about the individual poems, the general opinion about the *Appendix* is very different from that of 25 or 30 years ago, when widespread acceptance of the collection as Vergilian by Rand, DeWitt, Frank, Rostagni, and others resulted in the writing of new biographies of Vergil and his poetic development. The pendulum has swung far in the opposite direction, and many scholars today deny Vergilian authorship to all the poems with the exception of a few of the *Catalepton* and consider most to be post-Vergilian imitations. This is, in general, more characteristic of German scholars than of American and Italian, on whom the earlier views of Rand, Frank, and Rostagni have perhaps made a deeper impression.[10]

The important new critical edition of the entire *Appendix* is that by R. Giomini, *Appendix Vergiliana: Testo, introduzione e traduzione* (Firenze 1953). The edition is characterized by the collation of many mediaeval MSS and by the rejection of many emendations proposed by earlier editors, but Giomini's own text has received unfavorable comment.[11] The editor does not discuss the problem of authenticity, but makes his own position clear, that the poems are not by Vergil. His introduction, chiefly on manuscripts, contains a useful bibliography (xliv-liii).

Several scholars have written about the collection as a whole or discussed various poems. Arnaldi, 167-229, insists on the authenticity of the *Culex* but rejects most of the others; the *Aetna* and the *Dirae* are not Vergilian but date from the years of Vergil's youth; the *Moretum*. *Copa*, and *Ciris* are later and reveal the influence of Vergil. E. H. Clift, *Latin Pseudepigrapha: A Study in Literary Attributions* (Baltimore 1945) 123-128, considers most of the poems authentic, and Richardson, 17-100, is convinced that the *Culex, Ciris*, and *Moretum* date from the period of Vergil's youth[12] and that the *Culex* is probably by Vergil.

E. Bickel, "Syllabus Indiciorum Quibus Pseudovergiliana et Pseudoovidiana Carmina Definiantur: Symbolae ad Cirim, Culicem, Aetnam," *RhM* 93 (1949-50) 289-324, examines the *Culex, Ciris*, and *Aetna* on the basis of the poet's knowledge of events, his imitation of other works, his use of language and meter, and rejects all three poems: the *Culex* is a spurious work of the late Augustan period, the *Ciris*, with its imitations of the *Aeneid*, is to be dated about 18 B.C., and the *Aetna* was composed after the time of Manilius, either late in Tiberius' reign or during the reign of Claudius; of the *Catalepton* only 1, 5, 7, and 8 are genuine.

Dornseiff, 7-44, disagrees with Bickel on many points: the *Aetna*, if not by Vergil, dates from the period of his youth; the *Culex* is also a neoteric work, but slightly later, perhaps written as a jest on the family tomb built by Octavian in 28 B.C.; it may be the work of Vergil, but this cannot be proved. Dornseiff comments also on

4

the *Catalepton* and accepts more poems as Vergilian than Bickel had done. F. Giancotti. "L' 'Appendix Vergiliana' e il tema fondamentale di Virgilio," *Maia* 4 (1951) 118-137, finds in the *Appendix* the same attitude toward fate, misfortune, and human suffering that is so characteristic of the poet's major works and accordingly favors Vergilian authorship.

The views of L. Herrmann, *L'âge d'argent doré* (Paris 1951) 43-109, are highly unorthodox: the *Priapea* and the *Catalepton* (except 2, 9, and 13) are by Martial: the *Copa* and the *Moretum* are by Petronius; the *Aetna*. *Ciris*, and *Cat.* 9 likewise date from Nero's reign and are the work of Lucilius Junior.

Büchner's recent discussion. 42-160, is most thorough: the *Culex* and the *Ciris* are both later than the publication of the *Aeneid*· the *Dirae* and the *Lydia* are two independent poems, the former composed about 40 B.C.. the *Lydia* somewhat later, but neither is by Vergil. The *Aetna* is probably to be dated between 65 and 79 A.D. Of the entire *Appendix*. Büchner accepts as genuine only *Catalepton* 5 and 8.

Several editions and articles on specific poems of the *Appendix* have appeared in recent years. R. E. H. Westendorp Boerma, *P. Vergili Maronis Libellus Qui Inscribitur Catalepton*. Pars Prior (Groningen 1949),[13] has an important edition (in 168 pages) of *Catalepton* 1-8; this work, an advance on earlier commentaries, contains a full bibliography (i-xiii), prolegomena (in Latin), text, translation (into English), and bibliography and notes (in Latin) on each of the eight poems; the editor accepts all eight as youthful works of Vergil.

For articles on the *Catalepton*. see F. Cupaiuolo, *Considerazioni e divagazioni sul Catalepton I* (Napoli 1943); L. Herrmann, "Was Martial the Author of *Catalepton* 2?", *TAPhA* 73 (1942) xxviiif. (possibly); W. E. Gillespie, "The subject of *Catalepton* III," *CJ* 35 (1939-40) 106-108 (no single person is meant, but several representatives of the type of conqueror); L. Alfonsi, "L' 'Ortensio' di Cicerone e il 'Catalepton V' di Virgilio," *RFIC* 19 (1941) 259-267 (Vergil was indebted to Cicero); J. Martin, "Vergil und die Landanweisungen," *WJA* 1 (1946) 98-107 (*Catalepton* 8 not the work of Vergil); R. E. H. Westendorp Boerma, "De Epigrammate Quodam Perplexo," *Ut Pictura Poesis: Studia Enk* (Leiden 1955) 215-226 (on *Catalepton* 11).

Theories concerning the *Culex* continue to vary widely. E. Bickel, "Die Athetese des Culex," *RhM* 89 (1940) 318-320, argues against Vergilian authorship and believes that the reference in the prooemium to Octavius, the later Augustus, caused the ascription of the poem to Vergil. A Dal Zotto, "La redazione greca del *Culex* . . . ," *Atti del V Congresso Nazionale di Studi Romani* 5 (1946) 215-221, on the contrary, attributes the poem to Vergil, assuming that he made Latin translations of both the *Culex* and the *Ciris* from the Greek poems composed by Parthenius. F. Giancotti, "Sulla cronologia e sulla dedica del 'Culex'," *Maia* 4 (1951) 70-76, likewise favors

Vergilian authorship for the *Culex* and, convinced that the numeral XVI in the Suetonius-Donatus Life should be emended, believes that XXI best gives the approximate date of composition. E. Fraenkel, "The Culex," *JRS* 42 (1952) 1-9, however, considers the poem a forgery from the time of Tiberius; the work contains imitations from Vergil's major works (the *bona pastoris* from *Georgics* 2 and the Roman heroes from *Aeneid* 6) and borrows also from Ovid; the work was a deliberate attempt to supply information about Vergil's early poetic activity and was wrongly accepted as genuine by poets of the Silver Age. A. Salvatore. "Prolegomena ad Criticam Culicis Editionem," *AFLN* 2 (1952) 11-44, discusses the text of the *Culex* and considers Vollmer the most reliable of earlier editors.

Three important works on the *Ciris:* H. Hielkema, *Ciris Quod Carmen Traditur Vergilii* (Utrecht 1941), provides an edition with text, translation (into Dutch), introduction and full commentary (both in Latin), and finds in many passages imitation of Vergil and Ovid. F. Munari, "Studi sulla 'Ciris,'" *Atti d. Accad. d'Italia, Memorie d. Cl. d. Scienze Mor. e Stor.*, 4 (Firenze 1944) 241-367, after a thorough investigation of language and content, also concludes that the *Ciris* was composed after Ovid. the poem being little more than a cento of material largely Vergilian, combined with imitations of Catullus, Lucretius, Ovid, and other poets. A. Salvatore, *Studi sulla tradizione manoscritta e sul testo della Ciris* (Napoli 1955), divides his work into two parts (115 and 156 pp.): the first, reprinted from *RAAN* 30 (1954), deals with manuscripts and editions, and devotes more than fifty pages to the newly discovered Graz fragment;[14] the second contains a commentary, followed by text and critical apparatus, with a final section on *Iuppiter magus* (*Ciris* 374) which originally appeared in *AFLN* 4 (1954) 25-39. H. Bardon, *REL* 33 (1955) 409-410, praises Salvatore's work and calls his text of the *Ciris* the best at the present time.

In the opinion of C. G. Hardie,[15] Fraenkel has "proved" that the *Culex* is not by Vergil, and Hielkema, Munari, and others, including S. Mariotti, "La *Ciris* .è un falso intenzionale," *Humanitas* 3 (1950-51) 371-373, have given strong support to a post-Ovidian date for the *Ciris;* Hardie points out that the author of the *Culex* was primarily interested in Vergil's ideas, whereas the *Ciris*-poet was attracted by Vergil's phrases and rhythms. W. Ehlers, "Die Ciris und ihr Original," *MH* 11 (1954) 65-88, attempts to reconstruct the Greek original of the

5

Ciris, and K. Oehler, "Zum Text der Cirisklage," *Philologus* 100 (1956) 140-147, opposes Sudhaus' frequently accepted transposition of 448-453 after 477.

The *Dirae* has been edited by C. van der Graaf, *The Dirae, with Translation, Commentary and an Investigation of its Authorship* (Leiden 1945), and the *Aetna* by E. Bolisani, *L'Aetna rivendicato a Virgilio* (Villafranca di Verona 1949). Van der Graaf discusses the metrical and stylistic peculiarities and rejects Jacobs' division of the *Dirae* into two poems, *Dirae* (1-103) and *Lydia* (104-183); he believes that the poem is earlier than the *Bucolics* and favors Vergilian authorship. But K. H. E. Schutter, "De Lydia et Diris carminibus," *Mnemosyne* 6 (1953) 110-115, thinks that we have here two poems, neither by Vergil. Bolisani's edition of the *Aetna* contains introduction, text, translation, commentary, and a brief critical appendix; the editor believes that the poem is an early work by Vergil. J. H. Waszink, "De Aetnae carminis auctore," *Mnemosyne* 2 (1949) 224-241, on the contrary, ascribes the work to Lucilius and dates it after 65 A.D. on the basis of imitations of Lucan and Seneca

4A. The Bucolics: General

Rose's *The Eclogues of Vergil* (above, note 2) provides the most thorough discussion of the problems of the poems and gives a useful summary of earlier literature, but the author's own conclusions must often be weighed with care.[16] For other studies, see Richardson, 101-132; Guillemin, 15-85; Perret, 14-48; Paratore, 70-176; Büchner, cols. 160-243.

M. Desport, "L'écho de la nature et de la poésie dans les Eglogues de Virgile," *REA* 43 (1941) 270-281, discusses Vergil's use of echo and song. E. A. Hahn (above, note 2), 196-241, writes on the characters and presents much of value also on chronology, arrangement, and allegory. Snell discusses Vergil's discovery of Arcadia as a poetic symbol, as a land set halfway between myth and reality.[17] The contrast between the pastoral Arcadia and life, between the dream world and reality, is treated by G. Barra, "Le Bucoliche e la formazione spirituale e poetica di Virgilio," *RAAN* 27 (1952) 7-31; Barra analyzes the poems on the basis of their originality and their relation to Theocritus, and gives their chronology as 2, 3, 5, 4, 6, 7, 8, 1, 9, 10; but see Rose, 251f.; Hahn, 199ff.; Hanslik, 8; Büchner, 234; these scholars agree that 2, 3, 5, 9, 1, 4, were composed in that order.

J. Ruelens, "Les saisons dans les Bucoliques de Virgile: Chronologie et composition," *AC* 12 (1943) 79-92, argues that the *Eclogues* were composed in the published order, from September of 41 to December of 38 B.C. and that no rearrangement was involved; but all others believe that the poems were rearranged for publication, with the odd-numbered poems dialogues, those with even numbers monologues (so Barra, 7; Duckworth A, 2). Richardson, 121, states that the interest in both form and content centers about 5, "the central panel of the grouping," and Hahn, 239ff., arranges the first nine Eclogues in three triads, the first (1, 2, 3) and third (7, 8, 9) presenting shepherds realistically, the second (4, 5, 6) containing more cosmic themes, with 5 as the central poem; 10 is a final poem blending the shepherds and realism of triads 1 and 3 with the gods and fantasy of triad 2.

The most controversial article on the structure of the *Eclogues* is that by P. Maury, "Le secret de Virgile et l'architecture des Bucoliques," *Lettres d'Humanité* 3 (1944) 71-147. Eclogues 1 and 9 (confiscations), 2 and 8 (love), 3 and 7 (singing matches), 4 and 6 (religion and philosophy) frame 5 (the dead and deified Daphnis);[18] the four poems on each side form the columns of a "bucolic chapel," with Caesar honored in the central shrine in the guise of the deified Daphnis, and Gallus honored in 10 at the entrance of the chapel. Maury believes that Vergil as a Neopythagorean developed numerous mathematical symmetries, with the total lines of 1-4 and 6-9 equalling 666, the numerical value of the names Caesar and Gallus. Perret, 14-18, accepts Maury's conclusions and considers his article one of the most important discoveries in modern Vergilian criticism; cf. also A. Wankenne, *LEC* 19 (1951) 388, note 16; against Maury and Perret, see J. Marouzeau, "Jeux de chiffres," *REL* 23 (1945) 74-76, 24 (1946) 77-78; E. de Saint-Denis, "Douze années d'études virgiliennes: l'architecture des 'Bucoliques'," *IL* 6 (1954) 139-147, 184-188, who prefers a simple alteration between dialogue and song; Becker, 315 ff., who favors a division of the *Eclogues* into two halves. On Maury and his critics, see now G. Stégen, *Commentaire sur cinq Bucoliques de Virgile* (Namur 1957; see below, note 19), who modifies Maury's conclusions and points out additional numerical symmetries.

4B. Individual Eclogues

1. G. Stégen, "L'unité de la *Première Bucolique*," *LEC* 12 (1943-44) 8-15[19] (on the dramatic aspects of the poem); cf. also F. Cupaiuolo, "Virgilio Bucolico," *GIF* 1 (1948) 323-330. R. Verdière, "Les amours de Tityre," *Latomus* 9 (1950) 273-282, supports Herrmann's view (above, note 6) that

6

Tityrus is Q. Caecilius Epirota. J. Michel, "Une allusion à la Paix de Brindes dans la première Bucolique (v. 59-66)?", *Latomus* 14 (1955) 446-453, dates the poem soon after the end of September, 40 B.C.

The identification of Tityrus in 1, the relation of 1 and 9, and the question of the restoration of Vergil's land have been treated by numerous writers; see Rose, 45-68, 228-233; Hahn, 220-226; S. Maugeri, "Breve considerazioni sulla cronologia della I e della IX Egloga virgiliana." *MC* 10 (1940), Saggi vari 41-49; J. Liegle, "Die Tityruskloge," *Hermes* 78 (1943) 209-231 (*Eclogue* 1 written in 41 B.C.; the *iuvenis* of 1.42 is not Octavian but L. Antonius, brother of the triumvir); J. Martin, "Vergil und die Landanweisungen," *WJA* 1 (1946) 98-107 (land not restored to the poet by Octavian); F. Bömer, "Tityrus und sein Gott," *WJA* 4 (1949-50) 60-70 (the *deus* is Octavian); H. Bennett, "The Restoration of the Virgilian Farm," *Phoenix* 5 (1951) 87-95[20] (Vergil's farm successfully restored).

J. J. Savage, "Vergil's Musing Tityrus, II," *CB* 28 (1951-52) 19-20 (the *servitium* of 1.40 is *servitium amoris:* no reference to Tityrus as a slave); H. Wagenvoort, "Vergilius' Ecloga I en IX," *Mededelingen . . . Vlaamse Acad. v. Wetenschappen* 15 (1953) Nr. 3.[21]

Hanslik, 5-19, and Büchner, 160-166, 216-221, provide good summaries of earlier discussions: Hanslik dates *Eclogue* 1 in the fall of 40 B.C. and (against Liegle) identifies the *iuvenis* of 42 with Octavian; Tityrus is symbolic of Vergil; the plural in 45 and *primus* in 44 are to be explained as an imitation of Hesiod, *Theog.* 22ff.; Büchner shows that 1 is later than Horace, *Epode* 16; if, as most agree, *Eclogue* 4 is later than 1, we have here an added argument that 4 is Vergil's reply to Horace; cf. below, Sect. 4C.

J. Aymard, " 'Aut Ararim Parthus bibet aut Germania Tigrim' (Buc., I, 62)," *Latomus* 14 (1955) 120-122, shows that the symmetry of the verse extends to the rivers themselves, the Arar being noted for its gentle course, the Tigris for its rapidity.

2. See Stégen, *Etude* (above, note 19) 28-39.

3. E. G. Schauroth, "A Virgilian Riddle and its Source," *CW* 43 (1949-50) 8-10, suggests that 104f. refers to the height of the winter sun in the far North; J. J. Savage, "The Riddle in Virgil's Third Eclogue," *CW* 47 (1953-54) 81-83, believes that the passage refers to the small opening in the roof of the temple of Jupiter on the Capitoline. The meaning of 108-110 is discussed by G. Stégen, "Le jugement de Palémon," *LEC* 20 (1952) 345-357,

who explains *quisquis* as the readers of the poem who will feel sentiments similar to those expressed by Damoetas and Menalcas; Stégen is opposed by E. Derenne, "Le jugement de Palémon," *LEC* 21 (1953) 182-186.

4. See below, Sect. 4C.

5. Rose, 117-138, believes that Daphnis is not Caesar but merely Daphnis, the ideal shepherd; Hahn, 212-217, identifies Daphnis with Caesar, as does Maury (above, Sect. 4A). P. Grimal, "La 'Ve Eglogue' et le culte de César," *Mélanges Picard* (Paris 1949; = *RA* 29-32) I 406-419, maintains that the hypothesis of Caesar is the only possible interpretation of the poem; see also F. Bömer, "Ueber die Himmelserscheinung nach dem Tode Caesars," *BJ* 152 (1952) 35-40. On the structure of 5, see Stégen, *Etude* (above, note 19) 83-97.

6. According to L.Alfonsi, "Il mito di Sileno e la VI egloga di Virgilio," *A&R* 10 (1942) 93-99, the poem is Epicurean and combines Vergil's two loves, philosophy and poetry. D. van Berchem, "La publication du *de rerum natura* et la VIe Eglogue de Virgile," *MH* 3 (1946) 26-39, writes on echoes of Lucretius. On the importance of 6 and 10 for the poetry of Gallus, see H. Bardon, "Les élégies de Cornelius Gallus," *Latomus* 8 (1949) 217-228. J. B. Evenhuis, *De Vergilii Ecloga Sexta Commentatio* (The Hague 1955) concludes that the poem is based neither wholly nor in part on Gallus' poetry, and O. Skutsch, "Zu Vergils Eklogen," *RhM* 99 (1956) 193-201, considers it a catalogue of Alexandrian themes.

7. The poem is analyzed by U. Albini, "L'Ecloga VII di Virgilio," *Maia* 4 (1951) 161-166; see also Stégen, *Etude* (above, note 19) 98-106.

8. See Stégen, *Commentaire* (above, note 19) 57-91.

9. Cf. above on *Eclogue* 1. See also Arnaldi, 230-243, who considers 9 of basic importance for Vergil's poetic program and his use of symbolism; G. Stégen, "La neuvième Bucolique de Virgile," *LEC* 21 (1953) 331-342, who discusses the dramatic nature of the poem and compares its structure with that of 1.

10. Cf. above on *Eclogue* 6. See Snell (above, note 17) 295-299; E. Bréquet, "Les élégies de Gallus d'après le Xe *Bucolique* de Virgile," *REL* 26 (1948) 204-214; G. Stégen, "La composition de la dixième Bucolique de Virgile," *Latomus* 12 (1953) 70-76.

4C. The Fourth Eclogue

This much discussed eclogue continues to receive

7

far more attention than any other short poem in ancient literature: see Rose, 162-217, 253-265; Hahn, 206-212; J. Loft, "Vergils 4. Ekloge," *C&M* 5 (1942-43) 1-12 (the *puer* of 18, 60, and 62 is the son of Pollio, but 8, 48, and 54 refer to the expected son of a god); H. Mattingly, "Virgil's Fourth Eclogue," *JWI* 10 (1947) 14-19; H. Hommel, "Vergils 'messianisches' Gedicht," *Theologia Viatorum* 2 (1950) 182-212 (text, German translation, copious notes, thorough discussion of the structure and meaning of the poem); W. Krogmann, "Das Kind und der Komet," *C&M* 12 (1951) 51-77; Dornseiff, 44-63; Hartke, 264ff., 373ff.; G. Jachmann, "Die vierte Ekloge Vergils," *ASNP* 21 (1952) 13-62[22] (the poem contains two conflicting themes, the arrival of the Golden Age with the birth of the child, and the gradual coming of the age; 31-36 are an unsuccessful attempt to combine the two ideas); F. Altheim, *Römische Religionsgeschichte* (Baden-Baden 1953) II 146-163 (conception of the poem neither Greek nor Roman but derives from ancient Iran); A. Kurfess, "Vergils vierte Ekloge und die Oracula Sibyllina," *HJ* 73 (1954) 120-127; *id.*, "Vergils 4. Ekloge und christliche Sibyllen," *Gymnasium* 62 (1955) 110-112; Stégen, *Etude* (above, note 19) 40-82; E. Bickel, "Politische Sibylleneklogen," *RhM* 97 (1954) 209-228 (the Achilles of 36 is Octavian); Becker, 328-341 (analysis of the poem); Büchner, 175-193; Duckworth D, 287-290.

The view that the *puer* is the expected child of Octavian and Scribonia is favored by Hahn, Bömer, Hartke, Jachmann, Bickel, Hanslik, and Duckworth D; according to Hommel, Krogmann, and Stégen, the child is Asinius Gallus, son of Pollio. J. J. Savage, "Apollo-Hercules: Two Themes in the Fourth Eclogue," *Vergilian Digest* 2 (1956) 5-10, supports the theory that the child is the expected offspring of Antony and Octavia. Büchner, 191, believes that the *puer* is not a human child but a symbol of the Golden Age.

Scholars remain divided on the relation of *Eclogue* 4 and Horace's *Epode* 16. Those favoring Vergil's priority include Hartke, Dornseiff, Hanslik, Becker, and Stégen; see especially K. Barwick, "Zur Interpretation und Chronologie der 4. Ecloge des Vergil und der 16. und 7. Epode des Horaz," *Philologus* 96 (1944) 28-67, and H. Fuchs, "Zu einigen Aussagen des Horaz," *Westöstliche Abhandlungen: Festschrift Tschudi* (Wiesbaden 1954) 39-43. Arguments supporting the view that Vergil's poem is an answer to the *Epode* are given by W. Wimmel, "Ueber das Verhältnis der 4. Ecloge zur 16. Epode," *Hermes* 81 (1953) 317-344; *id.*, "Eine Besonderheit der Reihung in Augusteischen Gedich-

ten," *Hermes* 82 (1954) 213ff.; Bickel, 222f.; Büchner 184ff.; Duckworth D, 289f.

On the transposition of 23 after 20, see Büchner-Hofmann, *Lateinische Literatur und Sprache* (Bern 1951) 131 and note 2. The transposition is opposed by Barwick. Dornseiff, Hartke, Jachmann, and Becker. On 28-30, see J. Fabri, S.J., *"Molli paulatim . . . ," LEC* 13 (1945) 249-252; L. Herrmann, *"Paulatim flavescet campus," LEC* 14 (1946) 64, who interprets the miracle of 28 as referring to the Campus Martius and compares *Aen.* 6.872f. Bömer, 49, note 30, rejects the usual view of *incrementum* in 49 as a synonym of *suboles* and interprets the word as implying apotheosis, "an associate of the gods"; cf. *Aen.* 8.301.

Several discussions on the meaning of *decem menses* in 61 are summarized by N. I. Herescu, "Les 'decem menses' et les calculs chronologiques des Romains," *REL* 33 (1955) 152-165.[23] He explains the phrase as resulting from popular usage from the influence of the pre-Julian lunar calendar. On the reading and interpretation of 62, see E. Kalinka, *"qui = cui," Glotta* 30 (1943) 222f. (*qui* is dative singular, not nominative plural); J. Mesk, "Verg. Ecl. IV 62," *PhW* 64 (1944) 120 (*qui* is nominative, against Kalinka); Föschl, *AAHG* 3 (1950) 72 (the reading *qui non risere parenti* is necessary).[24] On 62-63, see P. Mingazzini, "La chiusa dell'ecloga quarta di Virgilio e il rito del lettisternio," *GIF* 1 (1948) 209-212.

5A. The Georgics: General

"The *Georgics* are probably the most perfect example of Roman poetry and manifest the finest union between invention and tradition" (Richardson, 173). Although they have received less attention in recent years than either the *Eclogues* or the *Aeneid*, much has been written on their content, structure, and style; see Richardson, 132-163 (chiefly on structure); Letters, 58-88; Guillemin, 89-184; Perret, 49-85; Paratore. 177-282; Büchner, 243-315. P. d'Hérouville in *Géorgiques I-II: Champs. Vergers, Foréts* (Paris 1942) completes what he calls a "free commentary" on the *Georgics*.[25]

For other discussions of Vergil's intention and achievement in the poem, see C. Saggio, "Virgilio georgico lombardo," *A&R* 9 (1941) 161-176; G. Vidoni, "Quadri e figure nelle Georgiche di Virgilio," *Antiquitas* 1 (1946) No. 2, 25-32; L. A. S. Jermyn, "Virgil's Agricultural Lore," *G&R* 18 (1949) 49-69 (on the sources of his agricultural knowledge and how he used them); L. P. Wilkinson, "The Intention of Virgil's *Georgics*," *G&R* 19 (1950) 19-28 (the poem is descriptive rather than didactic; it was not written to support a "back to the land" policy); E. Turolla, "Una poesia e una seconda poesia nelle 'Georgiche'," *GIF* 5 (1952) 314-329 (after the first book the *Georgics* move in the direction of the more severe and tragic style of the *Aeneid*).

The *Georgics* are viewed as a glorification of labor, and Knight, 113, considers the motto of the poem to be *labor omnia vicit improbus* (1.145f.). But H. Altevogt, *Labor improbus: Eine Virgilstudie* (Münster 1952; = *Orbis Antiquus*. Heft 8), opposes the usual interpretation of *improbus* as "persistent," "unremitting," and looks upon *labor* as evil, along

8

with *egestas* (cf. *Aen.* 6.276f.). L. Castiglioni, *Lezioni intorno alle Georgiche di Virgilio* (Milano 1947) writes on the chronology of the poem, the Aristaeus episode, and the work as an *Ascraeum carmen*.

For a discussion of imagery, see S. P. Bovie, "The Imagery of Ascent-Descent in Vergil's *Georgics*," *AJPh* 77 (1956) 337-358. On other aspects of language and style, cf. Arnaldi, 244-254; P. Bourgeois, "L'hellénisme, procédé d'expression dans les *Géorgiques* (III et IV)," *REL* 18 (1940) 73-94 (Vergil's use of Greek words and names; the poem is Greek as well as Italian); A. Ginnell, "Recherches stylistiques sur les Géorgiques de Virgile," *Mélanges Niedermann* (Neuchâtel 1944) 91-98; J. Bayet, "Un procédé virgilien: la description synthétique dans les 'Géorgiques'," *Studi Funaioli* (Roma 1955) 9-18.

For more technical aspects of the poem, see R. J. Getty, "Some Astronomical Cruces in the *Georgics*," *TAPhA* 79 (1948) 24-45 (on 1.215-230, 4.231-235 and 425-428); J. André, "Virgile et les Indiens," *REL* 27 (1949) 157-163 (on Vergil's geographical knowledge); R. T. Bruère, "Pliny the Elder and Virgil," *CPh* 51 (1956) 228-245 (on Pliny's attempt to censure and emend the poet's statements in the *Georgics*).

5B. Georgics: Individual Books

1. U. Albini, "Struttura e motivi del primo libro delle Georgiche," *SIFC* 25 (1951) 49-64, arranges Book 1 in three parts: 43-203, 204-310, 311-497. G. Le Grelle, S.J., "Le premier livre des *Géorgiques*, poème pythagoricien," *LEC* 17 (1949) 139-235, analyses the structure of the book on the basis of the "golden section" (the whole is to the greater part as the greater is to the lesser). He divides *Georgics* 1 into *Works* (43-203) and *Days* (204-462.5); these parts reveal the exact "divine proportion" (the ratio is 1.618); likewise the exordium and the epilogue in relation to the "foyer astronomique" (204-258) reveal this same proportion, as do the many subdivisions of the book which Le Grelle terms "chrysodes." Le Grelle, like Maury (above, Sect. 4A), believes that Vergil was a Neopythagorean and made much use of numerical symbolism; e.g., the *Works* and the *Days* (less the "foyer astronomique") total 365.5 lines, the number of the days of the year (cf. 463: *sol tibi signa dabit*), and the exordium and epilogue, with the "foyer astronomique," total 144, the square of 12, the months of the year; the sections on the temperate zones (50-203 and 259-437) add to 333, half of 666, the triangle of 36. This is an amazing and controversial article[26] which, even if valid only in part, throws new light on Vergil's method of composition and his use of proportion and harmony of structure.

Articles on various passages of Book 1: R. G. Getty, "*Liber et alma Ceres* in Vergil *Georgics* I, 7," *Phoenix* 5 (1951) 96-107.[27] discusses Vergil's mention of Liber and Ceres in place of the signs of the Zodiac, Libra and Virgo (rival claimants for the honor of being Octavian's natal sign). G. Herzog-Hauser, "Zum Prooemium I. der Georgica," *WS* 66 (1953) 113-117, points out that Octavian is honored by receiving the same amount of space (24-42) that is accorded to the gods (5-23); see also Hartke, 75-80. H. Mattingly, "Notes on Virgil," *CR* 56 (1942) 18-19, wrongly believes that Julius Caesar, not Octavian, is invoked in 24ff., as does Richardson, 159f. Duckworth D, 291ff., compares the treatment of Octavian in 24-42 with that in Horace, *Odes* 1.2. R. Beutler, "Zur Komposition von Vergils Georgica I 43-159," *Hermes* 75 (1940) 410-421, analyzes the structure and content of the passage, as does Altevogt (above, Section 5A) for 43-203. F. W. Walbank, "*Licia telae addere* (Virgil, *Georg.* I 284-286)," *CQ* 34 (1940) 93-104, explains *licium* as 'warp' and *tela* as 'loom.' L. A. S. Jermyn, "Weather-Signs in Virgil," *G&R* 20 (1951) 26-37, 49-59, writes on Vergil's use of Aratus and other sources in 1.351-460. M. P. Cunningham, "Note on Latin Poetic Imitation," *CB* 30 (1953-54) 41, 43f., compares 1.375-376 with the earlier versions of Aratus, Cicero, and Varro.

2. See G. de Plinval, "A travers le Livre II des Géorgiques de Virgile," *MH* 1 (1944) 77-86 (new interpretation of various passages); C. A. Disandro, "Nota virgiliana," *REC* 6 (1955) 33-49 (on the composition of 177-258). On 380-396 and its importance for early Roman festivals, see J. H. Waszink, "Varro, Livy and Tertullian on the history of Roman dramatic art," *VChr* 2 (1948) 224-242; E. de Saint-Denis, "A propos du culte de Bacchus (Virgile, Géorg., II, 385-396)," *RBPh* 27 (1949) 702-712; K. Meuli, "Altrömischer Maskenbrauch," *MH* 12 (1955) 206-235. According to Waszink, Vergil's description of rural festivals shows the influence of Varro; the passage refers, not to definite festivals (*Liberalia* and *Vinalia*), but to festivals in honor of Bacchus in general. Saint-Denis identifies the festival described by Vergil with the *Liberalia*, and Meuli rejects both the *Liberalia* and the *Vinalia* and favors the festival of the Lares, the *Compitalia*.

3. Hartke, 369f., states that 26-39, the middle portion of the prooemium (two cola of four verses each on history, two cola of three verses each on myth) are framed by two passages of nine verses each; cf. C. A. Disandro, "El proemio III de las Geórgicas," *AFC* 6 (1953-54) 57-73 (the prooemium of 48 verses is divided: 2, 14, 9, 14, 9).

4. K. Nawratil, "Zum vierten Buch der Georgica," *WS* 58 (1940) 112-119, argues that political-historical themes are combined with philosophy in *Georgics* 4 as in the *Aeneid; Georg.* 4. 149-227 anticipates the thought of *Aen.* 6.724ff. W. M. A. van de Wijnpersse, "Fragrantia mella," *Hermeneus* 22 (1950-51) 22-30, shows that Vergil, by portraying bees as tiny human beings, was able to

9

portray their spiritual life. On the political symbolism of *Georgics* 4, see Perret, 83-85, and H. Dahlmann, "Der Bienenstaat in Vergils Georgica," *Abh. der Geistes- und Sozialwiss. Kl., Akad. der Wiss. und der Lit.*, Mainz (Wiesbaden 1954) Nr. 10, 547-562. According to Dahlmann, the political and social system of the bees provides a model for the Roman people and a defense of the principate.

B. G. Whitfield, "Virgil and the Bees. A Study in Ancient Apicultural Lore," *G&R* 3 (1956) 99-117, writes on Vergil's knowledge of bees and his relation to other ancient writers, both earlier and later; Whitfield believes that Vergil relied largely upon his own experience and made less use of Aristotle, Theophrastus, and Varro than is commonly believed. R. T. Bruère, "The Garden Motive in Virgil's Fourth *Georgic*," *PAPhA* 71 (1940) xxx-xxxi, discusses the episode of the old man of Tarentum (125-146) and suggests that Vergil viewed gardening as a picturesque but exotic pursuit; writing at greater length on the subject would be out of place in a eulogy of the land of Italy; but see P. Grimal, *Les jardins romains à la fin de la république et aux deux premiers siècles de l'empire* (Paris 1943) 404-419, on Vergil's treatment of gardens in both the *Eclogues* and the *Georgics*.

P. Colmant, S.J., "Analyse de l'épisode d'Orphée," *LEC* 9 (1940) 39-43, and G. Norwood, "Vergil, *Georgics* IV, 453-527," *CJ* 36 (1940-41) 354-355, both give a structural analysis of 453-527; Norwood reveals a concentric pattern around the heart of the story (481-503 = f), as follows: a b c d e f e d c b a.[28] E. A. Havelock, "Virgil's Road to Xanadu," *Phoenix* 1 (1946) 1, 3-8; 2, 2-7; 1 Suppl. (1947) 9-18, compares the imagery and the romantic geography in the Aristaeus episode and Coleridge's work. C. M. Bowra, "Orpheus and Eurydice," *CQ* 46 (1952) 113-126, attempts to reconstruct the lost Hellenistic original by analyzing the story of Orpheus and Eurydice as we find it in Vergil and Ovid. A. Klotz, "Die Umarbeitung von Vergils Georgica," *WJA* 2 (1947) 140-147, discusses the difficulties at the end of the book and maintains that a passage praising Gallus appeared originally at the end of the Aristaeus story. Büchner, however, believes that the Aristaeus episode is a Hellenistic epyllion which was added later; this is supported by the fact that several verses in the second half of *Georgics* 4 appear also in *Aeneid* 1, where they are functional and therefore earlier; cf. Büchner-Hofmann, *Lateinische Literatur und Sprache* (Bern 1951) 116f.; see also Büchner, 293-297, where the author argues in favor of a second edition in 26 or 25 B.C., after the suicide of Gallus, when the Aristaeus episode replaced a passage praising Gallus (but as a writer of elegy, not as prefect of Egypt).

6A. The Aeneid: General[29]

See Letters, 89-156; Guillemin, 187-317; Perret 86-145; Paratore, 283-386; Büchner, 315-441.

The most significant book of recent years on the *Aeneid* is undoubtedly Pöschl's *Die Dichtkunst Virgils* (above, note 2) on the structure and symbolism of the poem, and especially on the characters of Aeneas, Dido, and Turnus; it perhaps contributes more to our understanding of and insight into Vergil's motives than any single book since Heinze's *Vergils epische Technik* of 1903, with which it often disagrees, and the importance of the book is attested by the numerous lengthy and favorable reviews.[30]

The following two books are devoted only in part to the *Aeneid*: C. R. Buxton, *Prophets of Heaven and Hell* (Cambridge 1945), looks upon Vergil, Dante, Milton, and Goethe as the four poets who present a universal vision of life, the past and the future as well as the present; as the poets who, above all others, deal with the problem of evil and the problem of salvation; and as the four "best spokesmen of our Western civilization." The book contains much of interest and value on Vergil's ideal of a world empire of justice and peace under Divine Will. C. M. Bowra, *From Vergil to Milton* (London 1945), studies the literary epics of Virgil, Camoëns, Tasso, and Milton; the introductory chapter (1-32) compares the oral epic of Homer with the written epic of Vergil, and the chapter on Vergil (33-85) discusses the poet's theme of the destiny of Rome and Aeneas as a symbolic character; the chapter is recommended for Bowra's analysis of the characters of Dido, Turnus, and Aeneas.

R. W. Cruttwell, *Virgil's Mind at Work* (Oxford 1947), also writes about the symbolism of the *Aeneid*, but he is less interested in the conscious and subconscious workings of the poet's mind than in the unconscious; this is a strange book with its paired chapter-titles (e.g., "Troy and Rome," "Vulcan and Vesta," "Hut and Hive," "Tomb and Womb"), with its emphasis on fire and bees and beehive-huts, with its balanced, almost rhythmical, prose.[31]

Minor books include G. Venturelli and G. Giovannini. *Osservazioni sull' Eneide* (Firenze 1953), a slight volume of comments on each book and (65-84) quotations from other Vergilian scholars; F. Sforza, *Il più prezioso tesoro spirituale d'Italia: L'Eneide* (Milano 1952), an expansion of the author's impossible theory in *CR* 49 (1935) 97-108 that the *Aeneid* was a bitter attack on Rome and Augustus, that Vergil portrayed Aeneas and the Trojans as treacherous and despicable and the Italians as loyal and chivalrous.[32]

For books of a more specialized nature, see A. Rostagni, *Da Livio a Virgilio e da Virgilio a Livio*

(Padova 1942),[33] on the chronology of the books of the *Aeneid* and the influence which Livy and Vergil exerted on each other; A. Montenegro Duque, *La onomastica de Virgilio y la antigüedad preitálica* (Salamanca 1949), on Rutulian and Etruscan names and the origins of the two peoples; P. J. Miniconi, *Etude des thèmes "guerriers" de la poésie épique gréco-romaine* (Paris 1951), esp. 73-82, 111-121; H. R. Steiner, *Der Traum in der Aeneis* (Bern 1952; = *Noctes Romanae* 5), on the importance of dreams for relating the human action to the divine purpose; G. Krókowski, *Quaestiones Epicae* (Wrocław 1951), on the manner in which Homer and Vergil handle simultaneous action, and particularly on the chronology of *Aeneid* 8-10.

M. Van Doren, *The Noble Voice* (New York 1946) 86-121, in a chapter more unsympathetic than understanding, believes that Vergil's "style is the one contribution he could make to European poetry"; that "Aeneas does not move under his own power any more than the poem does." F. R. Dale, *Character and Incident in the Aeneid* (1953),[34] likewise criticizes both events and characters, especially the Nisus-Euryalus episode in 9 and Vergil's portrayal of Aeneas in 4.

On the tragic nature of the poem, the problem of suffering, and the question of Fate and Free Will, see F. H. Cowles, "The Epic Question in Vergil," *CJ* 36 (1940-41) 133-142 ("Why should a good man suffer?"); H. G. Mullens, "Tragic Optimism in the *Aeneid*," *G&R* 11 (1941-42) 137-138 (Aeneas' good a social not a personal good); C. J. Ellingham, "Virgil's Pilgrim's Progress," *G&R* 16 (1947) 67-75 (Aeneas is the Religious Man, journeying from the City of Destruction to the Promised Land; the theme of the *Aeneid* is the deliverance of the world from war); W. H. Semple, "Aeneas at Carthage: A Short Study of *Aeneid* I and IV," *BRL* 34 (1951-52) 119-136 (on Aeneas as an agent of divine will); E. Turolla, "Le origini e le caratteristiche del tragico nella prima 'Eneide'," *GIF* 6 (1953) 114-133 (on the tragic elements of *Aeneid* 1-6 and their origins in Homer, Sophocles, and Euripides; the tragedy of Aeneas is greater and more significant than that of Dido); L. Feder, "Vergil's Tragic Theme," *CJ* 49 (1953-54) 197-209 (on the difficulties of Aeneas' mission and on Dido and Turnus as tragic characters); G. E. Duckworth, "Fate and Free Will in Vergil's *Aeneid*," *CJ* 51 (1955-56) 357-364 (the characters make their own decisions and suffer the consequences).

Several writers discuss Vergil's hatred of war and his realization that it brings sorrow and disaster to both sides alike: D. A. Cazzaniga, "Guerra e pace in Virgilio," *ScCatt* 71 (1943) 401-411; W. H. Alexander, "War in the *Aeneid*," *CJ* 40 (1944-45) 261-273; B. L. Ullman, "We Want a Virgilian

Peace," *CJ* 41 (1945-46) 1-3; G. E. Duckworth, "Vergil and War in the Aeneid." *CJ* 41 (1945-46) 104-107; L. A. Springer, "Vergil's Voice of Protest," *CW* 47 (1953-54) 55-57; W. H. Semple, "War and Peace in Virgil's *Aeneid*." *BRL* 36 (1953-54) 211-227.

For more technical articles, see C. Saunders, "Sources of the Names of Trojans and Latins in Vergil's *Aeneid*," *TAPhA* 71 (1940) 537-555 (the names are derived from Homer, classical myths, early Italian history, and many are chosen for their etymological significance); W.-H. Friedrich, "Exkurse zur Aeneis," *Philologus* 94 (1940-41) 142-174 (on the frenzy of Amata in 7, the speeches of Sinon in 2, and the Jupiter-Venus scene in 1.223ff.; this last Friedrich thinks Vergil would have omitted; against this, cf. Büchner, 320f.); J. Aymard, *"Immanem veluti pecora inter inertia tigrim,"* *RPh* 18 (1944) 69-83 (on hunting similes in the *Aeneid*); C. Bione, "Quando ebbe inizio la composizione dell' Eneide?" *Atti del V Congresso Nazionale di Studi Romani* 5 (1946) 170-177 (Vergil began the *Aeneid* about 26 B.C.; cf. Knight, 69); S. L. Mohler, "Sails and Oars in the *Aeneid*," *TAPhA* 79 (1948) 46-62 (on the performance of the Trojan ships under varying conditions of wind and weather; the ships were Augustan, not Homeric); cf. L. F. Smith, "Aeneas' Fleet," *CJ* 41 (1945-46) 328-331 (on the fate of the ships).

6B. *Aeneid: Individual Books*

1. A. Salvatore, *Sul primo libro dell' Eneide* (Nàpoli 1947) writes a scholarly analysis of the book. On the genuineness of the four verses (*ille ego . . . Martis*), said to have been removed by Varius, see G. Funaioli, " 'Ille ego qui quondam . . .' e Properzio, II, 34," *A&R* 8 (1940) 97-109[35] (against authenticity); D. van Berchem, "Au dossier d' 'ille ego,'" *REL* 20 (1942) 69-78 (compares passages in Horace, esp. *Satires* 2.1.13f.: *horrentia pilis agmina,* and accepts the four verses as genuine); L. Alfonsi, "Di Properzio II, 34 e della protasi dell' Eneide," *RFIC* 22-23 (1944-45) 116-129 (the four verses are an authentic statement of Vergil's change to a higher form of poetry and are echoed by Propertius and later poets); A. Rostagni, "Elementi autobiografici nell' epopea," *Belfagor* 1 (1946) 73-79,[36] (favors authenticity).

A. Pagliaro, " . . . *Troiae qui primus ab oris . . .*," *Studi Funaioli* (Roma 1955) 288-298, examines Vergil's use of *primus* and suggests that the word appears in *Aen.* 1.1 because a new era begins with Aeneas. E. de Saint-Denis, *"Graviter commotus* (Virgile, *Enéide* I, 126)," *Latomus* 5 (1946) 167-173, interprets *commotus* as 'shaken' rather than 'angered.'

On the interpretation of 1.462 and the question whether this famous line refers only to its specific context or has a universal significance, see J. J. H. Savage, "Mentem Mortalia Tangunt" *CW* 36 (1942-43) 90-91 (rhetorical coloring); A. Pagliaro, "Sunt lacrimae rerum," *Maia* 1 (1948) 14-128 (tears a product of the *res*); J. M. Kramer, "Aeneas 'lacrimae rerum' en het wenen van Odysseus," *Hermeneus*

11

23 (1951-52) 101-104 (emphasis on the suffering of war); H. Huisman, "Lacrimae Rerum," *ibid.* 122 (against Kramer); L. A. MacKay, "Three Notes on Vergil," *CW* 45 (1951-52) 257-258 ("tears are real things"); W. T. Avery, *"Mentem Mortalia Tangunt," CPh* 48 (1953) 19-20 (compares Aeschylus, *Agam.* 432); Feder (above, Sect. 6A) 199-202 (not an expression of universal sympathy); W. H. Alexander, *"Aeneid* I, 462: A New Approach," *AJPh* 75 (1954) 395-400 (compares *Iliad* 24); A. M. Cayuela, "Sunt lacrimae rerum," *Helmantica* 5 (1954) 71-94 (things have tears); L. F. Smith, "The *Res* of Vergil and *Aeneid* I. 462," *CJ* 50 (1954-55) 39-40 (*res* means "empire").

J. Mjöberg, "Virgil, Aen. 1: 608: *polus dum sidera pascet," Eranos* 42 (1944) 138-141, interprets: "as long as the pole-star leads the flock of stars to graze"; *polus* means pole-star, not heaven. T. T. Duke, "Vergil—A Bit Player in the *Aeneid?" CJ* 45 (1949-50) 191-193, suggests that Vergil appears in the character of Iopas in 740-747 and sings from his own *Georgics;* discussing this same passage, W. Kranz, "Das Lied des Kitharoden von Jaffa," *RhM* 96 (1953) 30-38, rejects the symbolic interpretation of Pöschl, 248ff., and believes that the song emphasizes the Oriental nature of Carthage.

2. C. Dolzani, "Valori drammatici ed elementi chiaroscurali del II libro dell' *Eneide," A&R* 9 (1941) 177-179, shows the effective contrasts of light and dark in the book, with fire at the end, both the fire of destruction and the fire on the head of Iulus—the presage of future glory. V. Ussani, Jr., "Eschilo e il libro II dell' Eneide," *Maia* 3 (1950) 237-254, discusses the influence of Greek tragedy and especially the *Persians* of Aeschylus on Vergil's treatment of the fall of Troy; Aeneas, often criticized for the small part he plays in 2, has the role of the messenger who describes the tragedy. A. Mazzarino, *Il racconto di Enea* (Torino 1955), analyzes 2 and summarizes ancient and modern estimates of its value. The richness and complexity of Vergil's thought are excellently revealed by B. M. W. Knox, "The Serpent and the Flame: The Imagery of the Second Book of the *Aeneid," AJPh* 71 (1950) 379-400; cf. also T. P. Howe, "Color Imagery in *Macbeth* I and II and the *Aeneid* II: A Padagogic Experiment," *CJ* 51 (1955-56) 322-327.

H. Kleinknecht, "Laokoon," *Hermes* 79 (1944) 66-111, explains the story of Laocoon (2.40-56, 199-245) as a *prodigium* of the wrath of the gods. G. Puccione, "Quae sit fiducia capto," *PP* 9 (1954) 431-438, interprets *fiducia* in 75 as *pignus.* G. E. Duckworth, "Magical Circles and the Fall of Troy," *CJ* 40 (1944-45) 99-103, suggests that the original purpose of the wooden horse was to cause a section of the wall to be demolished and thus to break its magic power.

On the interpretation of 2.255, see the following articles, each with the title *"Tacitae per amica silenti lunae":* G. Ponte, *GIF* 3 (1950) 44-56, A. Pagliaro, *PP* 6 (1951) 22-32, and A. di Prima, *Paideia* 6 (1951) 277-290.37 Ponte believes that the moon does not shine in 255, that the poet stresses the darkness of the night;

Pagliaro takes *tacitae lunae* as dative with *amica,* "in the silence which is dear to the quiet moon," i.e. to night; Di Prima interprets *luna* as *nox.*

B. Oliviere, "La musique d'un passage de Virgile (*Enéide,* II, 250-267)," *LEC* 18 (1950) 196-208, writes on rhythmical effects in the passage. R. Allain, "Une 'nuit spirituelle' d'Enée," *REL* 24 (1946) 189-198, examines Vergil's portrayal of Aeneas in 302-588; Aeneas' heroism is stressed at the expense of his piety, and the hero reveals his later realization of the futility of opposing the will of the gods. G. Wijdeveld, "De Vergilii Aen. II, 469 sqq.," *Mnemosyne* 10 (1941-42) 238-240, discusses the comparison of Pyrrhus to a serpent; the name Pyrrhus suggests the Greek dance *pyrriché,* as does the snake *arduus ad solem;* cf. Knox, 393-395. R. Allain, "Le merveilleux dans un épisode crucial de l' 'Enéide'," *LEC* 17 (1949) 321-334, treats the role of Venus in 589-631 and the relation of the gods to Fate; Aeneas wrongly believes that Helen and Paris alone are responsible for the Trojan war, and Venus' revelation prepares him for his divine mission. L. J. D. Richardson, "Facilis iactura sepulcri," *PIA* 46, Sect. C (1940) 85-101, suggests that *iactura* in 646 signifies renunciation, voluntary sacrifice, rather than simply 'loss'; cf. Allain in *LEC* 14 (1946) 161-165.

3. The story of Aeneas' wanderings has been condemned as uninteresting; inconsistencies with the other books have been noted, and many have believed that 3 was originally the first book and written in the third person. On these and other topics, see A. W. Allen, "The Dullest Book of the *Aeneid," CJ* 47 (1951-52) 119-123 (the book "is by no means dull"); W. H. Semple, "A Short Study of Aeneid, Book III," *BRL* 38 (1955-56) 225-240 (the book is diversified with incidents relevent to the main action); E. L. Highbarger, "A Roman Tale of the Sea: *Aeneid* III," *Classical Studies for A. D. Fraser* (Tuscaloosa 1956) 23-35; R. B. Lloyd, *"Aeneid* III: A New Approach," *AJPh* 78 (1957) 133-151 (Book 3 is "basic to our understanding of the structure of the first half of the epic").

E. de Saint-Denis, "La chronologie des navigations troyennes dans l' *Enéide," REL* 20 (1942) 79-98, reexamining the chronologies suggested by Heyne, Chabert, Mandra, and Constans and the problem of *septima aetas* (*Aen.* 1.755 and 5.626), suggests that Vergil in his final revision would have prolonged the first visit in Sicily.

W. Jens, "Der Eingang des dritten Buches der Aeneis," *Philologus* 97 (1948) 194-196, shows parallels and contrasts in the episodes at Thrace (8-68) and at Delos (69-120). R. B. Lloyd, *"Penatibus et*

Magnis Dis," *AJPh* 77 (1956) 38-46, writes on the allegorical relationship between Aeneas and Augustus; Aen. 8.679 echoes 3.12; in "On *Aeneid,* III, 270-280," *AJPh* 75 (1954) 288-299, Lloyd discusses geographical details and problems of the Aeneas legend. H. W. Parke, "The Sources of Vergil, *Aeneid,* III, 692-705," *AJPh* 62 (1941) 490-492, points out that three oracles are echoed in this passage.

4. H. L. Tracy, "Aeneid IV: Tragedy or Melodrama?" *CJ* 41 (1945-46) 199-202, maintains that Vergil was not wholly successful in combining drama and epic. E. Paratore's *Il libro de Didone* (Roma 1947) contains the material in the introduction of his 1947 edition of *Aeneid* 4 (above, Sect. 2). P. Scazzoso, "Il libro IV dell' Eneide," *Paideia* 4 (1949) 81-100, believes that the book is not really tragic since it lacks true dramatic action, in spite of external connections with Greek drama. R. G. Austin, *The Fourth Book of the Aeneid* (Oxford 1951) writes a sympathetic analysis and maintains that Aeneas too suffered deeply; cf. L. Reys, "Verhouding Dido en Aeneas," *Hermeneus* 24 (1951-52) 93-98 (modern criticism stresses love rather than national duty). J. Beaujeu, "Le mariage d'Enée et de Dido et la causalité historique," *Revue du Nord* (Univ. de Lille) 36 (1954) 115-119, says that Vergil's problem was to arrange a marriage that was not a marriage, one which Dido considered as such without Aeneas' being bound by it; the view of Guillemin, 253ff. (also in *REL* 26 [1948] 198f.) is rejected; *inceptos* in 316 means "put into effect" rather than "not achieved"; this view of *inceptos* is supported by inscriptional evidence.

For the legend of Dido and the founding of Carthage, and Vergil's use of earlier material, see C. C. van Essen, "Dido," *Hermeneus* 20 (1948-49) 167-170; A. M. Panaro, "I precedenti del quarto libro dell' Eneide: La formazione della leggenda di Didone," *GIF* 4 (1951) 8-32. E. Burck, "Das Bild der Karthager in der römischen Literature," in J. Vogt (ed.), *Rom und Karthago* (Leipzig 1943) 336-345, believes that Vergil has followed Naevius in combining the Dido story with the Punic conflict but is the first to treat Dido with sympathetic understanding; Dido has the characteristics of a Roman matron. T. B. DeGraff, "Dido—*Tota Vergiliana,*" *CW* 43 (1949-50) 147-151, maintains that Vergil, not Naevius, invented the Dido-Aeneas romance and created the character of Dido. W. C. McDermott, "Elissa," *TAPhA* 74 (1943) 205-214, examines the use of the names *Dido* and *Elissa* and suggests that *Elissa* may have been a name of affection applied to Dido by Aeneas.

A. E. Raymond, "What was Anchises' Ghost to Dido? (Vergil *Aeneid* 4. 427)," *Phoenix* 6 (1952) 66-68, justifies Dido's remark in 427 on artistic grounds; it is suggested by Aeneas' words in 351-353. According to Pöschl, 76-79, the *lacrimae* of 449 are those of Aeneas; cf. Knight, 205. V. Bongi.

"Apollonio Rodio, Virgilio ed Ennio," *Athenaeum* 24 (1946) 68-74, argues that Dido's dream in 465-468 is less indebted to *Argon.* 3.616-632 than to Ilia's dream in Ennius (35ff. Vahlen). R. Goosens, "Euménides ou Bacchantes (Virgile, *Enéide.* IV, 469)," *Latomus* 5 (1946) 75-78, defends Vergil's reference to *Eumenidum agmina;* Pentheus was no less mad than his mother and the other Maenads. E. Swallow, "Dido's Pyre," *CW* 45 (1951-52) 65-68, discusses Dido's deception of Anna and the household in 494ff.

5. E. Swallow, "The Strategic Fifth *Aeneid."* *CW* 46 (1952-53) 177-179, analyzes the book both as a charming interlude and as a preparation for the main purpose of the poem. For a discussion of the games, see W. H. Willis, "Athletic Contests in the Epic," *TAPhA* 72 (1941) 392-417; Büchner, 465-472 (*Anhang* by Mehl); the boat race in 114-285 is treated by A. M. Cayuela, "Un análisis literario escolar," *Helmantica* 4 (1953) 3-23. J. L. Heller. "Labyrinth or Troy Town?" *CJ* 42 (1946-47) 123-139, discusses the *Troiae lusus* of 5.545-603; the game performed by Roman youths on horseback has the peculiar geometrical design associated with the Labyrinth of Cnossus, the walls of Troy, and the evolutions of the Greek dance. For a thorough analysis of the earlier literature on the *Troiae lusus* and a bibliography from 1840 to 1952, see E. Mehl, "Troiaspiel," *RE* Supplb. VIII (1956) 888-905.

6. F. Aldao, "Significado espiritual del VIº libro de la *Eneida,*" *AILC* 3 (1945-46) 121-281, writes at length on the diverse elements in the book and its value as a summary of pagan eschatology. P. Grimal, "Le livre VI de l' Enéide' et son actualité en 23 av. J.-C.," *REA* 56 (1954) 40-60, describes the historical background of 6 and points out striking similarities between details in the book and the *ludi saeculares,* presented two years after Vergil's death; the analogies are to be explained by Vergil's knowledge of the plans for the festival. A. K. Michels, "Lucretius and the Sixth Book of the *Aeneid,*" *AJPh* 65 (1944), 135-148, points out many reminiscences of Lucretius' thought and expression in 6.

On the Sibyl of Cumae, see J. van Ooteghem, S.J., "L'oracle de la Sibylle au chant VI de l'Enéide," *LEC* 9 (1940) 14-17 (the prophecy in 83-97 does not fulfil the promise of Helenus in 3.458-460; *fortuna* in 96 is to be taken as *fortuna troiana*); J. F. Latimer, "Aeneas and the Cumaean Sibyl: A Study in Topography," *Vergilius* 5 (1940) 28-35; S. Eitrem, "La Sibylle de Cumes et Virgile," *SO* 24 (1945) 88-120 (legendary background; Vergil's description of the oracle and the sacrifices); H. Waszink, "Vergil and the Sibyl of Cumae," *Mnemosyne* 1 (1948) 43-58 (Vergil has combined the features of three earlier Sibyls into one).

A. K. Michels, "The Golden Bough of Plato,"

AJPh 66 (1954) 59-63, believes that the golden bough, like many other themes in *Aeneid* 6, derives from Plato; on the symbolism of the bough, see R. A. Brooks, *"Discolor Aura*: Reflections on the Golden Bough," *AJPh* 74 (1953) 260-280.

The Journey in the Underworld: H. L. Tracy, "Hades in Montage," *Phoenix* 8 (1954) 136-141, discusses the variety of source-materials: "a judicious mixture of *Märchen*, myth, and Roman institution." L. A. MacKay, "Three Levels of Meaning in *Aeneid* VI," *TAPhA* 86 (1955) 180-189, gives the three themes as the spiritual purification which fits Aeneas for his mission, the moral development underlying lives of heroic virtue, and the attempt to understand the nature and destiny of man. C. Murley writes on "The Classification of Souls in the Sixth *Aeneid*," in *Vergilius* 5 (1940) 17-27; cf. F. Norwood, "The Tripartite Eschatology of *Aeneid* 6," *CPh* 49 (1954) 15-26, who shows how Vergil has combined three underworlds, the Homeric, one where morals are predominant, and one of Roman heroes.

P. Jacob, C.I.C.M., "L' épisode de Palinure," *LEC* 20 (1952) 163-167, explains the contradictions between 6.337-383 and 5.835-871 by an original plan in which Palinurus was the helmsman of Orontes' ship in *Aeneid* 1; Vergil died before adjusting 6.337ff. to the new version in *Aeneid* 5. G. Carugno, "Gli aôroi nell' Antinferno virgiliano." *GIF* 6 (1953) 63-69, points out the uncertainty of the fate of the children prematurely dead (cf. 6.426-429). M. Treu, "Die neue 'Orphische' Unterweltsbeschreibung und Vergil," *Hermes* 82 (1954) 24-51, discusses the similarities between the newly discovered papyrus and *Aeneid* 6, especially 660-664 and 740-742; the differences are Vergilian and Roman. L. Alfonsi, "Precedenti dell' incontro di Enea ed Anchise," *Aevum* 29 (1955) 375-376, writes on 684-686 and 697-700; the meeting of Aeneas and Anchises is dependent on Cicero, *Somnium Scipionis* (*Rep.* 6.14). E. B. Stevens, "Aeneid 6.724ff. and Cicero's Hortensius," *CW* 36 (1942-43) 86-87, suggests that 724ff. to be indebted not only to Cicero's *Somnium Scipionis* and *Tusculan Disputations* 1.42, but also to the lost dialogue *Hortensius*. H. J. Rose, "Quisque Suos Patimur Manes," *HThR* 37 (1944) 45-48, suggests that *manes* in 743 means the land of ghosts, i.e. the otherworld; it is wrong to confuse *manes* in this passage with good and evil daimones (*genii*); cf. E. Magotteaux, "Mânes virgiliens et démon platonicien," *AC* 24 (1955) 341-351, who identifies *manes* in 743 with the Platonic *daimon*; *manes* means "destiny."

R. J. Getty, "Romulus, Roma, and Augustus in the Sixth Book of the *Aeneid*," *CPh* 45 (1950) 1-12, writes on Anchises' description of the Roman heroes in 756ff. and the manner in which Romulus foreshadows Augustus. Duckworth D, 304-308, analyzes the structure and content of 760-853 and compares the passage with the six Roman Odes of Horace. On the importance of 847-853 for an understanding of Roman culture in the time of Augustus, see F. Eggerding, "Parcere subiectis: Ein Beitrag zur Vergilinterpretation," *Gymnasium* 59 (1952) 31-52. F. Bömer, "Excudent alii," *Hermes* 80 (1952) 117-123, discusses the meaning of *excudere* in 847 and elsewhere in Vergil. On the interpretation of *instar* in 865, see E. Henschel, "Quantum instar in ipso," *Gymnasium* 59 (1952) 78 (the phrase means "how like he is to . . .").

E. L. Highbarger, *The Gates of Dreams: An Archaeological Examination of Vergil. Aeneid VI. 893-899* (Baltimore 1940; = *Johns Hopkins Univ. Stud. in Archaeology. No. 30*), provides a wealth of interesting and suggestive material on the background of the Gates of Dreams;[38] he believes that "the 'Gate of the Horns' is an Oriental concept of great antiquity, whose origin was lost even to the Greeks of Mycenaean times, though Homer reflects the idea. On the other hand, the 'Gate of Ivory' appeared to be an invention of the fertile Greek imagination" (vii); Aeneas' journey is *"an allegory of the soul's experiences* as it travels from heaven to earth and back again" (82); Highbarger seeks to explain the difficulty of 896 by saying that Vergil uses the gate of ivory both as the entrance to Orcus and the departure from Elysium. For later discussions of this passage, see T. J. Haarhoff, "The Gates of Sleep," *G&R* 17 (1948) 88-90 (*falsa ad caelum insomnia* are true visions which appear false to the world above); J. van Ooteghem, S.J., *"Somni portae,"* *LEC* 16 (1948) 386-390 (Aeneas departs through the ivory gate either because he was not a true shade, or to indicate that the departure was before midnight); Steiner (above, Sect. 6A) 88-96 (the underworld experience has a dreamlike character); F. M. Brignoli, "La porta d'avorio nel libro VI dell' 'Eneide'," *GIF* 7 (1954) 61-67 (the artistic importance of the ivory gate is this: Aeneas sees reality but it is like a dream to him and he does not realize its truth; cf. *Aen.* 8.730: *rerumque ignarus;* he must conquer through merit, not through preknowledge of destiny).

7-12. The articles on *Aeneid* 7-12 are few in number, an indication that far too many scholars and readers neglect the second half of the poem. C. J. Ellingham, "Nescioquid maius nascitur Iliade,"

14

G&R 11 (1941-42) 10-18, argues against the view that the second half of the *Aeneid* is "adulterated Homer"; Vergil's battle-victims are more sympathetically drawn. W. H. Alexander, *"Maius Opus (Aeneid* 7-12) "* (Berkeley 1951; = *Univ. Cal. Pub. Class. Philol.* 14, No. 5, pp. 193-214), believes that the second half of the poem is artistically superior to *Aeneid* 1-6; he views the story of Aeneas as the tragic tale of Everyman and the *Aeneid* as "a penetrating study of human existence." E. Turolla, "La seconda Eneide' e una determinazione di maniere diverse nell' opera virgiliana," *GIF* 7 (1954) 97-112. analyzes the structure and content of *Aeneid* 7-12 and praises Vergil's achievement, especially in Book 12. G. d'Anna, *Il problema della composizione dell' Eneide* (Roma 1957), building upon the theory of Paratore (above, note 2) 310ff. that parts of *Aeneid* 6 and 8 were written before first, argues that *Aeneid* 7-12 were composed before 1-6 and that Propertius referred to 7-12 when he said in 2, 34, 65f. that something greater than the *Iliad* was being born.

7. E. Fraenkel, "Some Aspects of the Structure of Aeneid VII," *JRS* 35 (1945) 1-14, writes on 37-45 as the exordium of *Aeneid* 7-12, Juno's soliloquy in 293ff. and the parallelism with 1.37ff., Allecto's activity, and the catalogue (641ff.) in relation to the Homeric catalogue. An appendix discusses the problem of Allecto and Ennius' Discordia; on this, see also W. F. J. Knight, "The Integration of Allecto," *CJ* (Malta) 3 (1948) 3-4. M. von Duhn, "Die Gleichnisse in den Allectoszenen des 7. Buches von Vergils Aeneis," *Gymnasium* 64 (1957) 59-83, examines the similes in 376-384, 460-466, 528-530 as introductory symbols for the later course of the war. H. T. Rowell, "Vergil and the Forum of Augustus," *AJPh* 62 (1941) 261-276, suggests that the palace of Latinus in 170-189 with its statues and trophies of war resembled the later Forum of Augustus and that Vergil had been consulted about the plans for the great national monument; cf. A. Degrassi, "Virgilio e il Foro di Augusto," *Epigraphica* 7 (1945) 88-103, who dates the installation of the statues in the niches of the hemicycles after 9 B.C.

8. F. Bömer, "Studien zum VIII. Buche der Aeneis," *RhM* 92 (1944) 319-369, considers the three important episodes to be those of Cacus (184-279), the archaeology of Latium (306-368), and the shield (626-728); the high point of the book is the prodigy (520-540); Bömer gives an analysis of the book and stresses its unity. Cf. N. Terzaghi, "Sulla composizione dell' VIII canto dell' Eneide," *Atti del V Congresso Naz. di Studi Romani* 5 (1946) 265-273.

G. Watson, *"Aeneid* viii. 215-217," *CR* 4 (1954) 99-100, interprets *colles clamore relinqui* as "the hills are left behind by the sound," that is, the sound echoes from the hills. A. Y. Campbell, "Virgil, *Aeneid* viii. 215-218— and its 'E-hoes'," *CR* 5 (1955) 137-139, supplies *impleri* with *colles* and reads *colles clamore propinqui.*

The significance of Hercules in 8 is treated by H. Fraenkel, "The Key Lines (VIII 185-89) for the Cacus Episode in the Aeneid," *Miscellanea Galbiati* (Milano 1951) I 127-128, (Augustus, like Hercules. will be recognized as a new god if he delivers his people from dire jeopardy); A. Loyen, "Hercule et Typhée: A propos de Virgile, *Enéide* VIII, 298," *Mélanges Ernout* (Paris 1940) 237-245 (Hercules as a god and symbol of Virtue fights against the personification of evil).

On Aeneas at the site of Rome, see three articles by P. Grimal: "La colline de Janus," *RA* 24 (1945) 56-87 (the Janiculum of 8.358 is not the present hill across the Tiber but the *arx,* one of the summits of the Capitoline); "La promenade d'Evandre et d'Enée à la lumière des fouilles récentes," *REA* 50 (1948) 348-351 (Evander points out sites which recall monuments erected by Augustus); "Enée à Rome et le triomphe d'Octave," *REA* 53 (1951) 51-61 (Aeneas arrives at Rome on the very day in August when Octavian's triumph was celebrated in 29 B.C.; the book as a whole is a souvenir of the triumph).

G. Funaioli, "Sui versi 541-544 del libro VIII dell' Eneide," *Atti del V Congresso Naz. di Studi Romani* 5 (1946) 274-277,[39] discusses the sacrifices offered by Evander and Aeneas. J. J. Savage, "Catiline in Vergil and in Cicero," *CJ* 36 (1940-41) 225-226, suggests that Catiline is mentioned in 668f. because the conspiracy took place in the year of Augustus' birth.

9. P. Colmant, S.J., "L'épisode de Nisus et Euryale ou le poème de l'amitié *(Enéide,* IX, 176-502)," *LEC* 19 (1951) 89-100, discusses the composition and the characters. On Nisus' question concerning Fate and Free Will, see J. D. Jefferis, *"Aeneid* IX, 184f.," *CJ* 35 (1939-40) 484; R. Schaerer, "Sur deux vers de Virgile: Dieu sujet et Dieu attribut," *Mélanges Niedermann* (Neuchâtel 1944) 99-104; cf. Duckworth, *CJ* 51 (1955-56) 360f.

E. Breguet, "Virgile et les augures: à propos d'Enéide IX 324-328," *MH* 13 (1956) 54-62, discusses the ironical treatment of Ramnes in 9 and Vergil's attitude toward auguries elsewhere in the *Aeneid;* Ramnes as *rex* and *augur* resembles Aeneas, Romulus, and Augustus.

E. Zorzi, "Come muore Lico?" *SIFC* 25 (1951) 191-197, writes an analysis of 556-568.

10. A. Maréchal, "Sur la mort de Lausus (Virgile *Aen.* X, 811-832)," *Mélanges Ernout* (Paris 1940) 251-257.

11. C. W. Mendell, "The Influence of the

15

Epyllion on the *Aeneid,"* *YClS* 12 (1951) 205-226, shows that *Aeneid* 11 well illustrates the epyllion structure; the book is divided into three sections, each with a focal point: 1-224 around 100-138 (Aeneas' appeal for peace); 225-467 around 302-335 (Latinus' speech); 468-915 around 648-724 (deeds of Camilla); Mendell points out examples of the same technique in Books 4 and 7.

12. On Turnus, see below, Sect. 6C.

J. Fontenrose, "Apollo and Sol in the Oaths of Aeneas and Latinus," *CPh* 38 (1943) 137-138, discusses 161-215 and maintains that Apollo and Sol are not the same. A. H. F. Thornton, "The Last Scene of the *Aeneid,"* *G&R* 22 (1953) 82-84: Turnus, full of *furor* and *violentia* must die, cf. 6.853: *debellare superbos;* Aeneas is not to be viewed as a ruthless avenger.

6C. Aeneid: Characters[40]

General studies include E. Longi, *Personaggi virgiliani* (Palermo 1940), on Aeneas and Dido, Amata, Nisus and Euryalus, Pallas, Mezentius and Lausus, Camilla, and Turnus; E. C. Evans, "Literary Portraiture in Ancient Epic," *HSPh* 58-59 (1948) 201-205, on the portraiture of Aeneas, Dido, and Turnus; A. Pinto de Carvalho, "Galeria feminina da Eneida," *Kriterion* 33-34 (1955) 356-386, on Creusa, Lavinia, Andromache, Camilla, and particularly Dido.

Aeneas. See G. Funaioli, "La figura di Enea in Virgilio," *A&R* 9 (1941) 3-16;[41] G. Carlsson, "The Hero and Fate in Virgil's Aeneid," *Eranos* 43 (1945) 111-135 (on Aeneas' submission to a higher Power); J. N. Hritzu, "The Ideality of Aeneas," *CW* 38 (1944-45) 27-29; "A New and Broader Interpretation of the Ideality of Aeneas," *CW* 39 (1945-46) 98-103, 106-110 (on the humility and compassion of Aeneas and his pilgrimage as the pilgrimage of man, "striving to fulfill his divine mission of the gaining of the kingdom of heaven and the salvation of his own soul"); "Aeneas, the Noblest of the Romans," *CW* 42 (1948-49) 178-186; M. Hadas, "Aeneas and the Tradition of the National Hero," *AJPh* 69 (1948) 408-414 (Vergil's portrayal of Aeneas shows parallels to Hellenized oriental literature); C. Gargiulo, *La religiosità di Virgilio nella figura di Enea* (Messina 1950); J. W. Spaeth, Jr., "Hector's Successor in the *Aeneid,"* *CJ* 46 (1950-51) 277-280 (Aeneas has the role of Hector, Turnus that of Achilles); V. Pöschl, "Das Zeichen der Venus und die Gestalt des Aeneas," *Festschrift Regenbogen* (Heidelberg 1952) 135-143; H. L. Tracy, "The Gradual Unfolding of Aeneas' Destiny," *CJ* 48 (1952-53) 281-284; W. D. Anderson, "Venus and Aeneas: The Difficulties of Filial *Pietas,"* *CJ* 50 (1954-55) 233-238. H. Liebing, *Die Aeneasgestalt*

bei Vergil (Kiel 1953),[42] makes a thorough study of Aeneas' character, with copious reference to scholarly discussions; he opposes those who see a development in the hero's character.

Amata. S. Patris, I.E.J., "Une figure féminine de l'Enéide: Amata, reine des Latins," *LEC* 13 (1945) 40-54, attributes to Amata the Roman traits of energy, tenacity, and audacity.

Anna. E. Swallow, *"Anna Soror,"* *CW* 44 (1950-51) 145-150, writes on the importance of Anna's role in the tragedy of Dido and absolves her from blame.

Ascanius. See R. E. Coleman, "Puer Ascanius," *CJ* 38 (1942-43) 142-147; L. H. Feldman, "The Character of Ascanius in Virgil's 'Aeneid'," *CJ* 48 (1952-53) 303-313 (Vergil glorifies the promise of Roman youth for the future).

Dido. See H. N. Couch, "Nausicaa and Dido," *CJ* 37 (1941-42) 453-462; F. De Ruyt, "Infelix Dido!" (Virgile, *Eneide* VI, 450-476)," *LEC* 11 (1942) 320-324 (the tragedy of Dido is presented with psychological insight); C. A. Forbes, "Tragic Dido," *CB* 29 (1952-53) 51-53, 58 (on Dido as a symbol of tragic love and of the clash between East and West); Sister M. Loretta Margaret Killeen, I.H.M., "Character Analysis of Dido," *CB* 31 (1954-55) 53, 56-57.

Juno. C. W. Amerasinghe, " 'Saturnia Juno'—Its Significance in the *Aeneid,"* *G&R* 22 (1953) 61-69, views Juno as a tragic figure, guilty of hybris, and powerless to carry out her wishes, even though she is the daughter of Saturn. L. A. MacKay, *"Saturnia Juno,"* *G&R* 3 (1956) 59-60, likewise rejects the astrological implications of any reference to Saturn; the epithet "Saturnia" is applied to Juno chiefly where her activity is in defense of the old order and the native traditions of the *Saturnia. tellus.*

Mezentius. F. A. Sullivan, S.J., "Virgil's Mezentius," *Classical Essays . . . J. A. Kleist* (St. Louis 1946) 93-112, 118-120, shows that Mezentius, beginning as an *impius* warrior, is sympathetically portrayed as a tragic figure.

Turnus. See G. E. Duckworth, "Turnus as a Tragic Character," *Vergilius* 4 (1940) 5-17 (Turnus' real tragedy is his inability to live up to his ideals); E. L. Highbarger, "The Tragedy of Turnus: A Study of Vergil, *Aeneid* XII," *CW* 41 (1947-48) 114-124 (a tragic character not only because of his personal traits but because he is a victim of gradually increasing ill fortune); W. Ehlers, "Turnus," *RE* VII A (1948) 1409-1413; J. B. Garstang, "The Tragedy of Turnus," *Phoenix* 4 (1950) 47-58 (his tragedy is that he is driven to face death in an unequal

16

combat); R. M. Boltwood, "Turnus and Satan as Epic 'Villains'," *CJ* 47 (1951-52) 183-186.

6D. *Structure of the Aeneid*

H. L. Tracy, "The Pattern of Vergil's *Aeneid* I-VI," *Phoenix* 4 (1950) 1-8, describes the structural design and the contrasting color and tone values in the first six books; he criticizes Vergil for "fussiness" and thinks that the poet worked too hard for effects.

Perret, 111-120, writes on the architecture of the poem; he isolates *Aeneid* 6 from his structural analysis and believes that 5 concludes the story of Carthage. His analysis of 7-12 is unusual and interesting: he links together 7 and 8 as books of negotiations, 10 and 11 as books of combat; but 7 and 11 concern the Latins, 8 and 10 Aeneas' allies, Arcadians and Etruscans, while 9 and 12 are reserved for Turnus and Trojan valor.[43]

Conway's theory[44] of the alternation of the books of the *Aeneid*, the odd-numbered books being lighter, those of even numbers of a more serious and tragic nature, is stressed both by T. W. Stadler, *Vergils Aeneis: Eine poetische Betrachtung* (Einsiedeln 1942) and by Duckworth A, 5f., 10-15; Stadler looks upon the even-numbered books as books of depth, dealing chiefly with the hero, his mission, and Fate (systolic books), the other books (diastolic) being those of breadth, more concerned with other characters and events.

Vergil divided his epic into two halves (cf. *maius opus*, 7.45), and Duckworth shows that the second six books form a parallel panel to the first six, with various similarities and contrasts between the corresponding books 1 and 7, 2 and 8, 3 and 9, etc., e.g., on the head of Iulus (2.681ff.) and Augustus (8.680f.), Anchises on Aeneas' shoulders —symbolic of the past (2.721f.) and the shield on Aeneas' shoulder—symbolic of the future (8.729ff.).

But Vergil also arranged his epic in three parts;[45] this is emphasized by Stadler, Pöschl, and Büchner. Pöschl, 280, considers the three parts (1-4, 5-8, 9-12) to be "Dunkel—Licht—Dunkel," and Büchner, 418, summarizes the three parts as follows: 1-4, Aeneas in Carthage; 5-8, arrival in Latium and preparation for battle; 9-12, the conflict; see also W. A. Camps, "A Note on the Structure of the *Aeneid*," *CQ* 4 (1954) 214-215, who excludes 7.25-285 from his analysis and looks upon the central portion as composed of 5-6 and 8-9. It is better to view the three-fold division as a central portion (5-8) on the destiny of Rome, framed by two tragedies, that of Dido (1-4) and of Turnus (9-12).

6E. *The Trojan Legend*

On the rivalry between the families of Aeneas and Priam and the different versions of Aeneas' flight from Troy, see J. van Ooteghem, S.J., "Qui était Enée?" *LEC* 12 (1943-44) 118-126 (Vergil justified Aeneas's departure); V. Ussani, Jr., "Enea traditore," *SIFC* 22 (1947) 109-123 (Vergil substituted for the older tradition of *Aeneas proditor* that of *pius Aeneas*).

J. Perret rejects the evidence that both Stesichorus and Hellanicus knew the story of Aeneas' journey westward to Sicily or Italy, and in his 700-page book, *Les origines de la légende troyenne de Rome (281-31)* (Paris 1942), maintains that the Aeneas legend originated in the third century B.C. in connection with Pyrrhus, king of Epirus, who, considering himself a second Achilles, wished to wage a second Trojan War against the Romans, the descendants of the Trojans; Perret's theory is rejected by most scholars, e.g., P. Boyancé, "Les origines de la légende troyenne de Rome," *REA* 45 (1943) 275-290.[46]

On the Aeneas-Anchises statuettes found at Veii, see G. Bendinelli, "Gruppo fittile di Enea e Anchise proveniente da Veio," *RFIC* 26 (1948) 88-97. F. Bömer, *Rom und Troia: Untersuchungen zur frühgeschichte Roms* (Baden-Baden 1951), uses the statuettes as a means of dating the origin of the Aeneas legend in the late sixth century B.C., but agrees with Perret that the legend became a theme of Greek and Roman propaganda in the third century. Bömer also discusses problems concerning the Penates; cf. P. Boyancé, "Les pénates et l'ancienne religion romaine," *REA* 54 (1952) 109-115.

T. S. Duncan, "The Aeneas Legend on Coins," *CJ* 44 (1948-49) 15-29, shows the importance of ancient coins for the study of myth and history. A. Alföldi, *Die Troianischen Urahnen der Römer* (Basel 1957) treats of the early development of the Aeneas legend, especially among the Etruscans, and the important role played by Lavinium; for the later period he provides a wealth of numismatic evidence. W. Ehlers, "Die Gründungsprodigien von Lavinium und Alba Longa," *MH* 6 (1949) 166-175, writes on Vergil's use of earlier tradition in connection with the omens of the tables (*Aeneid* 3 and 7) and the sow with young (3 and 8). W. H. Fitzgerald, S.J., "The Wandering Aeneas," *CB* 28 (1951-52) 15-17, 20, discusses the development of the Aeneas legend and suggests that the story of a Trojan emigration to Italy may possibly have historical foundation. A. J. Gossage, "Two Implications of the Trojan Legend," *G&R* 2 (1955) 23-29, 72-81, maintains that Vergil builds up Aeneas' reputation as a fighter, e.g., in *Aen.* 11.281-292 (but in the *Iliad* Aeneas is coupled with Hector as a brave warrior far more often than Gossage appears to realize); the Romans are the descendants of a, vanquished people, but Rome takes vengeance on Greece for the sack of Troy; cf. *Aen.* 1.283-285, 6.836-840.

6F. *Geography and Archaeology*

On Cumae and the cave of the Sibyl, see P. O'R. Smiley, "In the Steps of Aeneas," *G&R* 17 (1948) 97-103 (stresses Vergil's accuracy in topographical details); J. H. Taylor, S.J., "With Vergil at Cumae," *CB* 29 (1952-53) 37-40 (describes the excavations of 1932).

For the topography and archaeology of the coastal district of the Roman Campagna and for descriptions of Ostia, Ardea, and Lavinium we are indebted to B. Tilly, *Vergil's Latium* (Oxford 1947).[47] The book is valuable in establishing the scene, ancient and modern, of *Aeneid* 7-12. Tilly rejects the traditional view that the oracle of Albunea (*Aen.* 7.81-101) was near Tivoli, ancient Tibur, and locates it at Zolforata, sulphur springs not far from Pratica di Mare, ancient Lavinium. M. Guarducci, "Albunea," *Studi Funaioli* (Rome 1955) 120-127, also argues against Tibur and places the grove in the vicinity of Ardea. F. A. Sullivan, S.J., "In Old Latium with Vergil and Livy," *CB* 29 (1952-53) 61-64, includes in his discussion the region of the Alban hills and lakes.

7A. *Vergil's Life and Works: General*

In addition to Büchner's comprehensive *RE* article, also published separately, recent books dealing with Vergil's life and works in general include Knight's *Roman Vergil*, Letter's *Virgil*, Guillemin's *Virgile*, Perret's *Virgile*, and Paratore's *Virgilio*.[48]

Knight has written a strange, somewhat disorganized book, with many challenging but unsupported theories;[49] he deals much with Vergil's use of earlier material, to which he applies the term "integration."[50] Letters writes for the general public rather than for the classical student or scholar; he stresses the importance of *Aeneid* 6 for the unity of the poem, and his sketchy treatment of 7-12 seems typical of the tendency to neglect the second half of the epic. Guillemin is interested in Vergil's poetic art and the unity of his thought; the poet founds Roman classicism by combining the two literary currents represented by Catullus and Lucretius.[51] Perret has much on chronology and structure, on political allusions and symbolism; his book is extremely informative and suggestive for its size and contains a useful 21-page bibliography arranged under appropriate headings.[52] Paratore's *Virgilio* first appeared in 1945; the second edition (1954) contains many references to and criticisms of Knight, Pöschl, and Guillemin; Paratore is concerned with ethical, religious, and political values; some of his many theories seem questionable, e.g., that the *Georgics* is an Epicurean poem written under the influence of Horace's pessimism, or that the Homeric element in the *Aeneid* is secondary and reached by way of Naevius and Ennius.[53]

J. Giono, *Les pages immortelles de Virgile* (Paris 1947), writes a long essay on Vergil and then gives, in French translation, selections from Vergil's works; J. Echave-Sustaeta, *Virgilio* (Barcelona 1947), writes a series of short essays, to accompany selections from Vergil (both in Latin and in Spanish translation). T. J. Haarhoff, *Vergil the Universal* (Oxford 1949), reprints with minor changes *Vergil in the Experience of South Africa* (Oxford 1931); the Introduction, "Universality in Vergil" is new; in this he refers to Knight's *Roman Vergil* as "our best modern book on the poet." G. Caiati, *Vita di Virgilio* (Padova 1952), discusses both life and works.

Two strange books are listed here as literary curiosities, without recommendation. F. Aussaresses, *Virgile journaliste* (Paris 1947), bases the material of the book on his earlier article, "Virgile et le Redressement romain," *Lettres d'humanité* 5 (1946) 149-185; he views Vergil as a writer of government propaganda for a program of Roman rehabilitation; much of the book is in the form of imaginary conversations between the author and Vergil, Maecenas, Agrippa, or Horace. P. Richard, *Virgile auteur gai* (Paris 1951), interprets Vergilian scenes and episodes as comedy, parody, or irony; Aeneas' adventures are laughable to the modern reader; the war scenes add to the comic effect; Anchises' words in *Aen.* 6.694 are worthy of Terence (cf. *And.* 106), etc. A better guide to Vergil's humor is provided by O. L. Wilner, "Humor in Vergil's Aeneid," *CW* 36 (1942-43) 93-94.

Of a scholarly and specialized nature are A. G. Blonk, *Vergilius en het landschap* (Leiden 1947), on the poet's description of scenery and his treatment of nature: reflective quiet in the *Eclogues*, life and movement in the *Georgics*, scenery used for comparisons in the *Aeneid*; and M. Desport, *L'incantation virgilienne* (Paris 1952; 486 pp.); on poetry as incantation and Orpheus the enchanter as Vergil's ideal of the poet; on this work, cf. Guillemin, *REL* 30 (1952) 418-420.

Each of the following books contains chapters on Vergil: J. Cousin, *Etudes sur la poésie latine: Nature et mission du poète* (Paris 1945), 110-124 (on Vergil and others as poets inspired by Apollo and the Muses; Augustan poetry is described as "æsthetic and political mysticism"; E. Henriot, *Les fils de la Louve: Etudes latines* (Paris 1949), 97-136 (critical analysis for the general reader; Vergil is Alexandrian, scholar, archæologist, prophet, psychologist, philosopher, and propagandist, but always the poetic artist to a supreme degree); G. Highet, *Poets in a Landscape* (New York 1957), 45-73 (on the poet's life and works in relation to the Italian

18

countryside which he knew and loved).

Short essays and articles include the following: J. Erskine, "Vergil," *CJ* 36 (1940-41) 390-400 (general appreciation; his message to us today); R. V. Schoder, S.J., "The Uniqueness of Vergil," *CB* 18 (1941-42) 59 (his understanding of the human soul); W. C. Korfmacher, "Vergil as Poet and Thinker in Latin IV," *CB* 23 (1946-47) 69-71; F. Klingner, "Virgil," in H. Berve (ed.), *Das neue Bild der Antike* II (Leipzig 1942) 219-245[34] (an important discussion of the *Eclogues*, *Georgics*, and *Aeneid*, with emphasis on Vergil as a poet; the art of Vergil and Horace differs strikingly from that of Catullus and Lucretius); F. Beckmann, *Mensch und Welt in der Dichtung Vergils* (Münster 1950; *Orbis antiquus*, Heft 1) (on the unity of Vergil's work; the Arcady of the *Eclogues*, the toil of the *Georgics*, and the action of the *Aeneid* are to be reconciled, for Aeneas is an Arcadian spirit and the ultimate goal of Fate is *otium*; the *pax Augusta* will restore the *Saturnia regna*);[35] J. Bayet, "L'expérience sociale de Virgile," *Deucalion* 2 (1947) 197-214 (Daphnis in *Eclogue* 5 is Caesar; in the *Georgics* hard work is the plan of Jupiter and human welfare comes from a rustic life; Aeneas is the archetype of the Roman *princeps* and the legends of the epic are oriented to the achievements of Augustus); K. Latte, "Vergil," *A&A* 4 (1954) 155-169 (on Vergil's poetic development from a disciple of the *novi poetae* to the leading representative of Augustan classicism).

7B. Religion and Philosophy[36]

N. W. DeWitt, "Virgil, Augustus, Epicureanism," *CW* 35 (1941-42) 281-282, suggests that the reason for Vergil's defection from Epicureanism was snobbery originating in Greece; Platonism and Stoicism were the two socially correct creeds. C. N. Cochrane, *Christianity and Classical Culture* (New York 1940), 61-73, writes on Vergil's philosophy of history and his conception of cosmic justice. E. Tavenner, "Roman Religion with Especial Relation to Vergil," *CJ* 40 (1944-45) 198-220, discusses Vergil's attitude toward and use of the old Roman religion. L. Herrmann, "Virgile a-t-il imité la Bible?", *AC* 14 (1945) 85-91, examines and rejects supposed influences of the Bible in *Eclogues*, *Georgics*, and *Aeneid*.

R. Allain, "Quelques aspects de l'unité de l'Enéide," *LEC* 14 (1946) 151-173; the *Aeneid* presents a unified philosophical conception; Stoicism is everywhere victorious over Epicureanism, and the allusions to Lucretius do not have the meaning usually attributed to them. K. Büchner, *Der Schicksalsgedanke bei Vergil* (Freiburg i. Br. 1946); on Fate,

the will of Jupiter, the role of Aeneas, Augustus as the fulfilment. A. Guillemin, "L'unité de l'oeuvre virgilienne," *REL* 26 (1948) 189-203; the religious philosophy of the *Aeneid* is the same as that of the *Georgics*: belief in a Divine Providence who acts without violating human liberty. W. P. Clark, "Vergil's Gods," *CW* 42 (1948-49) 50-55; on Vergil as a religious man and a philosophic poet. J. Perret, "Le polythéisme de Virgile," *Mélanges Picard* (Paris 1949; = *RA* 29-32) II 793-802; on Vergil's treatment of the gods and his relation to contemporary religious thought, especially that of Varro.

A. Wankenne, S.J., "Le thème de la mort chez Virgile," *LEC* 19 (1951) 230-234; "Le thème de l'au-delà chez Virgile," *ibid.* 384-390; illustrations from Vergil's poetry. P. Boyancé, "Le sens cosmique de Virgile," *REL* 32 (1954) 220-249; on Vergil's preoccupation with the cosmos and man's relation to it; Iopas in *Aen.* 1.740-746 is the type of cosmic poet that Vergil dreamed of becoming. M. E. Taylor, "Primitivism in Virgil," *AJPh* 76 (1955) 261-278; both chronological and cultural primitivism. M. L. Clarke, *The Roman Mind* (Cambridge, Mass. 1956) 66-88; philosophy and religion in the Augustan age.

7C. Rome and Augustus

The political aspects of Vergil's poetry are stressed by many writers; see H. Haffter, "Politisches Denken im alten Rom," *SIFC* 17 (1940) 97-121, on the political ideals of Vergil and his contemporaries and their indebtedness to earlier Roman thought; A. Graf Schenk von Stauffenberg, "Vergil und der Augusteische Staat," *WG* 9 (1943) 55-67,[37] on Vergil's references to Augustus and Rome; in *Eclogue* 4 the birth of the child is to be understood as symbolic of the Golden Age (cf. Büchner above, Sect. 4C); O. B. Roegele, *Die Botschaft des Vergil* (Heidelberg 1947), on the gods, Fate, and the Roman *imperium*; H. J. Rose, *Aeneas Pontifex* (London 1948),[38] on Aeneas as a pontiff and as symbolic of Augustus; F. Beckmann, *Der Friede des Augustus* (Münster Westf. 1951, 2d ed. 1954), on Aeneas as symbolic of Augustus, who is representative of the Roman virtues and founder of the *pax Augusta*; J. Wytzes, *Vergilius: De Dichter van het Imperium* (Kampen 1951), on Vergil's conception of *imperium*, the importance of *pietas* and *fatum*, the divinity of Augustus; in spite of his high ideals Vergil's outlook is pagan rather than Christian.

F. Bömer, "Vergil und Augustus" (above, note 2) writes an important and comprehensive article on Vergil's references to Augustus and the problem of his divinity. F. Klingner, "Virgil und die geschichtliche Welt," *Römische Geisteswelt.* I (3d ed., München 1953) 275-293, discusses Vergil's conception of history and his praise of Augustus. P. Lambrechts, "La politique apollinienne' d'Auguste et le culte impérial," *NClio* 5 (1953) 65-82, stresses the importance of Apollo and Augustus in Vergil's works. J. Oroz, "Virgilio, poeta del 'imperium'," *Helmantica* 4 (1953) 251-277, writes on the divine mission of Rome and the necessity of *imperium*. P. de Jonge, "De aanvaarding van het Principaat door Livius en Vergilius," *TG* 66 (1953) 39-55, compares the attitudes of the two writers. W. C. Korfmacher, "*Vergilius Redivivus*," *CW* 47 (1953-54) 1-4, discusses Vergil's ideal of peace and justice under Roman rule.

Most recent are the following: C. G. Starr, "Virgil's Acceptance of Octavian," *AJPh* 76 (1955) 34-46 (Vergil did not accept Octavian until about 40 B.C.); L. Pepe, "Virgilio e la questione dinastica," *GIF* 8 (1955) 359-371 (Vergil's emphasis on Marcellus and the Claudian line); P. Grimal, *Le siècle d'Auguste* (Paris 1955) 58-71 (on the independence of Vergil and Horace, on the *Aeneid* as a poem of Rome and its origins, and as an instrument of reconciliation between the two halves of the Empire); W. C. Korfmacher, "Vergil, Spokesman for the Augustan Reforms," *CJ* 51 (1955-56) 329-334 (on the nature of the reforms and Vergil's support of them); A. Dalzell, "Maecenas and the Poets," *Phoenix* 10 (1956) 151-162 (the source of inspiration in politics was Vergil rather than Maecenas); U. Knoche, "Zur Frage der epischen Beiwörter in Vergils Aeneis," *Festchrift Bruno Snell* (München 1956) 89-100 (on the significance of the epithets *pius* and *pater* for the Romans of Vergil's day).

7D. Vergil and Horace

The relation of the two poets is treated under three headings: (1) as spokesmen for the Augustan regime, (2) as creators of Augustan poetry, (3) as friends who influenced each other's poetry (on *Eclogue* 4 and *Epode* 16, see above, Sect. 4C).

1. H. Oppermann, "Das römische Schicksal und die Zeit des Augustus," *HZ* 164 (1941) 1-20, compares Vergil, Horace, and Livy in their treatment of Rome and Augustus. E. K. Rand, *The Building of Eternal Rome* (Cambridge, Mass. 1943) 50-80, views Vergil and Horace as builders of the "ideal empire." M. A. Levi, *Il tempo di Augusto* (Firenze 1951) 183-214, discusses the importance of Vergil and Horace for the cultural life and the political ideals of the Augustan age. G. Andrés, "Virgilio y Horacio, colaboradores a la Paz octaviana," *Helmantica* 3 (1952) 101-125. C. Koch, "Roma Aeterna," *Gymnasium* 59 (1952) 128-143, 196-209; this is an important article on the Augustan idea of *Roma aeterna* as seen in Vergil, Horace, and Livy, and on

Augustus as a second Romulus.

2. F. Klingner, *Dichter und Dichtkunst im alten Rom* (Leipzig 1947; = *Leipziger Universitätsreden*, Heft 15),[59] writes on tradition and originality in Vergil and Horace and the artistic nature of their poetry. E. Fraenkel, "Carattere della poesia augustea," *Maia* 1 (1948) 245-264, discusses Vergil and Horace as the creators of Augustan poetry, their style and their regard for structure and symmetrical proportion. L. Pepe, "Virgilio giudice di se stesso," *GIF* 8 (1955) 97-104, compares the attitudes of Horace and Vergil toward Greek poetry; there is no reference to literature in *Aen.* 6.847ff., and Vergil affirms the superiority of his own poetry. F. Bömer, "Beiträge zum Verständnis der augusteischen Dichtersprache," *Gymnasium* 64 (1957) 1-21, discusses Horace's and Vergil's choice of words, compares *Odes* 3.30 and *Aen.* 6.847ff., and stresses the simplicity of Vergil's style.

3. E. L. Highbarger, "Vergil and Horace, Friends," *Vergilius* 6 (1940) 38-40, discusses the indebtedness of each to Homer. C. T. Murphy, "Vergil and Horace," *CB* 18 (1941-42) 61-64, cites parallels in their poetry to prove the close relationship of the two poets throughout their lives. A. Kurfess, "Vergil und Horaz," *ZRGG* 6 (1954) 359-364, suggests that Horace parodies *Eclogue* 4 in *Epode* 16, *Georg.* 2.458ff. in *Epode* 2, and *Eclogue* 8 in *Epodes* 5 and 17 and *Sat.* 1.8. A. Rutgers van der Loeff, "Horatius bij Vergilius," *Hermeneus* 26 (1955) 163-165, considers *Aen.* 12.517-520 a reminiscence of *Epode* 2, but thinks that Vergil otherwise was not influenced by Horace. Duckworth, "*Animae Dimidium Meae*: Two Poets of Rome" (above, note 2), analyzes the influence of Vergil and Horace on each other, especially in dealing with political and imperial themes (*Eclogue* 4 and *Epode* 16; *Georgics* 1 and *Odes* 1.2; *Aeneid* 6 and *Odes* 1.12, 3.1-6; cf. the echoes of Vergil in *Carm. Saec.* and *Odes* 4).

7E. Varia

On Vergil's attitude toward home and travel, see E. Janssens, "Virgile et l'esprit d'aventure," *Latomus* 5 (1946) 103-109 (passages illustrating the poet's interest in travel and adventure); X. Tilliette, "Virgile et la maison," *LEC* 15 (1947) 15-30 (Vergil's love of a simple home and garden); G. Tronquart, "Le sens profond du retour à la terre chez Virgile," *BAGB* 3 (1953) 3, pp. 37-41 (Vergil's plea for a return to country life in *Georgics* 2); A. Tomsin, "Virgile et l'Egypte," *AC* 22 (1953) 412-418 (Vergil accompanied Maecenas to Egypt in 29 B.C., hence the accuracy of the Nile descriptions in *Georg.* 4.287ff., *Aen.* 8.711ff.).

Vergil's relation to Roman art is discussed by E. L. Highbarger, "Vergil and Roman Art," *CW* 36 (1942-43) 87-89 (Vergil's use of architecture, sculpture, vases, and painting in his poetry); "Graeco-Roman Shepherds and the Arts," *CJ* 39 (1943-44) 366-368 (the art objects in *Eclogues* 3 and 7 may reflect actual life); L. A. Holland, "Aeneas-Augustus of Prima Porta," *TAPhA* 78 (1947) 276-284 (suggests that the artist was inspired by the description of Aeneas in *Aen.* 12.311ff.; the *princeps* has the costume and attributes of Aeneas); A. Lesky, "Amor bei Dido," *Festschrift Egger*, II (Klagenfurt 1953) 169-178 (Amor on Dido's knee is inspired by earlier art).

On the Vergil-Menander controversy, see R. Carpenter, *Observations on Familiar Statuary in Rome* (Roma 1941; = *MAAR* 18), 96-101 (the head ascribed to Menander is undoubtedly Roman and probably to be assigned to Vergil; the three portraits on the *Ara Pietatis Augustae* are suggested as those of Propertius, Vergil, and Horace); R. V. Schoder, S.J., "Found: A Portrait of Vergil?" *CB* 19 (1942-43) 1-2 (accepts Carpenter's views); V. M. Scramuzza, "Livy in the *Ara Pietatis Augustae?*" *CPh* 38 (1943) 240-245 (accepts Vergil as the central figure and believes that the other two are Livy and Horace); R. Herbig, "Zum Menander-Vergil-Problem," *MDAI(R)* 59 (1944) 77-87 (the head is Roman and dates from 30-25 B.C., but is not necessarily Vergil's); Carpenter, "A Contribution to the Vergil-Menander Controversy," *Hesperia* 20 (1951) 34-44 (on the characteristic marks of the many versions of the head and the reasons for ascribing it to Vergil); cf. J. F. Crome, "Il volto di Virgilio," *Atti e Memorie, Accad. Virg. di Mantova* 28 (1953) 5-24 (13 plates), who also attributes the head to Vergil.

8. *Style, Language, Meter*

General discussions include those by Knight, 180-281 (see above, note 49); J. de Echave-Sustaeta, *Estilística Virgiliana* (Barcelona 1950), on conditional clauses, hypotaxis, elliptical forms, parataxis; L. R. Palmer, *The Latin Language* (London 1954) 111-118, on poetic vocabulary, archaisms, introduction into epic of rhetorical devices (antithesis, anaphora, homoioteleuton, chiasmus); Büchner, 227-231 (*Eclogues*), 299-305 (*Georgics*), 409-417 (*Aeneid*).

Style. On various aspects of Vergil's poetic style, see W. F. J. Knight, "Repetitive Style in Virgil," *TAPhA* 72 (1941) 212-225 (Vergil in his mature work used repetitions more spontaneously, especially in passages of emotion); cf. Knight, "Pairs of Passages in Virgil," *G&R* 13 (1944) 10-14; L. P.

Wilkinson, "Onomatopoeia and the Sceptics," *CQ* 36 (1942) 121-133 (illustrations, chiefly from the *Georgics*); K. Büchner, "Der Superlativ bei Horaz,"[60] *Hermes* 79 (1944) 113-126 (Horace's use compared with Vergil's); P. Turnbull, "Vergil: Painter with Words," *CJ* 42 (1946-47) 97-101 (use of line and pattern, contrast of color, feeling for texture); J. S. Th. Hanssen, "Virgilian Notes," *SO* 26 (1948) 93-125 (93-112, on Vergil's imitation of lines and phrases of earlier poets; the common source in many cases is meter and the Latin language and way of thinking; 113-125, examples of plays upon the etymological meaning or origin of a word); A. Wankenne, S.J., "L'hypallage dans l'oeuvre de Virgile," *LEC* 17 (1949) 335-342 (especially *Aen.* 2.255, 6.268);[60a] M. L. Clarke, "Rhetorical Influences in the *Aeneid*," *G&R* 18 (1949) 14-27 (on rhetorical devices, especially in the Venus-Juno debate in *Aeneid* 10 and the Drances-Turnus debate in 11; the poet's art is such that we are not annoyed by his rhetorical effects); M. P. Cunningham, "Some Principles of Latin Phrasing: Quintilian 11.3.35-38 on Aeneid 1.1-3," *CW* 47 (1953-54) 17-22; N. I. Herescu, "Iucunditas in situ," *AC* 22 (1953) 89-93 (on choice of words and position in the verse).

Language. See A. Ernout, "Notes et Discussions," *RPh* 66 (1940) 143-166 (lists of Vergilian words and their appearance in later Roman authors); J. Marouzeau, "Virgile linguiste," *Mélanges Ernout* (Paris 1940) 259-265 (etymological value of words); W. S. Maguinness, "The Singular Use of *Nos* in Virgil," *CQ* 35 (1941) 127-135; J. S. Th. Hanssen, "Remarks on Euphony-Cacophony, and the Language of Virgil," *SO* 22 (1942) 80-106; S. Whately, "Noises Off: Some Sound-Effects in Virgil," *G&R* 14 (1945) 17-28; F. De Ruyt, "Note de vocabulaire virgilian: *somnia et insomnia*," *Latomus* 5 (1946) 245-248 (on *Aen.* 4.9 and 6.896); see now V. Ussani, Jr., *Insomnia: Saggio di critica semantica* (Roma 1955), 75-113 (on *Aen.* 4.9) 115-153 (on *Aen.* 6.896); S. and R. Werner, "Zur Neubildung von Substantiven auf -*men* bei den Dichtern der augusteischen Zeit," *MH* 6 (1949) 29-32 (*fundamen, libamen, gestamen, luctamen, stramen, munimen,* and *solamen* first appear in Vergil and are to be ascribed to him); cf. G. Pasquali, "I sostantivi in -*men*," *MH* 7 (1950) 227 (the words in -*men* were not invented by Vergil but belong to colloquial speech); R. J. Bastian, S.J., "Side-Lights on Emotion in Virgil," *CB* 27 (1950-51) 61-63 (on the effectiveness of words such as *nequiquam, moritura*); F. Bömer on *excudere*, see above, Sect. 6B (*Aeneid* 6); F. Bömer, "Der Akkusativus Pluralis auf -*is*, -*eis*, und -*es* bei Vergil," *Emerita* 21 (1953) 182-234; 22 (1954) 175-210 (a detailed study to determine

Vergil's spelling of the words); H. Hommel, "Secum tenere c. accus.," *Hermes* 82 (1954) 375-378 (on *Aen.* 1.675); E. Fraenkel, "Urbem quam statuo vestra est," *Glotta* 33 (1954) 157-159 (the famous "inverse attraction" in *Aen.* 1.573 is not merely an archaism but has a poetic effect; cf. the echo in 4.655).

Meter. See R. G. Kent, "A problem of Latin prosody," *Mélanges Marouzeau* (Paris 1948) 303-308 (on final syllables with short vowel and single final consonant made long by position before an initial vowel through retention of the final consonant as word-final, instead of carrying it over to the initial syllable of the following word); A. H. Ashcroft, "Vergil's Hexameter Line," *G&R* 20 (1951) 97-114 (on Vergil's effective use of line-endings, caesura, diaeresis, elision, alliteration, assonance, etc.); H. Drexler, "Hexameterstudien," *Aevum* 25 (1951) 435-466, 512-547 (a detailed study of the structure of Vergil's hexameter and comparisons with other Roman poets; 18 tables of statistics); V. P. Naughton, "Metrical Patterns in Lucretius' Hexameters," *CQ* 2 (1952) 152-167 (Lucretius a forerunner of Vergil in his use of homodyned and heterodyned lines); G. Michenaud, "Les sons du vers vergilien," *LEC* 21 (1953) 343-378 (a detailed study of Vergil's use of alliteration and the sound-effects gained by the repetition of certain letters).

9. Interpretation and Text Criticism

V. Ussani, Jr., "Un contributo alla critica del testo Virgiliano," *Atti d. Accad. naz. d. Lincei* 347 (1950), *Memorie, Cl. d. scienze mor., stor. e filol.* 8, 3, 2, pp. 85-171, attempts to determine the nature of the early text of Vergil by a detailed comparison of Vergilian lines and phrases appearing in the *Punica* of Silius Italicus. The fact that Silius agrees now with M. and now with P indicates that even in the first century A.D. numerous variant readings were already in existence; the evidence of Silius, who was a faithful imitator, should be decisive when M and P disagree with each other, or with the other manuscripts.

Eclogues. R. Verdière, "Virgilianum," *Latomus* 10 (1951) 279-280, reads in 1.65 *rabidum certe veniemus Araxen,* cf. *Aen.* 8.728; N.-O. Nilsson, "Ad Verg. ecl. 5.15," *Eranos* 53 (1955) 199-200, favors *iubeto certet,* the reading of P; A. Barigazzi, "Ad Verg. ecl. VII, 25 et Euphor, 140 P. (A.P. VI, 279)," *SIFC* 24 (1950) 29-31, prefers *crescentem.*

Georgics. G. Puccioni, "Varianti del testo virgiliano," *Maia* 6 (1953) 154-161, reads *Atho* in *Georg.* 1.332; V. Paladini, "Virg., G., II, 344: . . . *Frigusque caloremque* o . . . *Frigusque calorque?*" *SIFC* 21 (1946) 113-115, prefers the archaic neuter *calor;* W. H. Semple, "Virgil, *Georg.* iii 116-117," *CR* 60 (1946) 61-63, interprets *gressus glomerare* as "to add step to step in succession"; E. de Saint-Denis, "Notes sur le livre IV des *Géorgiques.*"

REL 28 (1950) 193-211, discusses 95-100 (meaning of *horrent*), 110-111 (*falx saligna*), 141 (defends the reading *pinus*). 203-205 (retains order of verses), 228-230 (*ora fove*), 260-263 (sense of *stridit*), 293 (*coloratis Indis*), 386 (meaning), 418-421 (*sinus reductos*); cf. his new edition of the *Georgics* (above, Sect. 2); R. Verdière, "Vergilianum," *Latomus* 9 (1950) 378, suggests *castris* for *rostris* in *Georg.* 4.74; if *rostris* is retained, it means 'platform'; F. R. Dale, "Virgil, *Georgics* iv. 229-230," *CR* 5 (1955) 14-15, interprets *ora fove* as "protect your face."

Aeneid. The following articles each discuss more than one passage: G. Wijdeveld, "Vergiliana," *Mnemosyne* 10 (1941-42) 77-80 (*Aeneid* 1, 4, 6, and 7); A. Burger, "Note critique sur deux passages de l'Enéide," *Mélanges Niedermann* (Neuchâtel 1944) 81-90 (on *Aen.* 1.518; 6.806); A. Montenegro Duque, "Sobre dos vocablos de la Eneida," *Emerita* 14 (1946) 237-241 (read *Marus* in 9.685; *actor* or *auctor* in 12.94ff.).

A. Boethius, "Nixae aere trabes," *Eranos* 50 (1952) 147-148, reads *nixae* for *nexae* in 1.448-449; G. Puccioni, "Varianti del testo virgiliano," *Maia* 6 (1953) 148-154, argues for *ruit alta a culmine Troia* in 2.290; cf. V. Ussani, Jr., "De Verg. Aen., II, 290," *Maia* 7 (1955) 216-230 (rejects Puccioni's reading); L. A. MacKay, "Three Notes on Virgil," *CW* 45 (1951-52) 258, suggests *ruentis* for *ruentis* in 2.771; E. Paratore, "Briciole filologiche," *Studi Funaioli* (Roma 1955) 329-332, interprets *Aen.* 4.456 as two separate clauses; *est* is to be supplied with *visum* and *effata;* W. T. Avery, "*Aeneid* 6.242: The Latinity of *unde* and the Reading *Aornon,*" *CPh* 50 (1955) 257-258, considers the verse spurious.

L. Herrmann, "Troyens ou colombes, Aventiniens ou Clausiens?" *Mélanges Marouzeau* (Paris 1948))249-252, places 13 before 201 in Book 6 and 664-665 before 721 in Book 7; W. Plankl, "Eine crux Vergiliana," *Gymnasium* 60 (1953) 172-174, reads *signat* for *signant* in 7.4: cf. H. Heubner, "Eine vermeintliche crux Vergiliana," *Gymnasium* 61 (1954) 229-230 (against Plankl); W. F. J. Knight, "*Caeli convexa per auras,*" *CQ* 34 (1940) 129-130, opposes emendation of the phrase in 7.543 and believes that Vergil wrote the ungrammatical and untranslatable phrase; on *Aen.* 8.215, see Watson and Campbell (above, Sect. 6B: *Aeneid* 8); R. Goossens, "Les travestissements fantastiques du senex...," *Latomus* 6 (1947) 317-328, reads *Cynci* with Lejay in *Aen.* 10.186; S. Timpanaro, Jr., "Miscellanea," *ASNP* 18 (1949) 201-204, reads in this same verse *Cunare* and thinks that *Cinyri* is a conjecture of an ancient editor; A. Montenegro Duque, "*Antheum* por *Antaeum* en *Aen.* X 561," *Emerita* 15 (1947) 142-148, argues in favor of *Antheus.*

10. Vergil and Earlier Writers

Many books and articles already cited discuss Vergil's use of material from Greek and Latin poetry, e.g., Knight, 73-110, on integration of literary reminiscences (cf. also above, note 50); Rose, 24-44, 139-161 (Vergil and Theocritus); Paratore, 295-337 (Vergil and Homer); Pöschl, see Index, 285f.: "Homer and Vergil."

F. Mehmel, *Virgil und Apollonius Rhodius: Untersuchung über die Zeitvorstellung in der antiken epischen Erzählung* (Hamburg 1940), compares the portrayal of time in Homer and Apollonius and Vergil's relation to each. G. Herzog-Hauser, "Zum

Problem der imitatio in der lateinischen Literatur," *WS* 64 (1949) 124-134, defends Vergil's procedure (*Aeneid* 4 and Apollonius, Palinurus and Elpenor). F. Klingner, "Virgil," *L'influence grecque sur la poésie latine de Catulle à Ovide* (Geneva 1956; *Fondation Hardt: Entretiens sur l'antiquité classique*, II, 1953) 129-155, presents the general poetic background, with emphasis on Theocritus and Lucretius, and discusses Vergil's originality; cf. 156-166, a discussion of Klingner's paper by V. Pöschl, A. Rostagni, D. van Berchem, L. P. Wilkinson, and P. Boyancé.

Homer. C. Marchesi, *Motivi dell'epica antica* (Milano 1942) 33-41, on differences of technique and spirit between Homer and Vergil; L. J. D. Richardson, "Virgil and the Homeric Epithet," *G&R* 12 (1943) 1-14, on the difficulties of reproducing in Latin verse the compound adjectives of Homeric epic and the various expedients attempted by Vergil; W. F. J. Knight, *Vergil and Homer* (1950),[61] on integration of earlier material by both Homer and Vergil; L. Schley, "Vergils Homerisieren in der Aeneis," *Wiss. Zeitschr. der Univ. Leipzig, Ges.— & Sprachwiss. Reihe* 1 (1952-53) 3, pp. 89-117; W. Kühn, "Rüstungsszenen bei Homer und Vergil," *Gymnasium* 64 (1957) 28-59, a comparison of scenes of warriors putting on armor and a discussion of Vergil's originality; an "Anhang" treats the *prodigium*-scene in *Aen.* 8.520-540 and its importance for Aeneas' realization of *fatum.*

Aeschylus. See Ussani (above, Sect. 6B: *Aeneid* 2).

Bacchylides. E. Paratore, "Bacchilide e Virgilio," *WS* 69 (1956) 289-296, on parallels between *Epinician* 5 and *Aeneid* 6.

Apollonius. Cf. Mehmel, above. M. Hügi, *Vergils Aeneis und die hellenistische Dichtung* (Bern 1952; *Noctes Romanae* 4), devotes most of his volume to Vergil's imitation of Apollonius and seeks to show why and how he used the borrowed motifs. Certain features of the Dido episode are inspired by Apollonius but contain no verbal reminiscences; the epic character of *Aeneid* 4 derives from Homer, but the tragic and elegiac elements come from Apollonius who had introduced the love-motif into epic. Vergil expanded and changed what he borrowed to produce something different — and greater. For Apollonius' influence on Vergil, see also H. Herter, "Bericht über die Literatur zur hellenistischen Dichtung seit dem Jahre 1921; II Teil: Apollonius von Rhodos," *JAW* 285 (1945-46) 328-332.

Early Latin poetry. L. J. D. Richardson, "Direct citation of Ennius in Virgil," *CQ* 36 (1942) 40-42,

discusses the Ennian quotations in *Aen.* 6.841-846 and suggests that they be printed with quotation marks. W. B. Anderson, "The Aeneid and Earlier Latin Poetry," *PCA* 40 (1943) 9-12, examines briefly the influence of Naevius, Ennius, and Catullus.

Catullus and the "novi poetae." For the influence of the epyllion on the structure of the *Eclogues* and the *Georgics*, see Richardson (above, note 2) 101-173; on that of the *Aeneid*, see Mendell (above, Sect. 6B: *Aeneid* 11). E. Castorina, "Da Levio a Virgilio," *GIF* 2 (1949) 22-28, discusses the influence of the *novi poetae* on the *Appendix* and the *Eclogues.*

Lucretius. See Van Berchem (above, Sect. 4B: *Eclogue* 6); Michels (above, Sect. 6B: *Aeneid* 6); C. Bailey, *Virgil and Lucretius* (1947).[62]

Philodemus. J. I. M. Tait, *Philodemus' Influence on the Latin Poets* (Bryn Mawr 1941) 48-63, on Vergil as a member of the Epicurean school at Naples.

11A. Ancient Authors after Vergil

Propertius. See Funaioli and Alfonsi (above, Section 6B: *Aeneid* 1); L. Alfonsi, "Quaestiones propertianae," *Aevum* 18 (1944) 52-60 (reminiscences of Vergil in Propertius); A. La Penna, "Properzio e i poeti latini dell' età aurea," *Maia* 3 (1950) 209-236 (numerous allusions to Vergil); L. Alfonsi, "Il giudizio di Properzio sulla poesia virgiliana," *Aevum* 28 (1954) 205-221.

The popularity of Vergil's works in the early empire is attested by the discovery of 56 inscriptions and graffitti which cite passages from his poetry; see M. Della Corte, "Virgillio nell' epigrafia pompeiana," *Epigraphica* 2 (1940) 171-178 (13 from *Ecl.,* 2 from *Georg.,* 41 from *Aen.*).

Lucan. A. Guillemin, "L'inspiration virgilienne dans la *Pharsale*," *REL* 29 (1951) 214-217, compares 7.391-396 with *Aen.* 6.773-776; 6.785ff. with *Aen.* 6.824f.; 6.793-796 with *Aen.* 8.666-669; and 7.358-360 with *Georg.* 2.167-170; these reminiscences point up the basic differences between the two epics; Lucan's poem, and especially Book 7, is to the *Aeneid* as an end to a beginning, as death to birth. E. Malcovati, "Sul prologo della Farsaglia," *Athenaeum* 29 (1951) 100-108, maintains that the first seven verses are by Lucan and in the tradition of Vergilian epic.

Statius. G. Krumbholz, "Der Erzählungsstil in der Thebais des Statius," *Glotta* 34 (1954-55) 93-139; cf. 94-108 for a comparison of passages in Vergil and Statius.

23

Pliny the Younger. N. Terzaghi, "Tre fonti secondarie del Panegirico di Plinio," *Maia* 2 (1949) 121-127, suggests that Pliny in *Paneg.* 15.4 has in mind *Aen.* 8.337ff. and especially 366f.

Tacitus. J. J. H. Savage, "Germanicus and Aeneas Again," *CJ* 38 (1942-43) 166-167, points out that Germanicus' words on his death-bed (*Ann.* 2.71) recall *Aen.* 12.435f. Cf. G. B. A. Fletcher, "Some Certain or Possible Examples of Literary Reminiscence in Tacitus," *CR* 59 (1945) 45-50 (includes several from the *Aeneid*).

Apuleius. C. A. Forbes, "Charite and Dido," *CW* 37 (1943-44) 39-40, cites numerous parallels between *Metam.* 8.1-14 and *Aeneid* 4.

Constantine (?). A. Bolhuis, *Vergilius' Vierde Ecloga in de Oratio Constantini ad Sanctorum Coetum* (Ermelo 1950), compares the very bad Greek translation with Vergil's text of *Eclogue* 4 and shows that the commentary is based on the Greek translation and not on the Latin original; the purpose of both translation and commentary is to present Vergil's *Eclogue* as a prophecy of the coming of Christ. Bolhuis' dissertation suggests that the author, who shows no knowledge of Vergil's poem, was presumably not Constantine.

Augustine. Cf. P. Keseling, "Virgil bei Augustin," *PhW* 62 (1942) 383-384; "Nochmals Virgil bei Augustin," *PhW* 64 (1944) 95-96 (lists of parallel passages); I. Calabi, "Le fonti della storia romana nel *De civitate Dei* di sant'Agostino," *PP* 10 (1955) 274-294 (Augustine's use of Vergil and other writers).

Priscian. See C. A. Forbes, "Vergilian Echoes in Priscian," *CW* 38 (1944-45) 172.

Venantius Fortunatus. See S. Blomgren, "De Venantio Fortunato Vergilii aliorumque poetarum priorum imitatore," *Eranos* 42 (1944) 81-88 (lists of parallel expressions).

Vergilian centos. See M. F. A. Brok, "Litteraire lappendekens," *Hermeneus* 22 (1950) 46-54; N. Dane II, "The Medea of Hosidius Geta," *CJ* 46 (1950-51) 75-78 (a defense of the dramatic structure); S. Pricoco, "Valore letterario degli epigrammi di Damaso," *MSLC* 4 (1953) 19-40 (the epigrams of Damasus contain many reminiscences of Vergil but should not be considered centos).

Quintus of Smyrna. I have left to the last the problem of the influence of Vergil on Quintus of Smyrna, for this involves the extent to which the Greek world knew Latin literature and especially the works of Vergil. Some years ago I maintained that Quintus' treatment of the fall of Troy implied a knowledge of *Aeneid* 2,[63] and more recent articles have confirmed the interest of the Greeks in Vergil. The Greek translation of *Eclogue* 4 is mentioned above (under Constantine), and A. Kurfess, "Vergil und die Sibyllinen," *ZRGG* 3 (1951) 253-257, shows that the Sibylline oracles of the Empire have borrowed from Vergil's works and this he considers important for the question of Quintus' use of Vergil. A papyrus from Egypt of the third or fourth century contains a Latin imitation of *Aen.* 1.477-493, thus revealing an interest in the study of Vergil in the East; cf. R. Cavenaile, "Un pastiche de Virgile. le *P. S. I.* II 142," *LEC* 18 (1950) 285-288, and E. L. Hettich, "The Colt Papyrus Find from Auja," *Archaeology* 3 (1950) 31-33, reports the discovery in southern Palestine of a fragmentary codex of the *Aeneid* (most from Book 6) and also a glossary in double columns, words from *Aeneid* 4 with Greek translation; for a detailed description of these two papyri, see L. Casson and E. L. Hettich, *Excavations at Nessana II: Literary Papyri* (Princeton 1950) 2-78.[63a] It is not difficult, therefore, to agree with Keydell that Quintus read Vergil in the original Latin and took various motifs from him; see R. Keydell in *JAW* 272 (1941) 9-11; "Quintus Smyrnaeus und Vergil," *Hermes* 82 (1954) 254-256 (Quintus in 11.330-501 borrowed from *Aen.* 9.509-517). Kleinknecht (above, Section 6B: *Aeneid* 2) maintains that Quintus, in his treatment of Laocoon, is dependent on Vergil.

IIB. Ancient Lives

New editions of the Suetonius-Donatus *Life* have been published by A. Rostagni, *Suetonio "De Poetis" e biografi minori* (Torino 1944) 68-107 (with copious notes) and by C. Hardie, *Vitae Vergilianae Antiquae*, in the Oxford Classical Text series (1954), combined with a reprint of R. Ellis' *Appendix Vergiliana.* Hardie prints the other ancient *Lives* of Vergil and in the Praefatio discusses many problems concerning both the *Lives* and the *Appendix.* On the Suetonian *Life*, 11, see F. Hornstein, "Vergilius *Parthenias.*" *WS* 70 (1957) 148-152. Rostagni, 159-166, prints Probus' *Life* which he considers genuine and therefore important, since it antedates the Suetonian *Life.*

See also L. Agnès, "Sull' autenticità della 'Vita Vergilii' di Probo," *RFIC* 19 (1941) 169-178 (favors authenticity; the *Life* of Probus is earlier than and thus independent of the Suetonian *Life*); E. Paratore, *Una nuova ricostruzione del "De Poetis" di Suetonio* (Roma 1946, 2nd ed. Bari 1950) 127-283 (on interpolations of Donatus in the Suetonian *Life*, and errors in the *Life* attributed to Probus); *Sulla Vita Tibulli e le Vitae Vergilianae* (Roma 1947) (on

24

passages in the *Life* ascribed to Probus); A. Mazza-rino, "Sulla personalità di Sulpicio Apollinare," *SIFC* 22 (1947) 165-177 (the Sulpicius Carthaginiensis of the *Lives* is not the learned Sulpicius Apollinaris mentioned by Aulus Gellius); A. Rostagni, "Questi-oni biografiche," *RFC* 25 (1947) 1-17[64] (on the *scripta* in Vergil's *testamentum*; on the epigram of Sulpicius: there are two different epigrams, the one in the Donatus *Life* by Sulpicius Apollinaris, the other by a Servius Sulpicius Varus); H. R. Upson, *Mediaeval Lives of Virgil,* summary in *HSPh* 51 (1940) 330-331; "Mediaeval Lives of Virgil," *CPh* 38 (1943) 103-111 (on a new *Life* of Vergil in a ninth century manuscript and comparison with the other *Lives*).

11C. Ancient Commentators

A. Tomsin, *Etude sur le Commentaire Virgilien d'Aemilius Asper* (Paris 1952) seeks to reconstruct from later commentaries and grammatical works the text of Asper's commentary.

Much has been done on Servius and the Servius-problem since 1939. L. F. Hackemann, *Servius and His Sources in the Commentary on the Georgics* (New York 1940), attempts to show the true nature of Servius' interest in Vergil and of his scholarship and expository technique. N. Marinone, *Elio Donato. Macrobio e Servio, commentatori di Virgilio* (Vercelli 1946), discusses the parallels in Macrobius *Sat.* 1-3 to both Servius and Servius Dani-elis and concludes that they derive from a common source; he suggests that the source is Donatus and that the *scholia Danielis* therefore derive from Dona-tus' lost commentary. A. Santoro, *Esegeti virgiliani antichi: Donato, Macrobio, Servio* (Bari 1946), likewise argues that the source of the passages where Servius, Servius Danielis, and Macrobius are in ac-cord is none other than Donatus.

The books of Marinone and Santoro appeared in 1946; that same year saw the great event in recent Servian studies, the publication of Servius on *Aeneid* 1 and 2 by a committee headed by E. K. Rand, *Servianorum in Vergilii Carmina Commentariorum Editionis Harvardianae Vol. II* (Lancaster 1946). The editors in addition to Rand were H. T. Smith, J. J. Savage, G. B. Waldrop, J. P. Elder, B. M. Peebles, and A. F. Stocker. The edition, known as the "Harvard Servius," has the commentaries of Servius and Servius Danielis arranged in parallel columns; it thus marks a great improvement over the Thilo-Hagen Servius and has rightly been called "the first critical edition of the text in lucid form."[65] This monumental work will ultimately appear in five volumes, and the next volume (= Vol. III) is to be published in the near future; see A. H. Travis,

"Progress Report: Volume III of the Harvard Ser-vius," *Vergilian Digest* 2 (1956) 11-12.

Prior to the publication of the edition, the following dissertations and articles appeared as preliminary studies: J. P. Elder, *De Servii commentariis Danielinis, ut aiunt, in Aeneidos libros primum et secundum confectis,* summary in *HSPh* 51 (1940) 315-318; A. H. Travis, *De Servii Carminum Vergilianorum Interpretis Dicendi Rationibus,* summary in *HSPh* 51 (1940) 328-329; A. F. Stocker, "A New Source for the Text of Servius," *HSPh* 52 (1941) 65-97;[66] A. H. Travis, "Donatus and the Scholia Danielis: A Stylistic Comparison," *HSPh* 53 (1942) 157-169 (the style of DS differs from that of Donatus in his commentary of Terence, but the substance of DS may derive from Donatus' commentary of Vergil); cf. "Addendum to 'Dona-tus and the Scholia Danielis'," *CPh* 45 (1950) 38-39.

For brief descriptive accounts of the Harvard edition, see A. F. Stocker, "Epilegomena to Volume II of the 'Harvard Servius'," *TAPhA* 77 (1946) 323-324; J. P. Elder, "The New Servius," *Speculum* 21 (1946) 493-495; M. P. Odile, "Où en sont les recherches sur Servius?" *Association G. Budé, Congrès de Grenoble 21-25 sept. 1948: Actes du Congrès* (Paris 1949) 154-156. The rela-tion of DS to Servius and to Donatus will be discussed in the Prolegomena to Vol. I, to be published last. The editors are not committed to the opinion that the non-Servian elements in DS are pure Donatus. But cf. A. Santoro, "Il 'Servio Danielino' è Donato," *SIFC* 20 (1943-46) 79-104, who identifies DS with Donatus' lost com-mentary (cf. Marinone and Santoro, above).

More recent studies on Servius include S. A. Akielaszek, *A Preliminary Text of the Servian Com-mentary on the Eclogues of Vergil,* summary in *Fordham Univ. Diss.* 18 (1951) 48-50 (the relation of Servius and Servius Danielis, and a critical colla-tion of DS on the *Eclogues*); D. van Berchem, "Poètes et grammairiens," *MH* 9 (1952) 79-87 (the arrangement of topics in Donatus and Servius is traditional and goes back to Greek grammarians of the Hellenistic age, especially Crates); A. F. Stocker, "Notes on the Text of Servius on Aeneid III," *Clas-sical Studies Fraser* (Tuscaloosa 1956) 13-17; J. J. Savage, "Early Commentators on Vergil," *Vergilian Digest* 1 (1955) 14-15.

For discussions of Servius' comments on specific pas-sages in Vergil, see H. Mattingly, *"Dives Anagnia,"* NC 6 (1946) 91-96 (Serv. on *Aen.* 7.684f.; Mattingly suggests that Antony's mint was located at Anagnia); V. Ussani, Jr., "Un problema di esegesi virgiliana antica," *CPh* 21 (1946) 83-99 (on *bene* in Servius and Servius-Danielis); A. M. Honeyman, "Varia Punica," *AJPh* 68 (1947) 77-82 (on references to Dido in Servius and Servius-Danielis); V. Bulhart, *Text-kritisches zu Servius,* *Mnemosyne* 6 (1953) 64-65.

11D. Manuscripts

On the Graz fragment of the *Appendix*, cf. above, Sect. 3 and note 14.

A. Malaman, "Le 'Castigationes Virgilianae Lecti-onis' di Pierio Valeriano e il Codice Vaticano di Virgilio," *AIV* 100 (1940-41) 2B, 81-91. A. Dold,

"Ein neues Fragment der berühmten St. Galler Vergilhandschrift in Capitalis elegans aus dem 3. oder 4. Jahrhundert," *WS* 60 (1942) 79-86 (contains *Aen.* 6.656-659, 675-678, and 688-724, with 678 repeated after 695). A. Pratesi, "Sulla datazione del Virgilio Mediceo," *RAL* 1 (1946) 396-411 (the manuscript is to be dated in the last decade of the fifth century). J. Courcelle-Ladmirant, "Les miniatures inédites d'un Virgile du XVe siècle conservé à la Bibliothèque Vaticane," *BIBR* 25 (1949) 145-158 (the miniatures reveal the mediaeval interpretation of Vergil's poetry). V. Ussani, Jr., "Da un codice medievale delle Ecloghe di Virgilio," *Maia* 3 (1950) 289-296.

12. Vergil's Influence on Later Literature

Much on Vergil's later influence is to be found in G. Highet, *The Classical Tradition: Greek and Roman Influences on Western Literature* (New York 1949), see Index, 761: Vergil; J. A. K. Thomson, *The Classical Background of English Literature* (London 1948), see Index, 272: Virgil; *Classical Influences on English Poetry* (London 1951) 30-70, 75-78, 172-195; R. R. Bolgar, *The Classical Heritage and its Beneficiaries* (Cambridge 1954), see Index, 590: Virgil. Cf. also G. B. Beach, "Vergil's Influence," *Folia* 10 (1956) 19-26.

Middle Ages. A. S. Pease, "*Mantua me genuit,*" *CPh* 35 (1940) 180-182, on Roman and mediaeval imitations of the couplet. P. Courcelle, "Histoire du cliché virgilien des cent bouches (*Georg.* II, 42-44 = *Aen.* VI, 625-627," *REL* 33 (1955) 231-240: citations and versions down to the twelfth century. J. J. H. Savage, "*Insula Avallonia,*" *TAPhA* 73 (1942) 405-415: the etymology for *insula Avallonia* stems ultimately from *maliferae . . . Abellae* in *Aen.* 7.740. R. Foreville, "Aux origines de la Légende épique," *MA* 56 (1950) 195-219: influence of Vergil on the the *Gesta Guillelmi ducis Normannorum et Regis Anglorum* of Guillaume de Poitiers. R. Zitzmann, "Die Didohandlung in der frühhöfischen Eneasdichtung," *Euphorion* 46 (1952) 261-275. M. N. Pavia, "Virgil as a Magician," *CJ* 46 (1950-51) 61-64, on Vergil's debasement into a magician during the Middle Ages.

Dante. Cf. Buxton, above, Section 6A, and see G. Bagnani, "The Classical Technique: Virgil, Dante, and Pope," *Phoenix* 2 (1947-48) 2-14 (on the use of proper names); A. P. MacVay, "Dante's Strange Treatment of Vergil," *CJ* 43 (1947-48) 233-235 (Dante demeans Vergil by putting him under the power of the witch Erechtho and by excluding him from Paradise, although he admits Statius and others; Dante's expressions of high regard for Vergil are "mere lip-service"); R. V. Schoder, S. J., "Vergil in the *Divine Comedy,*" *CJ* 44 (1948-49) 413-422 (a defense of Dante's treatment of Vergil, against MacVay); J. H. Whitfield, *Dante and Virgil* (Oxford 1949) 61-106 (the importance of Vergil for Dante); G. L. Bickersteth, *Dante's Virgil. A Poet's Poet* (Glasgow 1951, = *Glasgow Univ. Publ.* 89) (on Vergil as a dramatic creation and as a human and tragic person); R. Palgen, "Le légende virgilienne dans la *Divine Comédie,*" *Romania* 73 (1952) 332-390 (Dante's Vergil is the Vergil of mediaeval legend); A. Bufano, "Quantopere Dantes Vergilium admiratus atque imitatus sit," *Latinitas* 2 (1954) 177-187; P. Renucci, *Dante, disciple et juge du monde gréco-latin* (Paris 1954); see especially 282-311 on the meaning of the Roman world, 337-350 on the importance of Vergil for Dante; cf. Bibliography, 451-455.

Chaucer. A. C. Friend, "Chaucer's Version of the Aeneid," *Speculum* 28 (1953) 317-323: where Chaucer departs from the *Aeneid*, he may have used the twelfth century *Ilias* of Simon Chèvre d'Or. K. F. Doherty, S. J., "Dido in Vergil and Chaucer," *CB* 31 (1954-55) 29, 32-35: how and why Chaucer's portrayal of Dido and Aeneas differed from Vergil's.

Camoes. See Bowra (above, Section 6A), 86-138; L. V. Sumner, "A Literary Descendant of the Aeneid," *CJ* 50 (1954-55) 291-293 (comparison of the *Lusiads* and the *Aeneid*).

Milton. See Buxton and Bowra (above, Section 6A); D. Bush, "Virgil and Milton," *CJ* 47 (1951-52) 178-182, 203-204 (on Milton's use of epic devices).

Eighteenth century. D. M. Low, *Virgil and the English Augustans* (London 1953),[67] discusses Vergil's influence in the period 1688-1744. H. Oppermann, "Schiller und Vergil," *Gymnasium* 58 (1951) 306-322, writes on the similarity of their ideas and their writings.

Wordsworth. See N. Watts, "Virgil and Wordsworth," *Dublin Review* 219 (1946) 134-147 (the two poets have much in common: sympathy for human suffering, love of nature, recognition of sense of duty, interest in the destiny and origin of the soul); K. F. Doherty, S.J., "The Vergilian Wordsworth," *CJ* 49 (1953-54) 221-225, 235 (on the Vergilian elements in *Laodamia*).

Tennyson. E. T. Healy, "Virgil and Tennyson," *Kentucky Foreign Language Quarterly* 2 (1955) 20-25.

C. A. Manning, "The Aeneid of Kotlyarevsky," *CW* 34 (1942-43) 91-93, shows that the *Aeneid* was the basis for the first work in modern Ukrainian literature (early 19th century); Aeneas and the Trojans are portrayed as Kozaks. A. Bougery, "Les Bucoliques de Virgile dans la poésie moderne," REL 23 (1945) 134-150, discusses the influence of the Eclogues from the Renaissance to the twentieth century.

Translators and Commentators. See M. I. Gerhardt, "Les premières traductions des Bucoliques," Neophilologus 33 (1949) 51-56; J. Stevens, S.J., "Un humaniste espagnol: le Père Juan-Luis de la Cerda, commentateur de Virgile," LEC 13 (1945) 210-221; G. L. Luzzatto, "Le prime traduzioni francesi di Virgilio," Maia 7 (1955) 46-68; "Guido di Pisa traduttore di Virgilio," Maia 8 (1956) 27-38; "Virgilio nelle traduzioni francesi de Louis Dúchemin e di Marcellus," Maia 4 (1951) 212-225; L. J. D. Richardson, "Canon Thornhill's Translation of the Aeneid," Hermathena 67 (1946) 68-72.

Vergil Today. E. J. Wood, Virgil and To-day (Leeds 1945), concludes his lecture by saying that Vergil "is timeless and ageless" and his "voice speaks to us to-day as clearly as it did to his own countrymen two thousand years ago." T. S. Eliot, "Vergil and the Christian World," The Sewanee Review 61 (Winter, 1953) 1-14, points out that Vergil's key words are labor, pietas, and fatum, but he just falls short of being an anima naturaliter Christiana. Perhaps the greatest recent tribute to Vergil is Eliot's lecture, What is a Classic? (London 1945), in which he states that "Virgil acquires the centrality of the unique classic: he is at the centre of European civilization . . . Our classic, the classic of all Europe, is Virgil."

13. Vergil Societies

T. S. Eliot's essay, What is a Classic? was delivered in 1944 as an address before the Virgil Society. This British society has been very active since its founding in 1943. Numerous local branches have been established, and the lectures and presidential addresses delivered during the past fifteen years number more than fifty. Many of these have been circulated in mimeographed form, either summarized or in toto, and about one-fourth of the lectures have been printed.[68] The lecturers are distinguished British scholars (e.g., C. Bailey, L. A. S. Jermyn, W. F. J. Knight, H. Mattingly, J. T. Sheppard, O. Skutsch, B. Tilly, J. M. C. Toynbee) and the subjects cover almost every aspect of Vergilian studies: the Appendix, Eclogues, Georgics, and especially the Aeneid (e.g., "Virgil's Dido," "The Problem of Dido and Aeneas," "Virgil's Aeneas," "The Aeneid as a Tragedy"), as well as

Virgil's later influence (e.g., "Dante's Virgil," "Virgil, Dante, and Mediaevalism," "Virgil, Dante, and the Res Romana," "Virgil and Wordsworth").

In America, the Vergilian Society, which was organized in 1937 with both an American Committee and an Italian Committee, came to a temporary halt in 1940 as a result of World War II, and its journal Vergilius ceased publication in December, 1940. Since the war, the Classical Summer School at Cumae has been resumed, with headquarters at the Villa Vergiliana at Cumae, and in 1955 the first issue of the post-war publication of the Vergilian Society appeared, under the title The Vergilian Digest. This contained "A Practical Bibliography for Study of the Aeneid" (4-13), and future issues will continue to publish bibliographies and articles on Vergil of current interest.

ADDENDA

This survey was completed on Aug. 5, 1957. Items which have since come to my attention have been inserted in successive installments at galley stage, as far as possible. The following titles, most of them recent, are keyed to the sections of the survey.

3. A. Salvatore (ed.), Appendix Vergiliana, I: Ciris-Culex (Turin 1957); "Note sul testo della Ciris," Latomus 16 (1957) 23-48; "Note sul testo del Culex," WS 70 (1957) 260-277.

4B. 3. R. Gustin, "La saison de la troisième Bucolique de Virgile," LEC 26 (1958) 138-142.

4C. P. Courcelle, "Les exégèses chrétiennes de la quatrième Eglogue," REA 59 (1957) 294-319; R. Waltz, "Sur la 4e Bucolique de Virgile," LEC 26 (1958) 3-20.

5A. P. Scazzoso, "Riflessi misterici nelle 'Georgiche' di Virgilio," Paideia 11 (1956) 5-28.

5B. A. O. Hulton, "Virgil Georg. 1. 489-492," CPh 52 (1957) 245-247; E. Burck, "Der korykische Greis in Vergils Georgica (IV 116-148)," Navicula Chiloniensis: Studia . . . Jacoby (Leiden 1956) 156-172; R. Lamacchia, "Simbolismo romano in alcuni studi recenti," A&R, N.S., 2 (1957) 150-156 (on Dahlmann, above Georgics IV).

6A. I. Del Ton, "Vergilius pacis vates," Latinitas 5 (1957) 91-98.

6B. R. B. Lloyd, "Aeneid III: A New Approach," AJPh 78 (1957) 133-151; "Aeneid III and the Aeneas Legend," ibid., 382-400; P. J. Enk, "La tragédie de Didon," Latomus 16 (1957) 628-642; P. R. Murphy, "Emotional Echoes of Aeneis One in Aeneis Four," CB 33 (1956-57) 20-21; D. H. Abel, "Medea in Dido," CB 34 (1957-58) 51-53, 56; E. Liechtenhan, "Nochmals Vergil, Aeneis IX 324-328," MH 14 (1957) 52-59 (on Breguet, above Aeneid 9); B. Tilly, "The topography of Aeneid IX with reference to the way taken by Nisus and Euryalus," ArchClass 8 (1957) 164-172.

6C. Aeneas. E. Burck, "Das Menschenbild im römischen Epos," Gymnasium 65 (1958) 121-146, especially 132ff.

7A. R. E. H. Westendorp Boerma, Vergilius (Groningen 1955).

7B. P. Tihon, S.J., "Approches religieuses de Virgile," LEC 26 (1958) 166-175.

CORRIGENDA

The reference to Klingner on p. 190 (col. 2, end) and in notes 54, 55, and 59 should read: *Römisches Geisteswelt* (3rd ed., München 1956).

GEORGE E. DUCKWORTH
PRINCETON UNIVERSITY

---

1. G. Mambelli, *Gli studi virgiliani nel secolo XX: Contributo ad una bibliografia generale* (Firenze 1940). This work, in two volumes, totals 1755 pages and lists 3952 items; the authors are arranged alphabetically and there are brief comments on many books and articles. Also in 1940 appeared the last of the bibliographical lists in *Vergilius*, "Recent Work on Vergil," selected by G. E. Duckworth; cf. *Vergilius* 4, 44-45; 6, 49-50 (see below, Sect. 13).

More recent bibliographies on earlier Vergilian literature are those by N. I. Herescu, *Bibliographie de la litterature latine* (Paris 1943) 139-164. and by S. Lambrino, *Bibliographie de l'antiquité classique*, 1896-1914, I (Paris 1951) 14-729.

2. I shall give page references to the separate publication, citing it merely as "Büchner." To avoid repetition of references in the survey, I shall also mention the following works by the name of the author only:

Arnaldi = F. Arnaldi, *Problemi di stile virgiliano* (Napoli 1941), reprinted in *Studi Virgiliani* (Napoli n.d.) 167-271. Page references are to the second printing in *Studi Virgiliani*.

Becker = C. Becker, "Virgils Eklogenbuch," *Hermes* 83 (1955) 314-349.

Bömer = F. Bömer, "Vergil und Augustus," *Gymnasium* 58 (1951) 26-55.

Dornseiff = F. Dornseiff, *Verschmähtes zu Vergil. Horaz und Properz* (Berlin 1951; = *Ber. über die Verhandl. der sächs. Akad. der Wiss. zu Leipzig*, Philol.-hist. Kl. 97, Heft 6).

Duckworth A = G. E. Duckworth, "The Architecture of the *Aeneid*." *AJPh* 75 (1954) 1-15.

Duckworth D = G. E. Duckworth. "*Animae Dimidium Meae*: Two Poets of Rome," *TAPhA* 87 (1956) 281-316.

Guillemin = A. M. Guillemin, *Vergile: Poète, artiste et penseur* (Paris 1951).

Hahn = E. A. Hahn, "The Characters in the *Eclogues*," *TAPhA* 75 (1944) 196-241.

Hanslik = R. Hanslik, "Nachlese zu Vergils Eclogen 1 und 9," *WS* 68 (1955) 5-19.

Hartke = W. Hartke, *Römische Kinderkaiser: Eine Strukturanalyse römischen Denkens und Daseins* (Berlin 1951).

Knight = W. F. Jackson Knight, *Roman Vergil* (London 1944; 2d ed. 1944).

Letters = F. J. H. Letters, *Virgil* (New York 1946).

Paratore = E. Paratore, *Virgilio* (Roma 1945; 2d ed. Firenze 1954).

Perret = J. Perret, *Virgile, l'homme et l'oeuvre* (Paris 1952).

Pöschl = V. Pöschl, *Die Dichtkunst Virgils: Bild und Symbol in der Aeneis* (Innsbruck 1950).

Richardson = L. Richardson, Jr., *Poetical Theory in Republican Rome* (New Haven 1944).

Rose = H. J. Rose, *The Eclogues of Vergil* (Berkeley 1942; = *Sather Classical Lectures*, Vol. 16).

3. Many items have been eliminated because of their highly specialized nature or their inaccessibility. I have omitted also most school editions, translations into languages other than English, numerous brief critical notes (some of the more significant are listed in Sect. 9), reprints of books and articles originally published before 1940, chapters on Vergil in histories of Latin literature, unpublished dissertations, and typewritten lectures issued for the use of university students (e.g., E. Paratore, *La poesia della giovinezza di Virgilio* [Roma, Corso Ufficiale 1949-50], and E. Turolla, *Ultima fase d'evoluzione nella poesia virgiliana: L'Eneide*, I-II [Venezia 1951-52]).

For a more complete bibliography from 1940 through 1955. see J. Marouzean and J. Ernst, *L'Année Philologique*. Vols. XV-XXVI. The abbreviations of *L'Année Philologique* are used for classical journals and university publications.

4. For editions of poems in the *Appendix Vergiliana*, see below, Sect. 3.

5. This Budé edition, which first appeared in 1942, replaces that by H. Goelzer (1925). For a detailed review of Saint-Denis' edition, see M. Desport in *REA* 45 (1943) 165-170.

6. The last-named edition must be used with care; Herrmann believes that Vergil's essential purpose in the *Bucolics* was to present in pastoral costume the literary figures of his day; hence Meliboeus in 1 is Valerius Cato, Daphnis in 5 is Catullus, Lycidas in 9 is Horace, etc. These and other identifications are the same as those proposed by Herrmann in his *Les Masques et les visages dans les Bucoliques de Virgile* (Bruxelles 1930). Furthermore, Herrmann makes numerous transpositions, e.g., in 2, 60-62 after 27; in 4, 60-63 after 17, 11-14 after 59, and 23 after 20 (on this last, see below Sect. 4C); 8.6-13 appear at the end of 4, and other *Eclogues* are rearranged with the utmost freedom.

Tescari reads *te* for *me* in 10.44, and in 4.62 favors *qui non risere parenti* (see below, Sect. 4C); the latter reading appears also in the edition of L. Castiglioni and R. Sabbadini, *P. Vergili Maronis Bucolica, Georgica* (Torino 1945), which contains the text of both *Bucolics* and *Georgics* with a critical apparatus.

7. Sabbadini's text of the *Aeneid* with commentary has also been reprinted (Torino 1945-47).

8. The English language school editions (most with vocabularies) include *Aeneid* 1, by J. Bithrey (Dublin 1948); 2, by J. E. Dunlop (London 1949); 3, by H. E. Gould and J. L. Whitely (London 1949); 2, 3, 5, 6, by M. Duggan and R. Foley (Dublin 1945); 8, by H. E. Gould and J. L. Whitely (London 1953); 9, by J. L. Whitely (London 1955); 12, by H. E. Gould and J. L. Whitely (London 1950); 12, by W. E. Gould and J. L. Whitely (Cambridge 1956). also *The Story of Camilla* (from 7 and 11) by B. Tilly (Cambridge 1956).

9. All interested in earlier editions and translations will find much of value in the new bibliography of G. Mambelli, *Gli annali delle edizioni virgiliane* (Firenze 1954). This work lists printed editions and translations to 1850 (the *Appendix* excluded) and comments on many editions,

especially the earlier ones. Translations are listed, not only in the major European languages, but also in Polish, Bohemian, Armenian, and others, and the volume contains ninety items of imitations, parodies, and centos.

10. Cf., e.g., the words of C. W. Mendell in 1951: "Today the majority of scholars accept much of the *Vergilian Appendix* for what it purports to be, the work of Vergil in his apprentice days" (*YClS* 12 [1951] 214); against this, see W. C. Helmbold, *AJPh* 74 (1953) 313.

11. Cf. reviews by E. Galletier, *REL* 32 (1954) 406-408; P. Frassinetti, *Athenaeum* 32 (1954) 271-274; A. Ernout, *RPh* 29 (1955) 47-54; R. T. Bruère, *CPh* 51 (1956) 33-36. Giomini replies to the criticisms of Frassinetti in "A proposito di una recensione," *Maia* 7 (1955) 153-156.

12. Cf. also B. Otis, *CW* 49 (1955-56) 155: "The poems represent the general 'neoteric' background of both Gallus and the 'young Virgil.' "

13. Cf. reviews by E. Galletier, *REL* 27 (1949) 311-314; R. Giomini, *Maia* 3 (1950) 147-160; W. Till, *Gnomon* 23 (1951) 424-428.

14. The Graz manuscript contains *Ciris* 338-497, *Catalepton* 14.7-12 and 14a.1-4, one of the *Priapea* usually excluded from the *Appendix*, *Copa* 1-38 (very fragmentary), and *Moretum* 11-50. See A. Haury, "Du nouveau sur l'*Appendix Vergiliana*," *REA* 55 (1953) 404-405; J. Krassler, "Das Grazer Fragment eines Vergil-Codex des 9. Jahrhunderts," *AAWW* 90 (1953) 186-188; E. Gaar, "Text und kritische Bewertung des Grazer 'Vergil'-Fragments," *ibid.* 188-231, who publishes the text and discusses the new readings. e.g., *mago Iovi* in *Ciris* 374, which he takes as a reference to Pluto. Salvatore, 127 ff., disagrees and considers *magus* an appropriate epithet for Jupiter in Crete.

15. "The Pseudo-Virgilian 'Ciris,' " a lecture delivered to the Virgil Society, Oct. 16, 1954 (see below, Sect. 13).

16. Cf. N. W. DeWitt, *CW* 36 (1942-43) 250f., E. L. Highbarger, *AJPh* 65 (1944) 200-205.

17. B. Snell, *The Discovery of the Mind*, trans. T. G. Rosenmeyer (Oxford 1953) 281-309, 322f. Snell's article, "Arkadien, die Entdeckung einer geistigen Landschaft," appeared first in *A&A* 1 (1944) 26-41, and was reprinted in *Die Entdeckung des Geistes* (2nd ed., Hamburg 1948) 268-293. See also B. Brugioni, "Antiarcadia Virgiliana," *MC* 10 (1940) 102-111; G. Jachmann, "L'Arcadia come paesaggio bucolico," *Maia* 5 (1952) 161-174.

18. This part of Maury's analysis seems sound; see Duckworth A, 3-5; Skutsch, *RhM* 99 (1956) 195-197.

19. This article appears in a revised form in G. Stégen, *Etude sur cinq Bucoliques de Virgile* (Namur 1955) 9-27; Stégen examines *Eclogues* 1, 2, 4, 5, and 7 from the standpoint of unity and avoids allegorical interpretations.

S.'s *Commentaire sur cinq Bucoliques de Virgile* (*3, 6, 8, 9, 10*) *suivi d'une vue d'ensemble sur tout le recueil* (Namur 1957) reprints, with some changes, his articles on *Eclogues* 3, 9, and 10 discussed below.

20. Also printed in *Studies in Honour of Gilbert Norwood* (Toronto 1952 = *Phoenix*, Suppl. Vol. I) 163-171.

21. Cf. reviews by Rose, *CR*, n.s. 4 (1954) 301; Westendorp Boerma, *Mnemosyne* 8 (1955) 77-79; see also Rose, "Some Second Thoughts on Vergil's Eclogues," *Mnemosyne* 7 (1954) 57-68. Wagenvoort's article has since been reprinted in English in his *Studies in Roman Literature, Culture and Religion* (Leiden 1956) 233-273.

22. This article appears also in a shortened form in *Arbeits-*

gemeinschaft für Forschung des Landes Nordrhein-Westfalen, Heft 2 (1953) 37-62.

23. See N. I. Herescu, "Au dossier des 'decem menses,' " *RPh* 20 (1946) 12-21; L. Halkin, "Le problème des *decem menses* de la IVe églogue de Virgile," *LEC* 16 (1948) 354-370; A. Oguse, "Decem Menses," *REL* 27 (1949) 60-63; R. Waltz, "Ordinal et cardinal: une 'règle' caduque," *REA* 51 (1949) 41-53.

24. Hommel, 195 note 1, supports the reading *qui non risere parenti* by a passage from the ninth century "In purificatione Sanctae Mariae," which echoes both 60-62 and 50, 52: *exulta, cui parvus / arrisit tunc, Maria, / qui laetari omnibus / et consistere / suo nutu tribuit.*

25. See his earlier *A la campagne avec Virgile* (2nd ed., Paris 1930); cf. also his series of articles: "La poésie des céréales dans les Géorgiques," *RPh* 15 (1941) 29-42; "Météorologie agronomique selon Virgile: Les vents," *LEC* 10 (1941) 321-328; "Virgile et l'olivier," *REA* 43 (1941) 262-269; "Virgile poète de l'olivier," *REL* 19 (1941) 142-146.

26. Cf. Föschl, *AAHG* 6 (1953) 1-4.

27. Reprinted in *Studies in Honour of Gilbert Norwood* (Toronto 1952; = *Phoenix*, Suppl. Vol. I) 172-183.

28. Cf. Richardson, 155, for a different arrangement of panels; both concentric patterns resemble the arrangement of the *Eclogues* (above, Sect. 4A). See also C. W. Mendell in *YClS* 12 (1951) 205-226 for similar patterns in *Aeneid* 11 (below, Sect. 6B).

29. The books and articles listed in Sects. 6A through 6F are concerned particularly with the *Aeneid*, but various aspects of the *Aeneid*, as of Vergil's other works, will appear in later sections, especially 7 through 10.

30. Cf. e.g., Paratore, *Maia* 4 (1951) 310-318; Klingner, *Gnomon* 24 (1952) 133-138; Hardie, *JRS* 42 (1952) 134-137; Bruère, *CPh* 47 (1952) 106-110. Less favorable are Clarke, *CR* 1 (1951) 356-361; Vretska, *AAHG* 6 (1953 30-36; these reviewers object to Pöschl's rigid dualism (order vs. chaos, reason vs. passion, Jupiter vs. Juno, Aeneas vs. Dido and Turnus) and the portrayal of Turnus as the *Staatsfeind*. See also F. Giancotti, "Per l'unità artistica dell' Eneide," *Atti Accad. Pontaniana* (Napoli) 4 (1950-52) 209-216.

31. Cf. reviews by Pease, *CJ* 44 (1948-49) 225-226; Duckworth, *AJPh* 70 (1949) 441-443; Woodbury, *CPh* 45 (1950) 119-121.

32. Cf. Knight, 300f.; Sforza's view is defended by W. S. Maguiness, "Some Reflections on the *Aeneid*" (1951); this work is a printed Virgil Society lecture (see below, Sect. 13).

33. Reprinted in ·A. Rostagni, *Scritti minori*, II. 2 (Torino 1956) 201-221. Cf. also M. Santoro, *I problemi della composizione dell'Eneide: Livio fonte di Virgilio* (rev. ed., Napoli 1947), who discusses the sources of the *Aeneid* and maintains that Books 7 and 8 were influenced by Livy.

34. A printed Virgil Society lecture (see below, Sect. 13).

35. Reprinted in G. Funaioli, *Studi di Letteratura Antica*, II, 1 (Bologna 1948) 149-166.

36. Reprinted in A. Rostagni, *Scritti minori*, II, 2 (Torino 1956) 190-200.

37. Pagliaro, "Ancora di 'Tacitae per amica silentia lunae'," *Paideia* 7 (1952) 24-26, objects to Di Prima's remarks in 289f. about his own theory.

29

38. See reviews by Schauroth, *CW* 35 (1941-42) 164-166; Johnston, *CJ* 38 (1942-43) 543-546; Pease, *CPh* 38 (1943) 60-61.

39. Reprinted in G. Funaioli, *Studi di letteratura antica,* II, 1 (Bologna 1948) 249-253, under the title, "Sopra un passo del canto ottavo dell' Eneide."

40. See also above, Sect. 6A: Bowra; Pöschl; articles on the tragic nature of the *Aeneid.*

41. Reprinted in G. Funaioli, *Studi di letteratura antica.* II, 1 (Bologna 1948) 255-274.

42. This is a typewritten dissertation of 197 large pages, single-spaced, which I have read on interlibrary loan. I list it here in the hope that it will soon be printed and made more available. Liebing's work is important not only for its study of Aeneas but for its analysis of the other characters in relation to Aeneas and for the many problems treated.

43. For details and criticisms of Perret's analysis, see Duckworth A, 7-10.

44. R. S. Conway, "The Architecture of the Epic," *Harvard Lectures on the Vergilian Age* (Cambridge, Mass. 1928) 129-149.

45. Horace's Roman Odes (3.1-6) also divide into both halves and thirds; cf. Duckworth D, 299-302.

46. Cf. Bérard, *JS* (1943) 116-130; Piganiol, *RPh* 17 (1943) 214-217; Bickerman, *CW* 37 (1943-44) 93-95; Momigliano, *JRS* 35 (1945) 99-104. Bayet, *REL* 20 (1942) 175-180, is more favorable.

47. Cf. also B. Tilly, "Vergilian Cities of the Roman Campagna," *Antiquity* 19 (1945) 125-134.

48. These works are listed, with full titles and place and date of publication, above, p. 89, n. 2, and have been cited in previous sections.

49. Cf. reviews by Butler, *JRS* 34 (1944) 162-163; Austin *CR* 59 (1945) 16-20; Pöschl, *AAHG* 3 (1950) "5-"9; Bignone, *Erasmus* 3 (1950) 31-35. Pöschl is especially critical of Chapter 5, "Language, Verse. and Style," but Bignone praises it as one of the best studies of Vergil's artistic technique.

50. See also W. F. J. Knight, "Poetic Sources and Integration," *Vergilius* 5 (1940) 7-16; "Integration of Plot in the Aeneid," *ibid.* 6 (1940) 17-25.

51. Cf. reviews by Perret, *RFL* 29 (1951) 393-396; Klingner, *Gnomon* 25 (1953) 95-97. Van Ooteghem, *LEC* 20 (1952) 270-271, criticizes Guillemin for ignoring the theories of Maury and LeGrelle (above, Sects. 4A and 5B), and considers LeGrelle's article the most important work on the *Georgics* in the past fifty years.

52. On Perret, see P. Boyancé, "Un nouveau Virgile," *REA* 55 (1953) 146-156; cf. reviews by Guillemin, *REL* 30 (1952) 415-418; Büchner, *Gnomon* 25 (1953) 98-100; Börner. *BJ* 153 (1953) 153-159; Hardie, *JRS* 43 (1953) 221-223; Williams. *CR* 4 (1954) 34-35. Both Guillemin and Perret are reviewed in detail by Eggerding, *Gymnasium* 61 (1954) 555-568.

53. Cf. reviews by Perret, *REL* 32 (1954) 373-375; Clarke, *CR* 5 (1955) 173-175; Marti, *CPh* 51 (1956) 62-64.

54. Reprinted in F. Klingner, *Römische Geisteswelt,* I (3d ed., München 1953) 221-255.

55. Cf. F. Klingner, "Die Einheit des Virgilischen Lebenswerke," *MDAI (R)* 45 (1930) 43-58 (reprinted in *Römische Geisteswelt.* I [3d ed.. München 1953] 256-2"4): Klingner likewise stresses the unity of Vergil's works but begins with the Roman elements of the *Aeneid* and finds the same political themes in the earlier works.

56. On the Pythagorean influence on Vergil, see Wankenne. *LEC* 19 (1951) 388 and n. 16, and cf. above on Maury (Sect. 4A) and LeGrelle (5B).

57. Reprinted in A. Graf Schenk von Stauffenberg, *Dichtung und Staat in der antiken Welt* (München 1948) 5-26.

58. This is *Vergilian Essays—No.* 2; see below, Sect. 13.

59. Reprinted in F. Klingner, *Römische Geisteswelt,* I (3d ed., München 1953) 142-172.

60. Also printed in *Lexis* 1 (1948) 199-214.

60a. E. A. Hahn, "A Source of Vergilian Hypallage," *TAPhA* 87 (1956) 147-189, shows how Vergil frequently violates the prosaic precision demanded by strict logic; her analysis stresses the use of *mixtus, medius,* verbs compounded with *trans,* and *cum inversum* clauses and alternative expressions.

61. The 1950 Presidential Address delivered to the Virgil Society; see below, Sect. 13.

62. The 1947 Presidential Address delivered to the Virgil Society; see below, Sect. 13.

63. G. E. Duckworth, "Foreshadowing and Suspense in the *Posthomerica* of Quintus of Smyrna," *AJPh* 57 (1936) 58-86. especially 84ff.

63a. Cf. E. G. Turner. "Half a Line of Virgil from Egypt," *Studi in onore di Calderini e Paribeni,* II (Milano 1957) 15"-161.

64. Reprinted in A. Rostagni, *Scritti minori* II, 2 (Torino 1956) 249-265.

65. A. Travis, *Traditio* 4 (1946) 442. For other reviews, both lengthy and favorable, see Bruère, *CPh* 43 (1948) 126-130; Silk, *AJPh* 69 (1948) 92-97; Mountford, *CR* 62 (1948) 137-139; Coulter, *Speculum* 23 (1948) 332-335; Marinone, *RFC* 77 (1949) 141-152; Robinson, *CW* 43 (1949-50) 230-237. The review by E. Fraenkel, *JRS* 38 (1948) 131-143, 39 (1949) 145-154, was not favorable.

66. Cf. also A. F. Stocker, *De Novo Codicum Servianorum Genere,* summary in *HSPh* 50 (1939) 123-126.

67. A Virgil Society lecture; see below, Sect. 13.

68. For printed lectures already cited, see above, notes 32, 34, 58, 61, 62, 67. For the opportunity to read the mimeographed lectures and summaries of lectures, I am deeply indebted to Prof. Robert J. Getty, of the University of Toronto.

Recent Work on Vergil
(1957-1963)
George E. Duckworth

from Volume 57, pp. 193-228

RECENT WORK ON VERGIL (1957-1963)[1]

TABLE OF CONTENTS

1. Preliminary Remarks. Bibliography

This survey of recently published books and articles on V. is a continuation of that for the years 1940-1956 which appeared in *CW* in 1958.[2] Scholarly interest in all aspects of Vergilian studies continues unabated, and again I regret that lack of space makes it impossible to comment on or even list all the works which have appeared since 1956. My bases of selection are similar to those of the first survey,[3] and the arrangement into sections is essentially the same. I am pleased that the 1940-1956 survey seemed of value, and I trust that this continuation will prove equally useful.

For recent foreign bibliographical articles, see V. Pöschl, "Der Forschungsbericht. Virgil," *AAHG* 12 (1959) 193-218; K. E. Laage, "Zur Vergillektüre im altsprachlichen Unterricht," *Gymnasium* 66 (1959) 539-556; D. Wiegand, "Die Natur bei Vergil und Horaz. Bibliographie für die Jahre 1920-1959," *Gymnasium* 67 (1960) 344-358; cf. also G. Radke, "Auswahlbericht zur augusteichen Dichtung," *Gymnasium* 66 (1959) 319-347, esp. 323-334.

2. Editions and Translations[4]

Editions. U. Boella, *Idillio e Tragedia. Dalle Bucoliche e dalle Georgiche di Virgilio* (Torino 1958): introduction, text, and commentary on *E.* 1, 4, 5, 9, 10 and selections from the *G.* P. V. Cova, *Arbusta Iuvant. Le Bucoliche e scelta delle Georgiche di Virgilio* (Torino 1961): text and commentary of *E.* complete and selected passages from the *G.;* the introductions (3-26, 155-169) discuss V. as an Alexandrian poet, his relation to Theocritus, and the nature and purpose of the *G.* Holtorf's *Bucolica,* the first volume of a new V. commentary, contains bibliography; introduction on V.'s life, works, and later influence; *Bucolics* (introduction, text, and commentary for each poem); and an *"Anhang"* on their language and meter.[5] Perret *B* provides a smaller edition of the *E.* with introduction, bibliography, text, and commentary.[6] Richter's *Georgica* is an important edition of 446 pages, with introduction, text, structural analysis of each book, and an extensive commentary. The work reviews the scholarly literature of the

past half-century and gives many new interpretations; it is essential for all future study of the *G.*[7] F. della Corte, *Virgilio, Le Georgiche, Libro IV* (Torino 1960): introduction, text, and commentary; the editor thinks that Book 4 was not part of V.'s original plan.[8]

J. Goette-K. Bayer, *Vergil. Aeneis und die Vergil-Viten* (München 1958): this edition of 1072 pages contains the *A.,* text and translation (German verse); the *Vitae* and testimonia, text and translation (German prose); a critical apparatus for the *A.* and the *Vitae;* and a lengthy index of proper names.[9] G. Pascoli, *Epos (Virgilio),* a cura di D. Nardo e S. Romagnoli (Firenze 1958): an edition of the *A.,* text and commentary of Pascoli (5th ed. 1938) corrected and modernized; the editors add text (of Sabbadini) and commentary for the portions omitted by Pascoli. W. E. Sweet, *Vergil's Aeneid. A Structural Approach* (Ann Arbor 1960): this, the first volume of a projected four-volume series on the *A.,* contains the text of 1 and 2, with a prose interpretation in Latin based on that by Ruaeus and selected Latin notes from Servius and Donatus.[10]

For important editions of individual books, see R. D. Williams, *P. Vergili Maronis Aeneidos Liber Tertius* (Oxford 1962): introduction, text, bibliography, commentary, and index; the text is that of Hirtzel (OCT) but Williams indicates in his notes where he prefers a different reading or punctuation;[11] A. Schmitz, *Infelix Dido. Etude esthétique et psychologique du livre IV de l'Enéide de Virgile* (Gembloux 1960): text and detailed analysis of 4 (rhythm, language, structure, psychology of characters, parallels with ancient writers both before and after V.);[12] R. D. Williams, *P. Vergili Maronis Aeneidos Liber Quintus* (Oxford 1960): similar to Williams' edition of 3;[13] M. Delaunois, *Virgile. Le chant VI de l'Enéide* (Namur 1958): text, commentary, suggested essay topics, and a historical and mythological lexicon of proper names; the esthetic and literary commentary (40-134), consisting of short analyses of each section of the book, frequently compares V. with modern French writers.[14]

Translations. G. Johnson, *The Pastorals of Vergil. A Verse Translation of the Eclogues,* with an Introduction and Notes by L. R. Lind (Lawrence 1960): an accurate and smooth-flowing version, occasionally a bit free; Lind in the introduction points out that Vergil resembles T. S. Eliot in allusiveness, Robert Frost in simplicity of symbolism, and W. B. Yeats in his carefully created music.[15] C. Day Lewis, *The Eclogues of Virgil* (London 1963), translates in a six-stress line, the meter of his versions of the *G.* and *A.*, but for the songs in *E.* 3, 5, 7, and 8 uses the meter of English and Irish folk songs. H. A. Hedges, *The Georgics of Vergil. The Farmer: A Psalm of Italy by a Roman Poet* (New York 1959): hardly to be recommended; e.g., Hedges translates 4.488f. *(cum subita incautum dementia cepit amantem, / ignoscenda quidem, scirent si ignoscere manes)* as follows: "when an incautious dementia seized the lover,/for pardoning Hell knew how to do."[16]

To the four *A.* translations listed in Duckworth, *Survey* 92 (2), four more are now to be added, all in verse: by M. Oakley, *Virgil's Aeneid* (Everyman's Library, London 1957), with notes by the translator and an introduction by E. M. Forster; by P. Dickinson, *The Aeneid* (Mentor Classics, New York 1961), who appends a short essay on "Vergil and the Aeneid"; by T. H. Delabère May, *The Aeneid by Vergil* (Bantam Books, New York 1961), edited and with an introduction by M. Hadas, who has modernized the archaisms in Delabère May's version; most recently by L. R. Lind, *Vergil's Aeneid* (Midland Books, Bloomington 1963), with introduction ("Vergil and the Meaning of the *Aeneid*"), bibliography, and notes. All four translations seem readable and accurate. Dickinson's version is praised for its rapidity and condemned for its use of rare words, colloquialisms, and occasional errors. The most poetic are perhaps those by Oakley and Lind, and the latter is especially recommended for the excellent introduction and useful notes.[17]

On earlier verse translations of the *A.*, see R. G. Austin, *Some English Translations of Virgil* (Liverpool 1956), who points out the disadvantages and defects of the ballad meter, the Spenserian stanza, the English hexameter, blank verse, and the heroic couplet, and praises Day Lewis' version (in a flexible six-stress line), in spite of its colloquialisms. On the translations of Humphries and Day Lewis, see also Lind, *Aeneid*, Introduction, xxi f.

3. Appendix Vergiliana

Duckworth *MS*, 218f.; *SP*, 93-96: the mathematical ratios in the *Appendix* favor the authenticity of the *Culex* and argue for the unity of the *Dirae-Lydia;* for a suggested method of testing authorship by means of a statistical analysis of the patterns of alliteration, see Herdan (below, Sect. 8: *Style*).

C. Soltero González, *El "Apéndice Virgiliano"* (Quito 1958), uses the criterion of internal evidence to show that, except for *Catalepton* 5 and 8, none of the poems in the *Appendix* can be by V.; they lack the proportion, sensitivity, sustained perfection, and good taste of the authentic works.[18] A. Salvatore, *Appendix Vergiliana. I. Ciris - Culex* (Torino 1957); *II. Dirae [Lydia] - Copa - Moretum - Catalepton* (Torino 1960): each volume contains preface (on MSS and textual problems), bibliography, text, brief notes, critical apparatus, and index. Salvatore's text is praised by many reviewers.[19] L. Herrmann, *Le second Lucilius* (Bruxelles-Berchem 1958) [= *Collection Latomus*, Vol. 34]: text, critical apparatus, and translation (French) of *Catalepton* 9, the *Ciris*, and the *Aetna*. Herrmann ascribes these poems (along with others, including the *Octavia*) to Lucilius Junior, friend of the younger Seneca, and views *Catalepton* 9 as the dedication to the *Ciris*.[20] E. Bolisani, *Dall' "Appendix Vergiliana": I Catalepton e le Dirae tradotti e commentati* (Padova 1958): introduction (the poems are authentic, and the *Dirae* and *Lydia* are separate poems), text, translation (Italian), notes, testimonia, and index. On the *Culex* and *Ciris* as later imitations, if not intentional forgeries, see A. Ronconi, "Introduzione alla letteratura pseudoepigrafa," *SCO* 5 (1955) 15-37; F. W. Lenz, "Über die Problematik der Echtheitskritik," *Altertum* 8 (1962) 218-228. See Haarhoff, however (below, Sect. 7E).

Culex. E. Bolisani, "Il *Culex* dell'*Appendix Vergiliana* e il *Virgilio Maggiore*," *AIV* 116 (1957-58) 171-200: text, translation (Italian) and a comparison of passages with V.'s authentic works; Bolisani argues that V. composed the *Culex*. M. Schmidt, *Vergil. Die Mücke* (Berlin 1959) [= *Schriften und Quellen der alten Welt*, Band 4]: introduction, text and critical apparatus, translation (German), and notes; Octavius is the later Augustus and the tomb of the gnat is V.'s parody on the mausoleum of Augustus, erected in 28 B.C.; xvi in the Donatus-Suetonius Life is an error for xli.[21] The *Culex* is accepted as authentic not only by Bolisani and Schmidt, but also by K. Mras, "Vergils Culex," *Altertum* 7 (1961) 207-213, who believes that the poem was dedicated by V. to his school friend, the Octavius Musa mentioned in *Catalepton* 4 and 11.[22] Wimmel, 307f., considers the *Culex* post-Vergilian and discusses the author's indebtedness to V. and Propertius.

P. Frassinetti, "Per l'esegesi del *Culex*," *RFIC* 38 (1960) 32-52: interpretation or emendation of 18 passages. W. T. Avery, *"Culex* 174: un emendamento," *RFIC* 38 (1960) 165-169, compares *A.* 6.417-418 and reads *ingentem* rather than *ingens* in *Culex* 174; the line is hypermetric, as in *A.* 7.160 and *G.* 1.295. O. Novarese, "Un verso tormentato: *Culex* 174," *Helikon* 1 (1961) 515-518, opposes Avery and accepts the traditional reading *ingens*, frequently used by V. at the end of a hexameter. G. Cambier, *"Culex* v. 198," *Latomus* 18 (1959) 171: the reading *quod erat tardus* is a reminiscence of *G.* 3.424 (*tardosque. . .orbis*); Cambier, *"Culex,* v. 318," *Latomus* 19 (1960) 130, supports the reading *fluminibus* by citing *A.* 2.301ff.

Ciris. A. Haury, *La Ciris. Poème attribué à Virgile* (Bordeaux 1957): introduction, bibliography, text, translation (French), critical apparatus, and notes; Haury argues for Vergilian authorship.[23] E. Bolisani, "Dall' *Appendix Vergiliana:* la *Ciris* e il *Virgilio Maggiore,*" *AIV* 117 (1958-59) 1-48: text, translation (Italian), and a comparison of passages with V.'s authentic works to support the author's view that the *Ciris* is by V.; he seeks to refute the arguments of Munari.[24] A. Rostagni, "Il 'Panegirico di Messalla' e i componimenti a Messalla dedicati nell'appendice vergiliana," *RAL* 14 (1959) 349-355: the author of the *Panegyricus* is indebted to the *Ciris* (and, to a lesser degree, to *Catalepton* 9). I. Cazzaniga, *Ciris* (Milano 1961), on the poetic background of the epyllion, MSS and textual problems, and comparison with Ovid; the poet of the *Ciris* is to be assigned to the time of Tiberius, after the *floruit* of Ovid. The fact that the conclusion (538-541) = *G.* 1.406-409 may have caused someone to write the name *Vergili* in the margin or beneath, and this was wrongly added to *explicit Ciris.* D. Knecht, "De 'Ciris' en Ovidius," *AC* 31 (1962) 236-251, however, argues from the comparison of parallel passages in the *Ciris* and Ovid that Ovid knew and imitated the epyllion.

I. Cazzaniga, "Osservazioni critiche intorno ad alcuni passi della 'Ciris'," *SIFC* 32 (1960) 125-145; emendation or discussion of 20 passages; "Il v. 117 della Ciris," *PP* 15 (1960) 53-56. F. R. D. Goodyear, "Two Passages in the 'Ciris'," *PCPhS* 6 (1960) 32-34: emendations of 139-141 and 359-361. L. Alfonsi, "Nota a *Iuppiter Magus*," *RFIC* 35 (1957) 74-76: the epithet *magus,* guaranteed for *Ciris* 374 by the Graz MS, is supported by a reference in Martin of Braga, *de correctione rusticorum,* 7. I. Cazzaniga, "Intorno al verso 376 della Ciris. 'Amyclaeo spargens altaria thallo'," *PP* 14 (1959) 453-457. P. Maas, "Ciris 434," *Maia* 9 (1957) 223-224.

Moretum. A. A. Wiersma-Buriks, "Moretum," *Hermeneus* 32 (1960-61) 80-90: text, translation (into Dutch), and a brief analysis, showing reminiscences of Ovid, V., and Homer. A. Salvatore, "Tradizione manoscritta e lingua del *Moretum,*" in Castiglioni, II, 835-857, stresses the importance of the readings of G (the recently discovered Graz fragment).

Dirae (Lydia). For the view that the so-called *Lydia* is a part of the *Dirae,* see above, Duckworth; Soltero González, 133ff.; Salvatore, II, ix f. Bolisani separates the two poems but accepts them as V's. A. Salvatore contributes two articles: "Sul testo della cosi detta *Lydia,*" *RCCM* 1 (1959) 376-393, on controversial readings and the style of the poem; the *Lydia* belongs with the *Dirae;* and "Note sul testo delle *Dirae,*" in Herrmann, 678-693, on the emendation and interpretation of numerous passages.

Copa. R. E. H. Westendorp Boerma, in two similar articles, "De Syrische Copa," *Hermeneus* 29 (1957-58) 114-118, and "On Dating the *Copa,*" *Mnemosyne* 11 (1958) 331-338, agrees with Büchner that the *Copa* is not by V., but opposes his view that it is to be dated between Catullus and V. The author was influenced by V. and Horace, and esp. by Propertius, and perhaps composed the poem shortly after 16 B.C. Westendorp Boerma considers the *Copa* unique in Latin literature for its animation and charm.

Catalepton. J. W. Zarker, "Catullus 18-20," *TAPhA* 93 (1962) 502-522, favors the Catullan authorship of two *Priapea* (*Catalepton* 2* and 3*) on the basis of both the ancient evidence and the structure of the two poems. E. J. Barnes, "*Priapea* 3.3 (*App. Verg.*)," *CPh* 57 (1962) 33-34: for *formitata* read *formata arte.*

L. Herrmann, "Le livret pseudo-virgilien de Martial," *Latomus* 21 (1962) 781-793: a reconstruction of the order of the *Catalepton* (written by Martial with the exception of 2, 9, and 13) and their distribution in eight pages or columns of 18 verses each, followed by an edition of the poems in their new order with critical apparatus, translation (into French) and Index. M. Schmidt, "Anordnungskunst in Catalepton," *Mnemosyne* 16 (1963) 142-156: on the content and arrangement of the collection; Schmidt argues for authenticity (with the exception of 9, which replaced a short poem to Messalla), and favors a division (by Varius) into 6 + 3 + 6.

E. V. Marmorale, "Appunti e osservazioni su alcuni 'catalepton'," *Pertinenze e Impertinenze* (Napoli 1960), analyzes several poems in detail, all of which he ascribes to V. 1 (85-96): a metrical exercise in the form of a riddle modeled upon a Hellenistic epigram, perhaps by Philodemus. 2 (97-113): *tau, min, sphin* have not only the grammatical significance attributed to them, but are truncated words which indicate that Annius Cimber killed his brother by strangling him with a rope. 3 (114-137): the poem refers not to one of the persons already suggested (Alexander, Mithridates, Phraates, Antony, Pompey) but to Scipio Africanus; the details (including exile) best correspond to his career. 4 and 11 (138-159): youthful tributes to his friend Octavius Musa in the style of Catullus; *Romana historia* (11.6) means Roman legends treated in verse, as Octavius was a poet, not a prose historian. 5 (160-182): V. studied at the school of Siro in Rome, before the philosopher went to Naples; the *portus* of line 8 is metaphorical, referring to the haven of Epicurean "felicità," and the poem is to be dated not later than 50 B.C. 8 (182-193): Marmorale dates the poem in 41 B.C. and believes that *patria* in line 4 is Rome, not Mantua. Both the villa and V.'s tomb are to be located at the beginning of the Vomero, two miles from the n.w. gate of Naples.

Also on 5, see Wimmel, 132 f., 148; K. F. C. Rose, "On Catalepton 5," *RhM* 104 (1961) 95, who reads *prosa non Achaica* in line 2; W. Richter, "Catalepton 5,2," *WS* 74 (1961) 156-159, reads *rhopo non Achaico.* Rostagni (below, Sect. 4B: *E.* 5) favors V.'s authorship of *Catalepton* 9, but cf. Schmidt above. On 10, see R. Syme, "Sabinus the Muleteer," *Latomus* 17 (1958) 73-80; Sabinus is to be identified with C. Calvisius Sabinus, a *novus homo*, who commanded a mobile column under Caesar in 48 B.C. and later held office as praetor (presumably in 46) and consul (in 39); R. E. H. Westendorp Boerma, "Adnotationes ad Verg. Catalepton 10," *Mnemosyne* 14 (1961) 233-238, who discusses the reading of lines 19 and 22, and argues against a lacuna after line 19.

Aetna. A new critical edition by W. Richter, *Aetna* (Berlin 1963): introduction, text, critical apparatus, and translation (German). Richter discusses and emends various passages in "Erwägungen zum Aetna-Text," *Philologus* 107 (1963) 97-115. See also G. Cambier, "Notes de lecture," *Latomus* 22 (1963) 97-99.

4A. The Bucolics: General

See Holtorf, 38-46; on the indebtedness of the *E.* to Horace's *Epode* 16, see Wimmel (below, Sect. 4C); on Maury's theory of the structure of the *E.*, cited in Duckworth, *Survey* 123 (4A), see Perret *V*, 29-33; also Perret *B*, 6-8, with modifications in the total number of verses (cf. below, Sect. 4B: *E.* 8); on mathematical ratios in the *E.*, see Duckworth *MS*, 196 ff.; *SP*, 39 f., and esp. Brown, 67-73. Brown examines the structure and content of several

passages in both *E.* and *G.* on cosmogony and astronomy and finds therein number symbolism (esp. 216, the number of completion) and the Golden Section.[25] The sources of inspiration for V.'s use of number and proportion are to be sought in Greek scientific poetry, esp. by Eratosthenes and Aratus, whose *Phaenomena* provides a direct model for *G.* 1.

R. Poggioli, "The Oaten Flute," *HLB* 11 (1957) 147-184, writes on the nature of pastoral poetry in general and the pastoral ideal—a retreat from civic responsibility to a private realm of love and friendship, of poetry and music. M. de Oliveira Pulquério, "A expressao do amor nas *Bucólicas* de Virgilio," *Humanitas* 6-7 (1957-58) 1-20, analyzes the treatment of love (also the language and style) in *E.* 2, 8, and 10, examines V.'s relation to Theocritus, and maintains that love and nature are fused by V. in a lyrical unity. F. Trisoglio, "Le Bucoliche virgiliane come momento idillico-estetico," *RSC* 8 (1960) 289-310, describes the elegance, charm, and humanity of the *E.*; human passions form the fundamental theme, but not on a tragic level. In a time of political turmoil V. portrayed the advantages of country life.

M. Dolç, "Sobre la Arcadia de Virgilio," *EClás* 4 (1957-58) 242-266, discusses V.'s relation to Theocritus and his originality, esp. in the creation of a pastoral Arcadia, both realistic and allegorical. This Arcadia owes much to Roman gardens and is localized on the Palatine which was sacred to the memory of Evander, the shepherd king from Arcadia in Greece; *A.* 8 is a commentary on the *E.* A. Balil, "Apostilla topográfica a la Arcadia de Virgilio," *EClás* 5 (1959-60) 96-98, rejects the identification of V.'s Arcadia with the Palatine. On the nature of the pastoral Arcadia and V.'s use of Theocritus, see also Musurillo (below, Sect. 6A) 39 f., and (esp. in *E.* 9) C. Marchesi, "Pastorale virgiliana," *Helikon* 1 (1961) 19-27. W. C. Korfmacher, "Classical Type Characterization: The Pastoral Phase," in Ullman, 60-68, writes on the portrayal by Theocritus and V. of old men, young men, and young women as types. E. De Michelis, "Sulle egloghe di Virgilio," *Arcadia. Atti e Memorie* 4 (1961) 19-41, discusses the individual *E.* and considers 1 and 9 the most beloved and the most autobiographical; he stresses not only the psychology of the poems but also their linguistic elegance.

4B. Individual Eclogues[26]

1. H. Altevogt, "Die erste Ekloge Vergils im Unterricht," *AU* Heft 9 (1956) 5-23: an analysis of the poem and its significance as an introduction to V.'s desire for peace as seen in the *G.* and *A.* K. Wellesley, *Virgil's Home* (1957) [= VS Lect. Summaries, No. 41], rejects the identification of Tityrus with V.; the poet lost his farm and never regained it (on the location of his birthplace, see below on *E.* 9). S. A. Oscherow, "Tityrus und Meliboeus (Zur Frage des Ideengehalt von Vergils erster Ekloge)," *AAntHung* 5 (1957) 201-207 [in Russian, with German summary, 208]: the two characters embody two attitudes of the poet. Meliboeus represents his protest at the confiscations, Tityrus his hope that Octavian will save the farmers. V. at this date is already the official singer of the Augustan Age; see also L. A. MacKay, "On Two Eclogues of Virgil," *Phoenix* 15 (1961) 156-158 (V. sympathizes with Meliboeus, thereby criticizing the government's land policy), and A. D. Leeman, "Toelichting bij Vergilius' Eerste Herderszang," *Hermeneus* 33 (1961-62) 220-225 (V. suggests that his fortune is that of Tityrus, but his heart is with Meliboeus); cf. Holtorf, 40 f., 128 f. (V. gives thanks to the *iuvenis*, i.e., Octavian, for the preservation of his home). C. Vandersleyen, "Virgile poète de la paix: le sens de la 1re et de la 4me Bucolique," *LEC* 31 (1963) 265-274, finds in both *E.* 1 and 4 a desire for peace but disapproval of Octavian; in 1 Meliboeus is the main character and the theme is the suffering of displaced persons.

2. J. J. H. Savage, "The Art of the Second *Eclogue* of Vergil," *TAPhA* 91 (1960), 353-375, on the structure of the poem and its literary and political symbolism. Corydon = Domitius Marsus, Damoetas = Aemilius Macer, Amyntas = Tibullus. Corydon favors the themes of Damoetas, reflecting contemporary political situations which appeared in *E.* 3; see below. L. Alfonsi, "Dalla II alla X Ecloga," *Aevum* 35 (1961) 193-198, on V. as an Epicurean and his portrayal of love in 2 (the earliest eclogue) and 10 (the latest).

3. J. J. H. Savage, "The Art of the Third *Eclogue* of Vergil (55-111)," *TAPhA* 89 (1958) 142-158, on the poem's literary and political symbolism. Palaemon = Octavian, Menalcas = V., Damoetas = Aemilius Macer; Galatea stands for Sextus Pompey, Amaryllis for Antony. The main theme of the poem is the need to guard the harbors of Italy against the inroads of Sextus Pompey. One difficulty with Savage's ingenious interpretation of *E.* 2 and 3 is that he must date them in late 39 or 38 B.C.; most scholars consider them V.'s earliest pastorals; see Duckworth, *Survey* 123 (4A).

D. E. W. Wormell, "The Riddles in Virgil's Third Eclogue," *CQ* 10 (1960) 29-32, rejects the solutions of Savage and others,[27] and suggests that more than one correct answer is possible for each of the two riddles in 104-107; the first refers to Archimedes' orrery in Rome, or to Posidonius' planetarium, probably in Rhodes; the second has two answers likewise, "in Rhoetea" or "in Lacedaemon." W. Krenkel, "Zu Vergil, Ecl. 3, 104-105, und seinem Erklärer Asconius Pedianus," *Wiss. Zs. der Univ. Rostock* 8 (1958-59) 27-32,[28] favors explaining the first riddle as the grave of Caelius of Mantua;[29] the *grammatici* mentioned by Asconius are Bavius and Maevius (3.90). See Brown, 39-40 (supports Wormell).

4. See below, Sect. 4C.

5. Daphnis most probably symbolizes Caesar, according to Holtorf, 40, 175 ff.; cf. Perret *B*, 57. A. Rostagni, "Virgilio, Valgio e . . . Codro. Chi era costui?" in Castiglioni, II, 807-833, identifies Codrus, mentioned in 5.11 and 7.22 ff., with Messalla, praised by V. in *Catalepton* 9. Holtorf, 205, and Perret *B*, 59, consider it unnecessary to view Codrus as a real person, but L. Alfonsi, "Codro Euforioneo," *Aegyptus* 40 (1960) 315-317, supports Rostagni by linking Codrus with the circle of Euphorion; the pastoral-erotic-elegiac nature of Messalla's compositions argues for the identification Codrus-Messalla.

6. Several important attempts to explain the nature of the poem have appeared in recent years. Z. Stewart, "The Song of Silenus," *HSPh* 64 (1959) 179-205, examines earlier theories and concludes that 6 "is a survey of types of poetry, especially — perhaps solely — types for which Rome had inherited a taste from Alexandria." The types in 31-86 are scientific, genealogical, epyllion, tragedy, elegy (hence Gallus), metamorphoses, and *paedika*. Epic and bucolic are represented in 1-12, comedy in 13-20. C. G. Hardie, *Eclogue VI* (1960) [= VS Lect. Summaries, No. 50], views 6 in the context of V.'s poetic development. The poem contains the germ of the *G.*, the Ascraean song, and here the pipe of Hesiod is given to Gallus. The unity of 6 is shown by the adaptations from Callimachus both in the proem and in the poem proper, and by the mention of Apollo throughout. The themes are not pastoral but, like *E.* 4, portray the Golden Age (in 6 enjoyed, lost, and regained). Wimmel, 132-148, maintains that the introduction (1-12), modeled upon the *Aitia* prologue of Callimachus, marks the beginning of the Augustan "Apologetik," and he compares the use of the same motif by Horace, Propertius, and Ovid. The passage concerning Gallus (64-73) corresponds to the dream in the beginning of the *Aitia*. J. P. Elder, *"Non iniussa cano. Vir-*

gil's Sixth Eclogue," *HSPh* 65 (1961) 109-125, agrees with Skutsch[30] that the poem is a catalogue of Alexandrian themes, but suggests that it contains also V.'s declaration of his poetic inspiration and a brief for his own kind of pastoral. Elder stresses the importance of Hesiod for Alexandrian poetry and for Callimachus in particular. Marchesi (above, Sect. 4A), however, thinks that V. in 6 was inspired by Lucretius rather than by Greek models; the poem contains a series of scenes in which love predominates. La Penna, 216-223, explains 6, with its themes moving from chaos through the *Saturnia regna* to myths of passion and tragedy, as modeled upon the poetry of Hesiod, where almost all the same themes appear. V. has used a Hesiodic scheme as his basis for a new philosophy and new poetry; Gallus is not an intrusion but is portrayed as an *alter Hesiodus*. Coleman (below, Sect. 5B: *G.* 4) says: "Apart from this Gallus episode the medley sung by Silenus forms a kind of catalogue of the themes favoured by the poets of the Alexandrian School, both Greek and Roman." Coleman regards both 6 and 10 as *laudes Galli*. On Golden Mean ratios in 6 and the identification of Silenus with Parthenius, see Brown, 62-67, 127-132. E. de Saint-Denis, "Le chant de Silène à la lumière d'une découverte récente," *RPh* 37 (1963) 23-40, examines in detail earlier attempts, both philosophical and literary, to explain the content and structure of 6 and to find unity therein;[31] he rejects the identification of Silenus with Parthenius or Siro and, on the basis of a Silenus mosaic found in 1960 at Thysdrus, Tunisia, and probably inspired by *E.* 6.13 ff., suggests that Silenus represents poetic inspiration of the highest type, hence the combination of cosmogonic and mythological themes.

7. See above, under 5.

8. J. B. Trapp, "The Owl's Ivy and the Poet's Bays. An Enquiry into Poetic Garlands," *JWI* 21 (1958) 227-255: from 8.12-13, where V. wove plants into a crown, later poets derived their acquaintance with the idea of poetic coronation and the materials fit for it. Perret *B,* 93, rejects 8.76 and also 28A, inserted by editors as a balancing refrain. His total for 6-9 is 331 verses, instead of 333 as in Maury and Perret *V;* the rejection of 76 and 28A is justified, according to Duckworth, *AJPh* 83 (1962) 447, note 11.

9. See Heurgon (below, Sect. 7B). Wellesley (above, *E.* 1) locates V.'s birthplace neither at Pietole nor in the Carpenedolo area but at Bande n.w. of Mantua; the poet spent his youth along the Mincio near Montaldo. L. Herrmann,

"Le domaine rural de Virgile," *Latomus* 19 (1960) 533-538, likewise rejects both Pietole and Carpenedolo; *E.* 9.7-10 favor a site west of Montichiari. E. Medori, "Con Virgilio alla ricerca del 'Vicus Andicus,' " *RSC* 10 (1962) 51-58, believes that the scenery of the *E.* is essentially Mantuan and that Pietole Vecchia is to be identified with ancient Andes. K. Vretska, "Vergils neunte Ekloge," *AU* 6, Heft 2 (1963) 31-46: analysis of structure and content.

10. See Alfonsi (above, under 2). Winniczuk (below, Sect. 7D: *Cornelius Gallus*) 140 ff., compares various passages in 10 with similar erotic themes in Roman elegy. J. Hubaux, "Parthenius. Gallus. Virgile. Properce," in *Propertiana,* 31-38, writes on elegiac themes in the song of Gallus and their use by Propertius in 1.8; *Parthenios* in *E.* 10.57 is an allusion to the poet Parthenius, friend of Gallus and V.[32] V. A. Estevez, S.J., "Pastoral Disillusionment: *Ecloga* 10," *CB* 38 (1961-62) 70-71: Gallus, abandoned by his love, turns for help to the imaginative pastoral world; disillusioned, he finally rejects it. His successive and emotional states give to the poem a psychological unity. W. Steidle, "Zwei Vergilprobleme. 1. Die Götter in Georgica I 5b-23. 2. Zum Verständnis der 10. Ecloge," 311-320, 320-334 in R. Muth (ed.), *Serta Philologica Aenipontana* (Innsbruck 1962) [= *Innsbrucker Beiträge zur Kulturwissenschaft,* 7-81]: analysis of 10 as a catalogue of the verses of Gallus and its relation to Theocritus.

4C. The Fourth Eclogue

See Holtorf, 41-43, 160-172; Perret *B,* 47-55; Savage (below, Sect. 6B: *A.* 6); Courcelle (below, Sect. 11A: *Christian Writers*).

J. Gagé. "A criança na IV ecloga e sua educação mística. Ensaio de interpretação," *Rev Hist* 8 (1954) 17-77:[33] on the subject matter of the poem and its religious background (esp. Neo-Pythagoreanism); the "secular" child, Saloninus, who is both human and divine, as a new Hercules, and his father, Asinius Pollio, compared to Amphitryon; history of the poem from Augustus to Constantine and the Christian interpretation given to it. C. G. Hardie, *The Fourth Eclogue* (1957) [= VS Lect. Summaries, No. 42], surveys the recent scholarship on the problems of 4, and interprets *scelus nostrum* (13) as the tendency to civil war inherited from Romulus. Dante goes as far as possible in giving a Christian interpretation to the poem. R. Waltz, "Sur la 4me Bucolique de Virgile," *LEC* 26 (1958) 3-20, writing on V.'s aim and achievement, considers the poem unique but the least successful of the *E.;* he traces the development of the Messianic idea in late antiquity, including the objections of St. Jerome. E. Paratore, "Il bimillenario della guerra di Perugia e della pace di Brindisi," *StudRom* 8 (1960) 523-534, suggests that V. probably learned Messianic ideas from the Jewish ambassadors who came to Rome with Herod the Great, friend of Asinius Pollio. H. Wagenvoort, "Indo-European Paradise Motifs in Virgil's Fourth Eclogue," *Mnemosyne* 15 (1962) 133-145, thinks that the Romans knew more than they cared to display concerning the Indo-European idea of an earthly paradise and a former contact between gods and men. The motif of oaks dripping honey (30) is well-known from Norse mythology and V. had in mind the Indo-European Tree of Life; grapes growing on thorns (29, cf. 3.89) are characteristic of paradise, as are red and yellow sheep.

Cumaeum carmen in 4.4 is usually taken as a reference to the prophecy of the Sibyl (so Holtorf), but see G. Radke, "Vergils Cumaeum carmen," *Gymnasium* 66 (1959) 217-246: there is no evidence that V. speaks of the Sibyl of Cumae in 4 (which resembles Sibylline oracles neither in form nor in content) or that the official Sibylline oracles were connected with Cumae prior to *A.* 6; according to Varro they came from Erythraea. The alternative explanation of *E.* 4.4 in both Philargyrius and Ps.-Probus is the correct one: *Cumaeum carmen* is the poem of Hesiod of Kyme; this tradition is probably derived from Aemilius Asper who composed a commentary on V. in the 2nd cent. and was interested in Hesiod. Just as Catullus 64, Horace, *Epode* 16 (earlier than *E.* 4), and others echo Hesiod's view of the Golden Age, so V. in 4.4. refers to Hesiod. For echoes of Hesiod in *E.* 4, see also La Penna, 223-225. The transposition of 23 after 20, already suggested by Büchner, Snell, and others, is favored by G. E. Duckworth, "The Cradle of Flowers (*Ecl.* 4.23)," *T.APhA* 89 (1958) 1-8: line 23 (with the reading *fundet*) states that the earth will put forth flowers as a cradle, an interpretation which is supported by the *Vita* of Focas, 26.f.

The relation of *E.* 4 and Horace's *Epode* 16 continues to attract the attention of scholars.[34] The priority of Horace is maintained (rightly, in my opinion) not only by Radke but by Hardie, Reckford (below, Sect. 7B) 82 and n. 33, Paratore (*Epode* 16 composed during the Perusian war, *E.* 4 after the peace of Brundisium in 40 B.C., W. Wimmel, "Vergils Eclogen und die Vorbilder der 16. Epode des Horaz," *Hermes*

89 (1961) 208-226, Vandersleyen (above, Sect. 4B: *E.* 1), and N. Strosetzky, "Vergil, 4. Ekloge, und Horaz, 16. Epode, im Unterricht," *AU* 6, Heft 2 (1963) 5-30. Wimmel answers C. Becker who argued in *Hermes* 83 (1955) 314-349 that *Epode* 16 contained echoes of several *E.* and could not be dated before 39 B.C.; according to Wimmel, the epode shows the direct influence of Theocritus, Lucretius, and Catullus, and the *E.* are indebted to Horace. Strosetzky accepts Wimmel and points out that V.'s *te duce* (13) must be later than *me vate* (*Epode* 16.66). Those who favor the priority of V. include E. Fraenkel, *Horace* (Oxford 1957) 50-52; J. Perret, *Horace* (Paris 1959) 113, who dates the epode about 32 B.C.; Ryberg (below, Sect. 7B) 116 f.; R. Crahay and J. Hubaux, "Le Pô et le Matinus," in Castiglioni, I, 451-471: Horace in his series of *adynata* parodies *E.* 4; the Po flooding the peaks of Matinus would mean the end of the world. Both A. La Penna, "La lirica civile di Orazio e l'ideologia del principato," *Maia* 13 (1961) 98-105, and P. Grimal, "A propos de la XVIe 'Epode' d'Horace," *Latomus* 20 (1961) 721-730, date *Epode* 16 in 38 B.C., at the renewal of hostilities between Sextus Pompey and Octavian. W. C. Helmbold, "Eclogue 4 and Epode 16," *CPh* 53 (1958) 178, suggests that the similarities in the two poems may be the result of earlier discussion by the poets, in which case the date of composition (i.e., the question of priority) is unimportant.

The identity of the *puer*: Waltz (above) and Kerényi (below, Sect. 12: *Nineteenth Century*) 19 f. believe that the *puer* is Asinius Gallus, the son of Asinius Pollio, while Gagé identifies him with a younger son, Saloninus; according to Leglise (below, Sect. 6B: *A.* 1) 17, the child is Marcellus, and Perret *B* suggests Asinius Gallus or Marcellus. Hardie, Holtorf, and Zabulis (below, Sect. 7C) favor the view that the *puer* is Octavian and Scribonia.[35] See G. Radke, "Aurea funis," *Gymnasium* 63 (1956) 82-86, on *de caelo demittere*: Lucr. 2.1153 f., Cicero's dream about Octavian (in Suet. *Aug.* 94.9), and *E.* 4.7, where the *nova progenies* is to be identified with the *puer;* Radke argues for the view that the young Caesar is meant. Strosetzky agrees with Büchner (see Duckworth, *Survey* 125 [4C]) that the *puer* is a symbol of the Golden Age, but believes that V. at the same time refers to Octavian. J. Holtermann, "Der Friedensgedanke in der augusteischen Dichtung," *AU* 6, Heft 2 (1963) 78-93, rejects the theory that the *puer* is a human child and sees in both *E.* 4 and *Epode* 16 the direct influence of the prophecies of Isaiah; he discusses the Messianic interpretation given to the poem by the Church Fathers.

There is still no agreement on the interpretation of 60-63. Waltz, Holtorf, Ernout (review of Perret *B* in *RPh* 36 [1962] 262 ff.), and P. Meylan, "Zum Schluss von Vergils Vierter Ekloge," *MH* 20 (1963) 21, read *cui non risere parentes* in 62; Holtorf, Ernout, and Meylan interpret *risus* in 60 as the laughter of the child, with 62 referring to the response of the parents (Meylan stresses the fact that *parentes* includes the mother as well as the father). N. I. Herescu, "Le souvenir d'une berceuse dans le IVeme Eglogue de Virgile," *Orpheus* 4 (1957) 125-130, and Parret *B* read *qui non risere parentes* with Quintilian; according to Herescu, the passage has the language and style of a nursery song, one characteristic of which is that the child smiles at its parents; he and Perret *B* compare Catullus 61.219 f. (*dulce rideat ad patrem/semihiante labello*), as does Westendorp Boerma (below, Sect. 10: *Catullus*) 56, who suggests that V. is imitating Catullus. P. Maas, *Textual Criticism* (Oxford 1958) 36 f., says that *parentes* after *qui* is nonsense and favors the conjecture *parenti*. On *decem menses* in 61, see O. Neugebauer, "*Decem Tulerunt Fastidia Menses*," *AJPh* 84 (1963) 64-65: V.'s terminology is plain; nine-month children are born after ten (sidereal) months.

J.-G. Préaux, "Constatations sur la composition de la 4e bucolique de Virgile," *RBPh* 41 (1963) 63-79, discusses the structure of the poem, esp. the reason for the total of 63 lines (63 as a critical age being suitable for a birthday poem), and the composition in sections of seven lines, with the central portion (18-45) of 28 lines, a perfect number; line 39 makes an important transition from the earlier *fraus* to the fullness of the Golden Age and with 1-39 as major, the poem reveals the Golden Mean ratio (39/63 = .619.)[36]

5A. *The Georgics: General*

See Holtorf, 46-51, and (for a detailed structural analysis) Richter, 78-114, 408-412. Another important work on the structure and meaning of the poem is that by C. A. Disandro, "Las Geórgicas de Virgilio. Estudio de estructura poética," *Bol. Acad. Argentina de Letras* 21 (1956) 517-601; 22 (1957) 51-107, 175-230, 467-511. These four articles total 243 pages, and it is unfortunate that they have not been published together as a book and made more available. The material is divided into six parts: Prólogo (517 ff.), a summary of the earlier views of Sabbadini, Jahn, Witte, Burck, Drew, Schmidt, Klingner, and Richardson; I. Las Geórgicas, poema didáctico (537 ff.), on V.'s indebtedness to earlier writers, esp. Hesiod, Lucretius, and Cicero (*De Senectute, De Re Publica*); II. La estructura del poema (51 ff.), on the main sections 1-2 and 3-4, with each book divided into two parts, and on the numerous

links which bind together the books; III. Los elementos compositivos (175 ff.), on the relation of the descriptions and episodes to the main didactic themes; IV. Designio poético y estilo didáctico (467 ff.), esp. on the structure of the prooemia of 1 and 3;[37] and Conclusiones (505 ff.), in which the author stresses the lyrical nature of the poem and its value as the glorification of reality.[38] G. E. Duckworth, "Vergil's *Georgics* and the *Laudes Galli*," *AJPh* 80 (1959) 225-237, also discusses the structure and content of the poem (esp. the universal nature of the conclusions: 1. War; 2. Peace; 3. Death; 4. Resurrection). The story of Aristaeus and the regeneration of the bees is a necessary part of the poem and must not be viewed as an addition after the death of Cornelius Gallus; see Sect. 5B: *G. 4*. On mathematical ratios in the *G.*, see Duckworth *MS*, 194 ff.; *SP* 36-44; and esp. Brown, 11-22, who discusses also V.'s use of symbolic numbers and analyses in detail several important astronomical passages; see 23-61.

For various aspects of the poem, see J. Schilling, "Remarque sur les *Géorgiques*," *BAGB* (1961) 226-227: the work contains 2187 verses (if we reject 4.338 as an interpolation); this number is 3 to the 7th power and cannot be accidental; D. R. Dudley, "*Saturnia Tellus*," *PCA* 58 (1961) 24-25: "The *Georgics* are not born of a wish to serve imperial propaganda, nor of a romantic longing for an idealized past; they rest on the solid achievement of the farmers of Italy"; W. S. Maguinness, "Les *Géorgiques* de Virgile," *BAGB* (1962) [= *Lettres d'Humanité* 21], 441-451, on the purpose and nature of the poem (not merely a didactic work on farming but an esthetic and intellectual treatment of man and nature, with numerous digressions to provide charm, variety, and a more universal interest); K. Herbert, "The Vergilian Smile," *CO* 40 (1962-63) 8-11, on V.'s affection for life and nature in their sunnier aspects, as seen in the *G.*; R. Gustin, "La rhétorique dans les *Géorgiques*," *LEC* 30 (1962) 318-325, on oratorical themes and devices (commonplaces, comparisons, transition formulas) in 2.136-176, 458-540; 4.125-148.

La Penna, 225-247, stresses the influence of Hesiod's *Works and Days* upon the *G.*, seen not only in structure (Book 1), style, and verbal echoes, but in V.'s emphasis on the divine law of *labor* and the return of the Golden Age. The author also touches upon the importance of Aratus (Stoicism) and Lucretius (language and style rather than philosophical doctrine); see below, Sect. 10: *Lucretius*. On V.'s use of Nicander, see Sect. 10: *Nicander*.

5B. *Georgics: Individual Books*[39]

1. Brown, 41-61, explains *clarissima mundi / lumina* in 5-6 as "the entire group of seven *vagantes stellae*" headed by Mercury, with whom

Octavian (24 ff.) is associated. F. Rebelo Gonçalves, "A Deusa Telure na Invocação das Geórgicas," Euphrosyne 3 (1961) 91-110, argues that tellus in 7 is the goddess Tellus and compares Ovid, Fasti 1.671-678; Stat. Theb. 8.303-307. On the gods in 5b-23 and V.'s relation to Varro, see Steidle (above, Sect. 4B: E. 10). P. Colaclidès, "Labor Improbus," Platon 11 (1959) 207-208, examining the use of labor and improbus elsewhere in V.'s works, concludes that improbus in 146, in the context with egestas, means "evil" rather than "unceasing"; the passage should be compared with A. 6.437, not 6.276f.[40] R. Gustin, "Labor improbus (Virg. Géorg. I, 121-159)," LEC 28 (1960) 278-285, analyzes the passage and discusses its importance in revealing the general nature of the G. and the poet's profound knowledge of man. V. here repudiates Arcadian idleness and rejects the Golden Age. On labor improbus, see also Perret V, 68-74; L. P. Wilkinson, "Virgil's Theodicy," CQ 13 (1963) 75-84, on the antecedents and value of the idea of labor, and its relation to the G. as a whole. For acrostic signatures in 1.424-437 and 2.315-342, see Brown, 102-112. 1.503-504 are considered by Richter (ad loc.) as a later insertion, after Actium. G. Barra, "All'indomani di Nauloco (Virg. Georg. I, 503-04)," AFLN 7 (1957) 39-56, disagrees and argues that the verses in question belong to the original ending of the book, composed just after the battle of Naulochus (36 B.C.), when V. felt both confidence in Octavian and uncertainty about the future.

2. On 458-542, see Wimmel (on 3.1-48); Fenik (below, Sect. 7D: Horace). On the felixfortunatus passage (490-494), see Stewart (above, Sect. 4B: E. 6) 185 (the doctrine is part Epicurean, part Empedoclean); cf. Richter (ad loc.); Heurgon (below, Sect. 7B); and Duckworth SP, 74 (on the Pythagorean nature of the passage). Ryberg (below, Sect. 7B) 123 ff., thinks that V. gives up hope of attaining the pinnacle of poetry achieved by Lucretius; Sullivan (below, Sect. 7B) 404, disagrees and takes the prayer to the Muses seriously; V. hoped to describe rerum causas at a later date.

3. The prooemium of 3 has received considerable attention. See Disandro (above, Sect. 5A). Wimmel, 167-187, points out numerous parallels and contrasts between 2.458-542 and 3.1-48 and comments on the Lucretian elements in both passages. He analyzes the prooemium of 3 in detail as an "apologetisches Stück" influenced by Callimachus, and suggests that the templum (16) refers to the extant A., not to

an earlier plan for a historical epic about Octavian; cf. Duckworth MS, 188, note 6; SP, 14: V.'s desire to portray Caesar in medio (16) is actually fulfilled in the epic as we have it. But Hardie (above, Sect. 4B: E. 6), 7 f., believes that the proposed work was to be a historical poem in the style of Ennius and that V. had not yet thought of Aeneas as his hero. N. Terzaghi, "Sulla seconda edizione della Georgiche," Athenaeum 38 (1960) 132-140, maintains that V. wrote the prologue of 3 at the time of the second edition, when he substituted the Orpheus-Eurydice story for the laudes Galli (see below on G. 4). U. Fleischer, "Musentempel und Octavianehrung des Vergil im Proömium zum dritten Buche der Georgica," Hermes 88 (1960) 280-331, presents a thorough and important analysis of 1-48 as a literary prooemium referring to the G., into which V. inserted a glorification of Octavian by changing the original temple of the Muses to a temple honoring the Roman leader. The change in the prooemium was made in 29 B.C., when V. decided to compose a historical epic on Octavian's achievements. On the events described in 25-33, see Meyer (below, Sect. 7C). P. Grimal, "La mention de l' 'Invidia infelix' dans le prologue au livre III des Géorgiques," summary in REL 40 (1962) 33-34, argues, from V.'s rejection of the Epicurean doctrine of Invidia, that 3.26-39 were added in 30-29 B.C., the remainder of the prooemium having been composed in 34 B.C. On 3. 41, see J.-G. Préaux, "Tua, Maecenas, haud mollia iussa," RBPh 37 (1959) 92-103: V.'s attitude toward Maecenas is not one of servility; the words haud mollia refer to the difficulty of writing the G., a work very different from the molles versus of the E. Préaux examines similar passages, esp. with mollis and iussa, in Horace and Propertius and elsewhere in V.

K. Meuli, "Scythica Vergiliana. Ethnographisches, Archäologisches und Mythologisches zu Vergils Georgica 3, 367 ff.," Schweizerisches Archiv für Volkskunde 56 (1960) 88-200: the Scythian hunting scene described in 371-375 implies the use of some form of snowshoe; since such hunting is possible only with skis, V.'s source, a Greek ethnographic writer of the 5th cent. B.C., apparently knew of people who hunted on skis. This predates by a thousand years the earliest literary reference to skis.

4. See F. X. Quinn, S.J., "Vergil and Today's Bee Culture," CB 34 (1957-58) 4-5, 7 (the accuracy and modernity of V.'s knowledge of bees); T. J. Haarhoff, "The Bees of Virgil," G & R 7 (1960) 155-170 (V.'s interest in bees, their activity and their divinity); M. Roberty,

41

"Labor Improbus," *CO* 37 (1959-60) 28-29 (the importance of *labor* in 4 as the bond of union in the community of the bees; V. teaches a lesson to humanity of dedication and responsibility to the community); S. Blankert, "Notes on Virgil *Georgics* IV 25-90," *Mnemosyne* 12 (1959) 233-251 (observations based on a reasonable knowledge of bees and familiarity with the state of that knowledge in V.'s time).

A. Le Boeuffle, "Quelques Observations sur Virgile, *Géorgiques*, IV, 234 sq.," *REL* 39 (1961) 100-105, discusses the difficulties in taking *Piscis* in 234 as the zodiac constellation *Pisces* (cf. Richter, *ad loc.*) and agrees with Servius that it refers to the more brilliant constellation, Piscis Australis, bringer of storms and tempests (cf. *aquosus*), hence opposed to the Pleiades, symbol of spring. This theory had already been rejected by R. J. Getty, *TAPhA* 79 (1948) 34 ff. See Brown, 27-31, who reads *fustis* (club of Orion) in 234 instead of *Piscis*; cf. *aquosus Orion* in *A.* 4.52.

The most discussed problem of the poem in recent years is that of the *laudes Galli*, with several scholars continuing to accept the tradition of a second edition of Book 4, and others denying the existence of such an edition. The position of Richter, 11-13, 107-114, is unusual: he believes in changes in the second half of 4 (praise of Egypt and mention of Gallus replaced by the Orpheus episode) but there was no second edition as such. The *G.* as read to Octavian in 29 B.C. was unfinished. V. continued work on the poem during the early years of his composition of the *A.* (of the parallels between *G.* 4 and *A.* 1, those in the *A.* are the earlier) and finally published the *G.*, with the revised ending of 4, in 26 or 25 B.C. On the improbabilities of Richter's theory, see Burck, *Gnomon* 31 (1939) 229 ff.

Those who accept the theory that praise of Gallus was removed in a second edition include Lallemant, 284 f.: Gallus had perhaps written earlier on the theme of Orpheus, and V., by inserting the Orpheus story in 4 after the death of Gallus, paid a more discreet tribute to his friend; Winniczuk (below, Sect. 7D: *Cornelius Gallus*): the original *laudes Galli* concerned his political and military activity; Terzaghi (above, on 3) and Cova (above, Sect. 2: *Editions*): the praise of Gallus was replaced by the Orpheus-Eurydice story; Della Corte (above, Sect. 2: *Editions*) xiv-xxvii: V. was working on *A.* 1 when he revised *G.* 4 (hence the echoes of *A.* 1); the revision consisted of removing some reference to Egypt and perhaps mention of Gallus as prefect; T. J. Haarhoff, "Vergil and Cornelius Gallus," *CPh* 55 (1960) 101-108: the first edition praised Gallus as a poet;[41] V. sub-

stituted the Orpheus story, an Alexandrian tale such as Gallus might have written; the new ending thus contains subtle praise of Gallus and an implied criticism of Augustus; R. Coleman, "Gallus, The Bucolics, and the Ending of the Fourth Georgic," *AJPh* 83 (1962) 55-71: the Aristaeus epyllion itself is such a poem as Gallus wrote and admired, and the Orpheus-Eurydice story (the central panel of the epyllion) is an expression of V.'s grief at the tragic death of his friend.

Although Lallemant, Haarhoff, and Coleman all accept the existence of a second edition, their conviction that the extant conclusion of 4 is an oblique tribute to Gallus gives support to those scholars who reject Servius' account of a change in the second half of the book. See F. Klingner, "Catulls Peleus-Epos," *SBAW* Heft 6 (1956), esp. 72-77; Disandro (above, Sect. 5A) 225 ff.; Duckworth (above, Sect. 5A) 233 ff. Klingner and Disandro stress the incoherent nature of Servius' testimony, and both Disandro and Duckworth argue from the unified structure of the poem that the Aristaeus and Orpheus stories must have been part of the original conclusion. Fleischer (above, on 3) suggests that the Aristaeus and Orpheus stories were meant to refer to the literary interests of Gallus, and that Servius misunderstood an earlier statement that the end of 4 contained *laudes Galli*. Maguinness (above, Sect. 5A) also rejects Servius and thinks that the parallel passages in the *A.* echo those in the *G.* P. Händel, "Vergils Aristaeus-Geschichte," *RhM* 105 (1962) 66-91, examines the Aristaeus and Orpheus stories and finds them free of the flaws often ascribed to them. He considers them the original ending of 4, from which a short statement about Gallus may have been removed, and explains the story of the second edition as the result of the wrong insertion of a *nunc* (cf. Serv. *in G.* 4.1), which in turn led to a shift in the meaning of *commutare* (cf. Serv. *in E.* 10.1). The present conclusion with the Aristaeus and Orpheus stories may well be a tribute to Gallus, as has been suggested; furthermore, if Gallus himself had written a poem about Orpheus, V.'s version on the same theme, recalling his friend's poetic achievement, could explain the garbled account in Servius; see Duckworth *TD*, 120-122. It is unnecessary to assume, as do Lallemant and Coleman, that the Orpheus story was composed to honor Gallus *after* his death.

6.A. The Aeneid: General

Pöschl's valuable book, *Die Dichtkunst*

Virgils,[42] is summarized by A. Gillingham in *Vergilius* 5 (1959) 18-28, and is translated into English by G. Seligson under the title, *The Art of Vergil. Image and Symbol in the Aeneid* (Ann Arbor 1962). Also on the artistic unity and imaginative scope of the *A.* as a work of symbolic creation, see H. Musurillo, S.J., *Symbol and Myth in Ancient Poetry* (New York 1961), esp. 120-126. On the *A.* as an allegory, see below, Sect. 7C. M. R. Ridley, *Studies in Three Literatures: English, Latin, Greek, Contrasts and Comparisons* (London 1962) 57-67, criticizes V.'s delineation of character and handling of narrative but finds true greatness in his verbal artistry and expression of emotion; he is "beyond all others the poet of the pathos of two things, the inevitable and the unattainable" (67). New books include F. Sbordone, *Esegesi Virgiliana antica e moderna* (Napoli 1962), on the composition of the *A.*, the character of Aeneas, and ancient commentators; and Buchheit's important and well-documented work on the significance of Juno for the meaning and structure of the epic, V.'s emphasis on the Italian origin of Dardanus, and the Carthage-Rome antithesis in *A.* 1 and 7; Buchheit touches upon many important topics; see below, esp. Sects. 6B: *A.* 7, 8; 6C: *Juno*; 10: *Naevius*.

Holtorf, 51-68, analyzes the *A.*, stressing Fate as a leitmotif. R. Speaight, *The Virgilian Res* (London 1958)[43] discusses the timeless values of the poem in the light of V.'s use of *res* and esp. his view of *res Romana* (Augustan peace vs. *lacrimae rerum*). In *A Modern Virgilian. A Memorial Lecture to Monsignor Ronald Knox delivered to the Virgil Society* (London 1958), Speaight gives the essence of several lectures on the *A.* delivered by Ronald Knox in 1912 but still unpublished, dealing with *pietas*, divine purpose, freedom of will, V.'s eschatology. On the nature of *pietas* and its importance in the *A.*, see also H. Dörrie, "Pietas," *AU* 4, Heft 2 (1959) 5-27.

Various aspects of V.'s art are treated in the following articles: E. Wistrand, "Virgil's Palaces in the Aeneid," *Klio* 38 (1960) 146-154: the house of the demons (6.273-289) is similar to the Greek house of the type of the Vitruvian gynaeconitis; the royal palace of Priam (2.437-558) also represents a Greek house such as described by Vitruvius, but modified to correspond to Roman ideas of a princely dwelling; I. Trencsényi-Waldapfel, "Das Bild der Zukunft in Aeneis," *StudClas* 3 (1961) 281-304: a comparison of the allusions to the future in the *A.* with those in Homeric epic (more concerned with the past), in the *Oracula Sibyllina*, which V. knew and used, and in Lycophron's *Alexandra*, also employed as a source by V.; H. Dent, "The Aeneid: Background and foreground," *Orpheus* 8 (1961) 3-7: V. was able to enrich his poem

by associations with earlier legend and later history (to his own day): T. Greene, "The Norms of Epic," *CompLit* 13 (1961) 193-207: the imagery, hero, structure, and language of epic poetry, with references to the *A.*; J. E. Rexine, "Fire Symbolism in the *Aeneid*," *CO* 39 (1961-62) 1-2: fire, the dominant symbol of the poem, has aspects both destructive (Troy, Dido) and constructive (Ascanius, Lavinia, Vesta and Rome); E. A. Douglas, "The Realism of Virgil," *PVS* 1 (1961-62) 15-24 [= VS Lect. Summaries, No. 55]: the poet's realistic and impartial treatment of his characters and of Rome; G. F. Osmun, "Night Scenes in the *Aeneid*," *Vergilius* 8 (1962) 27-33; A. E. Miller, "Dreams and Visions in the *Aeneid*," *CO* 40 (1962-63) 42-44; B. Fox, "The Light Touch in the *Aeneid*," *CO* 40 (1962-63) 37-39.

6B. Aeneid: Individual Books[44]

1. P. Leglise, *Une oeuvre de pré-cinéma, l'-Enéide. Essai d'analyse filmique du premier chant* (Paris 1958), shows that V. has presented the events of Book 1 as does a modern writer of film scenarios; the analysis, scene by scene, contains much of critical and esthetic value and throws new light on V's use of Homer.[45] On 1-33, see Buchheit, 13-22. L. L. Luisides, "Il 'Numen laesum' nell' Eneide di Virgilio," *Platon* 11 (1959) 63-82, discusses the phrase *quo numine laeso* in 1.8 (which looks ahead to Books 7-12 as, by *hysteron proteron*, the following *quidve dolens* refers to 1-6); *numen* signifies the will of the gods and the manifestation of their approval of Aeneas' arrival in Latium (cf. 7.119); *numine laeso* in 1.8 describes Juno's attempt to nullify the divine will, as does *perverso numine* in 7.584. A J. Gossage, "Aeneas at Sea," *Phoenix* 17 (1963) 131-136: analysis of 92-98 and a defense of Aeneas' character. A. Deman, "Virgile et la colonisation romaine en Afrique du Nord," in Grenier, I, 519-526: Aeneas' arrival at Carthage (418-438) contains allusions to the new Carthage of Caesar and Augustus (Colonia Iulia Concordia Karthago). E. Kraggerud, "Vergil über die Gründung Karthagos," *SO* 38 (1963) 32-37: to the numerous allusions in *A.* 1 to the hostility between Rome and Carthage and Rome's ultimate victory we should add the double meaning in 445, *facilem victu*, which to the Romans would suggest "easy to overcome." R. D. Williams, "The Pictures on Dido's Temple (*Aeneid* I. 450-93)," *CQ* 10 (1960) 145-151: on the arrangement of the scenes—balancing pairs, with the central portion (deaths of Rhesus and Troilus, supplication of Pallas and Priam) stressing Greek cruelty and Trojan doom; Troilus in 474-478 is described as ambushed while without defensive armor.

2. B. Fenik, "Parallelism of Theme and Imagery in *Aeneid* II and IV," *AJPh* 80 (1959) 1-24, shows that 2 and 4 represent major crises or tests for Aeneas and in each book he is forgetful of divine will. Deceit and trickery are prominent in both books, and fire is the dominant image in each. Verbal parallels appear, esp. in the deaths of Priam and Dido. J. A. S. Evans, "*Aeneid* 2 and the art of the theater," *CJ* 58 (1962-63) 255-258, believes that V.'s indebtedness to drama and stage technique includes not only characterization and dramatic irony, but also (1) attention to atmosphere, light and shade, scenic background, (2) skill at constructing dramatic scenes. *A.* 2 is divided into two acts on the basis of contrasting scenery and lighting.

R. G. Austin, "Virgil and the Wooden Horse," *JRS* 49 (1959) 16-25, analyzes 1-267. The Laocoon scenes complement each other; omission of either or both would have weakened the Sinonepisode and shattered the structure of the story of the horse; see also Duckworth *SP*, 90 f. Austin, pointing out that the horse contained only nine men (listed in groups of three), explains *primus* (263) as meaning that Machaon came out first. A. Lesky, "Zwei Kataloge der Aeneis," in Castiglioni, I, 531-542, argues for the same interpretation of *primus*, but implies that there were more than nine men in the horse. He compares the list of warriors in 339-346 with that in 259-264.

On the famous Helen episode in 567-588, see N. L. Hatch, "The Time Element in Interpretation of *Aeneid* 2. 575-76 and 585-87," *CPh* 54 (1959) 255-257: no contradiction between *sceleratus* (576) and *merentis* (585) to support the arguments against authenticity; *sceleratus* represents Aeneas' later judgment, years after the event described; R. G. Austin, "Virgil, *Aeneid* 2. 567-88," *CQ* 11 185-198, who analyzes the arguments for and against authenticity, examines the linguistic problems, and concludes that the lines are by V., but perhaps not in their final form; Duckworth *MS*, 215, and *SP*, 85 f., who uses the mathematical ratios in *A.* 2 as an added argument for the genuineness of the Helen episode.

3. R. B. Lloyd, "*Aeneid* III: A New Approach," *AJPh* 78 (1957) 133-151, examines the nine episodes (divided into three groups of three each), the revelations they contain, and the importance of Anchises as interpreter of the revelations. The subtle relationship of the various episodes and also their importance in establishing the pattern for the structure of 1-6 indicate that the book was planned and executed with meticulous care. See Lloyd (below, Sect. 6E). G. d'Anna, *Ancora sul problema della composizione dell'Eneide* (Roma 1961), disagreeing with Lloyd and Duckworth, maintains that 3, told in the third person, was originally the first book and was followed by the funeral games (present

5), with the present 1 the original third book.[46]

4. See Fenik (above, on 2). W. Milch, "Das vierte Buch der Aeneis als examplarische Lektüre im Gymnasium," *AU* Heft 9 (1956) 24-40, analyzes 4 as a tragedy (in three acts; the second and third acts begin with the arrival of Mercury, 238 ff. and 554 ff.) and its importance, as Aeneas' greatest trial, for the poem as a whole. The author expresses his indebtedness to Pöschl's *Die Dichtkunst Virgils* and views both Dido and Aeneas as tragic characters. On the *A.* as a tragedy in five acts (plus a bipartite central core, 173-218, 219-295), see P. MacKendrick, "The Pleasures of Pedagogy," *CJ* 54 (1958-59) 194-200. F. L. Newton, "Recurrent Imagery in *Aeneid* IV," *TAPhA* 88 (1957) 31-43, discusses the images which represent the passion of love as warfare (or capture of a city), as a wound (with special reference to the hunt), and as fire. D. R. Bradley, "Swords at Carthage," *CPh* 31 (1958) 234-236: the sword of 646 is Aeneas' gift to Dido and is the same as that of 507; exchange of swords is implied by 261-262 and 579-580, presumably references to a sword which Aeneas received from the queen.

5. G. Monaco, *Il libro dei ludi* (Palermo 1957), discusses the chronological problem of 5, its spiritual and poetic significance, and gives a complete literary analysis of the book.[47] M. C. J. Putnam, "Unity and Design in *Aeneid* V," *HSPh* 66 (1962) 205-239, also analyzes the structure and content of 5 with particular stress on its unity and significance. The boatrace suggests in comic form the final stages of Aeneas' journey (loss of pilot, narrow escape from shipwreck, and safe arrival at destination); the burning of the ships and the death of Palinurus symbolize the end of Aeneas' wandering by sea. E. Wolff, "Der Brand der Schiffe und Aeneas' Wiedergeburt," *MH* 20 (1963) 151-171, discusses the relation of 5 to other books, esp. 1, 4, and 6.

On specific passages in 5, see J. Bayet, "Les Cendres d'Anchise: Dieu, Héros, Ombre ou Serpent? (Vergile, Enéide V 42-103)," in Rohde, 39-56: the funeral rites for Anchises have an authentic Latin character unique in the *A*, and V. carefully observes the archaic terms appropriate to the *Parentalia;* Anchises is attached to the world of the dead and is not to be considered divine; G. Bellardi, "Un esempio di *imitatio* in Virgilio," *Maia* 14 (1962) 187-208: analyses of *Il.* 23.653-699 (also *Od.* 18.1-116), Apollonius, *Arg.* 2.1-97, Theocritus 22, and *A.* 5.362-484; V., reworking the earlier material and introducing much originality both in stylistic features and in the psychological aspects of character and situation, has made the spirit of the episode truly his own; H. Morland, "Zu der Bogenschützenepisode in der Aeneis," *SO* 37 (1961) 58-67: the four contestants (490-499) are listed according to age, beginning with the *iuvenis* Hippocoon and ending with the aged Acestes; J. L. Heller, "A Labyrinth from Pylos?" *AJA* 65 (1961) 57-62: the labyrinthlike movements of the equestrian game in 580-587 make V.'s subsequent reference to the Cretan labyrinth something more than a poetic comparison.[48]

6. See Heurgon (below, Sect. 7B); Courcelle (below, Sect. 11A: *Christian Writers*). M. Delaunois, "La richesse humaine du chant VI de l'Enéide," *LEC* 26 (1958) 327-341, writes on the eternal values of the main themes: suffering, death, religion, destiny beyond the grave. B. Otis, "Three Problems of *Aeneid* 6," *TAPhA* 90 (1959) 165-179, discusses the inconsistency between the "mythological" and the "theological" Hades (they express the difference between the past and the future), the antithesis between V.'s other-wordly doctrine and his emphasis on Rome, and the two Gates of Sleep (Aeneas, not being a *vera umbra*, could not leave by the Gate of Horn; his Hades vision is a false dream and not to be taken as literal reality).

P. J. Enk, "De labyrinthi imagine in foribus templi Cumani insculpta," *Mnemosyne* 11 (1958) 322-330: many commentators have overlooked the significance of the Cretan scenes and the labyrinth (20-33); the latter symbolizes the *regnum mortuorum* (*hic labor* in 129 recalls 27). V. knew from Varro and other writers the close connection of labyrinths with tombs and the underworld, and he mentioned the Cretan labyrinth specifically because of the role of Minos as a judge of the dead (cf. 432). On the nature of the golden bough, see H. Wagenvoort, "De gouden tak," *Hermeneus* 31 (1959-60) 46-52, 72-79, 92-100: the magical character of the bough in 6, and its appearance elsewhere in ancient art and literature and in legends and fairy tales throughout Europe; J.-G. Préaux, "Virgile et le rameau d'or," in Dumézil, 151-167: the symbolic meaning of the bough; for Aeneas (and for Augustus likewise) it was a guarantee of immortality and resurrection furnished by the protection of Diana and Apollo; R. Merkelbach, "Aeneas in Cumae," *MH* 18 (1961) 83-99: (1) the similarities in the meeting of Aeneas and the Sibyl in *A.* 6 and Tibullus 2.5; (2) the golden bough and its relation to Aeneas and the destiny of Rome (by breaking off the bough Aeneas is designated as king of the Latins); (3) V. in 70 and 792 f. refers to the *ludi saeculares;* the festival was originally scheduled for 23 B.C. but was postponed because of the illness and death of Marcellus, hence the many parallels between *A.* 6 and the secular games.

J. Van Ooteghem, S.J., "Une scène de sacri-fice dans le sixième chant de *l'Enéide*," in Herrmann, 767-773, discusses the sacrifice to the infernal deities in 237 ff., and esp. the four young bulls (243) which are offered, not to Hecate, but to the *Stygius rex* (252); the two parts of the sacrifice (killing of victims and offering of burned flesh) are indicated by *primum* (243) and *tum* (252). The number four, considered a bad omen, was believed suitable for sacrifices to underworld divinities. R. Turcan, "La catabase orphique du papyrus de Bologna," *RHR* 150 (1956) 136-172, points out the similarities between the papyrus and 6.428-437, 621-624; these indicate that V. knew either the text of the papyrus or that from which the newly-discovered catabasis is derived. The papyrus is discussed also by C. A. Disandro, "Una nueva fuente para el libro VI de la Eneida," *Humanitas* (Tucumán, Argentina) 3. No. 9 (1957) 117-125, who believes that *A.* 6 (esp. 660-664) is indebted to an Orphic poem of the Hellenistic age. For an analysis of 616-620, see D. Kuijper, "Phlegyas Admonitor," *Mnemosyne* 16 (1963) 162-170. J. J. H. Savage, "The Cyclops, the Sibyl and the Poet," *TAPhA* 93 (1962) 410-442, writes on the description of Tartarus in 562-624 (= 63 lines, the obverse of the Sibyl's song in *E.* 4) with its Cyclopean imagery and the political symbolism in the portrayal of the damned (who suggest Antony and Sextus Pompey, destroyed by Octavian as the Cyclopes had been slain by Apollo); in 791-853 (also = 63 verses) Anchises' description of a future golden age contains several thematic and structural parallels to *E.* 4. J. Sheehan, "Catholic Ideas of Death as Found in Aeneid VI," *CF* 16 (1962) 87-109, compares V.'s Limbo (426-429), Hell (548-634), Elysian Fields (637-665), and Purgatory (735-751) with the teachings of the Catholic Church and esp. with those of the early Church Fathers. H. Trümpner, "Die Eschatologie bei Vergil im Unterricht. Aeneis VI 703-751," *AU* 4, Heft 2 (1959) 46-68, gives an analysis of Anchises' account of the origin of the world and the nature of life after death.

New discussions of the meaning of *quisque suos patimur manis* in 743 have appeared: see L. Herrmann, 'Musée et l'Enéide," in Deonna, 263-268: Herrmann disagrees with Magotteaux' suggestion that *manes* means *daimones*,[49] and interprets the word as "death," reading *potimur* instead of *patimur;* he assigns 743-744 to Musaeus by placing the lines before 673-676, and also transposes 645-647 after 664; Musaeus is the *Threicius sacerdos;* Woodcock (below, Sect. 6C: *Aeneas*) 10, takes 743 as meaning that individual responsibility does not cease at death; Haarhoff (below, Sect. 6C: *Aeneas*) 8, interprets: "we each of us bear his own spiritual fate, a fate not imposed on us externally but made by our acts and thoughts;" P. Boyancé, "Sur le discours d'Anchise (*Enéide*, VI, 724-751)," in Du-

45

mézil, 60-76: 743 refers to a purgatory beyond death. V.'s doctrine of the *igneus vigor* from heaven (730) is found also in Philo of Alexandria, but Philo has punishment by passions in the present life. So the Neo-Platonists, e.g., Macrobius (*Comm. in somn. Scip.* 1.10.17), interpret 743 as *inferos in his corporibus*. V. in *veterum malorum supplicia* (739 f.) probably refers to the Orphic belief that this life is already an expiation of more ancient crimes.

J. Hubaux, "Vingt vers sur Auguste," *BAB* 43 (1957) 408-423, points out the anti-Greek sentiment in *A.* 6, including that in 847-850. The praise of Augustus in 788-807 is wrongly placed in the text; Numa should follow Romulus, and the Augustus-passage should have the place of honor at the end of the procession of heroes, after 846. Only then is the praise of Rome in 851-853 truly appropriate.[50] In 6.852 we should read *paci*, not *pacis;* see Fraenkel (below, Sect. 11C). L.-F. Rolland, "La Porte d'Ivoire (Virgile, *Enéide*, VI, 898)," *REL* 35 (1957) 204-223, examines and rejects the explanations of Servius, Highbarger, and Everett, and argues that 893-898 differ much from *Od.* 19. 562-567. The gate of horn is for *umbrae verae*, the dead who visit the living during their sleep or who return to earth for reincarnation; to leave unnoticed (by Hermes?) Aeneas must depart by the gate of ivory. Haarhoff (below, Sect. 6C: *Aeneas*), 13 ff., explains *falsa insomnia* (896) as false to men in the normal world, to those who have not had the experience that can form the basis of reality. See also Otis on 6 (above).

7-12. W. S. Anderson, "Vergil's Second *Iliad*," *TAPhA* 88 (1957) 17-30, shows that V. exploits Homer fully by equating the Latin conflict in 7-12 with the Trojan War. The first but wrong impression is that Turnus will be an *alius Achilles* and Aeneas a *Paris alter*. Actually, V. unites the personalities of Achilles, Agamemnon, and Menelaus in Aeneas and makes Turnus a poignant combination of Paris and Hector. Abrahamson (below, Sect. 10: *Homer*) does not deny the influence of the *Iliad* in 7-12 but considers that in one sense the *Odyssey* is the archetype of the *A.* as a whole; as *Od.* 13-24 deal with the hero's struggles after his return home, so *A.* 7-12 describe Aeneas' struggles for a new home. W. H. Semple, "The Conclusion of Virgil's *Aeneid:* A Study of the War in Latium, with Special Reference to Books XI and XII," *BRL* 42 (1959-60) 175-193, discusses V.'s use of Homeric material and the structural arrangement in 7-12, esp. the manner in which the final duel is postponed to the end by (1) the insertion of episodes which contribute little to the action (e.g., Hercules and Cacus, Nisus and Euryalus, the story of Camilla's life) and (2) the manipulation of the plot (e.g., removal of Turnus from battle in 10, breaking of truce and wounding of Aeneas in 12). Semple views the final combat as an anti-climax after the reconciliation of Jupiter and Juno.

Lallemant, 264-268, and Duckworth *TD*, 110-117, point out numerous parallels, book by book, between *A.* 7, 9-12 and *Mahābhārata* 5-9; e.g., arrival in or return to promised land, embassy, desire of aged king (Latinus, Dhrtarāstra) for peace, outbreak of war, catalogue (*A.* 7, *M.* 5); aristeia of warrior later overwhelmed by arrows (*A.* 9, *M.* 6); catalogue, aristeia of youth (Pallas, Abhimanyu) and his tragic death, death of warrior (Mezentius, Drona) mourning loss of son (*A.* 10, *M.* 7); mourning for the dead youth (*A.* 11, *M.* 7); Drances' likeness to Karna (*A.* 11, *M.* 8); and the final day of battle (*A.* 12, *M.* 9) in which many striking similarities appear both in the course of events and in the words and actions of Turnus and Duryodhana. It seems most probable that V. knew and used the Sanscrit epic; cf. Lallemant, 281-287, Duckworth *TD*, 124-127.[51]

7. K. J. Reckford, "Latent Tragedy in *Aeneid* VII, 1-285," *AJPh* 82 (1961) 252-269: the beginning of 7 contains forebodings of tragedy; by looking backward to Troy and Carthage (1-4), to which it is bound by verbal and imagistic echoes, and forward to the Latin wars, the death of Turnus, and the future greatness of Rome, it plays a significant part in unifying the *A.* S. G. P. Small, "The Arms of Turnus: *Aeneid* 7.783-92," *TAPhA* 90 (1959) 243-252: the descriptions of the Chimaera and of Io have symbolic value; they reveal Turnus' innermost deficiencies and foreshadow his ultimate fate; see also Buchheit, 108-115. R. D. Williams, "The Function and Structure of Virgil's Catalogue in *Aeneid* 7," *CQ* 11 (1961) 146-153: the catalogue is introduced at a moment of high tension and both the pageantlike presentation and the variety of scenes prevent diminution of interest. The subject matter—the Italian element—is vitally important, and the emphasis on Greek origins keeps alive the Trojan War theme. Structurally the catalogue has three parts and twelve groups (the attached episode about Camilla is disregarded): a central portion (Caeculus through Ufens), stressing Italian peoples and places, is framed by two groups of three episodes each. Mezentius and Turnus are the great warriors, Aventinus and Virbius are picturesque figures of Greco-Roman mythology, the twins and Umbro take us into a strange world of magic and myth.

8. See above, Sect. 4A (Dolç, Balil). On Evander's farewell to Pallas, see Manton (below, on *A.* 11); Gonnelli (below, Sect. 10: *Catullus*). H. Schnepf, "Das Herculesabenteuer in Virgils Aeneis (VIII 184 ff.)," *Gymnasium* 66 (1959) 250-268: the purpose of the Hercules-Cacus episode is not merely to

46

explain the Hercules cult at the *ara maxima*, as in Livy. V., like Horace, links Hercules and Augustus: Hercules is the mythical counterpart of Augustus as bringer of peace and as a mortal deified. The episode thus anticipates and enriches the description of Augustus' triumphs as depicted on the shield. H. Bellen, "ADVENTUS DEI. Der Gegenwartsbezug in Vergils Darstellung der Geschichte von Cacus und Hercules (Aen. VIII 184-275)," *RhM* 106 (1963) 23-30: the victory of Hercules over Cacus recalls Octavian's victory over Antony and Cleopatra and suggests that Augustus is like Hercules is a god; cf. esp. 200-201: *attulit et nobis . . . aetas auxilium adventumque dei.* Buchheit, 116-133, argues that Hercules and Cacus symbolize Aeneas and Turnus.

9. On the names Nisus, Euryalus, and Hyrtacus, see Mørland (below, Sect. 9: *Language*); on the relation of the Nisus-Euryalus episode to the *Rhesus,* see Fenik (below, Sect. 10: *Euripides*), 54-96.

10. On Pallas and Abhimanyu, see Lallemant, 273 ff.; Duckworth *TD,* 98-103.

11. See below, Sect. 6C: *Camilla* (Huxley, Rosenmeyer). G. R. Manton, "Virgil and the Greek Epic: the Tragedy of Evander," *AUMLA* 17 (1962) 5-17, believes that Evander's farewell to Pallas in 8 and his lament on his son's body in 11.152-181 are derived from the lost *Aethiopis* (Nestor and funeral of Antilochus). Lallemant, 274, and Duckworth *TD,* 100 f., suggest that Evander's speech in 11 is modeled upon that of Arjuna after the death of Abhimanyu in *Mahābhārata* 7.

12. See Lallemant, 266-270; Duckworth *TD,* 103-110, 114-117; Semple (above, on *A.* 7-12). A. Alföldi, "Hasta—Summa Imperii. The Spear as Embodiment of Sovereignty in Rome," *AJA* 63 (1959) 1-27, esp. 20 ff.: the oath scene on gold coins struck from 209 B.C. portrays Aeneas and Latinus; cf. the *foedus* in 161-215. "Latinus, in the older and better tradition, did not swear on a sceptre, but on the spear"—the sign of the *imperium.* K. Büchner, "Vergils Aeneis," in Castiglioni, I, 103-126, explains, with illustrations drawn chiefly from 12, the *A.* as a dramatic-symbolic-historical epic; he stresses the significance of *sacra, foedus, leges, ius* (313-317) and *virtus, verus labor, fortuna, exempla, memoria, praemia virtutis* (435-440).[52] On the reconciliation of Jupiter and Juno in 791 ff., see Buchheit, 133-143.

6C: *Aeneid: Characters*

On Aeneas and Dido, see Milch (above, Sect. 6B: *A.* 4); Fenik (below, Sect. 10: *Euripides*), esp. 216-230. On Aeneas and Turnus, see Anderson (above, Sect. 6B: *A.* 7-12).

T. A. Dorey, *Virgil's Attitude to Youth and Age* (1959) [= VS Lect. Summaries, No. 46], finds Priam, Evander, Latinus, and Anchises (before his death) unsympathetic characters and old age viewed as an unhappy time (contrary to Cicero's picture in *De Senectute*). The young men are romantic and attractive, with the exception of Iulus ("rather a vague characterless figure"). Duckworth *TD,* 81-88, discusses the relation of Aeneas and Turnus to Achilles and Hector. For the similarities of V.'s characters to those of the *Mahābhārata* (Aeneas and the Pāndavas, Latinus and Dhrtarāstra, Drances and Karna, Pallas and Abhimanyu, and esp. Turnus and Duryodhana), see Lallemant, 269-275; Duckworth *TD,* 93-110 (cf. above, Sect. 6B: *A.* 7-12). According to Sister Mary Columba, S.C.L., "Vergilian Epithets in the Development of Plot," *CJ* 58 (1962-63) 22-24, the epithets applied to the characters depict qualities of intellect and modes of acting, and often affect the plot by arousing pity and fear.

Aeneas. L. A. MacKay, "Achilles as Model for Aeneas," *TAPhA* 88 (1957) 11-16, considers Achilles as more important than Odysseus or Hector as a model for Aeneas; it was not the confident warrior of the early books of the *Iliad,* but the later Achilles, obsessed by his mission, upon whom V. based his hero. P. J. Enk, "La tragédie de Didon," *Latomus* 16 (1957) 628-642, surveys and criticizes earlier views about Aeneas and Dido; Aeneas is not cold and insensible, but has a deep love for the queen and deserves our sympathy as much as Dido does. E. C. Woodcock, *Virgil's Philosophy of Religion* (1957) [= VS Lect. Summaries, No. 44], presents an analysis of Aeneas' actions and a defense of his character. Aeneas is an essentially religious man who believes in a divine purpose in the universe. Others fail because of their passions and faults and because they misinterpret or fail to realize their duty. Aeneas has human weaknesses also but his belief in the divine purpose is stronger than theirs. Other writers who defend Aeneas are D. J. Leigh, S. J., "Aeneas: True Man of True Emotion," *CB* 35 (1958-59) 65, 67-69 (Aeneas is the most misunderstood hero in literature; although a man of peace he has a vibrant personality characterized by powerful emotions); D. R. Dudley, "A Plea for Aeneas," *G & R* 8 (1961) 52-60 (the understanding of his character is essential to an appreciation of the epic);[53] M. B. McNamee, S.J., *Honor and the Epic Hero. A Study of the Shifting Concept of Magnanimity in Philosophy and Epic Poetry* (New York 1960): Chapter 4, "Dutiful

47

Aeneas, the Typical Roman Hero," 51-74 (Aeneas, as a personification of Roman duty, compared with the heroes of Homer, esp. Achilles).

The religious aspects of Aeneas' character are stressed also by the following: F. A. Sullivan, S.J., "The Spiritual Itinerary of Virgil's Aeneas," *AJPh* 80 (1959) 150-161, analyzes the chief stages of Aeneas' spiritual journey as a religious hero. In the early books he is human in his greatness and his frailty; the journey in 6 represents a purification and illumination, but not until 8 does he receive from Heaven the spiritual energy necessary for his destined task. T. J. Haarhoff, "The experience of Aeneas as a test of faith," *Orpheus* 6 (1959) 5-15, discusses the nature of Aeneas' *pietas* and the manner in which it is tested. According to P. Grimal, *Pius Aeneas* (VS Lecture, London 1959), Aeneas was never a pious man in the modern sense. *Pietas,* dealing with religion rather than morality, was necessary for Aeneas as the instrument of the gods and as the prototype of the perfect Roman. V.'s conception of his hero had the deepest possible roots in Roman religious soil. In his sacerdotal character Aeneas was also the prototype of the Roman *princeps.* D. J. Harrington, S.J., "Unity of the *Aeneis: Dum Conderet Urbem," CB* 37 (1960-61) 81-84, believes that Aeneas' vocation provides the unifying principle of the epic. U. Knoche, "Heldengestalten der Aeneis," in Rohde, 115-132, writes on V.'s conception of the epic hero, the heroic qualities of the leading characters, esp. Aeneas, and the manner in which they differ from those in Homer. Aeneas is a new type of hero, the father of his country (cf. 12.166), whose character is intimately connected with the historical, religious, and philosophical ideas of the poem. B. E. Levy, "Homer, Apollonius, and the Origins of Aeneas," *Vergilius* 7 (1961) 25-29, admits that Aeneas reflects the spirit of Augustan Rome but finds in his personality certain significant traits of Homer's Odysseus and Telemachus and of the Jason of Apollonius. J. B. Garstang, "*Deos Latio:* Western Asia Minor and the Gods of Latium," *Vergilius* 8 (1962) 18-26, believes that, in spite of his *pietas,* Aeneas neglects the worship of Juno; this is the crime on account of which he deservedly incurs her anger and hostility. His neglect is linked with the worship of Cybele which, closely associated with the Trojans, is set in artistic opposition to the worship of Juno. V. disapproved of Cybele and was tacitly criticizing those who favored her cult.

Also on Aeneas, see above, Sects. 6A (Musurillo, Sbordone), 6B: *A.* 1 (Gossage); below,

Sects. 7C (Coleiro, McClure), 10: *Homer* (Berman, Williams).

Anchises. R. B. Lloyd, "The Character of Anchises in the *Aeneid," TAPhA* 88 (1957) 44-55: Anchises' character develops from *A.* 2 and 3, where he is a leader and the interpreter of divine will, to 5 and 6, where he is present in spirit and becomes truly a *divinus,* having penetrated the great truths of human existence. Ancient commentators wrongly considered Anchises a *divinus* before his death; see H. T. Rowell, "The Scholium on Naevius in *Parisinus Latinus* 7930," *AJPh* 78 (1957) 1-22. On Anchises, see also Lloyd (above, Sect. 6B: *A.* 3); Bayet (above, Sect. 6B: *A.* 5).

Arruns. See Rosenmeyer (below, under *Camilla).*

Ascanius. L. H. Feldman, "Ascanius and Astyanax: A Comparative Study of Virgil and Homer," *CJ* 53 (1957-58) 361-366.

Camilla. S. G. P. Small, "Virgil, Dante and Camilla," *CJ* 54 (1958-59) 295-301, points out the weaknesses of Camilla (unbridled violence, love of war, vanity) which resemble the shortcomings of Nisus, Euryalus, and Turnus. All had to die that the future could be born; hence the four characters are mentioned together by Dante. H. H. Huxley, "*Virgo Bellatrix*" (1960) [= VS Lect. Summaries, No. 52], compares Camilla with other warrior maidens (in Quintus of Smyrna, Valerius Flaccus, and Silius Italicus) and praises her impetuosity and courage. T. G. Rosenmeyer, "Virgil and Heroism: *Aeneid* XI," *CJ* 55 (1959-60) 159-164: the striking but solitary figure of Camilla is thematically related to a major motif in the poem: the motif of heroism in a nonheroic world. Her fate is contrasted with that of her slayer Arruns.

Cybele. See Garstang, above under *Aeneas.*

Dido. See above, Milch; Fenik; Enk (under *Aeneas*). D. H. Abel, "Medea in Dido," *CB* 34 (1957-58) 51-53, 56: the relation of Dido as a tragic heroine to Greek tragedy and esp. Euripides; the differences between Dido and the Medeas of Euripides and Apollonius. H. Rupprecht, "Dido oder Elissa. Eine Vermutung über den Gebrauch dieser Namen bei Vergil und Ovid," *Gymnasium* 66 (1959) 246-250: V. uses the name *Dido* when he thinks of the queen's connection with Aeneas, but chooses the Punic name *Elissa* to stress her relationship with the dead Sychaeus. This same distinction appears clearly in Ovid's poetry. G. Williams, "Poetry in the Moral Climate of Augustan Rome," *JRS* 52 (1962) 28-46: see 43-45 on Dido in love and the central problem of her tragedy. She is portrayed as *univira,* in the style of Roman matrons.

Helen. J. B. Garstang, "The crime of Helen and the concept of *fatum* in the *Aeneid,*" *CJ* 57 (1961-62) 337-345: Homer and the Greek tragic dramatists had emphasized the crime of Helen as motivating the subsequent misfortunes of the Greeks and Trojans. V. stressed the same crime since it helped the idea of continuity between the *Iliad* and the *A.* and provided one link in the chain of cause and effect culminating in the Roman *imperium.*

Juno. See Garstang (above, under *Aeneas*). W. S. Anderson, "Juno and Saturn in the *Aeneid,*" *SPhNC* 55 (1958) 519-532: *Saturnia* as applied to Juno connotes both sympathy for the old Italy (so MacKay; see Duckworth, *Survey* 159 [6C: *Juno*]) and an extreme hatred of the new Italy as represented by Aeneas' destiny. She is wrong in her one-sided love for old Italy. Although Saturn in 7.202-204 is considered responsible for absence of law among the Latins, in 8.321 f. he is said to have brought law and order to Latium. In the final reconciliation Juno accepts the necessity of law. On Juno's role in the *A.,* see Buchheit, esp. 59-85; on the reconciliation, Buchheit, 133-143.

Latinus. See Buchheit, 86-100.

Saturn. See above, under *Juno.*

Turnus. See above, Anderson; Duckworth *TD;* cf. Crahay and Hubaux (below, Sect. 6E), esp. 173-176; Guercio (below, Sect. 7A). F. X. Quinn, S.J., "Another View of Turnus," *CB* 35 (1958-59) 25-26, praises Turnus for his military genius, calm deliberation, *pietas,* courage, and mercy to the conquered foe; Aeneas achieves real greatness by conquering such a genuine hero. Many readers will disagree with this estimate, esp. as regards Turnus' "calm deliberation" and his "mercy to the conquered foe."

6D. Structure of the Aeneid

On the structure of individual books, see above, Sect. 6B (Lloyd on 3, Milch and Mac-Kendrick on 4, Putnam on 5). On the similarity of the structure of *A.* 7, 9-12 and *Mahābhārata* 5-9, see Lallemant and Duckworth (above, Sect. 6B: *A.* 7-12).

G. E. Duckworth, "The *Aeneid* as a Trilogy," *TAPhA* 88 (1957) 1-10: the central and important third of the poem (5-8), stressing Italian and Roman themes and ending with the description on the shield of Augustus' victories and triumphs, is framed by both the tragedy of Dido (1-4) and the tragedy of Turnus (9-12). The even-numbered books in each third are linked by parallels and contrasts.[54] The use of Homeric material in 5-8, where long episodes are adapted

for historical and nationalistic purposes, differs from that elsewhere in the epic. Buchheit (71 ff., 173 ff.) stresses the parallels and contrasts in 1 and 7, but opposes (192) the view of the *A.* as a trilogy. W. A. Camps, "A Second Note on the Structure of the *Aeneid,*" *CQ* 9 (1959) 53-56: two units of the *A.,* 1-4 and 7-12, are borrowed from the *Odyssey* and the *Iliad* respectively; 5-9, with counterparts to celebrated Homeric episodes, contain many allusions to Rome and things Roman, Books 7-9 belong both to the plot-unit 7-12 and to the central mosaic 5-9.[55] G. E. Duckworth, "Tripartite Structure in the *Aeneid,*" *Vergilius* 7 (1961) 2-11: each book has three main divisions and in most instances each main division subdivides into three subordinate parts; the central portion of the second main division often contains a theme of importance to the epic as a whole.

Duckworth *SP* presents in revised form his views on the architecture of the *A.*—the parallelism of the halves (see *AJPh* 75 [1954] 1-15 and Duckworth, *Survey* 185 [6D]), the *A.* as a trilogy, and the tripartite divisions and subdivisions of each book. His analysis of the books leads to the discovery that the exact or approximate Golden Section appears not only in the main divisions and subdivisions but also in short speeches and episodes, and is most frequently achieved by the Fibonacci series (1, 1, 2, 3, 5, 8, 13, 21, 34, 55, . . .) or multiples thereof. He finds the same Golden Mean ratios in the *E., G.* (discovered for *G.* 1 by Le Grelle; see Duckworth, *Survey* 126 [5B: *G.* 1]), the *Appendix Vergiliana,* and also in Lucretius, Catullus, and Horace, thus showing that mathematical ratios and structural proportion are as important in literature as in art and architecture. The dozens and hundreds of Golden Mean ratios in the *A.* provide a control for a number of textual problems: the much-discussed half-lines (of which probably only one-fourth would have been completed in the final revision), interpolations and so-called spurious passages, suggested transpositions, even matters of paragraphing and punctuation. The mathematical composition of the poem favors a close adherence to the readings of the best MSS. The conclusions, presented in full in Duckworth *SP,*[56] are summarized in Duckworth *MS.*

6E. The Trojan Legend

R. B. Lloyd, "*Aeneid* III and the Aeneas Legend," *AJPh* 78 (1957) 382-400: V.'s careful selection and adaption of the various legends concerning Aeneas' wanderings in order to give structure and meaning to *A.* 3; J. A. Brinkman,

S.J., "The Foundation Legends in Vergil," *CJ* 54 (1958-59) 25-33, on the Aeneas and Romulus legends, their genesis and earlier growth, and their historical validity; S. Ferri, "Apollo Sminteo e Apollo di Vei," in Deonna, 215-219: the companions of Aeneas (Otrusi-Etrusi = Etruscans) brought to Italy from Phrygia a statue of Apollo which was the model for the Apollo of Veii;[57] K. Schauenburg, "Aeneas und Rom," *Gymnasium* 67 (1960) 176-191: a discussion of 58 Greek vases with pictures of Aeneas and Anchises departing from Troy (late 6th and early 5th cent. B.C.). Many of these vases are known to come from Etruria or South Italy and the majority are doubtless from the same source. The vases support Bömer's view[58] that Aeneas was well known in Etruria in the late 6th cent. and from there was taken to Rome. The Etruscans probably received the legend from Greeks living in Etruria, and the Romans stressed it because of the hero's *pietas*.

R. Crahay and J. Hubaux, "Les deux Turnus," *SMSR* 30 (1959) 157-212, give a detailed and important account of the complex legends concerning Turnus, Juturna, Evander, Latinus, and others, and their relation to the Aeneas legend. Turnus Herdonius of Aricia is another version of Turnus of Ardea (cf. the trios: Tarquinius Superbus—Mamilius—Turnus Herdonius and Latinus—Aeneas—Turnus); two elements are combined: (1) an Etruscan legend in which a person takes from a ruling king power and his daughter, and (2) a legend of a fire-bearing hero, associated with Italic myth, localized in south Latium, and connected with the Daunians of Apulia. For a discussion and criticism of the article, see E. Paratore, "Spicilegio polemico. VI. Sulla leggenda di Turno," *RCCM* 4 (1962) 92-97.

6F. Geography and Archaeology

See above, Sect. 6E (Brinkman, Schauenburg); Sect. 7C (Schäfer).

M. Guarducci, "Cippo latino arcaico con dedica ad Enea," *BMCR* 19 (1956-58) 3-13: a cippus discovered at Tor Tignosa (near Zolforata, probably V.'s Albunea) bearing the inscription *Lari Aeneae d (onum)* is evidence of an ancient cult of Aeneas and indicates that Aeneas was considered a *Lar* (*Lar* here signifies *heros;* the term followed by a proper name is unique). The inscription, dated in the late 4th or the first half of the 3rd cent. B.C., is the most ancient record of Aeneas in Latium. F. Castagnoli, "Dedica arcaica lavinate a Castore e Polluce," *SMSR* 30 (1959) 109-117:[59] at ancient Lavinium, where an archaic sanctuary with 13 altars has been excavated, a bronze dedication of the 6th or 5th cent. B.C., has also been found; it reads, from

right to left, "to Castor and Pollux" *(Castorei Podlouqueique)* and on the second line "the youths" *(qurois)*. See also R. Schilling, "Les fouilles récentes de Lavinium," *REL* 38 (1960) 75-77; F. Castagnoli, "Sulla tipologia degli altari di Lavinio," *BCAR* 77 (1959-60) 145-174 (description of the 13 altars and comparison with Greek and other Roman altars). B. Tilly, "Virgil's *Periplus* of Latium," *G & R* 6 (1959) 194-203: the description of the Italian coast from the Tiber to Terracina (sketched by V. in *A.* 7.797-802).

R. V. Schoder, S.J., *Vergil's Use of the Cumae Area* (1957) [= VS Lect. Summaries, No. 40]: history and geography and V.'s poetic treatment of the area; H. W. Benario, "Cocceius and Cumae," *CB* 35 (1958-59) 40-41: V. perhaps refers in *A.* 6 to the tunnels made by Cocceius at Cumae; A. J. Gossage, "A Visit to Virgil's Country," *G & R* 6 (1959) 86-89: Cumae, Lake Avernus, and Baiae. On Cumae, see also A. G. McKay, "The Greeks at Cumae," *VergDig* 3 (1957) 5-11; E. T. Salmon, "Samnite and Roman Cumae," *VergDig* 4 (1958) 10-15.

7A. Vergil's Life and Works: General

See Holtorf, 19-71. Perret *V* presents a general survey with many illustrations and translations of selected passages into French verse.[60] C. Saggio, *Catullo Cicerone Virgilio* (Alpignano 1959) 151-208, on V.'s life and poetry (esp. *E.* and *G.;* the *A.* will be treated more fully later); V. as a poet of Lombardy, and his universal qualities (understanding of love, evil, suffering, toil). For general surveys, see also K. Büchner, *Römische Literaturgeschichte* (Stuttgart 1957) 290-308, and *Humanitas Romana. Studien über Werke und Wesen der Römer* (Heidelberg 1957) 147-175. Büchner's monumental *RE* article on V. (see Duckworth, *Survey* 89 [1]) has now appeared in an Italian translation: *Virgilio. Edizione italiana a cura di M. Bonaria* (Brescia 1963); see esp. Bonaria's bibliography (573-598). *Virgil. A Study in Civilized Poetry* by B. Otis is scheduled for publication by Oxford in 1964.

V. Pöschl, "The Poetic Achievement of Virgil," *CJ* 56 (1960-61) 290-299, praises V. highly; the poems achieve "a synthesis of ancient civilization" but they are still more "the summary of an inner civilization," the moral ideals of the Greeks and the Romans. The *A.* contains in addition new modes of human behavior (e.g., the tact and discretion of the characters) and new poetic forms (architectural composition with symmetrical and contrasting patterns; the introduction of lyric moods and symbolism). In 1957 Woodcock (above, Sect. 6C *Aeneas*) said: "The very volume of Virgilian criticism proves that Virgil was a great poet, and no individual critic has ventured to contradict outright the verdict of nineteen centuries." One eminent critic has now ventured to do just this: R. Graves, "The Virgil Cult," *The Virginia Quarterly Review* 38, No. 1 (1962) 13-35, criticizes V. both as a poet and as a man, and maintains that all have been wrong in their judgment—not merely T. S. Eliot, but "the whole line of Virgilians from Propertius to Augustine, from Augustine to Dante, from Dante to Dryden, and from Dryden to Alfred Lord Tennyson, who survived into Mr. Eliot's childhood."[60a] For an excellent statement of the traditional view, see Townend (below, Sect. 12: *Vergil Today*).

T. J. Haarhoff, *Vergil, Prophet of Peace (With Some Reference to Dante)* (London 1956): V.'s desire for peace and his regretful acceptance of strife and suffering as a necessary prelude to peace;[61] on V.'s *pietas* and hatred of war, see also A. Guercio, "Vergilius, 'pius vates at Phoebo digna locutus,' " *Latinitas* 6 (1958) 292-299. For Meyer's view that V. favored a policy of foreign conquest, see below, Sect. 7C. R. Enking, "P. Vergilius Maro Vates Etruscus," *MDAI (R)* 66 (1959) 65-96: the preface to the *Vita* of Phocas calls V. a *vates Etruscus* and the *Vita Noricensis* describes him as *natus genere Tusco;* cf. *A.* 10.201-203 on Mantua: *Tusco de sanguine vires.* The Etruscan nature of many passages in the *A.* and Servius' many allusions to Etruscan law and religion support the view that V. was of Etruscan descent and that his epic was a poem not only of the ancestors of Augustus but also of the might and grandeur of Etruria. E. Zinn, "Elemente des Humors in augusteischer Dichtung," *Gymnasium* 67 (1960) 41-56, 152-155: on humor in the *E.* and *A.*, see 46 ff., 153 f. A. J. Gossage, "Vergil in Exile," *PVS* 1 (1961-62) 35-45 [= VS Lectures, No. 57]: V.'s poetry is colored by his own inner experience—a sense of exile (= eviction from his native home in 42 B.C.). Aeneas reflects V.'s own dilemma—the incompatibility between the hateful aspects of Rome and the peace of Arcadia. Two articles by W. F. Jackson Knight deal with V.'s poetic art: "Vergil's Secret Art," *PVS* 1 (1961-62) 1-14 [= VS Lectures, No. 54], on the poet's deliberate use of verbal manipulation and ambiguity ("negative capability") and of balance and symmetry;[62] "Poetic Sources and Integration—Continued," *Vergilius* 8 (1962) 2-7, on V.'s procedure in structure and language and the extent to which it was in part deliberate, in part unconscious.[63]

7B. *Religion and Philosophy*

See above, Sect. 6B: *A.* 6 (esp. Delaunois, Sheehan, Boyancé); Sect. 6C: *Aeneas* (Woodcock, Sullivan, Haarhoff, Garstang); according to Woodcock, Jupiter represents the Divine Purpose which mortals accept or reject at their peril. See also below, Sect. 11A: *Christian Writers* (Courcelle), *Claudian* (Martin), *Boethius* (Jackson Knight).

On Roman religion in the time of V., see K. Latte, *Römische Religionsgeschichte* (München

1960) [= Müller-Otto, *Hdb. d. Altertumswiss.* 5 Abt. 4 Teil], esp. 213 ff. ("IX. Neue Formen") and 294 ff. ("XI. Die Augusteische Restauration"). O. Esan, "Vergil's Religion," J. Ferguson (ed.), *Nigeria and the Classics* (Ibadan 1957) 39-55, writes on the religious elements in the *E.* (the hope that the Divine can produce an ordered society), the *G.* (exhortation to faith in a supreme Deity), and the *A.* (written to restore a right relationship between man and the Divine). *A.* 6.724 ff. resemble "the Christian doctrine of original sin and need for purification through baptism and the particularly Roman Catholic doctrine of purgatory" (cf. Sheehan, above Sect. 6B: *A.* 6). J. M. Dougherty, S.J., "Vergilian 'Fate' as Cosmic," *CB* 34 (1957-58) 65, 67, comments on the different meanings of *fatum* (individual destiny and a more universal concept—the ruling element of the cosmos) and finds the divine pattern of fate and world history a predominant theme in the *A.* and one of its main unifying elements. I. S. Ryberg, "Vergil's Golden Age," *TAPhA* 89 (1958) 112-131: on the literary and philosophical background of the Golden Age and V.'s treatment of the theme in *E.* 4, the *G.*, and esp. the *A.*, where the new *aurea saecula* combine the earlier reign of Saturn and the imperial ideals of peace and justice; see also K. J. Reckford, "Some Appearances of the Golden Age," *CJ* 54 (1958-59) 79-87; Zabulis (below, Sect. 7C). W. F. Jackson Knight, *Some Divine Monitions and Revelations in Vergil* (1958) [= VS Lect. Summaries, No. 45]: V.'s treatment of legendary and religious themes of divine intervention and his ability to put poetic values before ritual exactitude.

J. Heurgon, "Virgile, la poésie et la vérité," *IL* 10 (1958) 68-72: on V.'s interest in historical reality and philosophical truth as more important than pure poetry; this is seen esp. in *E.* 9, *G.* 2.490 ff. *(felix . . . fortunatus)*, and *A.* 6. All his life V. sought a coherent philosophical doctrine without finding it, hence his desire, after completing the *A.*, to devote the remainder of his life to philosophy. L. Alfonsi, "L'epicureismo nella storia spirituale di Vergilio," *Epicurea in memoriam Hectoris Bignone* (Genova 1959) 167-178, on Epicurean themes in V.'s poetry, esp. in the *E.* (irrationality of love, desire for *otium* and *laetitia*); cf. Alfonsi (above, Sect. 4B: *E.* 2). H. M. Howe, "The Gods and the Garden," *Vergilius* 6 (1960) 24-28: V. in the *A.* attempts to apply the teachings of Epicureanism in a new way. M. W. Edwards, "The Expression of Stoic Ideas in the *Aeneid*," *Phoenix* 14 (1960) 151-165: V.'s use of Stoic expressions (e.g., *fata sequi*) and his indebtedness to and conflict with

Stoic philosophy; his pity and admiration for human suffering contradict the Stoic view of man and fate. J. Pearson, "Virgil's 'Divine Vision,' (*Aeneid* 4.238-44 and 6.724-51)," *CPh* 56 (1961) 33-38: V.'s religious and philosophical ideas and their sources; Avernus, the descent into which is *facilis* (6.126), is the world we live in; *lumina* (4.244) refers to the comprehension which the soul gains at death, and also to the reawakening of Aeneas to a realization of his destiny. F. A. Sullivan, S.J., "Some Virgilian Beatitudes," *AJPh* 82 (1961) 394-405: V. and the problem of human happiness; V. found the beatitude-formulas in the Greek poets but derived the content of the beatitudes from the older Greek and Hellenistic philosophers. T. J. Haarhoff, *The Law of the State and the Law of the Spirit in Vergil and Euripides* (mimeographed lecture, Johannesburg 1962), on the nature of God and ideal justice.

7C.   Rome and Augustus

See above, Barra (Sect. 5B: *G.* 1), Fleischer (Sect. 5B: *G.* 3), Deman (Sect. 6B: *A.* 1), Schnepf and Bellen (Sect. 6B: *A.* 8); see below, Thornton (Sect. 10: *Catullus*), Avery (Sect. 11B).

M. L. Paladini, "A proposito della tradizione poetica sulla battaglia di Azio," *Latomus* 17 (1958) 240-269, 462-475: the battle of Actium as treated by V. (*A.* 8.671 ff.), Horace (*Epode* 9 and *Odes* 1.37), and Propertius (3.11).[64] E. Coleiro, "Allegory in the Aeneid," *Journal of the Faculty of Arts* (Royal Univ. of Malta) 1 (1959) 159-174, looks upon the *A.* as an allegory, as a kind of political pamphlet in which V. by means of Aeneas and the Trojan past idealizes Augustus (the former "scheming, hypocritical, autocratic Octavian") and the Roman present. Links between Aeneas and Augustus include *A.* 6.69-74 (temple of Apollo), 1.259 f. and 12.794 f. (foreshadowing of Augustus' deification), emphasis on Aeneas' *pietas,* his arrival at Pallanteum on August 12. M. McClure, "Vergil and Augustus— A Query," *CO* 38 (1960-61) 7-8: Aeneas symbolizes Augustus and has the virtues (summed up in *pietas*) which Augustus wished reborn in his people. But did Augustus fail "to live up to the republican ideals Vergil cherished? Is this why Vergil ordered the poem burned?" G. K. Zabulis, "Saturnia tellus of Vergil (On the Formation of the Ideology of the Augustan Age)," *VDI* No. 72 (1960) 111-123 [in Russian, but a full summary appears in German in *BCO* 7 (1962) 166-180]: on the political ideals of Augustus as expressed in V.'s works, esp. the desire for peace, the return of the Golden Age, and the praise of Italy as the *Saturnia tellus* (cf. *E.* 4.6; *G.* 2.173

ff.; *A.* 6.791 ff., 11.252 ff.) ; V. praises the activity of Augustus and identifies the *pax Augusta* with the reign of Saturn in Italy. M. Schäfer, "Zum Tellusbild auf der Ara Pacis Augustae," *Gymnasium* 66 (1959) 288-301: the famous frieze does not portray "Italia" but "Tellus"; it is, however, a *Saturnia tellus* of peace under Augustus, the *orbis pacatus* (cf. *E.* 4.17) to which V. alludes in *A.* 6.852. H. J. Mette, " 'Roma' (Augustus) and Alexander," *Hermes* 88 (1960) 458-462, on Augustus as Alexander in *A.* 6.792-805 and in Horace, *Odes* 3.3. H. D. Meyer, *Die Aussenpolitik des Augustus und die Augusteische Dichtung* (Köln 1961) [= *Kölner historische Abhandlungen,* Band 5] 17-32, examines the various passages in V. referring to Augustus' campaigns and foreign conquest, e.g., *G.* 3.25-33 and *A.* 8.724-728; both passages refer in part to actual events, in part to deeds still to be performed. V. has a vision of world conquest and gives to the Roman claim to world rule its classical expression.

7D.   Vergil and Other Augustan Poets[65]

Cornelius Gallus. See above, Sect. 5B: *G.* 4. On the life and poetry of Gallus and his role in V.'s poems (*E.* 6, 10; *G.* 4), see L. Winniczuk, "Cornelius Gallus. Poet and Statesman," *Eos* 50 (1959-60) 127-145; A. Lima da Costa, "Cornelius Gallus e a elegia latina," *Romanitas* 3-4 (1961) 331-339.

Varius Rufus. See Savage, below on *Horace.* J.-P. Boucher, "L'oeuvre de L. Varius Rufus d'après Properce II, 34," *REA* 60 (1958) 307-322: Lynceus, to whom 2.34 is dedicated, is Varius; Propertius praises the poetic achievements of both V. and Varius in the same elegy. A. Rostagni, "Il *De Morte* di L. Vario Rufo," *RFIC* 37 (1959) 380-394, discusses the Epicurean nature of the *De Morte* of Varius Rufus and the four fragments (preserved by Macrobius) which are echoed by V. (*E.* 8.85-88; *G.* 2.506, 3.115-117; *A.* 6.621-622).

Horace. See above, Sect. 4C (on *E.* 4 and *Epode* 16) ; Sect. 6B: *A.* 8 (Schnepf) ; Sect. 7C (Paladini, Mette). On the language of V. and Horace, see below, Sect. 8: *Language* (Börner, Wilkinson).

J. J. Savage, " 'Flentibus Amicis'—Horace, *Sat.* 1.5.93," *CB* 36 (1959-60) 1-4, 9-10: Diomedes' grief at the loss of his comrades (*A.* 11.272-274) supplies the clue to *Sat.* 1.5.93, in which Horace perhaps alludes to an epic by Varius Rufus on the deeds of Diomedes. B. Kytzler, "Das früheste Aeneis-Zitat," in Rohde, 151-167: the earliest reference to the *A.* is not Propertius, 2.34.59-66, but Horace, *Sat.* 2.1.8-15 (ten words identical with those in *A.* 2.8-15, almost in the same sequence, with the main theme announced in line 11 in each passage). Horace here follows V., and the beginning of *A.* 2 is thus chronologically the earliest part of the epic. Horace in his later *recusationes* names the poet who can write the desired work; here he does not name a writer, but by echoing the *A.* hints that V. is the person to describe *Caesaris invicti res.* B. Fenik, "Horace's First and Sixth Roman Odes and the Second Georgic," *Hermes* 90 (1962) 72-96: the many parallels between *Odes* 3.1 and 6 and *G.* 2.458 ff. indicate that the two odes are two phases of a single conception. Horace planned 1 and 6 to frame the Roman cycle as a whole. Fenik rejects Dornseiff's view that the parallels imply a criticism of V. by Horace. On *A.* 12.791 ff. and Horace, *Odes* 3.3, see Buchheit, 145-150.

Tibullus. See Merkelbach (above, Sect. 6B: *A.* 6). W. T. Avery, "The Year of Tibullus' Death," *CJ* 55 (1959-60) 205-209: the epigram of Domitius Marsus does not say that Tibullus died in 19 B.C., and Ovid implies (*Am.* 1.15; 3.9) that Tibullus died after the publication of the *A.*, in 16 at the latest. H. C. Schnur, "When Did Tibullus Die?" *CJ* 56 (1960-61) 227-229, examines Avery's arguments and considers them insufficient to upset the customary dating of the death of Tibullus. Avery, "Tibullus' Death Again," *ibid.* 229-233, refutes Schnur and reaffirms his view that Tibullus died in or after 18/17 B.C., after the publication of the *A.* W. Wimmel, "Tibullus II 5 und das elegische Rombild," in Rohde, 227-266: Tibullus' indebtedness in 2.5 to *E.* 4, *G.* 2.513 ff., and the Evander episode in *A.* 8.

Propertius. See above, Wimmel (Sect. 3: *Culex*); Westendorp Boerma (Sect. 3: *Copa*); Hubaux (Sect. 4B: *E.* 10); Paladini (Sect. 7C); also Boucher (under *Varius Rufus*), Kytzler (under *Horace*).

Wimmel, 216 f., discusses the indebtedness of Propertius in 3.1 to *G.* 3.1-48. R. Lucot, "*Domus Remi* (Properce IV, 1, 9-10)," *Pallas* 5 (1957) 63-70: Propertius, inspired by *A.* 1.291-293, designated by *domus Remi* the temple of Apollo on the Palatine, symbol of peace and concord. E. Paratore, "De Propertio Vergiliani carminis iudice," in *Properziana*, 71-82, writes on Propertius' estimate of the *A.* in 2.34.61-66. Opposing Alfonsi (*Aevum* 28 [1954] 205-221), he maintains that at the time of Propertius' poem only a small portion of the *A.* had been written, dealing chiefly with Augustus. Propertius as an elegiac poet would not have approved

or praised the Homeric elements in the poem so highly. F. Solmsen, "Propertius in his Literary Relations with Tibullus and Vergil," *Philologus* 105 (1961) 273-289, comments (281 ff.) on the echoes of *A.* 6 in Propertius 4.7 (apparition of Cynthia and her experiences in Elysium). Also on V. and Propertius, see R. Lucot, "*Cervix Aeneae* (*Prop.* IV, 1, 39-44)," *Pallas* 9 (1960) 171-175; P. Marty, "Cervix Aenae bis," *Pallas* 10 (1961) 55-58; R. Lucot, "Problèmes de création chez Properce," *ibid.*, 59-68.

Ovid. See Cazzaniga, Knecht (above, Sect. 3: *Ciris*); Rupprecht (above, Sect. 6C: *Dido*). Several articles discuss Ovid's indebtedness to V.; see L. Ramaglia, "La leggenda di Evandro," *RSC* 6 (1958) 59-62; F. Bömer, "Ovid und die Sprache Vergils," *Gymnasium* 66 (1959) 268-288; A. Grisart, "La publication des 'Métamorphoses': Une source du récit d'Ovide," *Atti del Convegno Internazionale Ovidiano* (Roma 1959) II, 125-156, esp. 141 ff.: the references in *Trist.* 1.7.11-40 to the escape of the *Metamorphoses* from destruction by fire are modeled upon the similar rescue of the *A.* from the fate requested by V. before his death; V. Pöschl, "L'arte narrativa di Ovidio nelle 'Metamorfosi,'" *ibid.*, II, 295-305: Ovid continues and develops the classical style of V. but surpasses him in rhetoric, realism, and psychological analysis; R. Lamacchia, "Ovidio interprete di Virgilio," *Maia* 12 (1960) 310-330: Ovid interprets and criticizes V. as he imitates him and should therefore be considered the first Vergilian critic of antiquity.

On V.'s *G.* and Ovid, see E. J. Kenney, "Nequitiae poeta," in N. I. Herescu (ed.), *Ovidiana. Recherches sur Ovide* (Paris 1958) 201-209 (echoes of the *G.* in the *Ars Amatoria*): A.-M. Guillemin, "Ovide et la vie paysanne (*Mét.*, 8, 626-724)," *ibid.*, 317-323 (influence of the *G.* on the idyllic story of Baucis and Philemon). I. K. Horváth, "Impius Aeneas," *AActHung* 6 (1958) 385-393, discuses the *carmen* and *error* (*Trist.* 2.207) which caused Ovid's exile and suggests that the portrayal of Aeneas as *impius* in *Heroides* 7 was a contributing factor.

7E. Varia

T. J. Haarhoff, "Virgil's Garden of Flowers and his Philosophy of Nature," *G & R* 5 (1958) 67-82, on the poet's feeling for plants and flowers as expressed in his poetry, including the *Culex* ("probably Virgilian") and the *Ciris* ("possibly Virgilian"). R. Gustin, "Le passé et l'habitude dans l'esthétique virgilienne," *LEC* 27 (1959) 362-368, on two categories of "the beautiful": (1) objects of antiquity and therefore of eternal value (V. stresses the ancient glories of agriculture in the *G.*, of cities in the *A.*), and (2) humble objects made beautiful because they are familiar (Meliboeus leaves his familiar surroundings in *E.* 1, and the Trojans lose theirs in *A.* 2).

C. Egger, "Virgilius an Vergilius?" *Latinitas* 6 (1958) 65-66, argues for *Vergilius* as the correct spelling. E. Bolisani, "Vergilius o Virgilius? L'opinione di un dotto umanista," *AIV* 117 (1958-59) 131-141: an examination of the evidence (including the arguments of Battista Spagnoli, called Mantovano, against Politian) supports *Virgilius* as the most common and most likely spelling of the poet's name.

W. H. Gross, "Vergilporträts," *RE* 2.R VIII B = 16 Halbband (Stuttgart 1958) 1493-1506, concludes with the statement that only new discoveries can bring us a convincing portrait of the most important Roman poet. V. Poulsen, *Vergil* (Bremen 1959) [= *Opus nobile*, Heft 12], accepts four portrait-busts as those of V. (two in the Ny Carlsberg Glyptotek in Copenhagen, two in the Lateran Museum); the identification of the so-called "Menander" with V. is now impossible. H. von Heintz, "Neue Beiträge zu V. Poulsen's Vergil," *MDAI (R)* 67 (1960) 103-110, adds a fifth portrait (in the Archäologischen Institut der Karl-Marx-Universität in Leipzig) but expresses doubt about the identification with V.; see J. C. Balty, *Latomus* 20 (1961) 920-921. J. Fink, "Virgil Among the Prophets and Confessors. Two Representations of the Poet in Bible Illustration," *Folia* 11 (1957) 3-17: portraits of V. in illuminated MSS of the 12th and 13th cent. The poet has been Christianized and wears a kind of Phrygian cap, characteristic in early Christian art of the youths in the fiery furnace and of the Magi adoring the Child; he is associated with the ancestors of Christ and the prophets of His Incarnation.

8. Style, Language, Meter

On the language and meter of the *E.*, see Holtorf, 253-302. J. Echave-Sustaeta, "Acotaciones al estilo de las Geórgicas," *Helmantica* 12 (1961) 5-26, discusses many features of *G.* 1 (word order, rhythmic effects, enclitics, hiatus, indirect questions, etc.). W. F. Jackson Knight, "Vergil's Latin," *AClass* 1 (1958) 31-44: a helpful analysis of V.'s arrangement of letters, words, and phrases (e.g., repetition, parataxis, archaism, ellipsis); his intellectual capacity, economy, and esp. variety of expression—one of the great secrets of his success. N. I. Herescu, *La poésie latine. Etude des structures phoniques* (Paris 1960), on euphony, the musical structure of the verse, alliteration, assonance, rhyme, and repetition, with numerous illustrations drawn from V.'s poetry.[66] L. P. Wilkinson, *Golden Latin Artistry* (Cambridge 1963), on verbal music (alliteration, assonance, etc.), expressiveness (in-cluding onomatopoeia), and verse rhythm in V. and contemporary poets; see esp. 74-83 on *G.* 1.43-392.

Style. W. D. Anderson, "Notes on the Simile in Homer and His Successors: I. Homer, Apollonius Rhodius, and Vergil," *CJ* 53 (1957-58) 81-87: in Apollonius and V. we have a swing from the universal toward the particular, from the objective toward the subjective. M. Coffey, "The Subject Matter of Vergil's Similes," *BICS* 8 (1961) 63-75, on the propriety and range of similes in Homer, Apollonius, and V.[67] H. and A. Thornton, *Time and Style. A Psycho-Linguistic Essay in Classical Literature* (London 1962) 65-70, esp. on the appositional form of expression.

On various aspects of metonymy, see the following articles by E. A. Hahn: "A Linguistic Fallacy (based on a study of Vergil)," in Whatmough, 53-64: apparent confusions of expression, or departures from strict logic, are frequent in poetry and esp. in V., who uses geographical and ethnological terms interchangeably; "Vergil's Linguistic Treatment of Divine Beings," *TAPhA* 88 (1957) 56-67; 89 (1958) 237-253: the first paper deals with the confusion of the god and his particular province or function; Part II treats of the confusion of the god and the special dwelling, symbol, or representation which man has provided in his name; "Body and Soul in Vergil," *TAPhA* 92 (1961) 193-219, on the linguistic fusion of the self with either the body or the soul and the resultant confusion of the body and soul with each other.

H. L. Tracy, "The Verb-Object Trope in Vergil," *Vergilius* 7 (1961) 12-18: the use of verbs and nouns to give the effect of metaphor. K. Quinn, "Syntactical Ambiguity in Horace and Virgil," *AUMLA* 14 (1960) 36-46: examples of such ambiguity in the *A.* are *tuta* (4.298) and *venis* (4.2). On parataxis, see I. Rodriguez and A. Ortega, O.F.M., "La parataxis en Virgilio," *Helmantica* 11 (1960) 437-459, on the development of the ideas and the relation between the parts, esp. abstract statement followed by concrete image; parataxis is essential to V.'s twofold conception of that reality; J. Marouzeau in two articles: "Sur un aspect de la corrélation en latin: Le cas de l'énoncé-fonction," *REL* 38 (1960) 172-181, on the paratactic use in V. of a second clause which has a functional relation (e.g., explanation, result) with the first; the second statement regularly begins with a verb, to underline the relationship; "Un cas particulier de l' 'énoncé-fonction': un cliché de construction chez Virgile," *REL* 39 (1961) 111-116, on the many instances where a statement begins with a verb (*est, sunt, stat, it, ibat, ruit, fugit, stupet*, etc.); V. here develops a stereotyped form of expression. H. Rupprecht, "Ueber Wortstellung als Hilfe zur Wortdeutung in der bukolischen Dichtung Vergils," *Gymnasium* 70 (1963) 19-23: the significance of certain words (e.g., *umbra, amor, poeta*) is determined by their position in the verse.

On various types of alliteration, see W. T. Avery, "The Onomatopoeia of *Aeneid* 3.699-715," *CJ* 54 (1958-59) 350-352, on the frequency of words which begin with the letter *h:* V. creates the effect of exertion and weariness; J. Marouzeau, "Un cas curieux d'allitération chez Virgile," *REL* 37 (1959) 114-117, on the surprisingly frequent alliteration of initial *v* in the *A.;* F. A. Sullivan, S.J., "Some Vergilian Seascapes," *CJ* 57 (1961-62) 302-309, on the use of color and sound effects, esp. alliteration and assonance, to depict the sights and sound of the sea; E. Merone, "L'allitterazione nelle Bucoliche di Virgilio," *Aevum* 35 (1961) 199-219: an analysis, poem by poem, of V.'s effective use of alliteration "con intento musicale e stilistico"; G. Herdan, *The Calculus of Linguistic Observations* ('s-Gravenhage 1962) [= *Janua Linguarum,* Ser. Maior IX] 80-85, on alliteration of the initial letter of verse lines; by a mathematical method "it may be regarded as established that the repetitions of initial verse line phonemes in Vergil's Georgics cannot only be regarded as a deliberate use of the device of alliteration, but as revealing a definite *pattern* through preference for repetition of line initials in gaps of a specified length. . . . A further statistical analysis of Vergil's work . . . may provide a new tool for decision in cases of disputed authorship" (85), such as the *Culex, Ciris,* etc.

Language. On epithets applied to the characters, see Columba (above, Sect. 6C). F. Bömer, "Beiträge zum Verständnis der augusteischen Dichtersprache," *Gymnasium* 64 (1957) 1-21, on the poetic vocabulary of Horace and V., esp. in *Odes* 3.30.1-5 and *A.* 6.847-853; V. uses words common in prose and prefers simple to compound forms; cf. Bömer above (Sect. 7D: *Ovid*). L. P. Wilkinson, "The Language of Virgil and Horace," *CQ* 9 (1959) 181-192: V. and Horace, unlike the *novi poetae,* did not favor archaisms, rare words, and compounds, but preferred ordinary words, often used in bold and clever combinations; both poets thus cultivated a style which had had advocates since the time of Euripides. L. A. MacKay, "The Vocabulary of Fear in Latin Epic Poetry," *TAPhA* 92 (1961) 308-316: an examination of V. *(A.)*, Ovid *(Metamorphoses)*, Lucan, and Statius; V. is the most temperate and the most varied in his use of words denoting fear. P. Miniconi, "La joie dans l' 'Enéide,' " *Latomus* 21 (1962) 563-571, on the use of words such as *laetus, laetitia, gaudium,* etc., and their artistic grouping by books: most frequent in *A.* 5 (23 times), also numerous in 1, 10, and 12; no such grouping appears in the *Iliad* or in Lucan.

H. Mørland contributes several articles on names: "Der Hyrtacide in der Aeneis," *SO* 32 (1956) 69-80, on the name Hyrtacus; he is the father both of Nisus (9.177, 234, 319, 406) and of Hippocoon (5.492, 503); verbal similarities couple Hippocoon and Nisus and indicate that the Nisus episode in 5 was composed before that in 9; "Nisus, Euryalus und andere Namen in der Aeneis," *SO* 33 (1957) 87-109, on the etymological significance of the names of the contestants in 5; in the boatrace the names of the leaders are closely connected with those of the ships; "Emicare in der Aeneis," *SO* 34 (1958) 43-44, on the use of *emicare,* esp. as applied to Euryalus in 5.337; "Zu den Namen in der Aeneis," *SO* 36 (1960) 21-29, on etymological wordplay, often subconscious, in the use of proper names, such as Caeneus, Evander, Lausus, Helenus, Pyrrhus, Coroebus, Virbius, Helenor; see also E. Kraggerud, "Einige Namen in der Aeneis," *SO* 36 (1960) 30-39, on etymological associations in proper names: Butes, Deiphobus, Abas, Anxur.

J. R. Gjerløw, "Bemerkungen über einige Einleitungen zur direkten Rede in Vergils Aeneis," *SO* 32 (1956) 44-68, on the use of *inquit, ait, fatur,* etc. R. Waltz, "Alma Venus," *REA* 59 (1957) 51-71: *almus* in Lucretius, V., and Horace means "nourishing," "helpful," "holy," but not "life-giving." H. Wagenvoort, "De praepositionis apud poetas Latinos loco," *AClass* 1 (1958) 14-20, on the order of the adjectives *summus* and *imus, solus* and *unus, totus* and *omnis;* when the adjective follows, it is almost always at the verse-end (cf. *A.* 2.65: *crimine ab uno*); in about two-thirds of the instances the adjective precedes (cf. 1.47: *una cum gente*). J. Campos, Sch.P., "Los 'Pluralia Poetica' en latin," *Helmantica* 10 (1959) 89-112 (numerous exx. from V.). A. Di Prima, "Le forme di genitivo Androgeō e simili in Virgilio," *Paideia* 15 (1960) 93-96, suggests that *Erebo* (*A.* 4.26) and *Tyro* (*A.* 4.36) are Greek genitives like *Androgeo* (*A.* 6.20). E. A. Hahn, "The Origin of the Greek Accusative in Latin," *TAPhA* 91 (1960) 221-238, esp. 233 ff.: V. was the first Roman poet to employ the Greek accusative with frequency; the construction continued to be rare in prose.

Meter. On the correspondence of mathematical ratios with the metrical patterns of Jackson Knight, see Duckworth *MS,* 219 f.; *SP,* 111-117. W. F. Witten, "Two Passages in the Third Book of the *Aeneid," G & R* 7 (1960) 171-172: 3.340 is the only hemistich where the sense is incomplete; Andromache's emotion chokes her and she is unable to complete the verse; so also Feldman (above, Sect. 6C: *Anchises*). The mathematical ratios in the *A.* indicate that about three-fourths of the half-lines were intentional; see Duckworth *MS,* 213 f.; *SP,* 77-80.

R. Lucot, "Un type d'hexamètre latin d'Ennius à Virgile," *Pallas* 3 (1955) 29-39: hexameters of the type of *A.* 4.448 *(tunditur, et magno persentit pectore curas)* are rare and are a Latin creation; the occurrences in V. are as follows: *E.* 9 (1/91), *G.* 23 (1/95), *A.* 77 (1/128). The static nature of this hexameter made it less suitable for rapid epic narrative. J. Soubiran, *"Intremere omnem* et *si bona norint.* Recherches sur l'accent de mot dans la clausule de l'hexamètre latin," *Pallas* 8 (1959) 23-56: the rarity of such clausulae in V. and other hexameter poets is explained by the desire to avoid a word accent on the first short of the fifth foot. R. Lucot, "Sur un type latin d'hexamètre (d'Ennius à Properce)," in Herrmann, 492-498: effective hexameters of the type of *A.* 2.3 *(infandum, regina, iubes renovare dolorem)* are extremely rare in Latin—nine instances in about 30,000 verses from Ennius through Propertius. The reasons for their infrequency are (1) the preponderance of the penthemimeral caesura, (2) the frequency with which a dactyl begins the hexameter, and (3) the emotional value which prevented the poets from using such a line too often. R. Lucot, "Une thème virgilien: Le lancer du javelot," *Pallas* 9 (1960) 165-170: relation of rhythm and meaning with verbs of hurling; e.g., initial *conicit* (*A.* 9.411, 10.646) expresses ease, but initial *coniecit* (2.545) and *contorsit* (2.52) imply great effort (appropriate in the cases of Priam and Laocoon). J. Soubiran, "Passion de Didon. Métrique de Virgile," *Pallas* 10 (1961) 31-53: the use of meter to express emotional values in *A.* 4. J. Hellegouarc'h, "Sur un type de vers virgilien," *REL* 40 (1962) 236-250: lines with a monosyllable preceding the penthemimeral caesura (cf. *A.* 1.35) have a stylistic reason, to place an emphasis on the word following the monosyllable.

J. Soubiran, "L'aphérèse de *est* chez Virgile," *Pallas* 5 (1957) 43-61, on prodelision of *est* after a vowel when it is an enclitic or has a weak semantic value; when *est* is emphasized it stands at the beginning of the verse or after a consonant. G. Cambier, "Le h-initial fait-il parfois position chez Virgile et chez d'autres poètes latins classiques?" *Latomus* 17 (1958) 360-361: words beginning with *h* are treated exactly as words with an initial vowel. N.-O. Nilsson, "Verschiedenheiten im Gebrauch der Elision in Vergils Eklogen," *Eranos* 58 (1960) 80-91, on the nature and frequency of elision in the *E.;* elisions are most numerous in 2 and 3, the earliest of the collection. M. Bonaria, "L'elisione parziale nella poesia latina," *Hermes* 90 (1962) 173-186, cites 11 instances in V. of *correptio,* or shortening in hiatus (e.g., *A.* 3.211; 5.261; 6.507).

9. Interpretation and Text Criticism

Eclogues. Holtorf and Perret *B* retain *Oaxen* in 1.65; A. Deman, "Virgile et la colonisation romaine en Afrique du Nord," in Grenier, I, 514-519, favors the correction to *Araxen,* and in *sitientes Afros* (1.64) sees a wordplay referring to the Sittiani, the companions of P. Sittius Nucerinus, colonizer in Africa. J.-G. Préaux, "Un contresens traditionnel sur Virgile, *Buc.* I, 56," *Latomus* 19 (1960) 724-735, and A. Deman, "Les oiseaux 'vendangeurs' de la Première Bucolique (vv. 56-58)," *Latomus* 20 (1961) 326-336, argue that *frondator* in 1.56 is a bird, but E. de Saint-Denis, "Encore le 'frondator' de la première églogue virgilienne: homme ou oiseau?" *Latomus* 21 (1962), 555-562, insists on the traditional interpretation of the word. R. Gustin, "La saison de la troisième Bucolique de Virgile," *LEC* 26 (1958) 138-142, argues, with citations from Latin poetry, that in 55-56 the season is spring (not summer, as favored by Cartault and others). Z. Stewart, "*Liquidi ignis* (Virgil, *Buc.* 6.33)," in Whatmough, 259-261, translates *liquidus* as "clear-flowing" or "bright-flowing," with emphasis on the first element. MacKay (above, Sect. 4B: *E.* 1) suggests that in 7.70 V. jests on *korydon,* "the crested lark," mentioned in Aristophanes *Birds,* 472, as "the first of all birds." According to E. Paratore, "Spicilegio polemico. V. Ad Verg. Buc. IX, 45," *RCCM* 4 (1962) 88-92, *si verba tenerem* in 9.45 has optative force ("if only I knew the words"); not knowing the *verba* Lycidas cannot recall the *numeros.*

Georgics. J. Mehler, "Wat betekent *tenuis* bij Vergilius Georg. II 93," *Hermeneus* 31 (1959-60) 169-170, suggests that *tenuis* means a *vinum crassum* that was thinned, and compares Horace, *Sat.* 2.4.52. V. D'Agostino, "A Virgilio, Georgiche 2, 317s. e 514," *RSC* 5 (1957) 153-155, reads *concretam* in 318 and *nepotes* in 514. G. Cambier, "Virgile, *Géorgiques,* IV, 131," *Latomus* 18 (1959) 459-463: on the interpretation of *vescum papaver.* E. A. Hahn, "*Nec Morti Esse Locum,*" *AJPh* 81 (1960) 73-75: *G.* 4.226 refers to immortality not just for the bees but for all living creatures. R. P. R. de Ravinel, "A propos du livre IV des *Géorgiques,*" *REL* 39 (1961) 94-99: notes on 96-98 (V.'s dependence on Varro; Columella's misunderstanding of V.), 116-117 (V. changes his direction; *traham* does not mean *contraham*), and esp. 287-294 (delete 291, *et viridem . . . harena;* the river in 292 f. is the Indus, not the Nile).[68]

Aeneid. M. Jacobelli, "Aeneidos protasis quomodo interpungenda et interpretanda," *Latinitas* 7

(1959) 55-60, punctuates 1-7 with a full stop after *litora* (3) and a semicolon after *iram* (4). S. H. Benedict, "Unusual Use of *Saevus* in *Aeneis* 1.99," *CB* 36 (1959-60) 23, follows Servius in taking *saevus* in an affirmative sense (as *magnus*), but see W. H. Alexander, "*Saevus* in *Aeneis* 1.99," *ibid.*, 45: *saevus* indicates how the warrior looked to his foe. P. Brommer and W. K. Kraak, "Notes sur Verg. *Aen.* I, 393-400," *Mnemosyne* 10 (1957) 56-57, on the flight of the swans and the comparison with the ships. J. Nováková, "Kritisches und Exegetisches zum Dichterwort *umbra*," *Eunomia* 1, 1 (1957) 11-15, favors Heyne's interpretation of *umbra* in 1.607 and 12.859. F. Martinazzoli, *Sapphica et Vergiliana. Su alcuni temi letterari della tradizione poetica classica* (Bari 1958) 81-141, discusses the *topos* of *homoiopatheia* (cf. Meleager *A.P.* 12.70 and *Lydia* 42 [= *Dirae* 145]), examines in detail the ancient and modern explanation of *A.* 1.630, and concludes that *non* goes with *disco* rather than with *ignara*. L. Alfonsi "Due note vergiliane," *Aevum* 34 (1960) 375-378, favors interpreting *cari* in 1.646 as *amantis* and compares 5.747 (for the second note, see below, Sect. 10: *Cicero*). W. Pötscher, " 'Sed magno Aeneas mecum teneatur amore' (Verg., *Aen.* I 675)," *Emerita* 26 (1958) 214-247: *mecum* means both "with me" (an allusion to Aeneas belonging to the family of Venus) and "with my help" (referring to Venus as the goddess of love).

H. M. Currie, "*Pervius usus*," *G & R* 6 (1959) 165: *usus* in 2.453 means "passage". A. Pagliaro, " 'Ipse manu mortem inveniam. . . .' (Verg. *Aen.* II, 645)," *Helikon* 1 (1961) 139-147: Anchises will beg the enemy to kill him; *manu* means "of my own initiative" both here and in 2.434. Wilton (above, Sect. 8: *Meter*) disagrees with Mackail's view that 3.353-355 would have been revised; the emphasis in both halves of 355 is on *auro*. J. M. Borowski, *Janus a Virgile*, *Aen.* IV. 37-38" (in Russian) in *Mélanges en l'honneur de W. F. Sitmarev* (Léningrad 1957) 74-76: *triumphis* in 4.37 is not ablative but dative of purpose (used ironically). On 4.244 and 6.126, see Pearson (above, Sect. 7B). N. D. Hinton, "Tears in *Aeneis* 4.449," *CB* 1961-62) 33-34: the tears are those of Aeneas, whose situation resembles that of Hercules in 10.464 f.; see Duckworth *SP*, 17, note 37. L. A. Holland, "The Attribute of Portunus and the Verona Scholion on Aeneid 5, 241," in Grenier, II, 817-823: Portunus is the ferry god, not god of the harbors; cf. Holland, *Janus and the Bridge* (Roma 1962) 141-178. F. H. Sandbach, "Virgil, Aeneid v.315 ff.," *CR* 7 (1957) 102-103: the phrase *simul ultima signant* (sc. *pedibus*) in 5.317 is to be taken with what follows ("as soon as they begin to trample the last stretch, . . . ").

J. Svennung, "Vergil, Aeneis 6, 96," *Eranos* 54 (1956) 195-201, argues for *qua* in 6.96 against *quam*, the reading of Servius, the best MSS. and most modern editors (Hirtzel in OCT reads *qua*); *qua* is supported by many similar expresions in V. and by the frequent presence of a false *-m* in the MSS. N. E. Collinge, "*Facilis Descensus*," *Phoenix* 13 (1959) 69-72:*Avernus* in 6.126 does not mean Hades; it is best to read *descensus Averni* (obj. gen.) and accept Henry's interpretation, "anyone can die." H. F. MacDonald, "Virgil's Migrating Birds," *G & R* 5 (1958) 185, explains 6.310-312 as meaning that the bird rested in Italy before cross-

ing the Mediterranean. K. Alt, "instar (Verg. Aen. 6, 865)," *MH* 16 (1959) 159-162: *instar* means "counter-weight," i.e., Marcellus is equal to all the *comites* about him.

J. G. Landels, "A Hellish Note," *CQ* 8 (1958) 219-220: in 7.514 *vocem* means "sound" or "note," not "voice," and *intendit* has the sense of *emittit*. V. L. Johnson, "The Case for Vergil's Venerable Pig," *Vergilius* 7 (1961) 19-21: the litter of thirty pigs (8.43-45, 81-85) originally symbolized the thirty days of the primitive month. W. A. Camps, "Aeneid VIII, 86-7," *PCPhS* 5 (1958-59) 22, interprets "Tiber calmed his stream which all that night had been in flood." To row up the Tiber would take only six or seven hours and they did not row during the night; the phrase *noctemque diemque* in 94 either is an oversight to be removed in revision or means merely "with unremitting effort." A. Y. Campbell, "More on Virgil, Aeneid viii. 215-218," *CR* 8 (1958) 15-16, favors *clamore propinqui* in 8.216 (rather than *clamare propinqui*, suggested by Peerlkamp); see Duckworth, *Survey* 157 (6B: *A.* 8). V. does not confuse the Ganges and the Nile when he speaks of *septem amnes* in 9.30, but refers to the seven streams of the Ganges, mentioned in *Mahabharata* VI.vi.48-49; the simile itself appears in *M.* VI. xix. 14; see Lallemant, 278-280; Duckworth *TD*, 118-120, and cf. above, Sect. 6B: *A.* 7-12. E. Laughton, "Virgil, Aeneid ix.119," *CR* 11 (1961) 5-6, reads *aequore* instead of *aequora;* the word means properly the sea's surface and is rare in the sense of "depths." H. Morland, "Ida (Aen. IX 177)—Berg oder Nymphe?" *SO* 35 (1959) 71-87: *Ida venatrix* is a nymph, an Oread, the mother of Nisus.

10. Vergil and Earlier Writers

On V.'s indebtedness to Homer, Greek tragedy, Plato, Lucretius, and Catullus, see Duckworth, *CJ* 56 (1960-61) 290-299 (cf. above, Sect. 7A).

Homer. Cf. Buchheit, 15 ff., 61 ff. See above, Sect. 6A (Trencsényi-Waldapfel); Sect. 6B: *A.* 1 (Leglise), *A.* 5 (Bellardi), *A.* 6 (Rolland); *A.* 7-12 (Anderson, Semple); Sect. 6C (Duckworth), *Aeneas* (MacKay, McNamee, Knoche, Levy), *Ascanius* (Feldman), *Helen* (Garstang); Sect. 6D (Duckworth, "Trilogy," Camps); Sect. 8: *Style* (Anderson, Coffey). See below under *Early Latin Poetry* (Ussani, Pascucci).

T. A. Dorey, "Homer and Virgil: the world of the dead," *Orpheus* 3 (1956) 119-122, on the contrast between Elpenor and Palinurus (Homer more realistic, V. more dramatic) and the difference in atmosphere (Homer builds up a greater sensation of horror); W. T. Avery, "Iliad 5. 837-39 and *Aeneid* 6. 412-14," *CPh* 53 (1958) 177-178; H.-J. von Schumann, *Träume der Blinden vom Standpunkt der Phänomenologie, Tiefenpsychologie, Mythologie und Kunst* (Basel 1959) [= *Psychologische Praxis*, Heft 25] 97-109, on dreams in the *Iliad*, *Odyssey*, and *A.;* V.'s dreams have a much stronger visual element than those of the blind Homer; E. Abrahamson,

"The Adventures of Aeneas," in *The Adventures of Odysseus. Literary Studies* (St. Louis 1960) 25-30, on the similarities and contrasts in the wanderings and struggles of Odysseus and Aeneas; the theme of both epics is Home Lost and Regained; A. A. Berman, *The Transmigration of Form: Recurrent Patterns of Imagination in the Odyssey and the Aeneid* [Diss. Summary], *HSPh* 65 (1961) 348-351, on the travels of Odysseus and Aeneas as psychological journeys, as expressing representative situations in human experience, esp. that of maturing; H. Naumann, "Homers Nekyia und ihr Gegenbild bei Vergil und Dante," *AU* 5, Heft 1 (1961) 89-103; R. D. Williams, *Virgil and the "Odyssey"* (1961) [= VS Lect. Summaries, No. 53]: *A.* 1 in structure is modeled on *Odyssey* 5-8; Aeneas at the start is a second Odysseus but in the course of the poem he steps from the heroic world of Homer to the world of Roman destiny; W. E. Gwatkin, Jr., "Dodona, Odysseus, and Aeneas," *CJ* 57 (1961-62) 97-102: the influence of Dodona upon Aeneas' visit at Buthrotum.

Hesiod. See above, Disandro (Sect. 5A), Wilkinson (Sect. 5B: *G.* 1). La Penna, 213-252, stresses the magnitude of Hesiod's influence on V.'s poetry, esp. *E.* 6 and the *G.* (see above, Sects. 4B and 5A). His views are discussed (253-270) by J. H. Waszink, F. Solmsen, P. Grimal, and others.

Aethiopis. See Manton (above, Sect. 6B: *A.* 11).

Tyrtaeus. I. Millán González-Pardo, "Una reminiscencia de Tirteo en Virgilio (Buc. V 78 = Aen. I 609)," *Emerita* 27 (1959) 53-58: V.'s verse is adapted from Tyrtaeus, line 31 of fragment 9D.

Alcman. R. Pfeiffer, "Von Schlaf der Erde und der Tiere (Alkman, fr. 58D.)," *Hermes* 87 (1959) 1-6, on the reminiscence of the passage in *A.* 4.522-527 as a guide to the correct reading in Alcman.

Sophocles. L. Alfonsi, "Pulchra Mors," *Latomus* 22 (1963) 85-86, suggests that the figure of *pulchra mors* (*G.* 4.218; *A.* 11.647; cf. 9.401) is derived from Sophocles' *Antigone*, esp. 96 ff.

Euripides. See above, Abel (Sect. 6C: *Dido*); Haarhoff (Sect. 7B). B. C. Fenik, *The Influence of Euripides on Vergil's Aeneid* (Ann Arbor 1960) [= Princeton Univ. dissertation, microfilmed], examines V.'s indebtedness to the *Hecuba, Andromache, Alcestis, Helen, Rhesus, Hippolytus,* and *Troades;* see above, Sect. 6B: *A.* 9; Sect. 6C.

Timaeus. T. S. Brown, "Timaeus and the *Aeneid*," *Vergilius* 6 (1960) 4-12, on the possible direct influence of Timaeus on V., in addition to indirect influence through Lycophron and Apollonius.

Lycophron. See Trencsényi-Waldapfel (above, Sect. 6A).

Theocritus. See above, Sects. 2 (Cova); 4A (Oliveira Pulquério, Dolç, Musurillo, Marchesi, Korfmacher); 4B: *E.* 10 (Steidle); 6B: *A.* 5 (Bellardi).

Callimachus. For V.'s indebtedness to the *Aitia*-prologue of Callimachus, see Wimmel (above, Sects. 4B: *E.* 6; 5B: *G.* 3).

Apollonius. See above, Sects. 4B: *A.* 5 (Bellardi); 6C: *Aeneas* (Levy), *Dido* (Abel); 8: *Style* (Anderson, Coffey).

Aratus. See Brown, esp. 96-104; La Penna (above, Sect. 5A).

Nicander. I. Cazzaniga, "A proposito di una presunta ironia virgiliana," *SIFC* 32 (1960) 1-17, on V.'s ironical use of Nicander, esp. in *G.* 1.388-389, and "Colori nicandrei in Virgilio," *ibid.*, 18-37, on Nicander's influence in *G.* 3.414-439, *A.* 5.268-280, and *E.* 6.43-44. On Nicander and *G.* 2.315-342, see Brown, 108-113.

Mahābhārata. Lallemant and Duckworth *TD* discuss the many parallels (in both characters and events) in *A.* 7, 9-12 and *Mahābhārata* 5-9 (see above, Sects. 6B: *A.* 7-12; 6C). The similarities are so numerous and so striking that V. must have known and used the Sanskrit epic, perhaps in a Greek version made accessible to him by Cornelius Gallus (Lallemant) or Parthenius (Duckworth).

Early Latin Poetry. V. Ussani, Jr., "Livio Andronico, *Odys.,* fr. 16 M," *Maia* 9 (1957) 144-153: V. in *A.* 1.92 has blended *Od.* 5.297-298 and Livius, fr. 16, which is probably a translation of the Homeric passage. On Naevius, see D'Anna 50-67 (above, Sect. 6B: *A.* 3); Rowell (above, Sect. 6C: *Anchises*); Buchheit, 23-57. M. Barchiesi, *Nevio Epico. Storia, Interpretazione, Edizione Critica dei frammenti del primo Epos latino* (Padova 1962), discusses *passim* V.'s indebtedness to Naevius (see Index, 589). G. Pascucci, "Ennio, *Ann.,* 561-62 V² e un tipico procedimento di *auxēsis* nella poesia latina," *SIFC* 31 (1959) 79-99, points out the changes in the Ennian *recusatio* (from *Il.* 2.488-492) as it appears in Hostius, Lucretius, V. (*G.* 2.43 = *A.* 6.625), and Ovid.

Cicero. See Disandro (above, Sect. 5A). Alfonsi, *Aevum* 34 (1960) 375-378, finds in *A.* 6.808-812 the influence of both Cicero and Livy. J. Hubaux, "Du Songe de Scipion à la Vision d'Enée," in Herrmann, 436-445: *extra anni solis-*

que vias (*A.* 6.796) recalls the *Somnium Scipionis* of Cicero. The praise of Augustus in 788-807 should follow 846. See Hubaux above (Sect. 6B: *A.* 6) and note 50.

Varro. See above, Steidle (Sect. 4B: *E.* 10); Disandro (Sect. 5A); Enk (Sect. 6B: *A.* 6). J. H. Waszink, "Agmina Furiarum," *HThR* 56 (1963) 7-11: *agmen* in *A.* 4.469 and 6.572 is perhaps to be explained by Varro's use of Agmentis as the name of one of the *Furiae.*

Lucretius. See above, Sects. 4B: *E.* 6 (Marchesi); 5A (Disandro, La Penna); 5B: *G.* 2 (Ryberg); 7B (Howe). For Lucretius' influence on *E.* 6 and the *G.* (2.458 ff. and 3.1-48), see Wimmel, 142 ff., 174 ff.; on Lucretius and *G.* 2, see Zabulis (above, Sect. 7C). B. Farrington, "Vergil and Lucretius," *AClass* 1 (1958) 45-50, shows that V.'s references to Lucretius' poem, esp. in the *G.,* reveal a double motive; admiration for his predecessor but rejection of his beliefs. Lucretius was indifferent to the history and mission of Rome, and his ideal of peace was very unlike V.'s more realistic attitude (*A.* 6.851-853). J.-P. Brisson, "Virgile et le rationalisme de Lucrèce dans le chant 1 des Géorgiques (43-203)," in R. Günther and G. Schrot (edd.), *Sozialökonomische Verhältnisse im alten Orient und im klassischen Altertum* (Berlin 1961) 64-75, believes that V. in *G.* 1 owes to Lucretius not only his language and imagery but much of his thought, e.g., the emphasis on *labor* (cf. Lucr. 5.206 ff.) in place of the Golden Age celebrated in *E.* 4.

Catullus. R. E. H. Westendorp Boerma, "Vergil's Debt to Catullus," *AClass* 1 (1958) 51-63, points out (1) verbal echoes, often fortuitous, (2) conscious imitation in phrase or line, and (3) adaptations of Catullan images, ideas, and situations. The influence of the longer poems 61, 62, and 64 is esp. noticeable. Of V.'s poetry, *E.* 4 and *A.* 4 owe most to Catullus. On V.'s indebtedness to Catullus 64, see also D. H. Abel, "Ariadne and Dido," *CB* 38 (1961-62) 57-61, and G. Gonnelli, "Presenza di Catullo in Virgilio," *GIF* 15 (1962) 225-253, who cites echoes of Catullus in the *Catalepton* as well as in the authentic works. The influence of Catullus 64 is seen esp. in *A.* 4 and 8 (Evander's farewell to Pallas). According to A. H. F. Thornton, "A Catullan Quotation in Virgil's *Aeneid* Book VI," *AUMLA* 17 (1962) 77-79, the echo of Catullus 66.39 in *A.* 6.460 is not incongruous, but suggests the deification of Aeneas and that of Augustus.

11.A. Ancient Authors after Vergil[69]

See Holtorf, 72-80, on Calpurnius Siculus, the Silver epic poets, Tacitus, Macrobius, St. Augustine, etc.

Inscriptions. R. P. Hoogma, *Der Einfluss Vergils auf die Carmina Latina Epigraphica. Eine Studie mit besonderer Berücksichtigung der metrisch-technischen Grundsätze der Entlehnung* (Amsterdam 1959): the influence is that of the *A.* only, but this is treated in full detail; the lines and phrases of the poem, with the repetitions and echoes in the inscriptions, are listed book by book in 221-343.[70] S. M. Bigorra, " 'Loci similes' virgilianos en epigrafes hispánicos de reciente aparición," *Emerita* 28 (1960) 317-326: Virgilian echoes in Latin verse epitaphs found in Spain too recently to be included in the material used by Hoogma. J. W. Zarker, "A Vergilian verse in the *Carmina Latina epigraphica,*" *CJ* 57 (1961-62) 112-116, examines *A.* 6.429 as it appears in about 80 verse inscriptions to express untimely death, and discusses the reasons for its popularity. W. Schmid, "Ein Vergilanklang in einer neupublizierten Inschrift aus Mactaris," *Philologus* 106 (1962) 277-280: the inscription, with change of number, repeats *A.* 1.269.

Calpurnius Siculus. M. Marchiò, "Un componimento georgico sulle orme di Virgilio: l'egloga V di Calpurnio Siculo," *GIF* 10 (1957) 301-314: *Eclogue* 5 of Calpurnius is an innovation in that it is not a pastoral but a georgic and is based chiefly on *G.* 3 of V.

Seneca. W. S. Maguinness, "Seneca and the Poets," *Hermathena* 88 (1956) 81-98: the majority of Seneca's quotations come from V. and Ovid, and those from V. are about four times as numerous as those from Ovid. Seneca often gives to the Virgilian passage a new meaning, usually a moral or allegorical implication lacking in the original context. G. Mazzoli, "Maximus poetarum," *Athenaeum* 40 (1962) 142-156: the *maximus poetarum* mentioned by Seneca, *De brevitate vitae,* 2.2 is not the poet suggested by previous scholars (Homer, Euripides, Menander, etc.) but V., and the sentiment is not a direct quotation but a rephrasing in prose of *G.* 3.66 f.

Valerius Flaccus. H. M. Currie, *Vergil and Valerius Flaccus* (1959) [= VS Lect Summaries, No. 48]: the many Vergilian imitations in the *Argonautica* should not blind us to Valerius' special spirit and peculiar ethos; he is most original in his romantic portrayal of Medea and her love for Jason. W. Schetter, "Die Buchzahl der Argonautica des Valerius Flaccus," *Philologus* 103 (1959) 297-308: Valerius imitates V. in dividing his work into two halves (cf. *A.* 7.44 f.

and *Arg.* 5.217) but gives more detail about the second half than V. does.

Statius. A. J. Gossage, *Statius and Vergil* (1959) [= VS Lect. Summaries, No. 47], on the indebtedness of Statius to V. in the *Silvae* (father-son relationship, sympathy for human suffering) and in the *Thebaid* (similarities in structure, character, and theme, e.g., vindication of *pietas* and *clementia*).

Tacitus. R. T. Bruère, "Ovid *Met.* 15. 1-5 and Tacitus *Ann.* 1. 11. 1," *CPh* 53 (1958) 34, on echoes in Tacitus of *A.* 1.33. N. P. Miller, "Virgil and Tacitus," *PVS* 1 (1961-62) 25-34 [= VS Lectures No. 56], on the frequency and significance of the Vergilian echoes; they are less numerous than some believe, but "Tacitus often makes deliberate and unexpected use of a Vergilian echo for his own purposes."

Juvenal. F. J. Lelièvre points out the manner in which Juvenal parodies V. for purposes of satire in "Parody in Juvenal and T. S. Eliot," *CPh* 53 (1958) 22-26, and in "Juvenal: Two Possible Examples of Wordplay," *ibid.*, 241-242.

Hosidius Geta. R. Lamacchia discusses the Vergilian cento, the *Medea*, in two long articles: "Problemi di interpretazione semantica in un centone virgiliano," *Maia* 10 (1958) 161-188, on changes of meaning in passages which Hosidius Geta took from V.; "Metro e ritmo nella *Medea* di Osidio Geta," *SIFC* 30 (1958) 175-206: metrical irregularities in the *Medea* result in part from the awkward juxtaposition of Vergilian hemistichs, but in most instances are to be explained by a rhythm based on word accent, to the neglect of quantity.

Nemesianus. B. Luiselli, "Il proemio del 'Cynegeticon' di Olimpio Nemesiano," *SIFC* 30 (1958) 73-95, on imitations of the *G.*, esp. 3.1-48, in *Cyneg.* 1-103.

Ausonius. M. R. Posani, "Reminiscenze di poeti latini nella 'Mosella' di Ausonio," *SIFC* 34 (1962) 31-69: the reminiscences of V. include those of *G.* 2.155 ff., *A.* 1.419 f., 6.32 f. (cf. *Mos.* 454-457, 324, 300-302, respectively).

Macrobius. See Townend (below, Sect. 12: *Vergil Today*).

Claudian. G. Martin, "Claudian, an Intellectual Pagan of the Fourth Century," in Ullman, 69-80: a comparison of the religious beliefs of V. and Claudian.

Boethius. W. F. Jackson Knight, "Virgilio, Plotino, Boezio," *Orpheus* 9 (1962) 3-19: the mystical nature of V.'s philosophy and its influence on Boethius.

Christian Writers. See above, Gagé, Holtermann (Sect. 4C); Sheehan (Sect. 6B *A.* 6); on St. Jerome, see Waltz (above, Sect. 4C). P. Courcelle discusses at length the religious and philosophical ideas of V. as interpreted by the Church Fathers from the 3rd to the 6th cent.; on *E.* 4, see "Les exégèses chrétiennes de la quatrième Eglogue," *REA* 59 (1957) 294-319; on *A.* 6, see "Les Pères de l'Eglise devant les Enfers Virgiliens," *AHMA* 30 (1955) 5-74, reprinted in a slightly abridged form and with less documentation as "Interprétations néoplatonisantes du livre VI de l'Enéide," *Recherches sur la tradition platonicienne* (Verona 1957) [= *Fondation Hardt: Entretiens sur l'antiquité classique*, III, Genève 1955] 93-136; see 125-136, a useful bibliography on *A.* 6 and its influence on later writers.

H. Hagendahl, *Latin Fathers and the Classics. A Study on the Apologists, Jerome and Other Christian Writers* (Göteborg 1958) [= *Göteborgs Universitets Arsskrift* 64 (1958) No. 2]. This book of 424 pages is devoted chiefly to Jerome, but deals also with Arnobius, Lactantius, Ambrose, and Augustine. Jerome's "quotations from Vergil are twice as numerous as those from all other poets together" (102) and outnumber those from his beloved Cicero; see 276-281 and *Index locorum*, 413-415. R. M. Grant, *CPh* 55 (1960) 70, calls the book "an invaluable contribution to the study of the classics in the early Christian period."[71] A. Salvatore, "Qua ratione Prudentius, aliqua *Cathemerinon* libri carmina conscribens, Horatium Vergiliumque imitatus sit," *AFLN* 6 (1956) 119-140: echoes of *E.* 4, *G.* 3 and 4, *A.* 1 and 4.

Quintus of Smyrna. M. Mondino, "Di alcune fonti di Quinto Smirneo: V. Quinto Smirneo e i poeti latini," *RSC* 5 (1957) 229-235, follows Noack against Heinze and believes that Quintus made direct use of the *A.* Numerous parallels are cited, including the Laocoon episode, where the punishment of Laocoon follows Sinon as in V. Holtorf, 79, and Buchheit, 193-197, also believe that Quintus was influenced directly by V. F. Vian, *Recherches sur les Posthomerica de Quintus de Smyrne* (Paris 1959), discusses in detail (esp. 55-74, 95-103) similarities and differences in *A.* 2 and *Posthomerica* 12-13, and favors the view that Quintus did not draw material from V.; the two poets used the same Greek source, not the Cyclic epics, but a later poem on the fall of Troy (possibly by Pisander). On the other hand, the discovery of several V. texts with Greek translations makes Quintus' knowledge of V. more likely and supports Mondino, Holtorf, and Buchheit against Vian; see Duckworth, *Survey* 232 (11A), on papyri, and below, Sect. 11D, on palimpsests.

11B. Ancient Lives

See Holtorf, 80-82; Götte-Bayer (above, Sect. 2); on the *Vita* of Focas, see Duckworth (above, Sect. 4C); Enking (above, Sect. 7A).

V. D'Antò, "Sviste ed errori nei dati cronologici di Suetonio e di altri biografi minori," *AFLN* 6 (1957) 117-143: many numerals in the Suetonian Lives are subject to correction: cf. 136 ff.: the Donatus-Suetonius *Vita* of V. should read XXVI, not XVI, for the composition of the *Culex;* XVI instead of XVII for the assumption of the *toga virilis;* cf. Schmidt (above, Sect. 3: *Culex*). W. T. Avery, "Augustus and the *Aeneid*," *CJ* 52 (1956-57) 225-229, reexamines the Donatus-Suetonius *Vita* (35) and argues that V. returned to Italy at the wish of Augustus and that the MS of the *A.* became imperial property before the poet's death. G. Marconi, "Il testamento di Virgilio," *RCCM* 3 (1961) 342-380, analyzes the statements in the Donatus-Suetonius *Vita* concerning V.'s death and will, and attempts to reconstruct the authentic wording of the testament. V. included the *A.* among the *scripta* (40) but ignored the poems of the *Appendix*. For a thorough discussion of Marconi's reconstruction, see R. Scarcia, "Il testamento di Virgilio e la leggenda dell'*Eneide*," *RCCM* 5 (1963) 303-321.

11C. Ancient Commentators

See Holtorf, 86-87; Sbordone (above, Sect. 6A), 53-69. On Servius, see above, Sect. 5B (on the second edition of *G.* 4); Enking (Sect. 7A); on Philargyrius and Ps.-Probus, see Radke (above, Sect. 4C).

J. Schwartz, "Quelques *Quaestiones homericae et vergilianae* chez les écrivains latins," in Herrmann, 698-701: the *grammatici* asked questions about the *A.* similar to those about the *Iliad* and *Odyssey;* these questions, apparently arranged in alphabetical order, are reflected in Juvenal 7.229 ff. N. Scivoletto, "La 'filologia' di Valerio Probo di Berito," *GIF* 12 (1959) 97-124: an examination of the testimony concerning Probus indicates that he was not as great a philologist as many modern scholars believe. The Servius citations do not support the theory that Probus composed an edition of V. with commentary. See, however, H. Womble, "The Servian Corpus and the Scholia of Pseudo-Probus," *AJPh* 82 (1961) 379-393: the scholia which bear the name of Probus are abbreviated extracts from a greater commentary which antedates Donatus and which may go back to Marcus Valerius Probus on Urbanus, commentator of V.'s works, cited by Servius eleven times, see W. Strzelecki, *RE* 2. R. XVII Halbband (1961) 982-986.

On the Harvard Servius and the publication of Vol. II (on *A.* 1 and 2), see Duckworth, *Survey* 233 (11C). Vol. III (on *A.* 3-5), under the editorship of A. F. Stocker, is scheduled to appear in 1964; the remaining volumes, I (*E.* and *G.*), IV (*A.* 6-8), V (*A.* 9-12), and VI (Epilegomenon and Index) are planned for publication in 1968 or later.

J. W. Jones, Jr., "Allegorical Interpretation in Servius," *CJ* 56 (1960-61) 217-226: examples in Servius of the four conventional forms of ancient allegorical interpretation: historical, physical, moral, euhemeristic; a fifth type of allegory *ex ritu Romano* appears in Servius-Danielis and perhaps reflects Donatus' earlier interest in Roman religion. R. B. Lloyd, "Republican Authors in Servius and the Scholia Danielis," *HSPh* 65 (1961) 291-341: in quoting from lost Republican authors the D scholia are superior to Servius in number of authors quoted, details of source given, length of quotations, and their accuracy where measurable. The evidence seems conclusive that the common source of S and D was the lost V. commentary of Donatus. The compiler of DS, adding to S from Donatus, was more faithful to the original than was S, but he did not preserve everything he found in his source. *Servii Grammatici in Vergilii Carmina Commentarii. Codex Leidensis B.P.L.52.* Introduction per G. I. Lieftinck (Amsterdam 1960) [= *Umbrae Codicum Occidentalium* I]: a reproduction of the MS which contains Servius' commentary on *A.* 5.93-573; 6.39-8.664; 10.775-11.262, dating from the end of the 8th cent.; *A.* 5.573-6.38 and 9.717-10.190, dating from the middle of the 9th.

For discussions of Servius' comments on specific passages in V., see G. H. Pagés, "*Quales Diomedis equi* (Seru. ad Aen. I 752)," *AFC* 7 (1959) 94-99: the horses of Diomedes of Thrace are identified with those captured by Diomedes in *Iliad* 10; E. Fraenkel, "Zum Text von Aeneis 6, 852," *MH* 19 (1962) 133-134: *pacis* in Servius on 6.852 is not a lemma but a shortening of the explanation given in the Floriacensis, one of the best sources of Servius-Danielis; there is no support in Servius for the reading *pacisque imponere morem;* V. Pisani, "Pisae," *PP* 14 (1959) 166-171: Servius on *A.* 10.179 f. and the tradition connecting Etruscan Pisae with Greece and Anatolia.

11D. Manuscripts

For a summary of the major and minor *codices,* see Holtorf, 82-86.

For palimpsests with text of V. and Greek translation, see G. Galbiati, "Del Virgilio diglotto," *Studi Storici in memoria di Mons. Angelo Mercati* (Milano 1956) [= *Fontes Ambrosiani* XXX] 195-200, and "Ancora del Virgilio Ambrosiano diglotto," *Studi in onore di Carlo Castiglioni* (Milano 1957) [= *Fontes Ambrosiani*

XXXII] 355-358, plus 8 pages of facsimiles: the Ambrosian palimpsest containing (under Arabic writing) *A.* 1.588-608, 689-698, 729-738 with Greek translation, written in 5th cent. uncials, attests the interest in Egypt in Latin literature and culture. E. M. Husselman, "A palimpsest fragment from Egypt," *Studi in onore di Aristide Calderini e Roberto Paribeni* (Milano 1957) II, 453-459: under a Coptic text (Wisdom of Solomon) are *G.* 1.229-237 and a Greek translation, beautifully written in small uncials of the 5th cent. The Latin text shows no variants from the Oxford text of Hirtzel.

J. de Wit, *Die Miniaturen des Vergilius Vaticanus* (Amsterdam 1959), describes in detail the miniatures of Vat. lat. 3225 and gives reproductions in black and white. The miniatures, to be dated at the end of the 4th cent. at the earliest, are originals in the sense that they were not taken from an earlier MS or from another cycle of V. illustrations.

R. Marichal, "Quelques apports à la tradition ancienne du texte de Virgile," *REL* 35 (1957) 81-84: graffiti and papyri give the earliest evidence for the text of V. The Augusteus (= Schedae Vaticano-Berolinenses), wrongly dated in the 2nd or 3rd cent., is not earlier than 350. J. J. H. Savage, "Sidelights on the History of Vergilian MSS in Capital Script," *VergDig* 4 (1958) 16-21, on the Mediceus and its *subscriptio* by the consul of 494. P. Avelino de Jesus da Costa, "Geórgicas de Virgilio (Fragmentos portugueses do século XI)," *Humanitas* 4-5 (1955-56) 220-245: the author discovered in Evora in 1946 two parchment sheets containing *G.* 3.226-277 and 382-433 and the scholia of Servius on the lines. The MS was probably brought to Portugal from some Beneventan monastery. The text does not agree with that in the *codices maiores* and perhaps derives from a different archetype. G. Serbat, "Un manuscrit de Virgile récemment découvert (ms. n° 54 de la Bibliothèque municipale d'Agen)," *RPh* 36 (1962) 51-61: the MS, written in an Italian humanistic hand of the 15th cent. and containing *E., G.,* and *A.,* was described in 1600 as having belonged to Julius Caesar Scaliger (died 1568); the absence of corrections in his hand argues against his ownership. K. V. Sinclair, "Some Late Manuscripts of the Works of Classical Authors," *Phoenix* 16 (1962) 276-280: the MSS listed include one of V. and Ovid (= MS 2 in the library of the University of Tasmania at Hobart), written by an anonymous scribe in a 15th cent. German *littera bastarda.*

12. *Vergil and Later Ages*
See Holtorf, 87-106.

Middle Ages. H. Haffter, "Walahfrid Strabo und Vergil," *ESHG* 16 (1958) 221-228: the influence of the *G.* and A. on the poetry of the 9th cent. abbot of Reichenau. E. Paratore, "Virgilio in Alessandro di Telese," *Studi Medievali in onore di Antonino di Stefano* (Palermo 1956) 425-427: references in Alessandro's *Alloquium ad regem Rogerum* to the medieval legend of V. as *dominus* of Naples; Alessandro reveals a knowledge of the text of both *G.* and *A.* G. Padoan, "Tradizione e fortuna del commento all' 'Eneide' di Bernardo Silvestre," *IMU* 3 (1960) 227-240, on the MS tradition of Bernard's commentary and its value as an allegorical interpretation. Bernard, following Fulgentius, believes that the *A.* presents the life of man and the truth of philosophy. W. Ziltener, *Chrétien und die Aeneis. Eine Untersuchung des Einflusses von Vergil auf Chrétien von Troyes* (Graz-Köln 1957): the 12th cent. Arthurian romances by Chrétien de Troyes *(Erec, Cligés, Lancelot, Yvain, Perceval,* and *Guillaume),* are modeled upon the *A.* both in their epic technique (repetition, contrast, reversal of situation, retardation, suspense, simultaneous action) and in their literary motifs (attempted suicide, storm at sea, night attack, battle scenes, catalogues, similes, etc.). Ziltener believes that Chrétien used V. directly and argues against an indirect influence through the contemporary *Roman d'Enéas.* On the indebtedness of Chrétien to V., see also F. E. Guyer, *Romance in the Making. Chrétien de Troyes and the Earliest French Romances* (New York 1954) *passim.* J. J. Savage, "Virgilian Echoes in the 'Dies Irae,'" *Traditio* 13 (1957) 443-451: the author (Thomas of Celano?) reflects certain turns of V.'s phrasing and thought.

Dante. See above, Hardie (Sect. 4C); Small (Sect. 6C: *Camilla*); Haarhoff (Sect. 7A); Naumann (Sect. 10: *Homer*). See Townend, below under *Vergil Today.* A. Ricolfi, "La Trasfigurazione cristiana delle porte dell'Ade virgiliano in Dante e il 'messo da cielo,'" *NRS* 42 (1958) 223-256. R. M. Haywood, "*Inferno,* I, 106-108," *MLN* 74 (1959) 416-418: the phrase "quell'umile Italia" in line 106 recalls *A.* 3.521-524; the names in Dante's passage refer to V.'s Italy as the creation of two originally opposed peoples.

Chaucer. J. Kleinstück, "Fortuna: Schlange und Skorpion," *ABG* 6 (1960) 278-291: echoes of *E.* 3.93 *(latet anguis in herba)* in Chaucer and other writers. W. C. McDermott, "Chaucer and Virgil," *C & M* 23 (1962) 216-217: Chaucer's "firy serpent venymus" is based on a misreading of *A.* 6.288.

The Renaissance. W. S. Maguinness, *The Thirteenth Book of the Aeneid* (London 1957),[72] on the content and poetic nature of the supplement by Maphaeus Vegius. He is guilty of imperfect proportion and excessive speechmaking, but his instinctive Vergilianism—amazing in a youth of twenty-one—is more a matter of form and expression and rhythm than of verbal reproduction. On Vegius' feeling for Vergilian ratios, see Duckworth *SP,* 110 f. On the life of

Vegius and the nature of his supplement, see also D. W. Blandford, "The Thirteenth Aeneid," *CO* 35 (1957-58) 64-65; in "Virgil and Vegio," *Vergilius* 5 (1959) 29-30, Blandford points out that the Thirteenth Book is an anticlimax and unnecessary, as the incidents are implicit in the *A.* To end the poem with Aeneas' personal fortune is to miss the whole point of the epic— the triumph of a nation.

C. Dionisotti, " 'Lavinia venit litora.' Polemica virgiliana di M. Filetico," *IMU* 1 (1958) 283-315: the attacks of the 15th cent. humanist Martino di Filettino, called Filetico, on contemporary scholars, esp. those who read *Lavinia venit litora* in *A.* 1.2. The two invectives "in corruptores latinitatis" were appended to his commentary of a selection of Cicero's *Letters.* E. Paratore, "La duplice eredità virgiliana nell' 'Arcadia' del Sannazaro," *Arcadia. Atti e Memorie* 4 (1961) 42-66: the "twofold inheritance" can be interpreted as the influence of V.'s spirit and style, as the combination of bucolic and erotic motifs, as the interweaving of the world of the *E.* and that of the *G.* Paratore stresses Sannazaro's indebtedness to the *G.* S. Shepard, "Scaliger on Homer and Virgil. A Study of Literary Prejudice," *Emerita* 29 (1961) 313-340, seeks to explain the bitter attacks of Julius Caesar Scaliger against Homer and his veneration for V. What Scaliger found in the *A.* came nearer to the Renaissance conception of aristocratic society than did the contents of the *Iliad* or *Odyssey.* V.'s universe is perfect, Homer's is full of flaws; Homer's characters are crude and irrational, V.'s are models of good behavior and of valor on the battlefield. V. as the perfect writer of didactic epic taught men how to behave in Renaissance life. M. J. Bayo, *Virgilio y la Pastoral española del Renacimiento (1480-1530)* (Madrid 1959): translations of the *E.* by Juan del Enzina and by Fray Luis de León; the influence of V. on the *E.* of Garcilaso, Gutierre de Cetina, and others; also on the "Diana" pastoral novels.

Sixteenth to Eighteenth Centuries. M. H. R. Pereira, "Alguns aspectos do classicismo de António Ferreira," *Humanitas* 8-9 (1959-60) 80-111: influence of V.'s *E.* on the 16th cent. Portuguese poet. R. Bady, "Un concours de poésie dans les *Essais,*" *BAGB* (1959) [= *Lettres d'Humanité* 18] 527-534, on Montaigne's interest in V., Horace, and other Latin poets; although cited less frequently than Horace, V. was for Montaigne the master of Latin poetry and of all poetry, and he considered the *G.* "le plus accompli ouvrage de la Poésie." Mrs. E. T. Dubois, *Some Imitations of Virgil in France in the 17th*

and *18th Centuries* (1957) [= VS Lect. Summaries, No. 38]: esp. the 17th cent. Latin poetry of Father Rapin: *Eclogae Sacrae, Eclogae Variae,* and *Hortorum Libri IV.*[73] W. S. Maguinness, "Virgil and Milton," *Romanitas* 3-4 (1961) 118-130: Milton's dependence on V., esp. in forms of expression, the structure of his epic, and his use of similes.[74] D. P. Harding, *The Club of Hercules. Studies in the Classical Background of Paradise Lost* (Urbana 1962) [= *Illinois Studies in Language and Literature:* Vol. 50]: the author throughout examines Milton's indebtedness to V. and concludes (134): *"Paradise Lost* remains . . . the finest commentary on Virgil's *Aeneid* ever written."[75] H. M. Richmond, "Polyphemus in England: A Study in Comparative Literature," *CompLit* 12 (1960) 229-242: the theme of the rustic wooer and the refined mistress from Theocritus, V., and Ovid to Marlowe, Ben Johnson, and other English poets; the "Renaissance outdistancing of classical traditions" illustrates changes in literary taste. M. L. Clarke, *Virgil in English Education since the Sixteenth Century* (1957) [= VS Lect. Summaries, No. 39]: the changes in classical education in the schools and universities, and the important role played by V.

Nineteenth Centry. K. Kerényi, *Vergil und Hölderlin* (Zürich 1957): Hölderlin's "Friedensfeier" and *E.* 4. H. F. Graham, "The Travestied Aeneid and Ivan P. Kotliarevskii, the Ukrainian Vergil," *Vergilius* 5 (1959) 5-11: poets have sought to remedy V.'s lack of humor by writing travesties of the *A.*; one of the best is by Kotliarevskii (1769-1838), written in Ukrainian and extremely important for the later development of Ukrainian literature. For the effect of V.'s thought and expression on Michelet, see E. de Saint-Denis, "Les souvenirs de Virgile dans le *Journal* de Michelet," *LEC* 28 (1960) 257-277, and "Virgile et la formation de Michelet," *BAGB* (1960) 272-284.

Translators and Commentators. See above, Padoan, Bayo. L. B. Hall, "Caxton's *Eneydos* and the Redactions of Vergil," *MS* 22 (1960) 136-147, writes on the nature of the medieval redactions, e.g., events related chronologically in the third person, suppression of most of *A.* 6, with Anchises' prophecies of Roman heroes transferred to the end as part of the later history of Rome. Caxton's *Eneydos,* published in 1490 and a translation of the *Livre des Eneydes,* represents an intermediate stage between the freedom of the earlier medieval adaptations and the direct translations which for the English tradition began with the Scottish version of Gavin Douglas.

63

L. Proudfoot, *Dryden's Aeneid and its Seventeenth Century Predecessors* (Manchester 1960), discusses Dryden's use of words, phrases, and lines in *A*. 4 which had appeared in earlier translations (by Vicars, Stapylton, Ogilby, Harrington, etc.) and the merits of his *Aeneid*, esp. its tone, diction, and style.[76] K. F. Doherty, S.J., "On Wordsworth's *Aeneid*," *CW* 54 (1960-61) 213-217: Wordsworth's unfinished translation compared with that by Dryden. E. de Saint-Denis, "Les *Variations* de Paul Valéry sur les *Bucoliques* de Virgile," *RPh* 32 (1958) 67-83, on Valéry's understanding and appreciation of the musical nature, the "force chantante," of the *E*.

Music and Opera. A. E. F. Dickinson, "Music for the *Aeneid*," *G & R* 6 (1959) 129-147, on the numerous operas, from the 17th cent. on, relating to stories concerning Aeneas and/or Dido. The best known today are Purcell's *Dido and Aeneas* (1689) and Berlioz' *Les Troyens* (1863). H. Wimmershoff, "Einige Betrachtungen zu Orpheus und Eurydike in antiker und moderner Dichtung," *Gymnasium* 64 (1957) 340-346, on Gluck's opera, *Orfeo ed Euridice* (1762), and Rilke's poem, "Orpheus, Eurydike, Hermes." M. O. Lee, "Orpheus and Eurydice: Some Modern Versions," *CJ* 56 (1960-61) 307-313: stage and/or film versions by Cocteau, Anouilh, Tennessee Williams, and Camus "attest the abiding popularity of the myth."

Vergil Today. G. B. Townend, "Changing Views of Vergil's Greatness," *CJ* 56 (1960-61) 67-77, examines the features of V.'s work which were meaningful to men of different ages, esp. to Macrobius in 400 (mastery of language and vast wisdom), to Dante in 1300 (style and thought; V. as poet, prophet, patriot, and guide), to Dryden and Pope in the early 18th cent. (classical perfection; dignity and restraint). Today T. S. Eliot stresses his universality and Jackson Knight analyses his style and verse, and both throw light on the real significance of his borrowings from and allusions to earlier poetry. V. is a pioneer for the modern symbolist poets. The greatness of his work, with its apparent contradictions and unresolved dilemmas, explains the fact that later ages have been able to find such diverse messages in the *A*.

13. Vergil Societies

The lectures delivered at the London meetings of the British Virgil Society, both printed (esp. the Presidential addresses) and mimeographed (either in full or in abbreviated form), are included above under the appropriate headings. Beginning with 1961-62, these lectures are published annually by the Society in the form of *Proceedings*. The first volume of *PVS* contains Lectures 54-57.

The name of the annual publication of the Vergilian Society of America was changed from *The Vergilian Digest* to *Vergilius*[77] in 1959 (Number 5). This publication contains each year not only articles on V. (listed above) but information about the activities of the Society— the sessions of the Classical Summer School at Cumae and the Classical Tours in central Italy and Sicily.

ADDENDA (Feb. 4, 1964)

This survey was completed on Sept. 25, 1963. The following titles have since come to my attention and are keyed to the sections of the survey.

1. A. G. McKay, "Vergilian Scholarship, 1962-3," *Vergilius* 9 (1963) 33-36.

2. Editions. R. G. Austin, *P. Vergili Maronis Aeneidos Liber Secundus* (Oxford 1963): introduction, text, and commentary.

3. Catalepton. R. E. H. Westendorp Boerma, *P. Vergili Maronis libellus qui inscribitur Catalepton*, Pars Altera (Assen 1963): bibliography, text, critical notes, commentary. On Part 1, published in 1949 and containing *Catalepton* 1-8, see Duckworth, *Survey* 116 (3). A. Salvatore, *Appendix Vergiliana. Epigrammata et Priapea* (Napoli 1963): text and commentary.

4B. G. Rohde, "Vergils fünfte Ecloge als Höhepunkt und Abschluss der frühen Eclogen," *Studien und Interpretationen zur antiken Literatur, Religion und Geschichte* (Berlin 1963) 117-139: analysis of *E*. 5, which Rohde considers an imitation not only of Theocritus' Thyrsis (1) but also of the Thalysia (7); Daphnis is only Daphnis, the creator of bucolic song, but Mopsus is to be identified with Theocritus, as Menalcas = V.

5A. C. Whitaker, "Vergil's Philosophy in the Georgics," *PVS* 2 (1962-63) 47-58 [= VS Lectures, No. 62]: V.'s attempt to bring his readers "to a fuller awareness of life than philosophies of an academic kind could offer."

5B. A. Magariños, "Más sobre el comienzo del libro III de las 'Geórgicas' y la 'Eneida'," *EClás* 7 (1962-63) 137-145: the prooemium of *G*. 3 as V.'s proclamation of a new type of poetry.

6A. H. Trümpner, "Die Aeneis des Vergil im Unterricht," *AU* 6, Heft 3 (1963) 5-49: analysis and interpretation of the *A*., with emphasis on 1.1-296, 4, 6.679-901, and 12.791-952. H. L. Tracy, "Seven Homecomings," *Vergilius* 9 (1963) 28-31: Aeneas' stops at Thrace, Crete, Buthrotum, and Carthage; his welcome by Acestes in Drepanum and by Latinus and Evander.

6B. 1. E. C. Reinke, "Vergil's *lacrimae rerum*," *CO* 41 (1963-64) 5-7: discussion of the interpretations of 1.462; *res* is to be translated "life." V. E. Hernández Vista, "La introducción del episodio de la muerte de Priamo: estudio estilistico," *EClás* 7 (1962-63) 120-136: analysis of 2.438-468. *4.* P. Considine, "The Sources of the Dido Story in Virgil's Aeneid," in J. Ferguson (ed.), *Nigeria and the Classics* 4 (1960) 53-73 [Ibadan 1961]: the sources are classified as legendary, literary, and psychological; Considine stresses the influence of Homer

64

and Euripides. *5.* R. Briggs, "Vergil. A Literary Appreciation with special reference to Book V," J. Ferguson (ed.), *Nigeria and the Classics* 3 (1959) 57-68 [Ibadan 1960]. *6.* J. B. Garstang, "Aeneas and the Sibyls," *CJ* 59 (1963-64) 97-101: on the Sibyls of the Mediterranean area and the reasons why V. allowed only the Cumaean Sibyl in his narrative (e.g., "he was unwilling to flatter the Etruscans more than necessary").

6C. Aeneas. E. M. Blaiklock, *The Hero of the Aeneid.* Inaugural Address to the Class. Assoc. of Auckland (1961). *Univ. of Auckland Bull.* No. 59, Classics Series No. 3.

6D. T. Halter, *Form und Gehalt in Vergils Aeneis. Zur Funktion sprachlicher und metrischer Stilmittel* (München 1963): an important Zürich dissertation of 120 pages, plus 8 tables, on symmetry in selected episodes (parallel and chiastic arrangements), metrical and syntactical responsion, and V.'s use of the "Siebenzahl." F. M. Brignoli, "Quid Vergiliani qui dicuntur *tibicines* in Aeneide componenda valuerint," *Latinitas* 11 (1963) 171-183: on V.'s method of composition; the *tibinices* were not, as is usually believed, temporary passages (e.g., the hemistichs) to be changed or emended, but two-line summaries (e.g., 1.102-103, 142-143, 157-158; 4.554-555, 571-572, 584-585) where the details were to be filled in later (the details being the *solidae columnae;* see the Donatus-Suetonius Life, 24).

6E. See above, Addenda, Sect. 6B, *A.* 6.

7A. Sir John Lockwood, "Virgil and his Critics," *PVS* 2 (1962-63) 1-8 [= VS Lectures, No. 58]: against Robert Graves' criticisms of V. and his poetry (see above, Sect. 7A), and a comparison of the views of Graves and T. S. Eliot. J. G. Landels, "Vergil and the Two Cultures," *PVS* 2 (1962-63) 33-46 [= VS Lectures, No. 61]: V.'s attitude toward science and art.

7B. J. A. Akinpelu, "Virgil and Philosophy," in J. Ferguson (ed.), *Nigeria and the Classics* 5 (1961) 42-53 [Ibadan 1962]: on the Stoic elements in V.'s poetry; the Epicurean (or Lucretian) influence was literary, not ideological. H. MacL. Currie, "The Sense of the Past in Virgil," *PVS* 2 (1962-63) 17-32 [= VS Lectures, No. 60]: on Stoicism and antiquarianism in the *A.*

7E. A. Balil, Sobre iconografía de Virgilio," *EClás* 7 (1962-63) 89-94.

8. Language. S. Mariner, " 'Traiectus lora' (Virg. 'En.' II 273)," *EClás* 7 (1962-63) 107-119: *traiectus* is passive, not middle. V. J. Herrero, "Virgilio y la pronunciación del latin," *EClás* 7 (1962-63) 162-182. J. A. Enríquez, "La lengua poética en la época de Augusto," *EClás* 7 (1962-63) 183-191. Sister M. M. Foley, S.C., "Color Imagery in the *Aeneid,*" *CO* 41 (1963-64) 13-14: V.'s use of *ater, albus, purpureus, caeruleus,* and *viridis* in *A.* 1-6.

Meter. J. Jiménez Delgado, C.M.F., "El hexámetro virgiliano," *EClás* 7 (1962-63) 146-161; on caesura and accent.

9. E. Fraenkel, "[Vergil] Aeneis 6, 242," *MH* 20 (1963) 234-236: verse 242, transmitted in R, is not imitated from Priscian, *Periegesis* 1056; Priscian is echoing an already interpolated text of V.

10. Homer. See above, Addenda, Sect. 6B, *A.* 4. W. S. Anderson, "On Vergil's Use of the *Odyssey,*" *Vergilius* 9 (1963) 1-8: imitations of the *Odyssey* in *A.* 1-6.

Euripides. See above, Addenda, Sect. 6B, *A.* 4.

Theocritus. See above, Addenda, Sect. 4B.

11A. Christian Writers. C.-G. Undhagen, "Zu einer Vergilreminiszenz in der sog. Vita Sancti Feliciani," *Eranos* 61 (1963) 45-54: on the citation of *A.* 4.174.

Quintus of Smyrna. R. J. Smutny, reviewing Vian, *Recherches,* in *CPh* 58 (1963) 257-260, agrees with Vian about "Quintus' complete independence of Latin literary influences."

11B. See above, Addenda, Sect. 6D.

11C. A. F. Stocker, "Servius Servus Magistrorum," *Vergilius,* 9 (1963) 9-15: Servius' commentary compared with the Servius Danielis (a more advanced commentary, but probably not by Donatus); see, however, Lloyd (above, Sect. 11C). Stocker recommends the use of Servius in V. courses; see Sweet (above, Sect. 2, *Editions*).

12. Sixteenth to Eighteenth Centuries. H. H. Huxley, "Virgilian Parodies and Imitations," *PVS* 2 (1962-63) 9-16 [= VS Lectures, No. 59].

GEORGE E. DUCKWORTH

PRINCETON UNIVERSITY

1. I am most grateful to the American Council of Learned Societies for a Grant-in-Aid which enabled me to work in the libraries of Rome during the summer of 1963 and to include in this survey many important books and articles not otherwise available.

2. *CW* 51 (1957-58) 89-92, 116-117, 123-128, 151-159, 185-193, 228-235, reprinted in 1958 by the Vergilian Society of America under the title, *Recent Work on Vergil. A Bibliographical Survey, 1940-1956.* Since the latter lacks page numbers, I shall give the *CW* page references to Duckworth, *Survey,* but shall add in parentheses the section in which the reference may be found.

To avoid repetition of bibliography in the new survey, I shall abbreviate certain works as follows:

Brown = E. L. Brown, *Studies in "Eclogues" and "Georgics"* (Bruxelles-Berchem 1963) [= *Collection Latomus,* Vol. 63]. A revision of *Studies in the "Eclogues" and "Georgics" of Vergil* (Ann Arbor 1961) [= Princeton Univ. dissertation, microfilmed].

Buchheit = V. Buchheit, *Vergil über die Sendung Roms. Untersuchungen zum Bellum Poenicum und zur Aeneis* (Heidelberg 1963) [= *Gymnasium Beihefte,* Heft 3].

Castiglioni = *Studi in onore di Luigi Castiglioni* (Firenze 1960). 2 vols.

Deonna = *Hommages à Waldemar Deonna* (Bruxelles-Berchem 1957) [= *Collection Latomus,* Vol. 28].

Duckworth *MS* = E. Duckworth, "Mathematical Symmetry in Vergil's *Aeneid,*" *TAPhA* 91 (1960) 184-220.

Duckworth *SP* = G. E. Duckworth, *Structural Patterns and Proportions in Vergil's "Aeneid"* (Ann Arbor 1962).

Duckworth TD = G. E. Duckworth, "Turnus and Duryodhana," *TAPhA* 92 (1961) 81-127.

Dumézil = *Hommages à Georges Dumézil* (Bruxelles-Berchem 1960) [= *Collection Latomus*, Vol. 45].

Grenier = *Hommages à Albert Grenier*, édités par M. Renard (Bruxelles-Berchem 1962) [=*Collection Latomus*, Vol. 58]. 3 vols.

Herrmann = *Hommages à Léon Herrmann* (Bruxelles-Berchem 1960) [= *Collection Latomus*, Vol. 44].

Holtorf = H. Holtorf, *P. Vergilius Maro. Die grösseren Gedichte. I. Einleitung. Bucolica* (Freiburg/München 1959).

Lallemant = J. Lallemant, "Une source de l'*Enéide*: le *Mahabharata*," *Latomus* 18 (1959) 262-287.

La Penna = A. La Penna, "Esiodo nella cultura e nella poesia di Virgilio," in *Hésiode et son influence* (Genève 1962) [= *Fondation Hardt: Entretiens sur l'antiquité classique*, VII, 1960] 213-252, with "Discussion," 253-270.

Perret B = J. Perret, *Virgile. Les Bucoliques* (Paris 1961).

Parret V = J. Perret, *Virgile* (Paris, 1959). This book should not be confused with the same author's *Virgile, l'homme et l'oeuvre* (Paris 1952); see Duckworth, *Survey* 188 and n. 52 (7A).

Properziana = *Miscellanea Properziana* (Assisi 1957) [= *Atti dell' Accademia Properziana del Subasio*, Serie V, N. 5].

Richter = W. Richter, *Vergil. Georgica* (München 1957).

Rohde = G. Radke (ed.). *Gedenkschrift für Georg Rohde* (Tübingen 1961) [= *APARCHAI. Untersuchungen zur klassichen Philologie und Geschichte des Altertums.* 4. Band].

Ullman = *Studies in Honor of Ullman*. Presented to him on the occasion of his seventy-fifth birthday (edited by L. B. Lawler, D. M. Robathan, W. C. Korfmacher) (Saint Louis 1960 [1957]).

Whatmough = E. Pulgram (ed.), *Studies Presented to Joshua Whatmough on His Sixtieth Birthday* ('s-Gravenhage 1957).

Wimmel = W. Wimmel, *Kallimachus in Rom. Die Nachfolge seines apologetischen Dichtens in der Augusteerzeit* (Weisbaden 1960) [= *Hermes Einzelschriften*, Heft 16].

The abbreviations of *L'Année Philologique* are used for classical journals and university publications. I add the following abbreviations: *AU* (=*Der altsprachliche Unterricht*); *CO* (= *The Classical Outlook*); *MLN* (= *Modern Language Notes*); *PVS* (=*Proceedings of the Virgil Society*); *VergDig* (= *The Vergilian Digest*); *VS* (= Virgil Society); see below, Sect. 13. To save additional space, I abbreviate *Eclogues, Georgics, Aeneid*, and Vergil as *E., G., A.*, and V. respectively. The titles of books and articles are not abbreviated.

3. I omit school editions of an elementary nature, translations into languages other than English, reprints of books and articles published before 1957; cf. Duckworth, *Survey* 90, n. 3 (1). Important items, even though inaccessible to many readers, are now treated as fully as possible. Also, I have added a few titles of 1956 or earlier which were not available for comment at the writing of the first survey.

4. For editions and translations of poems in the *Appendix Vergiliana*, see below, Sect. 3.

5. J. André, *RPh* 36 (1962) 159-160, calls Holtorf's edition a monumental work and praises the commentary as "soigné, riche, précis"; C. Becker, *Gnomon* 33 (1961) 96-97 and J.-G. Préaux, *Latomus* 22 (1963) 101-102, are less favorable.

6. See reviews by G. E. Duckworth, *AJPh* 83 (1962) 444-447; M. L. Clarke, *CR* 12 (1962) 145-146; A. Ernout, *RPh* 36 (1962) 260-265.

7. See reviews by J.-G. Préaux, *Latomus* 17 (1958) 546-547; E. Burck, *Gnomon* 31 (1959) 224-238.

8. See reviews by G. Cambier, *Latomus* 20 (1961) 856-857; V. D'Agostino, *RSC* 9 (1961) 100-101 (on the introduction only).

9. The work is praised by J.-G. Préaux, *Latomus* 18 (1959) 806-807, as unique and revolutionary; see also H.-J. Newiger, *Gnomon* 31 (1959) 561-563; A. Rostagni, *RFIC* 39 (1961) 207-209.

10. On the nature and purpose of the edition, see W. E. Sweet, "The Structural Approach Applied to Vergil," *Vergilius* 6 (1960) 15-23. Cf. reviews by R. G. Austin, *CR* 11 (1961) 297-298; H. E. Wedeck, *CW* 54 (1960-61) 64.

11. See reviews by J. W. Spaeth, Jr., *CW* 56 (1962-63) 52-53; W. A. Camps, *CR* 13 (1963) 167-169; R. T. Bruère, *CPh* 58 (1963) 184-186.

12. See reviews by J. van Ooteghem, *LEC* 28 (1960) 467-468; F. de Ruyt, *AC* 30 (1961) 246-247.

13. See reviews by R. Verdière, *Latomus* 19 (1960) 362-364; W. A. Camps, *CR* 11 (1961) 131-133; C. Hardie, *JRS* 51 (1961) 222-226; R. T. Bruère, *CPh* 56 (1961) 120-121.

14. Editions of individual books with notes in Italian include the following: A. Di Benedetto, *Virgilio, Eneide, Libro II* (Milano 1960), rev. by M. E. Bertola, *RSC* 8 (1960) 237-239; L. Bruno, *Virgilio Eneide, Libro quinto* (Milano 1958), rev. by V. D'Agostino, *RSC* 5 (1957) 296-297; P. V. Cova, *P. Virgilio Marone, Eneide, Libro sesto* (Brescia 1959), rev. by A. H. *Latomus* 19 (1960) 650-651; A. Tortoreto, *P. Virgilio Marone, Eneide, Libro ottavo* (Brescia 1958).

15. See review by G. Cambier, *Latomus* 20 (1961) 927-928.

16. Cf., however, E. W. Spofford, *CW* 53 (1959-60) 90, who commends the freshness and vitality of the translation in spite of occasional obscurity.

17. See, on Oakley: R. G. Austin, *CR* 9 (1959) 37-38, H. M. Toliver, *CJ* 56 (1960-61) 328-330; on Delabère May and Dickinson: J. J. Savage, *CW* 55 (1961-62) 124-125; on Dickinson: A. Dalzell, *Phoenix* 16 (1962) 216-217; R. M(arcellino), *CO* 40 (1962-63) 12.

18. See reviews (favorable) by A. Ramírez, *CJ* 54 (1958-59) 140-142; R. T. Bruère, *CPh* 54 (1959) 67-68; (less favorable) by G. Rochefort, *REL* 36 (1958) 312-314; A. Haury, *REA* 61 (1959) 493; H. Bardon, *Latomus* 18 (1959) 690.

19. See, on I, G. Cambier, *AC* 27 (1958) 201-203; R. E. H. Westendorp Boerma, *Mnemosyne* 12 (1959) 173-176; on II, G. Cambier, *AC* 30 (1961) 248-249; G. Rochefort, *REL* 39 (1961) 353-355; W. Morel, *Gnomon* 33 (1961) 363-365; on both volumes, E. J. Kenney, *CR* 12 (1962) 146-148. For Salvatore's

earlier work on the *Ciris*, see Duckworth, *Survey* 116 f. (3).

20. R. E. H. Westendorp Boerma, *Mnemosyne* 12 (1959) 178-180, considers the theories fantastic and the edition inaccurate and unscientific. For Herrmann's earlier statement of his view in *L'âge d'argent doré*, see Duckworth, *Survey* 116 (3).

21. See reviews (unfavorable) by L. Herrmann, *Latomus* 18 (1959) 805-806; A. Rostagni, *RFIC* 38 (1960) 79-81; E. J. Kenney, *CR* 11 (1961) 86.

22. Mras, "De Culicis auctore," in Castiglioni, II, 621-626, presents the same argument in a slightly different form.

23. See reviews (unfavorable) by R. E. H. Westendorp Boerma, *Mnemosyne* 12 (1959) 176-178; P. Frassinetti, *Athenaeum* 37 (1959) 236-240; P. van de Woestijne, *AC* 28 (1959) 419; (favorable) by E. Galletier, *REA* 61 (1959) 199-201.

24. On Munari, see Duckworth, *Survey* 116 (3).

25. Brown, 11-20, discusses in detail the work of Le Grelle, mentioned by Duckworth, *Survey* 126 (5B); cf. also Duckworth *SP*, 36 f. On Maury, see Brown, 68-70.

26. On the reading or interpretation of specific passages, see below, Sect. 9.

27. See Duckworth, *Survey* 124 (4B).

28. Krenkel's article, under the same title, appears in a shortened form in J. Irmscher and K. Kumaniecki *Römische Literatur der Augusteischen Zeit* (Berlin 1960) [= *Deutsche Akademie der Wissenschaften zu Berlin. Schriften der Sektion für Altertumswissenschaft*, 22], 36-38.

29. So Lind; see Johnson (above, Sect. 2: *Translations.*)

30. See Duckworth, *Survey* 124 (4B).

31. The recent analyses of Stewart and Elder are not mentioned.

32. The same article by Hubaux appears in Deonna, 269-277, under the title, "Les souhaits de l'amant délaissé. A l'occasion du bimillénaire de Properce."

33. Listed in *L'Année Philologique* 28 (1957) 215, where the pages are wrongly given as 17-27.

34. For earlier discussions, see Duckworth, *Survey* 125 (4C).

35. Lind (see Johnson above, Sect. 2: *Translations)* considers no identification satisfactory and suggests that V. is deliberately mystifying his readers.

36. See Duckworth (below, Sect. 6D). Préaux fails to mention that the numbers (24, 39, 63) are multiples by three of the Fibonacci series numbers, 8, 13, 21, which appear so frequently in both the *G.* and *A.*

37. On the prooemium of 3, see also Fleischer and Grimal (below, Sect. 5B: *G.* 3).

38. See reviews by J. Marouzeau, *REL* 36 (1958) 310-311; H. Bardon, *Latomus* 18 (1959) 186-187; cf. V. Pöschl, *AAHG* 12 (1959) 207.

39. On the reading or interpretation of specific passages, see below, Sect. 9.

40. See Altevogt in Duckworth, *Survey* 126 (5A).

41. So Büchner; see Duckworth, *Survey* 128 (5B).

42. See Duckworth, *Survey* 151 (6A).

43. The 1958 Presidential Address delivered to the Virgil Society; see below, Sect. 13.

44. On the reading or interpretation of specific passages, see below, Sect. 9.

45. See reviews by J. Delande, *LEC* 26 (1958) 306-307; A. H., *Latomus* 19 (1960) 641-642.

46. See reviews by G. Rochefort, *REL* 39 (1961) 308-310; P. Venini, *Athenaeum* 39 (1961) 407-409; R. Marache, *Latomus* 21 (1962) 219-220. For D'Anna's earlier work on the composition of the *A.*, see Duckworth, *Survey* 156 f. (6B: *A.* 7-12).

47. See reviews by W. H. Alexander, *CPh* 54 (1959) 147; G. Cambier, *Latomus* 16 (1957) 729-730; M. van den Bruwaene, *AC* 27 (1958) 200-201; W. Wimmel, *Gnomon* 33 (1961) 47-54; G. Bellardi, *A & R* 6 (1961) 113-119.

48. For Heller's earlier article on the *Troiae lusus*, see Duckworth, *Survey* 154 (6B: *A.* 5).

49. See Duckworth, *Survey* 155 f. (6B: *A.* 6).

50. This transposition violates the structure of Anchises' speech. Augustus, who as the second founder of Rome properly follows Romulus (cf. 1.275-296), concludes the first half of the procession; see G. E. Duckworth, "*Animae Dimidium Meae*: Two Poets of Rome," *TAPhA* 87 (1956) 304 ff. On the violence done to the mathematical symmetry of the poem by such transpositions, see Duckworth *MS*, 216; *SP*, 86 f.

51. On Duckworth *TD*, see V. D'Agostino, *RSC* 10 (1962) 270.

52. This article appeared also in *AU* 4, Heft 2 (1959) 28-45.

53. This article was distributed in 1958 as VS Lect. Summaries, No. 43.

54. On the parallels in 2 and 4, see Fenik (above, Sect. 6B: *A.* 2).

55. But the emphasis on Augustus at the end of 8 suggests that this is the climax of the central portion, and the importance of Turnus in 9 links this book with 10-12.

56. The book contains 7 Appendices and 27 Tables and Charts. For reviews, see G. B. Riddehough, *CJ* 58 (1962-63) 272-273; W. C. Korfmacher, *CB* 39 (1962-63) 63; K. G(ries), *CO* 40 (1962-63) 104-105; Fr. José Oroz, *Helmantica* 13 (1962) 387-389; R. J. Getty, *Vergilius* 9 (1963) 16-22; R. D. Williams, *CPh* 58 (1963) 248-251; J. van Ooteghem, *LEC* 31 (1963) 221; V. D'Agostino, *RSC* 11 (1963) 90-91; P. Miniconi, "Les proportions mathématiques dans l' 'Enéide,' " *Latomus* 22 (1963) 263-272. The criticism by J. F. Lockwood, *Virgil Now* (London 1961; a VS Presidential Address) appeared before the publication of Duckworth *MS* and *SP*, and was based entirely on a short notice in the *Washington Post* of May 1, 1960; see Jackson Knight, *PVS* 1 (1961-62) 1 ff.

57. See also S. Ferri, "L'inno omerico a Afrodite e la tribù anatolica degli Otrusi," in Castiglioni, I, 291-307: the story of Aeneas is not a Greek creation but was born in Anatolia and brought to Italy by the Otrusi-Etrusi about 1000 B.C.; Vena-Veina = Vei and Lavna = La-vinium are two cities which bear the name of the mother of Aeneas.

58. See Duckworth, *Survey* 186 (6E).

59. Not 109-136, as given in *L'Année Philologique* 30 (1959) 386.

60. See above, Sect. 1, note 2, under Perret *V.*, The book is praised for the originality of its thought and style by H. Le Bonniec, *Latomus* 20 (1961) 167; see also J. Marouzeau, *REL* 37 (1959) 295-296; H. Bardon, *REA* 62 (1960) 186-187.

60a. Cf. the almost identical criticism in Robert Graves, *Oxford Addresses on Poetry* (London 1962) 27-53 ("The Anti-poet"). The quotation given above does not appear in the Oxford Lecture.

61. A printed VS lecture; see below, Sect. 13.

62. On balance and symmetry in the *A.*, see also Duckworth (above, Sect. 6D).

63. A sequel to "Poetic Sources and Integration," *Vergilius* 5 (1940) 7-16.

64. This article, under the same title, is published as *Collection Latomus*, Vol. 35 (Bruxelles-Berchem 1958).

65. On the life of Maecenas and his importance for the literary careers of V., Horace, and Propertius, see J. Eberle, "Mäcenas, der Etrusker," *Altertum* 4 (1958) 14-24; P. Boyancé, "Portrait de Mécène," *BAGB* (1959) 332-344.

66. Reviewers disagree with many of the author's conclusions, but find much in the book that is profitable; see L. P. Wilkinson, *Gnomon* 33 (1961) 355-360; J. Marouzeau, *REL* 38 (1960) 353-356; C. A. Rapisarda, *Orpheus* 7 (1960) 205-209.

67. Cf. also M. Coffey, *Virgil and the Tradition of the Ancient Epic Simile* (1960) [= VS Lect. Summaries, No. 49].

68. If 291 is deleted, 292 f. more probably refers to the Ganges with its seven streams; see below on *A.* 9.30.

69. On V.'s contemporaries, see above, Sect. 7D.

70. See reviews by M. L. Clarke, *JRS* 49 (1959) 204-205; J. W. Zarker, *AJPh* 82 (1961) 108-11; cf. also G. Cambier, *Latomus* 18 (1959) 856-857; L. Nougaret, *REL* 37 (1959) 277-279; V. Buchheit, *Gnomon* 32 (1960) 424-428; H. Bardon, *RBPh* 39 (1961) 209-210.

71. See also reviews by M. Testard, *REL* 36 (1958) 331-333; C. Favez, *Latomus* 17 (1958) 558-560; S. L. Greenslade, *CR* 9 (1959) 262-263; J. Daniélou, *Erasmus* 12 (1959) 324-327; J. Fontaine, *REA* 61 (1959) 534-540; P. Courcelle, *Gnomon* 31 (1959) 173-175; H. I. Marrou, *RBPh* 38 (1969) 418-423.

72. A printed VS lecture.

73. For a more detailed anaylsis of the *Eclogae* of Father Rapin and their relation to V., see Mrs. Dubois, "A Neo-Latin Adaptation of Virgil's Eclogues to a Christian Theme," *DUJ* 17 (1955-56) 108-115.

74. An outline, under the same title, appears in VS Lect. Summaries, No. 51 (1960).

75. See review by R. T. Bruère, *CPh* 58 (1963) 253-257.

76. See reviews by R. G. Austin, *CR* 11 (1961) 228-230; D. Knecht, *AC* 30 (1961) 613-615; J. Byrne, S.J., *CW* 55 (1961-62) 90; I. Simon, *Latomus* 21 (1962) 184-185.

77. The name of the pre-war Bulletin of the Vergilian Society of which six numbers appeared between June 1938 and December 1940.

Recent Work on Vergil:
A Bibliographical Survey,
1964-1973

Alexander G. McKay

from Volume 68, pp. 1-92

RECENT WORK ON VERGIL
A BIBLIOGRAPHICAL SURVEY, 1964 - 1973

(A sequel to *Recent Work on Vergil (1940 - 1956)* and
Recent Work on Vergil (1957 - 1963) by George E. Duckworth)

CONTENTS   PAGE

I. PRELIMINARY REMARKS; BIBLIOGRAPHY

Literary appreciations of Vergil's works, new texts and commentaries, and translations during the past decade are remarkable for their number and quality. The bibliographer's task has grown with the appearance of new classical journals and with a pronounced vogue for Vergilian studies in every conceivable department. Karl Büchner's monumental Pauly-Wissowa article (VIIIA, cols. 1021ff.), published in 1955, remains informative but by no means final. Bibliographic studies of Vergiliana have multiplied in recent years.[1] *Vergilius*, the annual publication of The Vergilian Society of America, publishes regular lists of the year's work on Vergil. Token of the abiding popularity and importance of Vergil resides in the two periodicals which are devoted almost entirely to him, *Vergilius* and the *Proceedings of the Virgil Society*.

Restrictions of space and cost of production have imposed limits on the total number of books and articles and notices listed herein. Following the procedure of the late George E. Duckworth, I have accorded only brief mention to many of the items listed and often have had to be content merely with the citation. School editions, translations into languages other than English, reprints of books and articles published before 1964, and chapters on Vergil in histories of Latin literature and typewritten materials have been largely omitted. In addition, I have listed only material directly accessible to me through original copy, xeroxed material or microfilm, abstracts, or authors' correspondence. A debt of infinite thanks is owing to the libraries of McMaster University, The University of Toronto, Stanford University, The University of California at Berkeley, and The American Academy in Rome for unceasing favors and generous assistance throughout the compilation of this material.

To eliminate repetition of titles the following abbreviations will appear throughout:

Actas: *Actas del III Congreso Español de Estudios Clásicos* 2 vols. (Madrid 1968)
Anderson: W. S. Anderson, *The Art of the Aeneid* (Englewood Cliffs, N. J. 1969)
Bardon: H. Bardon and R. Verdière, *Vergiliana: Recherches sur Virgile* (Leiden 1971)
Bayet: *Hommages à Jean Bayet* (ed. Renard, Schilling) (Brussels 1964)
Camps: W. A. Camps, *An Introduction to Virgil's Aeneid* (Oxford 1969)
Dudley: D. R. Dudley (ed.), *Virgil* ("Studies in Latin Literature and its Influence"), (London 1969)
Higginbotham: John Higginbotham, *Greek and Latin Literature: A Comparative Study* (London 1969)
Highet: Gilbert Highet, *The Speeches in Vergil's Aeneid* (Princeton 1972)
Martyn: J. R. C. Martyn (ed.), *Cicero and Virgil: Studies in Honour of Harold Hunt* (Amsterdam 1972)

---

[1] The present bibliography complements G. E. Duckworth's "Recent Work on Vergil (1957-1963)," *CW* 57 (1963-64) 193-228, reprinted by The Vergilian Society under the title, *Recent Work on Vergil: A Bibliographical Survey, 1957-1963* (1964). *L'Année Philologique* (through Vol. XLI) remains an indispensable source. Additional titles and direction are also available elsewhere: *Bollettino di Studi Latini* 1 (1971); 2 (1972); 3 (1973); *George E. Duckworth: A Bibliography* (Princeton 1971); E. Fraenkel, *Kleine Beiträge zur klassischen Philologie*. II Bande (Rome 1964) s.v. Vergil, 139-44; 145-72; 173-80; 181-98; J. E. Heffner, M. Hammond, and M. C. J. Putnam, "A bibliographical handlist on Vergil's Aeneid," *CW* 60 (1967) 377-88; A. G. McKay, "Vergilian Bibliography," *Vergilius* 10 (1964) 40-44; 11 (1965) 40-47; 12 (1966) 39-45; 13 (1967) 35-41; 14 (1968) 16-27; 15 (1969) 42-52; 16 (1970) 33-39; 17 (1971) 13-21; 18 (1972) 16-30; 19 (1973) 33-40; V. Pöschl, "Virgil, 3. Fortsetz., 1 & 2 Teil," *AAHG* 21 (1968) 193-220; 22 (1969) 1-37; and R. D. Williams, *Virgil* (Greece and Rome New Surveys in the Classics, 1) (Oxford 1967), Supplement, 1971. I have deviated from the abbreviations of *L'Année Philologique* in the following instances: AJP, C&M, CP, HSCP, PVS, TAPA, UCCPh (Univ. of Calif. Publications of Class. Philol.), RCANE (Reports, Classical Association of New England).

McKay: Alexander G. McKay, *Vergil's Italy* (Greenwich, Conn. 1970; Bath, England 1971)
Otis: Brooks Otis, *Virgil, A Study in Civilized Poetry* (Oxford 1963)
Putnam *PA*: M. J. C. Putnam, *The Poetry of the Aeneid* (Cambridge, Mass. 1965)
Putnam *VP*: M. J. C. Putnam, *Virgil's Pastoral Art. Studies in the Eclogues* (Princeton 1970)
Quinn: Kenneth Quinn, *Virgil's Aeneid. A critical description* (London 1968)
Renard: *Hommages à Marcel Renard* (ed. J. Bibauw) 2 vols. (Brussels 1969)
Wilkinson: L. P. Wilkinson, *The Georgics of Virgil. A Critical Survey* (Cambridge 1969)
Williams: Gordon Williams, *Tradition and Originality in Roman Poetry* (Oxford 1968)

II. EDITIONS AND TRANSLATIONS

1. M. Geymonat (ed.), *P. Vergilius Maro: Opera* (post Remigium Sabbadini, Aloisium Castiglioni) (Torino 1973). Rev: Williams *PVS* 12 (1972-73) 54.
2. R. A. B. Mynors (ed.) *P. Vergili Maronis Opera* (Oxford 1969). Rev: Eden *PVS* 9 (1969-70) 106-109; Ernout *RPh* 44 (1970) 274-77; Kenney *JRS* 60 (1970) 259-61; Knecht *AC* 39 (1970) 603-604; Maguinness *CR* 21 (1971) 197-200; Stégen *Latomus* 30 (1971) 170-72; Townend "Virgil Unpunctuated," *PVS* 9 (1969-70) 76-86; Westendorp Boerma *Mnem* 26 (1973) 84-88.

Two superb editions of entire works by Mynors and Geymonat offer magisterial improvements. Hirtzel's *OCT* was no match for Sabbadini's judicious Italian counterpart. Mynors reports ninth-century MSS readings in his apparatus and elevates some important suggestions to textual authority. Notable conjectures in the text include *A* 3,684f. (Heinsius and Nisbet), *A* 5,505 (Slater), *A* 9,579 (Housman), *A* 11,173 (Bentley), and *A* 12,218 (Schrader). Townend's review article detects interesting changes and retentions in the punctuation. Townend concludes that the Vergilian line "is a natural unit, and there is a certain predisposition for the sense of a line to be self-contained to a considerable extent. When it is not, as continually happens in Virgil, the lead-on is pretty clear, and a firm break within a line is almost always heralded by a word which could not possibly be a continuation of the previous phrase." Geymonat follows the Sabbadini-Castiglioni text with respect and discrimination and improves and updates the *apparatus criticus* profiting by Mynors' researches (and Maguinness' review) throughout. Both editions provide an *Index Nominum*; Geymonat adds an invaluable *Conspectus codicum et subsidiorum* and a helpful *Praefatio*. Bibliotheca Teubneriana (Leipzig) has commissioned a revised edition of Ribbeck-Janell for completion by 1976.

3. M. Giammarco, *Publio Virgilio Marone: Le Bucoliche* (Pescara 1970).
4. J. u. M. Götte, K. Beyer (edd.), *Vergil, Landleben: Bucolica, Georgica, Catalepton, Virgil-Viten* (München 1970).
5. H. E. Gould (ed.), *Eclogae* (London 1967). Rev: Blandford *PVS* 6 (1966-67) 59; Grimm *CW* 61 (1968) 422.

Götte and Beyer provide excellent editions and translations with parallel texts. Gould offers a serviceable text for classroom use.

6. H. H. Huxley (ed.), *Georgics I and IV* (London 1963). Rev: Austin *CR* 14 (1964) 280-82; Coleman *JRS* 54 (1964) 243-44; Collinge *DUJ* 26 (1964-65) 111-12; Currie *PVS* 3 (1963-64) 50; Rose *CW* 59 (1965) 55; Thomson *Phoenix* 19 (1965) 327-30.

Huxley's college text provides a helpful introduction with an excellent account of the Vergilian hexameter and a brief account of 18th-century didactic writers in the train of V. The notes profit by Huxley's botanical and zoological expertise and are generally bright and relevant.

7. R. D. Williams (ed.), *The Aeneid of Virgil. Books 1-6* (London 1972).
8. R. D. Williams (ed.), *The Aeneid of Virgil. Books 7-12* (London 1973).
9. R. G. Austin (ed.), *P. Vergili Maronis "Aeneidos." Liber Primus* (Oxford 1971). Rev: Camps *JRS* 62 (1972) 230; Leach *CW* 66 (1972) 42-43; Oroz *Augustinus* 17 (1972) 434-36; Perret *RPh* 46 (1972) 334-335.
10. R. G. Austin, *P. Vergili Maronis Aeneidos. Liber II* (Oxford 1964). Rev: Camps *CR* 15 (1965) 178-80; Knight *PVS* 3 (1963-64) 44-47; Luck *Gnomon* 37 (1965) 51-55; Reinke *CJ* 60 (1964) 82-84; Robson *Phoenix* 19 (1965) 169-71; Sullivan *AJP* 76 (1966) 359-62; Westendorp Boerma *Mnem* 19 (1966) 434-37.
11. F. Speranza (ed.), *Virgilio: Eneide II* (Naples 1964).
12. M. Casali (ed.), *Virgilio, Eneide libro IV* (Torino 1971).
13. C. Soria (ed.), *P. Virgilio Marone, Eneide IV* (Buenos Aires 1971).
14. B. Tilly (ed.), *P. Vergili Maronis Aeneidos Liber IV* (London 1968).
15. B. Tilly (ed.), *P. Vergili Maronis Aeneidos Liber V* (London 1966).
16. H. E. Gould (ed.), *Aeneid, Book XI* (London 1964).

Austin and Williams continue their valuable contributions to the lecture room and seminar. Austin's edition of *A* 2 is altogether admirable for perceptive judgment and sound learning. Rhythm, alliteration and sound patterns are noticed throughout; V's sources are repeatedly and revealingly cited, and there is attention to archaeological detail also. Austin's edition of *A* 1 is marked by the same sensitivity and common sense, both powerful stimuli to scholars, young and old, and an exceptional addition to the Clarendon series. Williams offers a fresh-eyed approach to the entire *A* in his two Macmillan volumes which supersede Page's exegetical texts, bane and blessing of generations of classicists. Williams' two volumes provide cautiously updated texts together with graceful and perceptive commentaries which are well attuned to structure, thematic language, poetics, and the like. Relevant introductory material and bibliographies complement both volumes. Bertha Tilly's school editions of *A* 4 and 5 offer conventional, useful assistance to students. Gould's *A* 11 is a moderately stimulating introduction to a challenging book for novice and expert.

17. E. Cetrangelo (ed.), *Virgilio, Tutte le Opere* (Firenze 1966).
18. J. u. M. Götte (ed.), *Vergil, Sämtliche Werke: Aeneis, Bucolica, Georgica, Catalepton* (München 1971).

Cetrangelo's translation, with a contentious essay by Antonio La Penna, is a masterly version worthy of consultation by students for comparison with the original Latin. Götte's versions are faithful and adroit.

19. H. des Abbeyes, *Les Bucoliques* (Bruxelles 1966). Rev: Perret *REA* 69 (1967) 148-49; Stégen *RBPh* 41 (1967) 606-607.
20. H. Naumann (ed.), *Hirtengedichte* (München 1968).
21. E. de Saint-Denis, "Une traduction nouvelle des Bucoliques de Virgile en alexandrins rimés," *Bayet* 640-49.
22. H. C. Schnur, *Vergil, Hirtengedichte* (Stuttgart 1968).

Des Abbeyes' verse translation (with foreword by E. de Saint-Denis) competes on every count with the Budé version. Saint-Denis reviews des Abbeyes' rhymed alexandrines, along with versions by Paul Valéry, Pagnol, and Jacques Perret. Berg's text and translation (103) owe much to Sabbadini's edition. The verse translation attempts to reproduce V's 'rustic' ingenuousness through a modern American style and favors Otto Skutsch's observations (135) on symmetry. Naumann's parallel text translation includes selections from the *Appendix Vergiliana*, the Suetonian *Vita* and Donatus' introduction to the pastoral poems.

23. L. Firpo, *Virgilio, Le "Georgiche"* (Torino 1970). Rev: Davis *CP* 67 (1972) 304-306; Sewter *G&R* 17 (1970) 228.

24. F. Klingner, *Georgica* (Zurich 1963). Rev: Austin *RBPh* 43 (1965) 700-702; Burck *Gnomon* 36 (1964) 670-79; Gries *CW* 58 (1964) 22.

25. K. R. MacKenzie, *Publius Vergilius Maro: The Georgics*. Translated into English verse, with etchings by Nigel Lambourne (London 1969). Rev: *TLS* 69 (1970) 131; Wilkinson *CR* 22 (1972) 107-108.

26. H. Naumann, *Georgica: Vom Landbau* (München 1970).

27. D. R. Slavitt, *The Eclogues and the Georgics of Virgil*. Drawings by Raymond Davison (New York 1972).

Firpo's verse translation into Italian hendecasyllables contains excellent footnotes (particularly welcome on geography, historical allusions and mythology), but lacks the original Latin. The plates are exceptional: Codex Augusteus (Vat. Lat. 3256 and Berolinensis II 416), Vat. Lat. 3225, and Codex Romanus (Vat. Lat. 3867), the latter represented by three color plates with miniatures. Klingner's translation and commentary are exemplary. MacKenzie's verse translation has been widely acclaimed. Naumann provides a parallel text and repeats his earlier success with the pastoral poems. Slavitt rejects fidelity of reproduction in favour of verse meditations on the *E* and a verse reading of the *G* which is closer than his ruminations on the pastorals. Slavitt is convinced that the latter "twitches and breathes, sulks, rages, and sometimes rejoices the way Virgil's Georgics did."

28. J. W. Binns, "Modern Translations of the Aeneid," *Vergilius* 12, 21-22.

29. F. O. Copley, *The Aeneid: a verse translation* (Indianapolis 1965).

30. F. della Corte (tr.), *Virgilo, Eneide* (Milano 1967). Rev: Questa *RFIC* 96 (1968) 242-49.

31. L. L. Johnson, *Vergil, The Aeneid* (Lerwick, Shetland 1967).

32. C. Day Lewis, *On Translating Poetry* (Jackson Knight Memorial Lecture 2) (Abingdon-on-Thames 1970).

33. A. Mandelbaum, *The Aeneid: a verse translation*. With drawings by G. Davenport (Berkeley 1971). Rev: Anderson, *CW* 66 (1973) 354; Highet *Vergilius* 18 (1972) 53-55; Huxley, *CO* 50 (1973) 67; *TLS* (May 12, 1972) 550.

34. J. H. Mantinband, *The Aeneid* (New York 1964). Rev: Hulley *CW* 58 (1964-65) 56; Lind *CJ* 60 (1964) 139.

35. D. Silhanek, *Homer's Iliad and Vergil's Aeneid* (New York 1969).

36. D. A. S. John and A. F. Turnerfield, *The Voyage of Aeneas. Virgil, Aeneid Books I-VI* (London 1968).

37. C. Vivaldi, *Publio Virgilio Marone: L'Eneide*. 2 vols. (Milano 1970).

Patric Dickinson's prefatory remark to his earlier version, "A translator stands before the *Aeneid* in awe and love and with the certain knowledge that he is doomed to failure" matched Day Lewis' confession that "Though there is seldom any insuperable difficulty about putting into English what Virgil meant, it is all but impossible to convey how he said it." But the progression of translations gives no sign of abatement. Copley's verse translation favours an iambic pentameter line with an admixture of anapaests, dactyls and trochees as required. Otis provides an introductory essay for this modern version which finds its best competition with Mandelbaum's controversial offering. Anderson accorded Mandelbaum's translation surprised approbation; Highet condemned it as vapid and lifeless with an inadequate iambic pentameter line and a loss of the Vergilian music. Binns discusses four recent versions (Copley, Dickinson, Lewis, and W. F. J. Knight). Johnson's translation uses 14-line Spenserian stanzas and complex rhyme. Silhanek, John, and Turnerfield offer school texts; Vivaldi's Italian version provides parallel texts.

III. APPENDIX VERGILIANA

Texts, Critical Notes, Metrics

38. R. E. H. Westendorp Boerma, "Où en est aujourd'hui l'énigme de l'Appendix Vergiliana?" *Bardon* 386-421.
39. E. Courtney, "Notes on the Appendix Vergiliana," *Phoenix* 21 (1967) 44-55.
40. P. T. Eden, "Adnotatiunculae in Appendicem Vergilianam," *Mnem* 20 (1967) 285-92.
41. W. V. Clausen, F. R. D. Goodyear, E. J. Kenney, J. A. Richmond (edd.), *Appendix Vergiliana* (Oxford 1966). Rev: Cazzaniga *RFIC* 96 (1968) 339-54; Courtney *CR* 17 (1967) 42-46; Doeblin *CP* 63 (1968) 247-51; Eden *PVS* 5 (1965-66) 53-55; Ernout *RPh* 41 (1967) 109-15; Verdière *AC* 36 (1967) 670-72; Westendorp Boerma *Gnomon* 40 (1968) 259-68.
42. E. Courtney, "The textual transmission of the Appendix Vergiliana," *BICS* 15 (1968) 133-41.
43. G. E. Duckworth, "Studies in Latin Hexameter Poetry," *TAPA* 97 (1966) 67-113.
44. M. D'Eufemia, "Alcune osservazioni sui carmi dello pseudo-Virgilio," *RCCM* 14 (1972) 122-31.
45. R. O. A. M. Lyne, "A New Collation of the Graz Fragment," *WS* 6 (1972) 79-92.
46. A. Mazzarino, "Brevi note all'Appendix Vergiliana," *Helikon* 5 (1965) 536-37.

The new *OCT* Appendix Vergiliana supersedes Vollmer's Teubner edition (reprinted 1935) and Robinson Ellis' *OCT* (reprinted in 1954 with Colin Hardie's *Vitae Antiquae*). The editorial consortium produced judicious texts with different attitudes to the apparatus criticus. Kenney's interpretative comments, succinct and informative, are a welcome novelty. The Graz fragment is included in this compilation which is perhaps more critical than corrective. Courtney (42) offers a stemma and treats the MSS tradition of the Corpus as a whole. Duckworth's statistical study of metrics indicated to him that the *Culex* and *Moretum* were probably Vergilian, that the *Ciris* and *Dirae* were non-Vergilian, late Republican oeuvres, and that *Aetna* was post-classical. The Graz fragment, found in 1953, is subjected to close examination by Lyne who argues that the exemplar of G was composed in minuscules rather than capitals. Mazzarino treats the lost Trèves MS which contained much of the *Appendix* and 458 verses of the *Ciris*. Courtney (39) provides emendations and textual notes on 21 passages (including *Culex, Copa, Catalepton* and *Moretum*); Eden offers ten textual notes. Westendorp Boerma's concise and authoritative account of the *status quaestionis* since 1963 is indispensable for a general view of the problems of authorship and date. D'Eufemia researches the *loci similes* relative to poems in the *Appendix*.

Culex

47. A. A. Barrett, *The Poetry of the Culex*. Diss. Toronto, 1968. Summary in *DA*. 30 (1970) 4429A-4430A.

48. A. A. Barrett, "The Authorship of the Culex, an evaluation of the evidence," *Latomus* 29 (1970) 348-62.
49. A. A. Barrett, "The Topography of the gnat's descent," *CJ* 65 (1970) 255-57.
50. A. A. Barrett, "The catalogue of trees in the Culex," *CW* 63 (1970) 230-32.
51. A. A. Barrett, "The Praise of Country Life in the Culex," *PP* 134 (1970) 323-27.
52. A. A. Barrett, "Note on Culex 292," *CP* (1970) 43.
53. A. A. Barrett, "Donatus and the Date of the Culex," *CP* 67 (1972) 280-87.
54. W. Clausen, "The textual tradition of the Culex," *HSCP* 68 (1964) 119-38.
55. D. Güntzschel, *Beiträge zur Datierung des Culex* (Munster 1972).
56. R. Renehan, "Culex 163," *RhM* 112 (1969) 189-90.
57. O. Skutsch, "Culex 59, *HSCP* 72 (1967) 309-10.
58. G. Stégen, "Sur les vers 272-276 du Culex," *Latomus* 29 (1970) 744-49.

The Pseudo-Vergilian *Gnat* is a strong competitor for V's youthful hand. But *grammatici certant:* in favour, Duckworth and Barrett; against, Otis, Clausen, Courtney, and Lyne. Barrett (47) and Güntzschel offer detailed studies of the poem with thorough evaluations of the evidence for authorship. Barrett finds the gnat's *catabasis* markedly inferior to *A* 6 but detects a sophistication in the arrangement of trees in specific order with carefully designed roles (49, 50). Güntzschel's dissertation ranges more widely than Barrett's to include detailed Kriterien und Methoden zur Datierung des Culex; Das Verhältnis des Culex zu Ovid and Nachovidischen Dichtern; Literaturgeschichtliche Erwägungen; and Der Culex and die Dichter seit Lucan. Clausen (54) offers a new stemma with notes on nine passages and on word repetition. *Idae* (*Culex* 163) in Renehan's opinion denotes nothing more specific than *silva* or *mons silvester*. Skutsch examines the poem's structure and finds a parallel design between 58-78 and 79-97. Stégen associates the Tartarean criminals and death penalties with an Orphic context.

Ciris

59. M. L. Clarke, "The Date of the Ciris," *CP* 68 (1973) 119-21.
60. W. Clausen, "On editing the Ciris," *CP* 59 (1964) 90-101.
61. M. D'Eufemia, *Due studi latini: Il mito di Scilla nella Ciris. Caratteri e sviluppi della storiografia sallustiana* (Lecce 1969).
62. D. Knecht, *Ciris: authenticité, histoire du texte, édition et commentaire critique* (Bruges 1970). Rev: Boucher *REL* 49 (1971) 410-13; Ernout *RPh* 46 (1972) 154-56; Haury *Latomus* 31 (1972) 529-30.
63. D. Knecht, "Notice sur le texte de la Ciris contenu dans le codex Adalbertinus IV F 36," *AC* 37 (1968) 637-40.
64. R. O. A. M. Lyne, "The Dating of the Ciris," *CQ* 21 (1971) 233-53.
65. R. O. A. M. Lyne, "The *Recentiores* of the Ciris," *Proc. Cambr. Philol. Soc.* 197 (1972) 43-49.
66. R. O. A. M. Lyne, "The constraints of metre and the Ciris. A brief note," *Latomus* 28 (1969) 1065-67.
67. G. Runchina, "Sulla pretesta Octavia e le tragedie di Seneca," *RCCM* 6 (1964) 47-63.
68. A. Salvatore, "La Ciris e Virgilio," *Studi in onore di V. Falco* (Napoli 1971) 353-75.
69. A. Salvatore, "Ancore su la 'Ciris' e Virgilio," *Vichiana* 1 (1972) 82-84.

Duckworth (43) attributes the high frequency of spondaic lines to Catullian or late Republican influence, thereby lending support to Skutsch (1901) who attributed *Ciris* to Cornelius Gallus. But the contemporary vogue is to assign the poem to the early 1st century A. D. Clarke (59) agrees with Lyne (64) that the *Ciris* reference in the Donatus life is a departure from the Suetonian version. Clausen rejects Vergilian authorship in his assessment of *Ciris* editions in his critique of editions following the discovery of the Graz MS. Knecht's edition provides a useful critical commentary and a careful study of the unique readings of the Adalbertinus MS. But Knecht's study of the manuscript is challenged by Lyne (65) who constructs a provisional stemma. The exceptional use of *defigere, deturpare* and *denubere* indicates to Lyne that the author struggled with metrical constraints. Runchina accepts a post-Neronian date; Clarke (59) dates Ciris ca. 2nd century A. D. (possibly 139 A. D.). Salvatore favours the youthful V as author.

Moretum

Duckworth's study (43) underscores striking resemblances between the *Moretum, Culex* and *Eclogues.* Columella imitated V's authentic works and the *Culex* and *Moretum. Res Rustica* 10,433-36, indicates that he associated that "sidereus vates" with the *Moretum.* Duckworth hesitantly accepts its authenticity.

Dirae-Lydia

70. E. van den Abeele, "Remarques sur les Dirae et la Lydia de l'Appendix Vergiliana," *RhM* 112 (1969) 145-54.
71. E. Courtney, "Dirae 93," *CR* 18 (1968) 149.
72. E. Fraenkel, "The Dirae," *JRS* 56 (1966) 142-55.
73. F. R. D. Goodyear, "The Dirae," *Proc. Cambr. Philol. Soc.* 197 (1971) 30-43.
74. H. Heubner, "Zu römischen Dichtern," *Hermes* 93 (1965) 348-57.
75. H. A. Khan, "Dirae 93 again," *Mnem* 22 (1969) 159-64.

Duckworth (43) accepts both as a unit, with *Lydia* (104-183) as conclusion to the *Dirae*; he rejects Vergilian authorship but assigns it to a late Republican date. Van den Abeele challenges the unity of the poems and rejects both V and Valerius Cato as authors of the *Lydia.* The clash between bucolic and elegiac themes (*Dirae* vs. *Lydia*), with stylistic and metrical differences, argues against their merger. Courtney's reading of *Dirae* 93 is *iam novissima nobis.* Fraenkel's text and commentary expunges 41-42, 89-90, 95-96, and 103, and dissociates *Lydia. Dirae* in Fraenkel's view was composed after *E* 1 and 9 which were inspirational. Goodyear's study of *Dirae* is important. Heubner treats *Dirae* 172ff., *inter alia.*

Copa

76. W. F. Jashemski, "A Pompeian Copa," *CJ* 59 (1964) 337-49.
77. W. F. Jashemski, "The Caupona of Euxinus at Pompeii," *Archaeology* 20 (1967) 36-44.
78. L. P. Wilkinson, "Copa Today," *G & R* 12 (1965) 38-41.

Jashemski's study of a taverna in Pompeii provides appropriate context for the *Copa.* Murals and the design of the characteristic taberna contribute to our understanding of Pompeian pub psychology. Wilkinson's appreciation retains 18-19 and 21-23, and argues for a marriage of pseudo-Theocritean and popular Epicurean ingredients. He provides an entertaining paraphrase. Vergilian authorship for Wilkinson is impossible, but gratitude is owing to the anonymous poet for his saucy, entirely charming vignette.

Catalepton

79. G. I. Carlson, E. A. Schmidt, "Form and Transformation in Vergil's Catalepton," *AJP* 92 (1971) 252-65.

80. C. Conti, "Per l'esegesi dei 'Catalepton' virgiliani," *GIF* 3 (1972) 251-72.
81. M. Schmidt, "Anordnungskunst im Catalepton," *Mnem* 16 (1963) 142-56.
82. K. Vretska, "Gedanken über den jungen Virgil," *Gestalt und Wirklichkeit: Festschrift für F. Weinhandl* (Berlin 1967) 337-47.
83. R. E. H. Westendorp Boerma, *P. Vergili Maronis libellus qui inscribitur Catalepton, Pars Altera* (Assen 1963). Rev: Goodyear *CR* 14 (1964) 219; Herrmann *Latomus* 22 (1963) 848-49; Knecht *AC* 33 (1964) 205-206; Lloyd *AJP* 87 (1966) 248-49; Schmidt *Mnem* 18 (1965) 318-20; Till *Gnomon* 38 (1966) 164-69; Williams *CP* 59 (1964) 275-76.

Disputes over authorship continue to rage over these trifles, but in all likelihood here alone in the *Appendix* the youthful hand of the Mantuan may be detected (5, 10). Of their varied characteristics there is little doubt. Carlson and Schmidt respect the elements of humour, satire and parody (7, 8, 10). Conti provides a noteworthy exegesis. But students are deeply indebted to Westendorp Boerma for his superb edition with its consideration of authorship, critical notes and Latin commentary.

Catalepton 2

84. V. Buchheit, "Literarische Kritik an T. Annius Cimber," *Forschungen zur Römischen Literatur: Festschrift zum 60 Geburtstag von Karl Büchner* (ed. Wimmel) (Wiesbaden 1970) 37-45.
85. D. Romano, "Il significato del Catalepton 2 di Virgilio," *Ann. Fac. Magist. Univ. Palermo* (1969) 237-44.

Buchheit senses an invective against Antonian partisans reminiscent of Cicero's fulminations against Antony and Dolabella. Annius Cimber, the poem's tyrannus, and tyrannicide, was included in Cicero's raking fire (cf. Catullus 44).

Catalepton 3

86. E. Wistrand, "On the problem of Catalepton 3," *Arctos* 5 (1967) 169-75.
87. E. Courtney, "Catalepton 3.9-10," *CR* 19 (1969) 15.
88. J. W. Zarker, "Catullus 18-20," *TAPA* 93 (1962) 502-22.

Wistrand identifies the ruler with Phraates IV of Parthia and dates the epigram ca. 30 B.C., possibly by V's hand. Courtney substitutes *icta* for *hora*, predicate agreement with *mortalia*. Zarker assigns 2 and 3 to Catullus and comments on their structure according to the Golden Section.

Catalepton 8

89. G. Maurach, "Catalepton 8 and Hellenistic Poetry," *AC* 12 (1969) 29-46.

Maurach marshals a diversified battery of influences on *Catal. 8* — Lucretius, Catullus, the Neoterics and Hellenistic models.

Catalepton 10

90. E. Baer, "Iugum (zu Verg. Catal. 10, 18)," *MH* 26 (1969) 42-44.
91. H. A. Khan, "The Humor of Catullus, Carm. 4, and the theme of Virgil, Catalepton 10," *AJP* 88 (1967) 163-72.
92. L. Richardson Jr., "Catullus 4 and Catalepton 10 Again," *AJP* 93 (1972) 215-22.

Khan associates the *servus currens* personification of Catullus 4 with *Catalepton* 10 which transfers from personified object (ship as *servus currens*) to mule-driver. Richardson extols the brilliant little poem with its comic twists.

Catalepton 13

93.   G. N. Sandy, "A note on Virgil, Catalepton 13.6," *Mnem* 26 (1973) 286-88.

Sandy argues for retention of *adsim*; recorded abrasive insults will be at Luccius' side during the pillory.

Aetna

94.   F. R. D. Goodyear (ed.), *Incerti Auctoris Aetna* (Cambridge 1965).
95.   R. J. Dickinson, "Some Emendations in the Aetna," *PACA* 9 (1966) 77-80.
95a. H. Fuchs, "*Aetna* 255 ∕ 257," *Hermes* 101 (1973) 256.
96.   F. Weissengruber, "Zur Datierung der 'Aetna'," *WS* 78 (1965) 128-38.

Even Donatus expressed doubts (*de qua ambigitur*) about the authorship of *Aetna*. Language, style, metre and imitations all suggest a post-Vergilian date but prior to the eruption of Vesuvius in 79. Duckworth (43) finds striking resemblances between the metrical techniques of *Aetna* and the *Aratea* of Germanicus suggesting that the author of *Aetna*, hardly V, imitated the technique of Germanicus Caesar who was an admirer of V's *G*. Goodyear's edition, with Dickinson's corrections, offers a noteworthy introduction and commentary.

Epigrammata et Priapea

97.   R. Fuehrer, "Nuove cure per l'Appendix Vergiliana," *Maia* 20 (1968) 390-95.
98.   L. Herrmann, "Martial et les Priapées," *Latomus* 22 (1963) 31-55.

Fuehrer provides corrections and detailed comments on Armando Salvatore's edition (1963). Herrmann assigns the Priapean poems to Martial.

Elegiae in Maecenatem

99.   J. Diggle, "Elegiae in Maecenatem 129-132," *Latomus* 27 (1968) 175-80.

Diggle associates Hesperus and Hymenaeus with Venus who assisted their elevation to the sky.

IV.   ECLOGUES

A.   GENERAL STUDIES

100.   A. Espinosa Alarcón, "Bucolismo y vida," *Actas* II, 327-33.
101.   J. M. André, *L'Otium dans la vie morale et intellectuelle romaine des origines à l'époque augustéenne* (Paris 1966) 500-27.
102.   H. Bardon, "Bucolique et Politique," *RhM* 115 (1972) 1-13.
103.   W. Berg, *Early Virgil* (London 1973).
104.   J. Carrière, "Un procédé virgilien de 'mise en lumière': sa fortune," *LEC* 39 (1971) 329-33.
105.   J. Carrière, "Pittoresque et fin de vers dans les Bucoliques de Virgile," *Euphrosyne* 1 (1967) 173-81.
106.   R. G. Coleman, "Vergil and the Pastoral," *PCA* 69 (1972) 32-33.

107. R. Coleman, "Pastoral Poetry," *Higginbotham* 100-23 (esp. 116ff.).

108. F. Cupaiuolo, *Trama poetica delle Bucoliche di Virgilio* (Napoli 1969). Rev: Liénard *Latomus* 31 (1972) 617-18; Lesueur *REL* 48 (1970) 564-66; Zuccarelli *Athenaeum* 48 (1970) 459-63.

109. A. Dal Negro, "Il paesaggio nelle Ecloghe di Virgilio," *Annuario Liceo Maffei Verona* (1968) 27-40.

110. G. D'Anna, "La Bucoliche virgiliane," *Cultura e Scuola* 8 (1969) 27-35.

111. B. F. Dick, "Ancient Pastoral and the pathetic fallacy," *Comp Lit* 20 (1968) 27-44.

112. O. A. W. Dilke, "The hundred-line Latin poem," *Renard* 322-24.

113. J. de Echave-Sustaeta, "Contribución al estudio del tiempo en la poesía de Virgilio," *Actas* II, 317-26.

114. C. Fantazzi, *The Virgilian version of Pastoral*. Diss. Harvard University Summary in *HSCP* 71 (1966) 316-19.

115. C. Fantazzi, "Virgilian Pastoral and Roman Love Poetry," *AJP* 87 (1966) 171-91.

116. K. W. Gransden, "The Pastoral Alternative I," *Arethusa* 3:1 (1970) 103-22; "The Pastoral Alternative (concluded)," *Arethusa* 3:2 (1970) 177-96.

117. C. Griffiths, "Myricae," *PVS* 9 (1969-70) 1-19.

118. A. Grillo, *Poetica e critica letteraria nelle Bucoliche di Virgilio* (Napoli 1971).

119. C. G. Hardie, "Three Roman Poets," *The Romans* (ed. J. P. V. D. Balsdon) (New York 1966) 238-44.

120. J. J. Jensen, "An Outline of Vergil's Mathematical Technique," *SO* 45 (1970) 113-17. (*E* and *G*).

121. F. Klingner, *Virgil: Bucolica, Georgica, Aeneis* (Zurich 1967). Rev: Brisson *Latomus* 27 (1968) 459-62; Otis *Gnomon* 41 (1969) 554-74; Verdière *RBPh* 46 (1968) 1409-10.

122. G. Le Grelle, "Nombres virgiliens. Antécédents littéraires et présupposés mathématiques," *LEC* 33 (1965) 52-63.

123. P. Levi, "Arcadia," *PVS* 7 (1967-68) 1-11.

124. J. Michelfeit, "Das augusteische Gedichtbuch," *RhM* 112 (1969) 347-70.

125. B. Otis, "The eclogues: a reconsideration in the light of Klingner's book," *Bardon* 246-59.

126. Z. Pavlovskis, "Man in a Poetic Landscape: Humanization of Nature in Virgil's *Eclogues*," *CP* 66 (1971) 151-68.

126a. J. B. Pearce, *Themes and Motifs in classical pastoral poetry*. Diss. Univ. of Texas, Austin. Summary in *DA* 33 (1973) 5149A-5150A.

127. C. Pietzcker, *Die Landschaft in Vergils Bukolika*. Diss. Freiburg, 1965.

128. V. Pöschl, *Die Hirtendichtung Virgils* (Heidelberg 1964). Rev: Clarke *CR* 15 (1965) 180-82; Currie *PVS* 4 (1964-65) 73; Gries *CW* 58 (1964) 89; Luck *Latomus* 23 (1964) 852-54; Schmidt *DLZ* 89 (1968) 300-302; Skutsch *Gnomon* 37 (1965) 162-69.

129. R. Poggioli, "Naboth's vineyard or the pastoral view of the social order," *JHI* 24 (1963) 3-24.

130. M. C. J. Putnam, *Virgil's Pastoral Art. Studies in the Eclogues* (Princeton 1970). Rev: Smith *Phoenix* 25 (1971) 288; *TLS* (18 Dec. 1970) 488; Veremans *Latomus* 31 (1972) 524-26; Williams *CR* 22 (1972) 274-75; Witke, *AJP* 94 (1973) 96-98.

131. E. A. Schmidt, "Hirtenhierarchie in der antiken Bukolik," *Philologus* 113 (1969) 183-200.

132. E. A. Schmidt, *Poetische Reflexion. Vergils Bukolik* (München 1972).

133. M. A. M. Shaw, *Place in the Eclogues*. Diss. University of Texas, Austin, 1971. Summary in *DA* 33 (1972) 292A-293A.

134. O. Skutsch, "Symmetry and Sense in the Eclogues," *HSCP* 73 (1969) 153-70.

135. O. Skutsch, "The Singing Matches in Virgil and in Theocritus and the Design of Virgil's Book of Eclogues," *BICS* 18 (1972) 26-29.
136. P. L. Smith, "Lentus in umbra, a symbolic pattern in Vergil's Eclogues," *Phoenix* 19 (1965) 298-304.
137. P. L. Smith, "Vergil's *Avena* and the Pipes of Pastoral Poetry," *TAPA* 100 (1970) 497-510.
138. J. Soubiran, "Une lecture des 'Bucoliques' de Virgile," *Pallas* 19 (1972) 41-75.
139. P. Steinmitz, "Eclogen Vergils als dramatische Dichtungen," *A&A* 14 (1968) 115-25.
140. E. Vanderlinden, "La dépossession de Virgile," *LEC* 34 (1966) 35-38.
141. J. B. Van Sickle, "The Unity of the Eclogues. Arcadian Forest, Theocritean Trees," *TAPA* 98 (1967) 491-508.
142. L. P. Wilkinson, "Virgil and the evictions," *Hermes* 94 (1966) 320-24.
143. R. D. Williams, "The Eclogues (42-37 B.C.)," *Virgil* (Greece and Rome New Surveys in the Classics 1) (Oxford 1967) 6-13.
144. A. Wojcik, "De Amore infelici in tribus eclogis Vergilianis II, VIII, X descripto," *Eos* 58 (1969) 83-98.
145. D. E. W. Wormell, "The Originality of the Eclogues: *sic parvis componere magna solebam*," *Dudley*, 1-26.
See also *Otis, Putnam VP, Williams*.

The decade's publication on the Bucolics is remarkable in magnitude and valuable for significant advances in almost every department: metrics, structure, Theocritean elements, language, Vergilian originality, landscape, the pastoral tradition, etc. Berg, Fantazzi, Klingner, Otis, Pöschl and Putnam have made the most significant advances; considerable promise attaches to the developing research of Hardie, Leach, Segal, Smith and Van Sickle.

André's examination of Vergilian *otium*, earthly and cosmic, illuminates a basic element of the pastoral paradise. Bardon emphasizes V's introduction of politics and contemporary adulation into the Theocritean design. Bird is mainly concerned with the pastoral hero (Daphnis), the Roman (Octavian) hero (*E* 1 and 9) and the future hero (*E* 4) destined for roles in *G* and *A*. Berg traces reciprocal relationships between the poems and the poet's preoccupation with Hellenistic symbols which represented the poet and his activity. Carrière deals with a technical device (104) and peculiarities attaching to verse endings in the *E* book (105). Coleman studies parallelism in the *E* (106) and novel features of V pastoral (107).

Cupaiuolo's study of the *E* as poetic drama, with recollections of Hellenistic authors, is profitable and provocative. Landscape, whether idyllic, Sicilian or Italic, remains a problem of interpretation, as fiction or reality, suffused with poetic associations. Dick's studies of the pathetic fallacy and pastoral poetic mark new departures. Dilke's view of the standard length of bucolics and occasional poems of 100 verses is reflected in V's *E*; the variation lies between about 100 verses (= A) and 63-77 (= 3): ABAB ABABA. *Myricae, cano*, and *vates* indicate, for Griffiths, that V sought an archaic prophetic association for his pastorals, poems which reject neoteric ideals. Hardie's study of the *E* is searching and suggestive. Jensen finds a predilection for the unit of 3 in the *E*, 4 in the *G* (a controlling factor in the design of the poems) and in connection with names (Maecenas, Caesar, Mantua) in the *G*. Le Grelle steadfastly supports the mathematical thesis, promoted by Edwin Brown. Levi treats Arcadia as a conventional element. Pavlovskis' study of humanised nature is noteworthy.

Rupprecht and Smith both examine *umbra* in the *E* from the standpoint of meaning and association for the retreatist pastoralist. Shaw considers the spatial element in pastoral landscape description and favours a landscape perspective against which shepherds move and change, recalling tendencies in landscape painting. Skutsch argues that V was less concerned with symbolism than with symmetry in the construction of the E. Skutsch suggest columns of 15 lines, with 22 columns on the right and left supporting 10 columns, with 5 columns of E 5 and E 10. Skutsch also detects adaptations and modifications of Theocritus' *Idylls* 5, 8, and 6 in V's E 3, 7, and 8. V's *avena* Smith visualizes as an oatstraw monaulos, a rude country instrument, which intensifies the archetypal setting for the E and symbolizes the process of pastoral composition. Soubiran challenges Maury's compositional order of the E and favours an atmospheric progression from bucolic spring and summer through a seasonal progress of diminishing colour and warmth to death's cold (E 9, palinode to E 1). The E detail is a spiritual itinerary from bucolic song to life's bitter realities. The order of composition for Soubiran is 2, 3, 5, 9, 1, 4, 8 and then 6 and 7 (to correspond with 4 and 2), and finally, the architectonic finale, 10. E 1, 3, 5, and 9 are particularly susceptible to this sort of criticism, but unlike the mimes of Theocritus, they inhabit a never-never world. Van Sickle's study considers the unified nature of the E, the origins of Arcadian poetry, and Vergilian imitations of Theocritus (in E 4, 7, and 10). Williams treats the E as poems and questions Otis' detection of a balance of values: "the unrestrained world of haphazard forces of love and passion and frenzy, and the controlled world of moral stability." Williams prefers the singer as the unifying theme; V's ambitions for his métier are excellence in poetry, sweetness and symmetry. For Williams the E are about writing poetry. Wojcik's article treats the protagonists of E 2, 8, and 10 and finds Corydon the sole victor over unhappy love; his recourse is the country life, simplicity and sincerity, V's own solution. Wormell's perception of originality includes new dimensions transcending pastoral's earlier limits, new extensions in space identifiable with the autonomous world of his poetic imagination, new extensions in time by equating it with the Golden Age (past, present, or future) and a new focus of sanity and hope in Octavian Caesar with obligations on the part of the poet to society.

Finally, Otis' treatment of structure and Theocritean elements, political and poetic design, is masterly (716); his review essay of Klingner's book marks new insights and new appreciation on several fronts. Pöschl's study of E 1 and 7 provides a literary credo for V's bucolic writings. E 1 is subjected to a detailed analysis, followed by reflections on classicism in Roman literature, art, and architecture. E 7, for Pöschl, reveals V's aims in bucolic poetry through the poetic contest; Corydon is victor over Thyrsis in style, material and metre. Putnam's distinguished volume treats the E as a search to define the place of the individual in an intricate restrictive society, and as an exploration of the form and content of pastoral poetry. Spiritual freedom for poet and citizen is V's ethical sermon. Putnam sidesteps the popular approaches of allegory and structural patterning in favour of detailed studies of the poems from the standpoint of design, vocabulary, and imagery, with proper concern for their relationship and interactions through language and ideas.

B. INDIVIDUAL POEMS

Eclogue I

146. P. Boyancé, "Lectures virgiliennes. La première Bucolique," *BAGB: Lettres d'Humanité* 31 (1972) 495-502.
147. T. W. Burrows, "Virgil's First *Eclogue:* A Rhetorical Analysis," *CB* 47 (1970) 22-26.
148. W. Clausen, "On the date of the first Eclogue," *HSCP* 76 (1972) 201-205.
149. R. Coleman, "Tityrus and Meliboeus," *G & R* 13 (1966) 79-97.
150. B. F. Dick, "Vergil's pastoral poetic. A reading of the first Eclogue," *AJP* 91 (1970) 277-93.

151. P. Fedeli, "Sulla prima Bucolica di Virgilio," *GIF* 3 (1972) 273-300.
152. E. A. Fredricksmeyer, "Octavian and the unity of Virgil's first Eclogue," *Hermes* 94 (1966) 208-18.
153. A. Grisart, "Tityre et son Dieu. Des identifications nouvelles," *LEC* 34 (1966) 115-42.
154. J. Heurgon, "Tityre, Alfenus Varus et la 1re Églogue de Virgile," *CT* 15 (1967) (Mélanges d'archéologie et d'histoire offerts à Ch. Saumagne, Tunis 1967) 39-54.
155. L. A. MacKay, "Meliboeus Exul," *Vergilius* 17 (1971) 2-3.
156. R. M. Neilsen, "Virgil's Eclogue I," *Latomus* 31 (1972) 154-60.
157. U. Schindel, "Meliboeus Redux," *Hermes* 97 (1969) 472-89.
158. C. P. Segal, "Tamen cantabitis, Arcades. Exile and Arcadia in Eclogues One and Nine," *Arion* 4 (1965) 237-66.
159. A. Traina, "La chiusa della prima ecloga virgiliana (vv. 82-3); Appendix: La Struttura della IX Ecloga," *Lingue e Stile* 3 (1968) 45-57.

Clausen advances historical data to provide a more accurate date (35 B.C.). Coleman examines the characters of Tityrus and Meliboeus and rejects V's identification with Tityrus. Dick perceives the struggle between Tityrus and Meliboeus as a conflict between visions and between the real (M) and the ideal (T) worlds. Tityrus, like V, freed from *servitium amoris* (subjective love poetry) discovered Octavian and Rome, but tempers his historical awareness with sympathy for the unfortunate Meliboeus. Fedeli detects neoteric and Alexandrian poetic artifice combined with non-Alexandrian symmetrical structure and comments on V's juxtaposition of natural elements with the human condition and besetting problems. Fredricksmeyer discounts *E* 1 as an unqualified eulogy of Octavian. By indirection V offers an evaluation of Octavian's past acts, for good and for ill, and of his promise for the future as savior and force for good. The divine youth at the center, according to Fredricksmeyer, is harbinger of the future,a guarantee underscored by Tityrus' invitation to Meliboeus at the close. Grisart discards the *iuvenis deus*-Octavian identification as historically unacceptable. V's identification with Tityrus is irreconcilable, but Tityrus may be Eros, V's freedman secretary. Heurgon suggests that Etruscan customs persisted in Mantua; Tityrus, landholder according to Etruscan law, was counselled by P. Alfenus Varus, the distinguished jurist, to visit Rome to request *libertas.* MacKay argues that Meliboeus contemplates no return home but remote exile in a barbarous land. Ovid endured what Meliboeus feared. Neilsen studies town and country imagery in *E* 1. Segal's commentary on *E* 1 and 9 discounts history and present dilemmas in favor of a poetical, non-historical reading. Traina treats *E* 1 and 9 as evocations of cosmic order and chaos, of temporal associations, past and present. The fragments of lyric are recollections of a happier time past.

Eclogue 2

160. G. K. Galinsky, "Vergil's second Eclogue. Its theme and relation to the Eclogue book," *C&M* 26 (1965) 161-91.
161. Ph. Henze, "Formosus Alexis, formosam Amaryllida," *Caesarodunum* 5 (1970) 147-49.
162. A. LaPenna, "La seconda ecloga e la poesia bucolica di Virgilio," *Maia* 15 (1963) 484-92.
163. E. W. Leach, "Nature and art in Vergil's second Eclogue," *AJP* 87 (1966) 427-45.
164. G. Lenoir, "La deuxième Bucolique ou le rêve de Corydon," *Caesarodunum* 5 (1970) 151-54.
165. O. Skutsch, "The original form of the second Eclogue," *HSCP* 74 (1970) 95-99.

166. A. Traina, "Si numquam fallit imago. Riflessioni sulle Bucoliche e l'epicureismo," *A&R* 10 (1965) 72-78.

Galinsky contrasts Theocritus 11 and *E* 2 on the power of poetry, positive (*E* 1) and negative (*E* 2), and regards the contrasts as a leitmotif of the *E*. La Penna examines Theocritean elements in *E* 2 and argues for a compositional order of 9, 1, 6, 4, 2, 3, 5, 8,7,10. Eleanor Leach's study relates pastoral song and society to the real world; Corydon favours fantasy but returns, *nolens,* to nature. Parallels with Campanian wall-painting are suggestive. Skutsch's mathematics suggest that 45-55 were later additions when V desired to have *E* 2 and 8 total 181 lines; the artificial symmetrical structure of the poem suffered.

Eclogue 3

167. L. Braun, "Der Sängerstreit der Hirten in Virgils dritter and siebenter Ekloge," *Gymnasium* 78 (1971) 400-406.
168. F. Burckhardt, "Zur doppelten Enallage," *Gymnasium* 78 (1971) 401-21.
169. W. R. Nethercut, "Menalcas' answer. The hyacinth in Bucolic 3. 106-107," *CJ* 65 (1970) 248-54.
170. M. C. J. Putnam, "The riddle of Damoetas (Virgil, Ecl. 3, 104-105)," *Mnem* 18 (1965) 150-54.
171. C. P. Segal, "Vergil's Caelatum Opus. An Interpretation of the Third Eclogue," *AJP* 87 (1967) 297-308.
172. J. Veremans, *Eléments symboliques dans la IIIe Bucolique de Virgile. Essai d'interprétation* (Brussels 1969). Rev: Cleary *CW* 63 (1970) 172; Verdière *RBPh* 48 (1970) 129; Westendorp Boerma *Mnem* 25 (1972) 317-18; Williams *CR* 22 (1972) 109-10.

Braun enlarges Pöschl's study of *E* 1 and 7 with a stylistic and conceptual analysis of *E* 3 and 7. Burckhardt challenges Braun on *E* 3, 109ff. Nethercut treats Damoetas' riddle and relates it to Caelius (a Mantuan) and North Italy, where the hyacinth flourishes. Ajax and Hyacinth inform the symbol: Italy is on the verge of something new, but civil war (Ajax) and youth's destruction (Hyacinth) are deep-seated. Putnam explicates the riddle (104-105, 62-63) by associating *ulmas* (105) with the Greek city Olenos where the goat Amalthea, nurse of Jupiter, was born. Segal examines the cups and finds suggestions of the expanding framework of pastorals to come (4, 5, 6, and 10). Veremans discovers elaborate symbolism and allegory in the enigmatic pastorals. But Pollio's poetry conceived as something magical (28, 86), a mystagogue's product for *cognoscenti,* with infusions of Platonic thought and eros, is a desperate reading.

Eclogue 4

173. L. Berkowitz, "Pollio and the Date of the Fourth Eclogue," *UCCPh* 5 (1972) 21-38.
174. M. Bollack, "Le retour de Saturne (une étude de la IVe Églogue)," *REL* 45 (1967) 304-24.
175. V. D'Antò, "Il puer della IV ecloga virgiliana," *Latomus* 23 (1964) 258-70.
176. H. Drexler, "Zur 16. Epode and 4. Ecloge," *Maia* 16 (1964) 176-203.
177. J. Echave-Sustaeta, "Virgilio precursos. Exploración del mistero de la égloga IV," *Helmantica* 14 (1963) 421-61.
178. E. Flintoff, "Virgil, Eclogue 4.8-10," *CR* 23 (1973) 10-11.
179. H. C. Gotoff, "On the fourth eclogue of Virgil," *Philologus* 111 (1967) 66-79.
180. J. Grüber, "Marginalien zu Vergils vierter Ekloge," *Lemmata. Donum natalicium S. Ehlers* (Munich 1968) 58-65.

181. E. W. Leach, "Eclogue 4: Symbolism and Sources," *Arethusa* 4 (1971) 167-84.
182. H. J. Mette, "Vergil, Bucol. 4," *RhM* 116 (1973) 71-78.
183. M. Orban, "Virgile (Buc. IV, 28), un prodige en devenir," *LEC* 33 (1965) 127-39.
184. J. G. Préaux, "La quatrième Bucolique de Virgile," *JE* 36 (1963-64) 123-43.
185. R. Schmitt, "Vergils decem Menses und die indogermanische Anschauung von der Schwangerschaftsdauer," *Studi Linguistici in Onore di V. Pisani* (Brescia 1969) 903-10.
186. J. B. Van Sickle, "The Fourth Pastoral Poems of Virgil and Theocritus," *Atti e Memorie dell'Arcadia* Ser. 3., Vol. 5:1 (1969) 129-48.
187. J. B. Van Sickle, "Poetica Teocritea," *Quaderni Urbinati* 9 (1970) 82-97.
188. J. B. Van Sickle, *The Unnamed Child: A Reading of Virgil's Messianic Eclogue*. Diss. Harvard University. Summary in *HSCP* 71 (1966) 349-52.
189. A. Wojcik, "De IV ecloga Vergilii," *Meander* 25 (1970) 157-72.

Berkowitz regards Pollio's consulship as imminent, like the Golden Age, after the poem's completion. Bollack detects Theocritean influence (Herakliskos in *Idyll* 24) on the Wunderkind and rejects Roman identifications in favour of a philosophy of history. D'Antò favours Octavia's unborn child, the later Marcella. Drexler dates Horace's *Epode* 16 prior to *E* 4 and examines both carefully. Echave-Sustaeta regards Asinius Saloninus, Pollio's son, as *puer*, harbinger of a renaissance within the political imbroglio. Gotoff defines the poem as a *genethliakon* for one of V's circle, a reaction to Horace's pessimism in *Epode* 16. Grüber assigns *E* 4 to a double event: the beginning of Pollio's consulship on 1 January, 40 B.C., and the birth of his son, C. Asinius Gallus, at the end of December, 41 B.C. Leach's discussion of symbolism and sources is instructive. Mette favours the child of Octavia and Antony, one vested with traits of Antony and of Octavian-Augustus. Orban accents V's use of *paulatim* as indicative of a gradual solution to present problems. Préaux aligns Peace and *puer*, the cease-fire negotiated by Octavian and Antony at Brundisium and the projected offspring of Antony and Octavia. Van Sickle's dissertation is largely concerned with Catullus 64 and its relationship to *E* 4; elsewhere he reconsiders *E* 4 in relation to Theocritus *Idylls* 1-3, 5-7 (187) and attempts a synthesis of *E* 4 and *Idyll*-4 (186). Wojcik argues that *E* 4, designedly *paulo maiora*, retains its bucolic character.

Eclogue 5

190. W. Berg, "Daphnis and Prometheus," *TAPA* 96 (1965) 11-24.

Berg associates Daphnis *euergetes* of the bucolic world, with Prometheus, father of civilization and culture hero; Octavian was probably Daphnis' counterpart in V's troubled time.

Eclogue 6

191. L. Herrmann, "Non in iussa cano. Virgile, Bucoliques VI, 8," *Latomus* 23 (1964) 77-80.
192. E. W. Leach, "The unity of Eclogue VI," *Latomus* 27 (1968) 12-32.
193. K. J. McKay, "Frustration of anticipation in Vergil, Eclogue vi?" *Antichthon* 6 (1972) 53-59.
193a. J. A. Notopoulos, "Silenus the Scientist," *CJ* 62 (1967) 308-309.
194. E. Paratore, "Struttura, ideologia e poesia nell'ecloga VI di Virgilio," *Bayet* 509-37.
195. J. Perret, "Sileni theologia," *Bardon* 294-311.

196. J. Perret, "Autour de la sixième bucolique," *REL* 46 (1968) 5-6.
197. C. P. Segal, "Virgil's sixth Eclogue and the problem of evil," *TAPA* 100 (1969) 407-35.
198. C. P. Segal, "Two Fauns and a Naiad?" (Virgil, Ecl. 6,13-26)," *AJP* 92 (1971) 56-61.
199. W. Spoerri, "Zur Kosmogonie in Vergils 6. Ekloge," *MH* 27 (1970) 144-63.
200. W. Spoerri, "Antike Vergilerklärer und die Silenoskosmogonie," *MH* 27 (1970) 265-72.

Silenus' theology and philosophy are major concerns of critics. Segal's searching article (197) assesses love, war and nature in *E* 6 and 10. Silenus, a merger of Dionysian and Apollonian elements, betokens the power of poetry to generate a cosmos which contains the dualities of the world and man's experience. Love and nature surpass evil through poetry in *E* 6; but the negative elements of amor, war, and nature are dominant in *E* 10. Segal also identifies Chromis and Mnasyllus as fauns rather than shepherds (198). Notopoulos traces V's Silenus to Theopompus; the satyr's scientific knowledge was traditional as early as the 5th century (*Oxyrh. Pap.* 8, 1083). Spoerri treats Epicurean cosmogony and rejects Zeph Stewart's eclectic theory. Herrmann's preference for *in iussa* suggests to him that *E* 8, 11-2 (*iussis carmina coepta tuis*) must refer to Pollio's request for an epic to add lustre to his consulship. Leach analyses the poem's triple concern with man, nature, and poetry, the basis of the poem's unity. Perret (195) comments on the doctrine of metempsychosis, both Platonic and Ennian, in *E* 6 and *A* 6; mystical elements and Dionysian allusions are also ingredients.

Eclogue 7

201. E. E. Beyers, "Vergil, Eclogue VII, a theory of poetry," *AClass* 5 (1962) 38-47.
202. H. Dahlmann, "Zu Vergils siebentem Hirtengedicht," *Hermes* 94 (1966) 218-32.
203. H. Fuchs, "Zum Wettgesang der Hirten in Vergils siebenter Ekloge," *MH* 23 (1966) 218-23.
204. W. R. Nethercut, "Vergil and Horace in Bucolic 7," *CW* 62 (1968) 93-98.
205. J. J. H. Savage, "The art of the seventh Eclogue of Vergil," *TAPA* 94 (1963) 248-67.
206. J. Veremans, "La métrique en fonction de la compréhension des textes latins (Virgile, VIIe Bucolique)," *JE* 37 (1964-65) 35-57.
207. P. Wuelfing von Martitz, "Zum Wettgesang der Hirten in der siebentem Ekloge Vergils," *Hermes* 98 (1970) 380-82.
208. S. V. F. Waite, "The Contest in Vergil's Seventh Eclogue," *CP* 67 (1972) 121-23.

Beyers assumes that V instructs his readers to reflect on the implications of etymology, word positions in the verse-line, and the resultant music. Dahlmann argues, *contra* Pöschl, that Thyrsis is not inferior to Corydon as master of style and metrics, but his Theocritean coarseness, objectionable to V, is the cause of his defeat. Fuchs treats Dahlmann's article (202), Perret's strophic reconstruction and Horace's verdict on the *E* in general terms. Savage analyses the content and structure of *E* 3 and 7 and conceives them as a unit; Codrus (*E* 7) is identified with Maecenas. Nethercut favours Savage's suggestion that Thyrsis is identifiable with Horace. Von Martitz senses a revolution in *E* 7: Thyrsis, one-time embodiment of pastoral poetry, a gross, naive representative of Theocritean pastoral, finds his sophisticated successor in Corydon. So character, behaviour, and usages determine the contest's outcome.

Veremans' metrical analysis of *E* 7 suggests that V caricatured an alien poetic genre with eccentric manifestations. Waite ascribes Corydon's victory to his sensitivity and more compelling sentiment.

Eclogue 8

209. B. Andriani, "Divagazioni astronomiche sull'egloga VIII de Virgilio," *RAAN* 39 (1964) 213-23.
210. G. W. Bowersock, "A Date in the Eighth Eclogue," *HSCP* 75 (1971) 73-80.
211. L. Braun, "Adynata und versus intercalaris im Lied Damons (Vergil, Ecl. 8)," *Philologus* 113 (1969) 292-97.
212. P. Levi, "The dedication to Pollio in Virgil's eighth eclogue," *Hermes* 94 (1966) 73-79.
213. P. Levi, "Zu Vergils achter Ekloge," *Hermes* 99 (1971) 126.
214. A. Richter, *Virgile, la huitième bucolique* (Paris 1970). Rev: Clarke *CR* 22 (1972) 275-76.

Richter's important monograph considers the thematic and structural balance of the two *carmina* as vital to the poem's artistic unity. *Indignus amor* and *carmen* (both bucolic song and magic incantation) are controlling themes of the poem whose structural coherence surpasses the literary *contaminatio*. Richter is more concerned with mood, atmosphere, and character than with symbolic meaning. Andriani detects confusion in V's astronomical knowledge of Lucifer-Hesperus. Bowersock shows that verses 6-13 do not refer to Pollio but to Octavian and so provides a later date (35 B.C.) which has implications for the entire corpus. Braun aligns *adynata* with the general despondency and final tragedy of *E* 8. The dedication to Pollio, in Levi's view (212) lacks authenticity on geographical matters; the attribution of a Jupiter formula to Pollio and stylistic factors raise questions (dispelled by Bowersock, 210).

Eclogue 9

215. G. Cipolla, "Political audacity and esotericism in the ninth Eclogue," *AClass* 5 (1962) 48-57.
216. E. de Michelis, "L'Egloga di Meri," *StudRom* 16 (1968) 269-79.
217. E. A. Schmidt, "Poesia e politica nella IX ecloga di Virgilio," *Maia* 24 (1972) 99-119.

Cipolla detects an anti-Octavian substratum. Michelis relates *E* 9 to the *E* and treats structural factors. Schmidt explores V's new conception of the poet-bard (*vates*) and the new relativity of poetry to the state. V's departures from Theocritus' *Thalysia* is signalled by his picture of men moving *in urbem* rather than away from the metropolis. *E* 9 is V's poetic apology for his new-style bucolic.

Eclogue 10

218. G. D'Anna, "Verg. ecl. 10, 44-5," *RCCM* (1971) 48-61.
219. H. L. F. Drijepondt, "La Xe Eglogue de Virgile, un avertissement bienveillant à Gallus," *AClass* 6 (1963) 149-50.
220. C. G. Hardie, "The Tenth Eclogue," *PVS* 6 (1966-67) 1-11.
221. D. A. Kidd, "Imitation in the Tenth Eclogue," *BICS* 11 (1964) 54-64.
222. H. C. Rutledge, "The Surrealist Tenth Eclogue," *Vergilius* 18 (1972) 2-9.

D'Anna examines Lycoris' detachment from Gallus and the *insanus amor* which caused it. Drijepondt regards *E* 10 as a message for Gallus urging him to reject elegy's heartache for simple, unadulterated bucolic pastimes. Hardie interprets E 10 in connection with E 6. Gallus, freed from Lycoris, was expected to favour more elevated poetry than elegy; but Gallus chose politics instead and committed political suicide. V, like Marsyas, recovered the Hesiodic pipe (G) which Gallus rejected. Rutledge sees E 10 as glorification of Gallus' elegiac art and V's pastoral genius. But Rutledge emphasizes that the poem's substance lies in the vagaries and various aspects of love. Fluidity, eroticism, simultaneous expression of several thoughts, are hallmarks of contemporary surrealism and herein lies its artistic unity. Kidd analyses V's *imitatio* technique, source of the poem's complexity, and outlines a unifying scheme.

V. GEORGICS

A. GENERAL STUDIES

223. E. Abbe, *The Plants of Virgil's Georgics. Commentary and Woodcuts* (Ithaca, N.Y. 1965). Rev: André *REL* 43 (1965) 541-42; Hentz *REA* 70 (1968) 200-202; Huxley *PVS* 5 (1965-66) 53 and *CR* (1966) 185-86; Kraak *Mnem* 21 (1968) 321-23; Lembach *Gnomon* 39 (1967) 193-96; Thomson *Phoenix* 20 (1966) 265.

224. A. Betensky, *The Literary Use of Animals in Lucretius' De Rerum Natura and Virgil's Georgics*. Diss. Yale University. Summary in *DA* 33 (1972) 2350A.

225. A. Bradley, "Augustan culture and a radical alternative. Vergil's Georgics," *Arion* 8 (1969) 347-58.

226. V. Buchheit, *Der Anspruch des Dichters in Vergils Georgika. Dichtertum und Heilsweg* (Darmstadt 1972).

227. M. R. Caroselli, *Le Georgiche virgiliane e l'agricoltura italica in età romana* (Milano 1970).

228. A. Cox, "Didactic Poetry," *Higginbotham* 124-61 (esp. 145ff.).

229. D. Y. Radaza S. J., *Symbols in comparative religion and the Georgics* (Logos 3) (Manila 1968).

230. M. Dolc, "Politica agraria y poesia en Virgilio," *EClass* 8 (1964) 120-39.

230a. J. R. Dunkle, "The hunter and hunting in the Aeneid," *Ramus* 2 (1973) 127-42.

231. R. R. Dyer, "Ambition in the Georgics: Vergil's Rejection of Arcadia," *Auckland Essays presented to E. M. Blaiklock* (Auckland 1971) 143-64.

232. B. Farrington, "Polemical Allusions to the De Rerum Natura in the Works of Vergil," *Geras: Studies presented to G. Thomson on the occasion of his 60th birthday* (ed. L. Varcl and R. F. Willetts) (Prague 1963) 87-94.

233. R. Fischer, *Das ausseritalische geographische Bild in Vergils Georgica, in den Oden des Horaz und in den Elegien des Properz* (Zurich 1968). Rev: Juhnke *Gnomon* 42 (1970) 520-22.

234. W. Frentz, *Mythologisches in Vergil* (Meisenheim 1967). Rev: Brisson *Latomus* 31 (1972) 1351-52; McKay *CW* 62 (1969) 194-95; Suys-Reitsma *Mnem* 24 (1971) 317-18.

235. R. Gandeva, "Die soziale Ideenrichtung der Georgica," *Studien zur Geschichte und Philosophie des Altertums* (ed. J. Harmatta) (Budapest-Amsterdam 1968) 145-61.

236. C. Hardie, *The Georgics: A Transitional Poem* (Abingdon-on-Thames 1971) (The Third Jackson Knight Memorial Lecture).

237. H. H. Huxley, "Fragment of an Anti-Georgic," *Vergilius* 16 (1970) 28.

238. R. Jourdoux, "La philosophie politique des Géorgiques d'après Livre IV (vers 149 à 169)," *BAGB Lettres d'Humanité* 30 (1971) 67-82.

239. R. Kettemann, *Vergils Georgika und die Bukolik* (Heidelberg 1972).

240. F. Klingner, *Georgica* (Zurich 1963). Rev: Burck *Gnomon* 36 (1964) 670-79; Gries *CW* 58 (1964) 22; Perret *Latomus* 23 (1964) 621.

241. J. W. Lackamp, "Vergilius' Georgica in het licht van de moderne land-bouw," *Hermeneus* 36 (1965) 245-54.
242. W. Liebeschuetz, "The Cycle of Growth and Decay in Lucretius and Virgil," *PVS* 7 (1967-68) 30-40.
243. A. G. McKay, "Applied Science and Humanity: A Study of Vergil's Georgics," *Chancellor's Lectures, Brock University, St. Catharines* (Canada) (St. Catharines, Ontario 1971) 23-33.
244. E. Maróti, "Zur Entstehung von Vergils Georgica," *ACD* 2 (1965) 25-31.
245. R. Martin, *Recherches sur les agronomes latins et leurs conceptions économiques et sociales* (Paris 1971).
246. G. B. Miles, *Virgil's Georgics on the Nature of Civilization*. Diss. Yale University, 1971. Summary in *DA* 32 (1971) 2073A.
247. J. Mountford, "The Architecture of the Georgics," *PVS* 6 (1966-67) 25-34.
248. A. Parry, "The Idea of Art in Virgil's Georgics," *Arethusa* 5 (1972) 35-52.
249. Karl-Heinz Pridik, *Vergils Georgica. Strukturanalytische Interpretationen* (Tübingen 1971).
250. M. Ruch, "Sensibilité virgilienne et psychologie animale," *Hum* (RES) 42 (1965-66) 1: 23-5; 2: 23-5; 3: 23-5; 4: 23-5.
251. M. Ruch, "Virgile et le monde des animaux," *Bardon* 322-27.
252. E. de Saint-Denis, "Mécène et la genèse des Géorgiques," *REL* 46 (1968) 194-207.
253. S. Shechter, *The Hellenistic Aition in Virgil's Georgics*. Diss. Harvard University. Summary in *HSCP* 69 (1965) 349-50.
254. R. G. Tanner, "The Georgics and Mark Antony," *PVS* 9 (1969-70) 86-105.
255. K. D. White, "Virgil's Knowledge of Arable Farming," *PVS* 7 (1967-68) 11-22.
256. K. D. White, *Roman Farming* (London 1970).
257. R. M. Wilhelm, *The Georgics. A Study of the Emergence of Augustus as Moderator Rei Publicae*. Diss. The Ohio State University, 1971. Summary in *DA* 32 (1971) 6400A.
258. L. P. Wilkinson, *The Georgics of Virgil: a Critical Survey* (Cambridge 1969). Rev: Anderson *CJ* 67 (1971-72) 76-78; Austin *JRS* 60 (1970) 262-63; Bishop *AUMLA* 34 (1970) 311-12; Burck *Gnomon* 42 (1970) 768-76; Currie *PVS* 9 (1969-70) 113-14; Lloyd *AJP* 93 (1972) 491-92; Martin *REL* 48 (1970) 568-71; Otis, "A New Study of the Georgics," *Phoenix* 26 (1972) 40-62; Putnam *CP* 65 (1970) 258-59; *TLS* 69 (1970) 131.
259. R. D. Williams, "The Georgics (36-29 B.C.)," *Virgil* (Greece and Rome Surveys in the Classics 1) (Oxford 1967) 14-22.
See also *Otis, McKay, Wilkinson, Williams.*

Addison's prefatory essay to Dryden's translation of the *Georgics* remarks that they are "a subject which none of the critics have sufficiently taken into their consideration." The recent spate of articles and monographs serves notice that this hitherto neglected masterpiece will shortly receive proper consideration. Wilkinson's book marked the awakening of English critics to the remarkable poems which he assessed as vividly descriptive with pleasure as their ultimate objective, not didactic sermonizing. Wilkinson stresses the deep personal feeling and philosophical tenor of the work and studies the religious, political and symbolic motifs which permeate the well-wrought lines. His comprehensive study of Nachleben is exemplary. Rhythm and diction are illumined and he provides a perceptive reading of the Aristaeus epyllion. Non-polemical and largely non-committal, Wilkinson is useful and enlightening. Otis' chapter (716) is more concerned with moral and philosophical intentions than with agricultural and descriptive aspects. His structural analyses reveal aesthetic patterns and artistic *variatio;* mood and intention are freshly explored. The Aristaeus myth, for Otis, is the ultimate synthesis of the omnipresent life-death-rebirth factor. Klingner explores symmetry and contrast in the *G*, multiple levels of meaning, reference and relationship, and the art of foreshadowing and subtle progression. Never abstruse or over-emphatic, Klingner's writing matches the 'refined pleasure' of the work under review.

Betensky analyzes V's animal words, his use of Lucretian language to express antithetical ideas of cultivation vs. spontaneous growth, order vs. *laetitia, segetes* vs. *pabula.* The farmer's happiness lies in the control of nature's fertility. Bradley reassesses the Orpheus myth as divorced from the work motif and productivity factor elsewhere in the Book; freedom rather than sublimation is V's tentative response to the contemporary crisis. Buchheit reaffirms the poetic, salvational character of *G.* Contemporary politics and agrarian problems remain a perennial concern of critics; agricultural techniques and botanical research are advanced by the studies of Abbe and White. Demetrio's work employs modern techniques (Eliade, Van der Leeuw, Tillich *et al.*) to show the *G* as basically a religious document. The symbol of earth is discussed in detail, along with *numina agrestium,* the Aristaeus episode, rites, sacrifices, water divinities, immortality and the Golden Age. Dyer treats the positive, creative force of *amor* apart from erotic love. Farrington argues that V consciously rejected Lucretius' political defeatism and pessimistic outlook on human progress. Fischer treats geographical digressions and associates them with a wider context. Frentz's study of the use of mythology in *G* is a conscientious literary study with wider implication. Gandeva finds the *G* more appropriate for the manorial estate than the field worker or small farmer class. Hardie studies the complex of themes in *E* 6 and new themes in *G* 1-3 as preface to the Aristaeus epyllion. The underworld theme elsewhere prepares for the ultimate treatment in *G* 4. Such preparation for Orpheus could hardly have been prelude to *laudes Galli.* Political, moral and mystical interpretations of the Aristaeus myth are countered and expanded by Hardie's poetical exploration. Ketteman's dissertation treats deliverance as a basic motif of both *E* and *G,* the meaning of *otium, molle,* and *dulce* in the *G,* and the tension between the conceptual Golden Age and the world of the *E* and *G.* Liebeschuetz shows how Lucretius' treatment of the cycle of growth and decline in organic and inorganic nature influenced V. McKay's lecture explores V's successful marriage between technology and poetry with its overtones for our present environmental and cultural crisis. Maroti senses V's partisanship for Octavian and reflections of Julian propaganda in *G.* Miles concentrates on control as problematical and central to V's poem; the context is agricultural but the implications are universal. Mountford studies the plan of *G* introductions and epilogues, form, balance and coherent design throughout and in particular episodes. Parry moves from *G* 3,49-71 to a wider study of poetic invention and variety in connection with external phenomena and concentrates on *G* 4 where the 'suite' of thought and expression is most evident. Pridik's structural analysis and interpretation is most concerned with *G* 1,1-203 and *G* 4,281-558. Ruch (251) assesses the aesthetic, moral and philosophical implications of V's treatment of animals, the poet's empathy with his creatures, the sounds of the animals, their sufferings, and their reflex actions (*amor, furor*). Saint-Denis is convinced that Maecenas prompted the *G.* Callimachean influence and the *aition* aspect of *G* concern Shechter (and Hardie). Programmatic passages are examined in relation to *E* 6 and to Callimachus and Lucretius. Tanner suggests that the *G* were originally designed to honour Mark Antony prior to 34 B. C. The Aristaeus epyllion, originally perhaps a panegyric on the land and social organization of Egypt, favourable to Antony and Cleopatra, was revised to provide instruction for Octavian's rule. Wilhelm highlights Octavian as founder (*auctor*) of a new order and prosperity in new *Saturnia regna;* Aristaeus appears in the likeness of Cicero's *moderator rei publicae,* counterpart to Octavian, regenerator of his state (*regnum*) and sole ruler.

B. INDIVIDUAL BOOKS

Georgics 1

260. R. Andriani, "Un punto oscuro nel primo libro delle Georgiche," *RAAN* 39 (1964) 225-30.
261. V. Buchheit, "Vergil in Sorge um Oktavian (Zu Georg. I, 498ff.)," *RhM* 109 (1966) 78-83.
262. K. Büchner, "Der Eingang der Georgica," *Bardon* 70-91.
263. G. Doig, "Vergil, Georgics I, 491-2," *AJP* 86 (1965) 85-88.
264. H. Drexler, "Zu Vergil, Georg. I, 118-159," *RhM* 110 (1967) 165-74.
265. A. German, "On Georgics I," *CJ* 65 (1969-70) 263-66.
266. J. G. Griffith, "Luna and Ceres," *CP* 63 (1968) 143-54.
267. J. Martyn, "False Modesty in Vergil," *Vergilius* 15 (1969) 53-54.
268. A. Ruiz de Elvira, "Los problemas del proemio de la Géorgicas," *Emerita* 35 (1967) 45-54.
269. W. Steidle, "Die Anordnung der Arbeiten im ersten Buch von Vergils Georgica," *RhM* 109 (1966) 135-64.
270. G. Zalateo, "Da Omero a Vergilio," *Arctos* 6 (1970) 120-26.

According to Andriani, V's astronomical use of Taurus (217f.) was partial. Buchheit examines the *epicedion* factor in 498ff., and treats V's imitation of Catullus 64, 35-42 at 505-14. Büchner's critical analysis of the Prooemium is important. Doig detects Greek ambiguities and suggestions at 491-92. Drexler finds discrepancies in V's theodicy (118-59). German lauds V's common sense and observation in light of present farming techniques. Griffiths advances Apuleius *Met.* 11,2 to support the Luna-Ceres equation (5ff.). Martyn treats *G* 1,80-1 and Juvenal's parody (3,321-2). Ruiz de Elvira treats zodiacal matters and V's debt to Aratus. Steidle discovers systematic (but not seasonal) design in the farmer's fieldwork and resources (160ff., 204ff.). Zalateo finds Homeric precedent for *G* 1,382 (*densis alis*).

Georgics 2

271. I. Borszák, "Von Hippokrates bis Virgil," *Bardon* 41-55.
272. G. Castelli, "L'Ideale della vita agreste in Georg. II, 458-542," *Fons Perennis: Saggi critici di Filol. classica in Onore di V. Agostino* (Torino 1971) 81-105.
273. J. R. C. Martyn, "Virgilius Satiricus," *Martyn* 169-91.
274. A. G. McKay, "Vergil's Glorification of Italy (*Georgics* 11, 136-74)," *Martyn* 149-68.
275. E. Paratore, "Su Verg. Georg. II, 498," *Acta Philologica, III, piae memoriae N. I. Herescu* (Rome 1964) 269-98.
276. J. J. H. Savage, "The Wine of Maron," *TAPA* 96 (1965) 375-401.

Borszák argues that V's delineation of Italy is indebted to Polybius and Poseidonius. The *Laudes Italiae* are associated with Varro, *DRR* I, 2, 3-6. Castelli studies the design of the farmer's life. McKay provides analysis and commentary and highlights engineering feats in Campania. Martyn studies 458-540 for satirical attacks on those perennial victims of the satirist's lash, greed, luxury, and vain ambition. Paratore associates *perituraque regna* (2,498) with Roman imperium. Savage connects the Spercheos River, Taygetus, and Mount Haemus with V's personal names: Maro (recalling the Spartan hero Maron and Maronian wine of Ismarus) and Vergilius (the Pleiades).

Georgics 3

277. P. Brind'Amour, "Virgile et le dressage des chevaux," *Phoenix* 26 (1972) 187-88.

278. F. Capponi, "Un irreale ornitologico? (Georg., 3,338)," *Bardon* 92-96.
279. P. Grimal, "Invidia infelix et la 'conversion' de Virgile," *Bayet* 242-54.
280. J. Heurgon, "L'épizootie du Norique et l'histoire," *REL* 42 (1964) 231-47.
281. W. Liebeschuetz, "Beast and Man in the Third Book of Virgil's *Georgics,"* *G&R* 12 (1965) 64-77.
282. R. Martin, "Virgile et la Scythie (Géorgiques III, 349-83)," *REL* 44 (1966) 286-304.
283. D. M. Pippidi, "Les premiers rapports de Rome avec les cités grecques de l'Euxin," *REL* 47 (1969) 24-25.
284. D. M. Pippidi, "Notes de lecture, XVIII: A propos de l'hiver en Scythie," *StudClas* 10 (1968) 242-43.
285. L. P. Wilkinson, "Pindar and the proem to the third Georgic," *Forschungen zur römischen Literatur, Festschrift zum 60. Geburtstag von Karl Büchner* (2 vols.) (Wiesbaden 1970) 286-90.

Borszák (271) treats the Scythian excursus (349-83), the tripartite pattern of geography (Scythia, Italia, Libya), and indebtedness to Hippocrates and Poseidonius (cf. Diod. 5,25-32). Brind' Amour reads *pransique* at 207. Capponi struggles with the unidentifiable acalanthis and links it, by association, with *G* 2,328. Grimal argues that the proem was composed in 34 and revised in 29. The 'Apolline' temple foreshadows Octavian's supremacy and the pedimental figures, token of the new theology, offer a Last Judgment design. Epicurean *invidia* yields to divine immanence in V's conception of the world. Heurgon speculates freely on time and locale for the Noric plague. Book 3, for Liebeschuetz, operates on several levels: as textbook, as description of animal and human life cycles, and as evocation of forces (internal passions and external factors) which shape and determine men's lives and those of the higher animals. The gods are absent as determining factors. Martin regards the Scythian excursus as rhetorical and imaginary in the first section, as precise and historical (the imminent invasion of Moesia, 29 B. C.) in the second section. Pippidi (283) studies 349-83 as evidence for Roman expansion and responds to Martin (282). Wilkinson's Appendix III (258) discusses Pindaric inspiration for the proem.

Georgics 4

286. S. Byl, "De quelques erreurs scientifiques dans la quatrième Géorgique de Virgile," *LM* 16-17 (1968) 9-16.
287. E. Coleiro, "Allegory in the IVth Georgic," *Bardon* 113-23.
288. M. Detienne, "Orphée au miel," *Quaderni Urbinati* 12 (1971) 7-23.
289. J. P. Elder, "Gallus and the End of the Fourth *Georgic;* or How Long did the Bees Buzz the Praises of Gallus?" *RCANE* (April 5, 1963) 11-12.
290. O. M. Lee, "Virgil as Orpheus," *Orpheus* 11 (1964) 9-18.
291. M. Ruch, "La capture du devin," *REL* 44 (1966) 333-50.
292. C. P. Segal, "Orpheus and the fourth Georgic: Vergil on nature and civilization," *AJP* 87 (1966) 307-25.
293. P. L. Tozzi, "Iscrizione latine sull'arte lanaria bresciana e Virgilio, Georgiche IV, 277-8," *Athenaeum* 49 (1971) 152-57.
294. A. Wankenne, "Aristée et Orphée dans les Géorgiques," *LEC* 38 (1970) 18-29.
295. D. S. Wender. "Resurrection in the fourth Georgic," *AJP* 90 (1969) 424-36.
296. D. E. W. Wormell, "Apibus quanta experientia parcis: Virgil Georgics 4,1-227," *Bardon* 429-35.

Byl is critical of details in V's bee kingdom. Coleiro finds double allegory, one underlying the bee community, the other in the Aristaeus episode. Aristaeus' *crimen* towards Eurydice symbolizes Gallus' misdemeanor to Augustus; loss of bees and *amicitia* are the penalties. But Gallus could have shared Aristaeus' pardon with a more contrite attitude. Coleiro dates the second edition ca. 26 B. C. Detienne uses the techniques of a comparative religionist and treats the symbolic associations of honey and the Aristaeus episode. Elder is inclined to accept Servius' verdict about the revised version. Identification of Orpheus with V is Lee's deduction in his structural and allegorical study of the Aristaeus episode. Ruch argues that analogies between Livy 5,15 and Aristaeus' capture of the prophetic Proteus may have Etruscan overtones. Segal finds different attitudes to nature in Aristaeus and Orpheus; both frame the essentially tragic life of the bees. There is a thematic contrast of man and bees and a stylistic contrast between the two sections of the book, a Lucretian and a more Homeric, more characteristically Vergilian, half. Segal underlines the contrast between the 'real' world of the bees and the 'ideal' world of myth and poetry which is filled with death and disaster. Tozzi's remarks on *aster amellus*, a purple flower favoured by bees, and on a relevant artifact, endorse the accuracy of V's topography and geography of Cisalpine Gaul. Wankenne rejects Servius' comment on the Gallus eulogy; the present text evidences no haste and considerable maturity. Wender associates *G* 4 with *E* 3: there is no eternal life for Man but the farmer can participate in the annual rebirth of nature and the Roman people may attain everlasting life after the pattern of the bees. Wormell argues that the bees bridge the gap between the agricultural tragedy of *G* 3 and the human tragedy of *G* 4.

VI. THE AENEID

A. GENERAL STUDIES

297. L. Alfonsi, "Il mito di Pasifae in Virgilio," *Mythos: Scripta in hon. M. Untersteiner* (Genova 1970) 33-36.

298. W. S. Anderson, *The Art of the Aeneid* (Englewood Cliffs, N. J. 1969). Rev: Davis *CompLit* 24 (1972) 93-94; Duckworth *AJP* 92 (1971) 343-45; Hamilton *CP* 66 (1971) 215-17; Hornsby *CW* 64 (1970) 26; Robson *Phoenix* 25 (1971) 293; Rutledge *Vergilius* 16 (1970) 41-43.

299. W. S. Anderson, "Pastor Aeneas. On pastoral themes in the Aeneid," *TAPA* 99 (1968) 1-17.

300. C. R. Beye, *The Iliad, the Odyssey, and the Epic Tradition* (New York 1966) 206-34.

301. D. W. Black, "Epic and Encomium," *PVS* 8 (1968-69) 38-48.

302. R. Bloch, "A propos de l'Enéide de Virgile. Réflexions et perspectives," *REL* 45 (1967) 325-42.

303. R. Bohn, *Untersuchungen über das Motiv des gelobten Landes in Vergils Aeneis und im Alten Testament* (Freiburg 1965).

304. S. P. Bovie, "Manus. Virgil's Portraiture of Human Hands," *Minnesota Review* 4 (1964) 513-20.

305. A. J. Boyle, "The Meaning of the Aeneid. A Critical Inquiry: Part I — Empire and the Individual: An Examination of the Aeneid's Major Theme," *Ramus* 1 (1972) 63-90.

306. J. P. Brisson, "Carthage et le fatum. Réflexions sur un thème de l'Enéide," *Renard* 162-73.

307. J. P. Brisson, "Temps historique et temps mythique dans l'Enéide," *Bardon* 56-69.

308. W. A. Camps, *An Introduction to Virgil's Aeneid* (Oxford 1969). Rev: Austin *JRS* 60 (1970) 261-62; Clarke *CR* 85 (1971) 47; Currie *PVS* 8 (1968-69) 68-70; Duckworth *AJP* 92 (1971) 124-26; Dunkle *CW* 63 (1970) 240; Griffin *Hermathena* 110

(1970) 93-94; Grimal *REL* 47 (1969) 603-604; Huxley *Phoenix* 25 (1972) 205-206; Putnam *CJ* 66 (1970-71) 278-80; Westendorp Boerma *Mnem* 25 (1972) 205-206.

309. G. Carlozzo, "Motivi virgiliani di morte," *Atti dell'Accad. di Scienze, Lettere e Arti di Palermo* 31 (1970-71) 1-40.

310. W. Clausen, "An interpretation of the Aeneid," *HCSP* 68 (1964) 139-47.

311. A. Cook, *The Classical Line: A Study in Epic Poetry* (Bloomington, Indiana 1966) 177-210.

312. H. MacL. Currie, "The Sense of the Past in Virgil," *PVS* 2 (1962-63) 17-32.

313. P. Damon, "Myth, Metaphor and the Epic Tradition," *Orbis Litterarum* 24 (1969) 85-100.

314. C. G. Davis, Jr., *The voyage, the chariot race, and the hunt: three motifs in Vergil's Aeneid.* Diss. The University of North Carolina. Summary in *DA* 27 (1967) 3025A.

315. C. G. Davis, "The Motif of the Hunt in Vergil's Aeneid," *Landmarks in Western Culture: commentaries and controversies* (edd. D. N. Baker, G. W. Fasel) (Englewood Cliffs, N. J. 1968) 204-14.

316. D. E. Eichholz, "Symbol and contrast in the Aeneid," *G&R* 15 (1968) 105-12.

317. W. Fauth, "Funktion und Erscheinung niederer Gottheiten in Vergils Aeneis," *Gymnasium* 78 (171) 54-75.

318. G. K. Galinsky, *The Herakles Theme. The Adaptation of the Hero in Literature from Homer to the Twentieth Century* (Oxford 1972) 126-52.

319. K. Gilmartin, "Hercules in the *Aeneid,*" *Vergilius* 14 (1968) 41-47.

320. J. Glazewski S. C., *The integration of epic convention into the narrative development of the Aeneid.* Diss. Fordham University. Summary in *DA* 31 (1970) 2895A.

321. M. Grant, "Virgil the European," *PVS* 3 (1963-64) 1-11.

322. B. Grassmann-Fischer, *Die Prodigien in Vergils Aeneid* (München 1966). Rev: Binder *Gymnasium* 76 (1969) 121-24; Dick *CP* 63 (1968) 237-38; Heimann *CJ* 63 (1967) 90-92; Liénard *Latomus* 26 (1967) 1040-42; Lloyd *AJP* 90 (1969) 381; van Straten *Mnem* 23 (1970) 93-94; Wlosok *Gnomon* 45 (1973) 245-49.

323. A. Grillo, *Il sogno nell'epica Latina, tecnica e poesia* (Palermo 1967).

324. T. J. Haarhoff, "The Element of Propaganda in Vergil," *AClass* 11 (1968) 125-38.

325. E. A. Havelock, "History and Counter-History in the *Aeneid,*" *Ventures: Magazine of the Yale Graduate School* (Spring 1967) 40-46.

326. G. Highet, *The Speeches in Vergil's Aeneid* (Princeton 1972). Rev: Currie *PVS* 12 (1972-73) 54-55.

327. R. Hornsby, "Pastor in the poetry of Vergil," *CJ* 63 (1967-68) 145-52.

328. R. Hornsby, "The Armor of the Slain," *PhQ* 45 (1966) 347-59.

329. U. Huebner, *Elegisches in der Aeneis* (Giessen 1968).

330. L. Johnston, "Hic pietatis honos?" *CB* 47 (1971) 73-75.

331. H. Koch, "Einige Anspielungen auf Hintergründige Sachverhalte in den ersten vier Büchern der Aeneis," *SO* 42 (1967) 113-26.

332. E. Kraggerud, *Aeneisstudien. Symbolae Osloenses Supplement* 22 (Oslo 1968). Rev: von Albrecht *Gnomon* 41 (1969) 822-24; Cleary *CW* 62 (1969) 360; Eden *PVS* 8 (1968-69) 60-62; Galinsky *AJP* 91 (1970) 479-82; McKay *Phoenix* 23 (1969) 408-10; Perret *Latomus* 28 (1969) 505-507; Putnam *CP* 64 (1969) 256-57.

333. W. Kuehn, *Götterszenen bei Vergil* (Heidelberg 1970). Rev: Hornsby *CW* 66 (1972) 44; Boyancé *Latomus* 32 (1973) 636-37.

334. W. A. Laidlaw, "Virgil, Aeneid," *N&C* 8 (1965) 18-27.

335. A. La Penna, "Spunti sociologici per l'interpretazione dell'Eneide," *Bardon* 283-93.

336. F. J. Lelièvre, "Two supernatural incidents in the Aeneid," *PVS* 11 (1971-72) 74-77.

95

337. A. Lesky, "Zu Katalogen der Aeneis," *Forschungen zur römischen Literatur. Festschrift zum 60. Geburtstag von Karl Büchner* (Wiesbaden 1970) 189-96.

338. G. Lieberg, "Vergils Aeneis als Dichtung der Einsamkeit," *Bardon* 175-91.

339. R. W. Lowe, "La dernière vanité de l'homme," *LEC* 38 (1970) 30-34.

340. A. G. McKay, "Dulcia limina," *Newsletter. Classical Assoc. Empire State* 8 (1972) 5 (Summary).

341. L. A. MacKay, "Hero and Theme in the Aeneid," *TAPA* 94 (1963) 157-66.

342. L. A. MacKay, "The Aeneid as Anti-Epic," *CW* 57 (1963-64) 94.

343. J. S. M. Maguinness, "Heroism in Virgil," *PVS* 10 (1970-71) 45-56.

344. W. S. Maguinness, "L'inspiration tragique de l'Enéide," *AC* 32 (1963) 477-90.

345. P. McGushin, "Aeneas' Lasting City," *Latomus* 24 (1965) 411-20.

346. M. A. Malissard, "A propos du livre de P. Leglise, une oeuvre de pré-cinéma: l'Enéide," *Caesarodunum* 6 (1971) 82-89.

347. F. Mench, "Film Sense in the Aeneid," *Arion* 8 (1969) 381-97.

348. B. Morris, "Virgil and the Heroic Ideal," *PVS* 9 (1969-70) 20-34.

349. J. H. Mozley, "Contact between gods and mortals in Virgil," *PVS* 5 (1965-66) 50-52.

350. W. R. Nethercut, "Invasion in the Aeneid," *G&R* 15 (1968) 82-95.

351. W. R. Nethercut, "Three Mysteries in the Aeneid," *Vergilius* 19 (1973) 28-32.

352. W. R. Nethercut, "The Imagery of the Aeneid," *CJ* 67 (1971-72) 123-43.

353. B. Otis, "The Originality of the Aeneid," *Dudley* 27-66.

354. B. Otis, "Virgil and Clio. A consideration of Virgil's relation to history," *Phoenix* 20 (1966) 59-75.

355. M. L. Owens, "Comprehensiveness and purpose in the Aeneid," *CB* 42 (1966) 87, 89-90.

356. E. Paratore, "La storia di Roma nella poesia epica latina," *RAL* (1970) 143ff.

357. A. Parry, "The Two Voices of Virgil's Aeneid," *Arion* 2 (1963) 66-80.

358. Z. Pavlovskis, "Gli Achei nell'Eneide," *RIL* 103 (1969) 315-38.

359. J. Perret, "Optimisme et tragédie dans l'Enéide," *REL* 45 (1967) 324-62.

360. J. P. Poe, "Success and Failure in the Mission of Aeneas," *TAPA* 96 (1965) 321-36.

361. J. R. T. Pollard, "Something odd about Virgil," *PVS* 7 (1967-68) 41-58.

362. M. C. J. Putnam, *The Poetry of the Aeneid. Four Studies in Imaginative Unity and Design* (Cambridge, Mass. 1965). Rev: von Albrecht *Gnomon* 38 (1966) 564-68; Austin *JRS* 57 (1967) 280-81; Clarke *CR* 16 (1966) 324-25; Henry *CP* 61 (1966) 143-48; La Penna *Maia* 20 (1968) 49-54; Lloyd *AJP* 88 (1967) 476-79; Perret *Latomus* 24 (1965) 671-72; Robertson *PVS* 5 (1965-66) 59-62; *TLS* (July 2, 1964) 567; Tracy *CJ* 61 (1966) 372-73.

363. K. Quinn, *Virgil's Aeneid. A critical description* (London 1968). Rev: von Albrecht *Gnomon* 42 (1970) 94-95; Anderson *CW* 62 (1968) 22; Brisson *Latomus* 27 (1968) 920-21; Clarke *CR* 18 (1968) 306-308; Lloyd *AJP* 91 (1970) 363-67; Otis *CJ* 64 (1969) 371-74; Perret *REL* 46 (1968) 494-96; Putnam *Vergilius* 14 (1968) 1-3; Stégen *RBPh* 47 (1969) 613-14; Sullivan *CP* 64 (1969) 123-25; Westendorp Boerma *Mnem* 23 (1970) 444-45.

364. K. Quinn, "The Tempo of Virgilian Epic," *Latin Explorations* (London 1963) 198-238.

365. K. Quinn, "Did Virgil Fail?" *Martyn* 192-206.

366. K. Quinn, V. Pöschl, M. D. Snyder, J. Clack, "Vergil Engaged," *CW* 66 (1972) 65-75.

367. K. Quinn, "Some Dying Words: Tragic Insight in the *Aeneid* and the

Question of Virgil's Competence," *AUMLA* 22 (1964) 178-90.
368. H. Rey, *Die Bedeutung der Nacht in der epischen Erzählung der Aeneis* (Hamburg 1967).
369. R. Rieks, "Die Tränen des Helden," *Silvae: Festschrift für E. Zinn* (Tübingen 1970) 183-98.
370. R. Ruch, "Le destin dans l'Enéide: essence et réalité," *Bardon* 213-21.
371. W. J. N. Rudd, "The citadel in the Aeneid," *PCA* 67 (1970) 30.
372. H. C. Rutledge, "Vergil's Daedalus," *CJ* 62 (1967) 309-11.
373. E. de Saint-Denis, "Le sourire de Virgile," *Latomus* 23 (1964) 446-63.
374. F. H. Sandbach, "Anti-antiquarianism in the Aeneid," *PVS* 5 (1965-66) 26-38.
375. R. A. Sarno, "Vergil, reluctant secularist," *CB* 44 (1968) 49-54.
376. C. P. Segal, *"Aeternum Per Saecula Nomen,* The Golden Bough and the Tragedy of History," *Arion* 4 (1965) 617-57; 5 (1966) 34-72.
377. C. P. Segal, "Circean temptations: Homer, Vergil, Ovid," *TAPA* 99 (1968) 409-42.
378. M. Sordi, "Virgilio e la storia romana del IV sec. a. C.," *Athenaeum* 42 (1964) 80-100.
379. F. A. Sullivan, "Tendere manus. Gestures in the Aeneid," *CJ* 63 (1968) 358-62.
380. F. A. Sullivan, "Volcanoes and volcanic characters in Virgil," *CP* 67 (1972) 186-91.
381. A. A. Takho-Godi, "Valeur stylistique des thèmes chthoniens dans l'Enéide de Virgile," *Bardon* 358-74.
382. R. G. Tanner, "Some problems in Aeneid 7-12," *PVS* 10 (1970-71) 37-44.
383. D. Thompson, "Allegory and Typology in the Aeneid," *Arethusa* 3:2 (1970) 147-54.
384. A. Thornton, "Why did Virgil compose a 'Homeric epic'?" *Prudentia* 3:2 (1971) 75-98.
385. H. L. Tracy, *"Fata Deum* and the action of the *Aeneid," G&R* 11 (1964) 188-95.
386. E. Vance, "Warfare and the structure of thought in Virgil's *Aeneid," Quaderni Urbinati* 15 (1973) 111-62.
387. C. Weber, "The diction for death in Latin epic," *Agon* 3 (1969) 45-68.
388. T. Wiesner, "Buskined Maro. Tragic elements in the Aeneis," *CB* 44 (1968) 65-69.
389. R. D. Williams, "The mythology of the Aeneid," *Vergilius* 11 (1965) 11-15.
390. R. D. Williams, "The purpose of the Aeneid," *Antichthon* 1 (1967) 29-41.
391. R. D. Williams, "Theme and Mood in the Aeneid," *BICS* 14 (1967) 110-11.
392. R. D. Williams, "The Aeneid (30-19 B.C.)," *Virgil* (Greece and Rome, New Surveys of the Classics 1) 23-44.
393. R. D. Williams, *Aeneas and the Roman Hero* ('Inside the Roman World') (Basingstoke and London 1973).
394. W. Wimmel, *"Hirtenkrieg" und arkadisches Rom. Reduktionsmedien in Vergils Aeneis* (München 1973).
395. W. Wimmel, *Zur Frage von Vergils dichterischen Technik in der Aeneismitte. Der Beginn der Feindseligkeiten in Latium* (Marburg 1969). Rev: Bardon *REA* 72 (1970) 197-98; Camps *CR* 22 (1972) 108-109.
396. A. Wlosok, *Die Göttin Venus in Vergils Aeneis* (Heidelberg 1967). Rev: Clarke *CR* 18 (1968) 308-309; Fredricksmeyer *CW* 62 (1968) 15; Galinsky *AJP* 91 (1970) 97-99; Knecht *AC* 37 (1968) 304-305; Liénard *RBPh* 47 (1969) 615-16; Perret *Latomus* 37 (1968) 304-305.
397. J. W. Zarker, "The Hercules Theme in the Aeneid," *Vergilius* 18 (1972) 34-48.

See also *McKay, Otis, Williams.*

Otis' study of the *Aeneid* is a major achievement in Vergilian research. According to Otis, the Odyssean Aeneid, the subjective narrative of an inner psychological struggle, precedes the Iliadic Aeneid where objective narrative advances Aeneas' vindication of *pietas* by his victory over the impious and frenzied foe; destiny (Jupiter-*fatum*) and counter-destiny (Juno-*furor*) are active within the fabric. Structural analysis discloses continuity of narrative; theme, mood, similes, recurrent phrases and the implications of action are Otis' concerns. The real plot of the epic is "the formation and victory of the *Augustan* hero." Cross-references and reverberations are central to Putnam's study of *A* 2,5,8, and 12. Tension between the pastoral world and the world of energy and violence is paramount; it ends, without resolution, with Aeneas' final action "leaving Turnus victorious in his tragedy." The accumulation of images and themes from V's repertoire to prove this final point (and others) has been challenged, but Putnam's observations are always illuminating and helpful. Quinn's essays on tempo and tragic insight are companions to his critical study of the *A*. Chapters on the heroic impulse, and the genesis and structure of the epic, precede the analyses of the separate books. Chapters on form, technique, and style, poetic diction, meter, and imagery are judicious and instructive. Anderson discusses each book, comments on themes and poetic techniques, Homeric allusions, heroism and the divine factor, metaphors and similes. A final chapter treats problems of translation and the Vergilian style. Camps' Introduction chooses the topical approach (e.g., the higher powers, principles of structure, poetic expression, echoes of history, etc.), to give a balanced, humane estimate of the epic.

Boyle explores the disparity between the ideology of empire and the practice, the disparity between achievement and cost which pervades the epic. V, in Boyle's argument, is concerned "to emphasize that it is a victory for the forces of non-reason and the triumph not of *pietas* but of *furor*." Clausen's interpretation concentrates on the melancholy hero and the larger design of the epic which enlists sympathy on the side of loneliness, suffering and defeat. Kraggerud discusses Aeneas' character and his relation to Fate, the problem of the length of Aeneas' stay in Carthage, and the funeral games of Anchises, the last the most important. Parry examines V's public and private voices: Rome's triumph, and the regret and nostalgia which are pervasive. Themes and motifs engage Bovie (descriptive imagery and symbolic significance attaching to human hands), Davis, Galinsky (whose chapter on Roman Heracles is original and important), Nethercut, Rudd, Sullivan, and Zarker. Conventions concern Glazewski, Hornsby, Anderson, Morris (who finds a decline in human and individual personality as cost of heroic endurance), Thornton (alert to moral instruction in the epic, Homer's poetry combined with a paedeutic) and Williams, whose searching essays are valuable on every count. Religious aspects are highlighted by Grassmann-Fischer on prodigies, Kuehn (on V's use of divine machinery), and Wlosok, whose study of Venus as force and character includes many structural and rhetorical problems.

Historical and political associations engage Haarhoff (the Dido episode), MacKay (341 — The Trojan War is civil war; Aeneas is a conscripted man in a "war-novel" where morality, human and divine, is questionable), Sordi, and Vance (on Aeneas' second thoughts and the interior states of heroes). Havelock's verdict is challenging: "If in the first six books, V remembered the agony and moral cost of the conflict with Carthage, in the last six...he puts on record his own interpretation of the civil wars of the first century B.C., which left Augustus to preside over a ravaged countryside, and an exhausted people."

Highet's analysis and classification of every speech include models, structural analyses, and their importance for characterization. V emerges as a master dramatist as well as an epic poet; the speeches offer some of V's most subtle and most powerful achievements in style and meter.

Cinematic aspects of V's art are detected by Malissard and Mench (who explores *A* 4,10, and 12 from the standpoint of a film-maker: montage, variation of viewing angle, alternation of close-up and distance-shot, etc.). Black stresses epinician features in the technique and spirit of the epic. Bloch treats Servius *ad Aen.* 1,422,411 and 3,42 (Polydorus). Eichholz studies *A* 1,740-47 and 748-49; and *A* 6,20-33, where Daedalus represents the failed creative genius as opposed to Aeneas whose creation will be momentous and durable. Grant finds that V discriminates against Asiatics but favours Greeks. Harrison opposes the oral poet's subtlety with V's counterparts (death of Turnus, Creusa's and Anchises' shades). Laidlaw's essay is general but competent. La Penna finds Homeric and contemporary models from the revolutionary age for Drances, Nisus and Euryalus. MacKay, Maguinness on tragic inspiration, and Wiesner on tragic elements, are useful. Nethercut examines the "mysterious" death of Palinurus, the gate of false dreams, and Turnus' rock (*A* 12,896-907), and assesses the invasion factor as an undercurrent to the Trojan mission and to Aeneas' dubious heroism and destiny. Pavlovskis (*contra* Grant) finds V antipathetic to the Greek-Achaean element although Augustan propaganda embraced all peoples. Pollard deals with problems attaching to the Laocoon episode, the shield of Aeneas, the Messianic Eclogue, etc., somewhat despairingly. The television debate involving Quinn, Pöschl and others (366) examines, *inter alia*, the characteristics of Aeneas, his limitations, his likeness to Augustus and his *humanitas*. Quinn (365) speculates on the original design of the epic and the poet's travails as he reworked his prose version into the final poem where shifts are sometimes evident and lend some element of confusion. Rieks studies lacrimose scenes in the epic; tears help to shape the structure of the poem. Saint-Denis treats the lighter side (never uproarious) and Perret touches the poles of optimism and pessimism. Rutledge analyzes Daedalus as symbolic master artist. Sandbach finds the anachronistic material background of ships, architecture, armour, and siege equipment lends support to the contemporaneity of the story. Chthonic themes, according to Takho-Godi, are symptoms of discordant, impetuous, irrational, and hidden factors and contribute substantially to the progress and meaning of the epic. Tanner submits *A* 7-12 to allegorical interpretation and provides some startling equations: Evander = Cicero, Cacus = Catiline, Achates = Agrippa, Drances = L. Munatius Plancus, etc. Thompson urges caution and careful distinction between allegory and typology as poet's motive. Wimmel treats *A* 5-8 as the Alexandrian center between the Odyssean (1-4) and Iliadic (9-12) portions and underscores the importance of pastoral and rural elements as minor motifs in the ultimate "quartet" of conflicts. Hornsby's article on the pastor complements Anderson's on pastoral themes. Elsewhere Hornsby attaches ominous associations to armour rather than valour or heroism; the wearing of someone else's armour suggests deceit and spells disaster. Otis (354) and Segal (376) are both concerned with V's view of history; Segal's discussion is profitable and influential; Otis comments on the Roman concern with the subjective, personal, uniquely temporal factor, unlike Homer and the Greeks; Augustine's Roman view of history's goal is religious; V's is more patriotic, political, or ethical. Sullivan's article on gestures complements Bovie's. Etna's eruption (*A* 3,571ff.) recalls Pindaric and Lucretian passages, and, as Sullivan shows, volcanic fire often appears in characterizations. Circe, in Segal's view (377), serves as mythical counterpart to Allecto, both of them brutalizing agents.

B. INDIVIDUAL BOOKS

Aeneid 1

398.   R. G. Austin, *"Ille ego qui quondam,"* *CQ* 18 (1968) 107-15.

399.   A. Fontãn, "Los poemas virgilianos los tres stili y il rota Vergili," *Actas* II 368-74.
400.   P. A. Hansen, "Ille Ego Qui Quondam . . . Once Again," *CQ* 22 (1972) 139-48.
401.   E. J. Kenney, "The incomparable poem the 'Ille Ego'," *CR* 20 (1970) 290.
402.   R. E. V. Pearce, "A note on Ille ego qui quondam . . .," *CQ* 20 (1970) 335-38.
403.   G. Stégen, "Le prologue de l'Enéide," *LEC* 39 (1971) 199-214.
404.   M. von Albrecht, "Die Kunst der Vorbereitung in Aeneis-Prooemium," *Antidosis. Festschr. für W. Kraus* (Wien 1972) 7-20.
405.   J. P. Bews, "Aeneid I and .618," *Phoenix* 24 (1970) 130-43.
406.   V. Buchheit, "Aeneas vor Karthago (Au. Aen. I, 419f., 441ff.)," *Gymnasium* 71 (1964) 429-33.
407.   A. J. Dunston, "Aeneid I and IV: The Artistry of the Prologue and of the Tragedy," *Arts. Journal of the Sydney University Arts Association* (Michaelmas Term, 1967) 22-35.
408.   G. K. Galinsky, "*Troiae qui primus ab oris* . . . (Aen. I,1)," *Latomus* 28 (1969) 3-18.
409.   T. Halter, "Vergils Aeneis-Proomium. Eine Deutung," *WS* 77 (1964) 76-109.
410.   E. L. Harrison, "Why did Venus wear boots? Some reflections on *Aeneid* 1, 314," *PVS* 12 (1972-73) 10-25.
411.   L. Herrmann, "*Crinitus Iopas* (Virgile, Eneide I,740)," *Latomus* 26 (1967) 474-76.
412.   B. Kiefer, "A note on Aeneid 1.495-504 and 4.141-150," *CJ* 67 (1971-72) 178.
413.   H. Koch, "Mathematische, symmetrische and rhythmische Komposition im 1. Buch der Aeneis," *SO* 45 (1970) 74-112.
414.   H. Koch, "Zur Gliederung von Aeneis I und IV," *Gymnasium* 73 (1966) 506-13.
415.   A. Pagliaco, "Sur lacrimae rerum," *Maia* 1 (1948) 114-128.
416.   C. Segal, "The Song of Iopas in the Aeneid," *Hermes* 99 (1971) 336-49.
417.   K. Stanley, "Irony and Foreshadowing in Aeneid I, 462," *AJP* 86 (1965) 267-77.
418.   H. P. Stahl, "Verteidigung des I. Buches der Aeneis," *Hermes* 97 (1969) 346-61.
419.   D. J. Stewart, "Sunt lacrimae rerum," *CJ* 67 (1971-72) 116-22. (Contrast 942).
420.   R. D. Williams, "The opening scenes of the Aeneid," *PVS* 5 (1965-66) 14-23.
421.   J. Wright, "Lacrimae rerum and the thankless task," *CJ* 62 (1967) 365-67.

The authenticity of the four verses (*ille ego . . . Martis*) allegedly removed by Varius, remains contested: Camps (308, Appendix 2), Austin, Kenney, and Fontãn argue against genuineness on grounds of MS authority, style, expression, and convention. Hansen and Stégen favour V's authorship; Pearce regards the lines as derivative from V. Editions should probably retain the lines in brackets.

Bews argues against Duckworth's subject divisions and discounts .618 ratios in *A* 1. Galinsky stresses the Italian aspect of V's epic with Aeneas replacing Ulysses. Von Albrecht and Halter consider the structure of the proem, the equilibrium of the verses. Herrmann identifies long-haired Iopas with Maecenas; his cosmological song, recalling the Orpheus-song in *Argonautica*, is treated by Segal in a larger context. Koch, contrary to Bews, supports Duckworth's mathematical thesis but also accents thematic design and common motifs and structural correspondences between *A* 1 and 4. Kiefer discusses the impossibility of a Dido-Aeneas union. Stanley detects prophetic assessment and tragic reflection in the temple pictures and forecast of later events. Stahl eliminates conflict between the two divine missions of Mercury and Amor. Stewart interprets *lacrimae rerum* as "the events of the past (which are dead and thus *mortalia*) do not lose their power to affect our minds in the present;" Wright favours Stanyhursts' 1582 translation of *A* 1,461-2. Williams examines themes, levels of meaning, imagery and moral values, and Jupiter's speech to Venus.

Aeneid 2

422. C. Bullock-Davies, "The image of the limen in Aeneid II," *G&R* 17 (1970) 135-41.
423. G. Dumézil, "La lance de Laocoon (Enéide, II,50-53)," *Hommages à M. Delcourt. Collection Latomus* 114 (1970) 196-206.
424. W. von Englehart, "Der vom Himmel gefallene Stern. Zu Vergil, Aeneis II, 692-700," *Hellas und Hesperien. Gesammelte Schriften zur Antike und zur Neueren Literatur* (edd. Bartels, Thurow, Zinn) (Stuttgart 1970) 459-75.
425. J. Foster, "Virgil, Aeneid II 446f.," *CR* 22 (1972) 304.
426. E. L. Harrison, "Divine Action in Book Two," *Phoenix* 24 (1970) 320-32.
427. J. M. Hoek, "Sino en Dido. Errare humanum," *Hermeneus* 36 (1965) 172-82.
428. A. de Marino, "La fine di Laocoonte e l'uccisione di Priamo nell' Eneide," *Vichiana* 4 (1967) 92-94.
429. J. M. Mir, "Laocoontis embolium. Aen. 2,40-50, 199-227," *Latinitas* 17 (1969) 96-112.
430. J. Mountford, "Tempo and Texture in Aeneid II," *PVS* 8 (1968-9) 26-38.
431. H. Paoletta, "Graecus ille dolis instructus et arte pelasga (Aen. II, 153)," *Latinitas* 16 (1968) 251-67.
432. G. Sanderlin, "Vergil's Protection of Aeneas in Aeneid II," *CW* 66 (1972) 82-84.
433. J. Sanz Ramos, "Notas al libro II de la Eneida," *EClás* 10 (1966) 149-68.
434. G. Stégen, "Une prétendue contradiction dans l'Enéide (II, 567-88)," *LEC* 35 (1967) 3-6.
435. H. Steinmeyer, "Die Laokoonszene in Vergils Aeneis (Aeneis II, 40-66 und 199-233)," *AU* 10 (1967) 5-28.
436. J. van Ooteghem, "Le sac de Troie chez Plaute," *LEC* 34 (1966) 51-54.

Bullock-Davies attaches thematic importance to thresholds which have tragic connotations deriving perhaps from Homer's "threshold of old age." Dumézil finds intimations of the October Horse in Laocoon's javelin throw. Von Englehart studies the star prodigy and its meaning. Foster translates 446f., "since they are fighting for their lives." Harrison is conscious of Iliadic influences in *A* 2,589ff., and traditional elements in the wooden horse episode include the Helen episode (authentic). Marino couples the Laocoon and Priam deaths as alpha and omega of Troy's tragedy. Marino senses tragic theater in both episodes, pity and fear, and ritual sacrifice. Mir's analysis of the Laocoon episode is exemplary. Mountford analyzes 626-31, 601-31, 54-56, 195-98, 203-11 etc., with attention to language variations and rhythmic response to changes in pace. Hoek and Paoletta study Sinon; Paoletta concentrates on *ambiguitas* and character originality. Steinmeyer contrasts V's Laocoon episode with Homer and Arctinus and accents novel dramatic, psychological and religious factors. Stégen retains the Helen episode as authentic. Van Ooteghem compares Plautus and V on the sack of Troy.

Aeneid 3

437. P. V. Cova, "Il tema del viaggio e l'unità del libro terzo dell' Eneide," *Aevum* 39 (1965) 441-73.
438. J. R. Dunkle, "Some historical symbolism in book three of the Aeneid," *CW* 62 (1969) 165-66.
439. J. Glenn, "Virgil's Polyphemus," *G&R* 19 (1972) 47-59.

440. R. E. Grimm, "Aeneas and Andromache in Aeneid III," *AJP* 88 (1967) 151-62.
441. G. Gutu, "Sur la composition du IIIe livre de l'Enéide," *StudClas* 9 (1967) 167-80.
442. A. G. McKay, "The Achaemenides Episode, Vergil, Aeneid III, 588-691," *Vergilius* 12 (1966) 31-38.
443. C. F. Saylor, "Toy Troy. The new perspective of the backward glance," *Vergilius* 16 (1970) 26-28.
443a. G. Thaniel, "A note on Aeneid 3.623-626," *CB* 50 (1973) 10-12.
444. H. L. Tracy, "Aeneas' Visit to Buthrotum," *Class. News & Views* (*EMC*) 11 (1967) 1-3.

Cova highlights the psychological wear and tear of the wanderings; Dunkle assesses them as reflection of Rome's experience and weariness with civil war. Glenn offers an incisive study of the Polyphemus incident. Grimm comments on divergence of viewpoints (300-343, 482-505) and the merits of the lines. Gutu defines Apollo's central importance in *A* 3 as response to Octavian's religious inclinations and detects a patriotic fervour and anti-Eastern viewpoint. McKay finds Parthian associations for the Achaemenides episode and argues for its late insertion. The passage has implications for Augustus' diplomatic coup in the East and vindicates his policy of restraint. Saylor and Tracy study the Buthrotum incident.

Aeneid 4

445. G. Ameye, "*Eadem impia Fama . . . detulit* (Virgile, Enéide IV, 298-299)," *REL* 44 (1966) 305-32.
446. A. A. Barrett, "Anna's conduct in Aeneid 4," *Vergilius* 16 (1970) 21-25.
447. A. A. Barrett, "Dido's Child: a note on Aeneid 4.327-330," *Maia* 24 (1973) 51-53.
448. J. M. Benario, "Dido and Cleopatra," *Vergilius* 16 (1970) 2-6.
449. P. Boyancé, "Virgile et Atlas," *Mélanges d'Histoire ancienne offerts à William Seston* (Paris 1973).
450. A. J. Boyle, "Homo immemor. Book 4 and its thematic ramifications," *Ramus I* (1972) 113-51.
451. G. S. Duclos, "Nemora inter Cresia," *CJ* 66 (1971) 193-95.
452. J. Ferguson, "Fire and Wound: the imagery of Aeneid iv.1ff.," *PVS* 10 (1970-71) 57-63.
453. G. H. Gellie, "Juno and Venus in Aeneid IV," *Hunt Studies* (ed. Martyn) 138-48.
454. C. H. Gordon, "Vergil and the Near East," *Ugaritica VI: Mission de Ras Shamra Tome XVII* (Paris 1969) 267-88.
455. J. N. Grant, "Dido Melissa," *Phoenix* 23 (1969) 380-91.
456. H. H. Huxley, " 'It' in Virgil," *Classical Folia* 27 (1973) 88-92.
457. H. H. Huxley, "Anna Achatae," *Latinitas* 17 (1969) 282.
458. G. Kilroy, "The Dido episode and the sixty-fourth poem of Catullus," *SO* 44 (1969) 48-60.
459. C. Kubik, "Gegenstände als Bedeutungssträger im 4 Buch der *Aeneis*," *AU* 13:5 (1970) 78-89.
460. A. La Penna, "Amata e Didone," *Maia* 19 (1967) 309-18.
461. J. Perret, "Amour et mariage dans l'épisode de Didon," *Bayet* 538-43.
462. K. Quinn, "The fourth book of the Aeneid. A critical description," *G&R* 12 (1965) 16-26.
463. G. Sanderlin, "Point of View in Virgil's Fourth Aeneid," *CW* 63 (1969) 81-85.

464. G. Stégen, *Le Plan de IV* ᵉ *livre de l'Énéide avec un commentaire* (Namur 1970). Rev: Cupaiuolo *BollStLat* 1 (1971) 502.
465 A. M. Tuppet, "Didon magicienne," *REL* 48 (1970) 229-58.
466. A. Wankenne, S. J., "La part des dieux dans le IVᵉ chant de l'Enéide; un principe d'explication psychologique," *LEC* 37 (1969) 162-66.
467. R. D. Williams, "Dido's reply to Aeneas (Aen. 4.362-387)," *Bardon* 422-28.

Quinn's article on V's dramatic masterpiece favours tripartite construction; Dido's retreat from reality and her gradual breakdown are underscored. Stégen's study is somewhat conventional. Sanderlin stresses the magnitude of Aeneas' sacrificial departure. Dido's character never lacks comment. Ameye finds vilification of Dido's *furor* in *eadem et impia* (298) with reference to *armari classem cursumque* (299). Barrett detects correspondences between Dido-Aeneas and Cleopatra-Caesar; Benario argues for V's familiarity with Cleopatra's characteristics and Horace's portrait (*Odes* 1,37). Boyle's wide-ranging article treats distraction, Aeneas *immemor*, and the inevitability of human failure. Duclos finds subtle allusion to the Ariadne legend and pertinence to Dido's tragedy in the Cretan references. Ferguson's study of fire and wound imagery notes the absence of the hearth-fire of domesticity and family life; wounds are associated with disease and hunt, both closely allied with Dido's symptoms and experience. Grant compares *G* 4,156-69 and *A* 1,430-6 and shows that the bee simile inspired a sequence of images about Dido. Huxley on *A* 4,402-7 examines the simile and comments on meter, lexicography and entomology. The similar careers of Dido and Amata concern La Penna and Zarker. Williams studies stylistic and metrical features of Dido's rhetorical speech as integral to her frenzied progression towards disaster. Gellie, Kubik, and Wankenne study divine interventions. Kilroy and Ferguson study Catullian influence (64), an important, influential factor. Gordon detects Near Eastern parallels in the Aeneas-Dido tragedy indicating that intercourse denoted marriage to Semitic minds. Perret discounts "Love Deceived" in favour of improper marriage vows properly broken, a vindication of Platonic eros. Witchcraft and character engage Tuppet.

Aeneid 5

468. S. Bertman, "The Generation Gap and Aeneid 5," *Vergilius* 17 (1971) 9-12.
469. G. K. Galinsky, "Aeneid V and the Aeneid," *AJP* 89 (1968) 157-85.
470. Sister Johanna Glazewski, "The Function of Vergil's Funeral Games," *CW* 66 (1972) 85-96.
471. H. A. Harris, "The games in Aeneid V," *PVS* 8 (1968-69) 14-26.
472. J. R. C. Martyn, "False Modesty in Vergil," *Vergilius* 15 (1969) 53-54.
473. H. Opperman, "Vergil, Aeneis V. 847 und die Palinurus episode," *Hermes* 99 (1971) 164-73.
474. T. E. V. Pearce, "Virgil Aeneid 5.279," *CQ* 20 (1970 154-59.
475. T. Smerdel, "La scena tragica di Palinuro," *ZAnt* 15 (1965-66) 350-64.
476. P. Somville, "Sur quelques vers de Virgile," *LEC* 39 (1971) 360-63.
477. G. Stégen, "Des régates dans l'Enéide (Virg. Aen. V,151-243)," *Latomus* 27 (1968) 600-609.
478. G. Stégen, "Un match de pugilat vu par Virgile (Énéide V,362-472)," *Bardon* 344-57.
479. G. Thaniel, "Ecce . . . Palinurus," *AClass* 15 (1972) 149-52.

Bertman notes the polarity of generations as symbolic, forceful exposition. Theme, events, references, and imagery, Galinsky suggests, offer analogues with the entire epic; Sicily's importance to Rome-Carthage relations and to the Trojan origins of Rome (Anchises, Eryx, Venus) is pendant to the national experience of Sicily and

Rome. Glazewski's account of the funeral games, imitation, invention, and applications is complemented by Harris' study of the sporting events, stock devices for entertainment, with some originality (boat race). Martyn scores V's aversion to earthy realism in *A* 5,353-58 (modelled on *Iliad* 23,777-81). Palinurus engages Oppermann, Smerdel (on tragic elements and design), Somville (V's sensitivity), and Thaniel who explores problematical links between *A* 5 and 6. Stégen's critiques of the boat race and boxing match explore structure and realism.

Aeneid 6

480. M. von Albrecht, "Vergils Geschichtsauffassung in der 'Heldenschau'," *WS* 80 (1967) 156-82.
481. M. von Albrecht, "Die Kunst der Spiegelung in Vergils Aeneis," *Hermes* 93 (1965) 54-64.
482. R. G. Austin, "Aeneid VI. 384-476," *PVS* 8 (1968-69) 51-60.
483. W. T. Avery, "The reluctant golden bough," *CJ* 61 (1966) 269-72.
484. J. J. Bray, "The ivory gate," *For Service to Classical Studies. Essays in Honour of Francis Letters* (Melbourne 1966) 55-69.
485. W. A. Camps, "The role of the sixth book in the Aeneid," *PVS* 11 (1967-68) 22-30.
486. J. H. D'Arms, "Vergil's cunctantem (ramum), Aeneid VI,211," *CJ* 59 (1964) 265-68.
487. F. Dupont and J. P. Neraudau, "Marcellus dans le chant VI de l'Enéide," *REL* 48 (1970) 259-79.
488. R. Hanslik, "Lokale inkonzinnitäten vor dem Palast des Hades in Vergils Aeneis vi," *Festschrift Karl Vetska* (edd. Ableitinger and Gugel) (Heidelberg 1970) 68-73.
489. L. Herrmann, "Le puer du sixième chant de l'Enéide," *Latomus* 24 (1965) 421-22.
490. W. F. Jackson-Knight, "Virgil's Elysium," Dudley 161-75.
491. Hans-Albrecht Koch, "Zum Verständnis von Vergil, *Aeneis* 6,205ff.," *WS* 81 (1968) 70-73.
492. E. Kraggerud, "Caeneus und der Heroinenkatalog, Aeneis VI,440ff.," *SO* 40 (1965) 66-71.
493. S. Kresic, "Le Rameau d'or chez Virgile," *EMC* 12 (1968) 92-102.
494. F. Loretto, "Die Gedankenfolge in Vergils Heldenschau," *Hans Gerstinger: Festgabe zum 80 Geburtstag* (Graz 1967) 41-51.
495. M. Lossau, "Bedingt episches iucundus bei Vergil," *Eranos* 68 (1970) 109-14.
496. H. Mörland, "Zu Aeneis VI,601ff.," *SO* 39 (1964) 5-12.
497. J. Perret, "Les compagnes de Didon aux Enfers (Aen. VI,445-449)," *REL* 42 (1964) 247-61.
498. R. Petzinger, "Patterns, proportions and paragraphing in Aeneid VI," *CW* 60 (1967) 313-15.
499. H. C. Rutledge, "The Opening of Aeneid 6," *CJ* 67 (1971-2) 110-15.
500. O. Seel, "Vergil und die Schuld des Helden (Aeneis VI.468)," *Verschlüsselte Gegenwart. Drei Interpretationen antiker Texte* (Stuttgart 1972) 95-110.
501. C. Segal, "The hesitation of the golden bough. A reexamination," *Hermes* 96 (1968) 74-79.
502. A. Setaioli, "Quisque suos patimur manes (Verg., Aen. VI,743)," *A&R* 12 (1967) 169-72.
503. A. Setaioli, "Noviens Styx interfusa," *A&R* 14 (1969) 9-20.
504. E. Skard, "Die Heldenschau in Vergils Aeneis," *SO* 40 (1965) 53-65.

505. F. Solmsen, "The World of the Dead in Book 6 of the Aeneid," *CP* 67 (1972) 31-41.
506. G. Stégen, "Le supplice de Phlegyas, Etude sur un episode de l'Enéide," *Latomus* 26 (1967) 118-22.
507. G. Stégen, "Le vestibule des Enfers (VI,273-294)," *Otia* 15 (1967) 75-79.
508. G. Stégen, "Les victimes aux enfers, Aen., VI,426-449," *LEC* 38 (1970) 230-36.
509. G. Stégen, "Virgile et la métempsycose (Aen. VI,724-751)," *AC* 36 (1967) 144-58.
510. E. Swoboda, "Zur Frage der Romanisierung, Aen. VI, 851f.," *AAWW* 100 (1963) 153-73.
511. G. Thaniel, "Vergil's Leaf-and-Bird Similes of Ghosts," *Phoenix* 25 (1971) 237-45.
512. H. Wagenvoort, "The Journey of the Souls of the Dead to the Isles of the Blest," *Mnem* 24 (1971) 113-61.
513. R. D. Williams, "The Pageant of Roman Heroes — Aeneid 6,756-853," *Martyn* 207-17.
514. R. D. Williams, "The Sixth Book of the Aeneid," *G&R* 11 (1964) 48-63.
515. R. D. Williams, "Virgil's Underworld — the opening scenes (Aen. 6.268-416)," *PVS* 10 (1970-71) 1-7.
516. J. W. Zarker, "Aeneas and Theseus in Aeneid VI," *CJ* 62 (1967) 220-26.

Camps assesses *A* 6 as V's response to *Odyssey* 11, a Roman counterpart designed to highlight Rome's destiny and accent Aeneas' piety to Anchises. Conflict exists between the divine benevolence towards the Roman state and cruelty towards its servants. Poetry, folklore, philosophy and religion merge in V's afterlife. Williams detects hope, patriotic fervor and clear insight in Aeneas' character in *A* 6. Petzinger follows Duckworth in the division of *A* 6,886-901, into three parts. The Bough continues to resist ultimate definition. Segal's large-scale study of the imagery of the bough (376) includes connotations of suffering and immortality, death associations, and pertinence to Misenus and Palinurus. D'Arms interprets the bough's reluctance as beauty's resistance to violence; Avery interprets *cunctantem* as pulled rather than severed; Kresic favours symbolic interpretation over alternative approaches; Segal interprets *cunctantem* as denoting the reluctant passage of primeval woods of mythical peacetime to historical reality. Hades and its denizens occupies Austin, who analyzes comic elements in the Charon interview and tragic features in the Dido encounter; Hanslik, who comments on Rhadamanthys' location; Perret, who studies the preliminaries to Dido's apparition; and Mörland, who treats V's originality in the punishments of Lapiths, Ixion, and Pirithous. Jackson Knight discovers two religions and two systems of belief about life and death, Platonic and Homeric. Setaioli argues that *A* 6,439 was inspiration for *G* 4,480. Solmsen argues that a tripartite scheme is irrelevant or inadequate over against a dual design. Solmsen also notes that the meaning of life is made apparent in a divine world scheme significantly prior to the galaxy of warriors and statesmen. Stégen (508) detects a structural pattern in the list of victims of destiny and love (426-39; 440-49). Thaniel answers Clarke's article (1006) on leaf- and bird-similes in connection with the Orphic catabasis. Williams illustrates V's method of employing traditional material as background for what is special and personal to himself and the poem. Williams deals mainly with the shapes at the entrance, Charon and his boat, and Palinurus' shade. Von Albrecht recalls the *Teichoscopia* (*Iliad* 3) as background to V's parade of heroes, a three-part progression (760-807; 808-53; 855ff.). The order is determined not by chronology but by types of influential men and prototypes. Dupont and Neraudau assess Marcellus' death as preparation for Rome's imminent rebirth. Herrmann regards Marcellus as *puer* of *E* 4. Skard suggests that *pompa funebris* practices (cf. Polybius 6,53) lie behind the marchpast of heroes rather than any Pythagorean or Orphic belief. Williams treats the pageant as an historical review. Setaioli (502) advances *Culex* 374: each soul meets its just deserts but all must enter Elysium and proceed towards their destiny. On metempsychosis Stégen (509) interprets *exinde* (743) as "from this earth" and reviews the composition of the passage (724-51). Rutledge examines Daedalus as mythological prototype of Augustus, as an *alter Aeneas* with a story as passionate as the Trojan hero's; Aeneas confronts Roman history rather than Minoan legend on the Shield (*A* 8). Theseus and Aeneas have similar life patterns, but Zarker attributes Theseus' failure to his lack of *pietas*.

Aeneid 7

517. R. Merkelbach, "Aineia nutrix," *RhM* 114 (1971) 349-51.
518. M. C. J. Putnam, "Aeneid VII and the Aeneid," *AJP* 91 (1970) 408-30.
519. E. Smith, "Latinus and the climax of Aeneid 7," *CB* 44 (1968) 85-87.

Putnam's study of metamorphosis in *A* 7 includes Circe, countryfolk, and peace and their brutal transformations. Aeneas is associated with *somnia vana* which exit by the gate of *falsa insomnia* and with the monsters which recur in *A* 8. Putnam argues that Aeneas at the close of *A* 10 and 12 himself undergoes a transformation from *pietas* to forgetfulness with respect to Anchises' injunctions. Merkelbach studies the obituary notice of Caieta.

Aeneid 8

520. C. Becker, "Der Schild des Aeneas," *WS* 77 (1964) 111-27.
521. J. T. Benade, "Enkele voorbeelde van Vergilius-imitatio in bk. VIII van die Aeneis," *Studies opgedra aan H. L. Gonin* (Pretoria 1971) 7-37.
522. G. Binder, *Aeneas und Augustus. Interpretationen zum 8 Buch der Aeneis.* (Meisenheim am Glan 1971). Rev: Perret *REL* 49 (1971) 439-40; Eden *JRS* 62 (1972) 221-23.
523. M. J. Cannon, S. J., "Vergil's Characterization in the Eighth *Aeneis*," *CB* 43 (1967) 85-87.
524. P. T. Eden, "The Salii on the Shield of Aeneas: Aeneid 8,663-6," *RhM* 116 (1973) 78-83.
525. D. E. Eichholz, "The shield of Aeneas. Some elementary notions," *PVS* 6 (1966-67) 45-49.
526. G. K. Galinsky, "The Hercules-Cacus episode in Aeneid VIII," *AJP* 87 (1966) 18-51.
527. G. K. Galinsky, "Hercules and the Hydra (Verg. Aen. 8,299-300)," *CP* 67 (1972) 197.
528. E. V. George, *Aeneid VIII and the Aitia of Callimachus.* Diss. University of Wisconsin. Summary in *DA* 28 (1967) 648A.
529. R. Girod, "Un western dans l'antiquité. Virgile, Enéide, VIII,175-275," *Caesarodunum* 4 (1969) 181-89.
530. J. G. Griffith, "Again the Shield of Aeneas (Aeneid VIII 625-31)," *PVS* 7 (1967-8) 54-65.
531. W. Heilman, "Aeneas und Evander im achten Buch der Aeneis," *Gymnasium* 78 (1971) 76-89.
532. G. Highet, "A Dissertation on Roast Pig," *CW* 67 (1973) 14-15.
533. W. Huebner, "Pontem indignatus Araxes (Verg. Aen. VIII,728)," *Lemmata Donum natalicium W. Ehlers* (Munich 1968) 103-110.
534. P. McGushin, "Virgil and the spirit of endurance," *AJP* 85 (1964) 225-53.
535. E. Paratore, "Hercule et Cacus chez Virgile et Tite-Live," *Bardon* 260-82.

536. A. Perutelli, "Un interpretazione dell'VIII libro dell' Eneide," *Maia* 25 (1973) 67-71.
537. J. Sanz Ramos, "La leyenda de Hercules y Caco en Virgilio y en Livio," *Actas* 2 389-400.
538. R. J. Rowland, "Foreshadowing in Vergil, Aeneid VIII, 714-28," *Latomus* 27 (1968) 832-42.
538a. D. West, *Individual Voices: Inaugural Lecture* (Newcastle Upon Tyne 1970), 14-17. (*A* 8,404-15).
539. M. Wigodsky, "The arming of Aeneas," *C&M* 26 (1965) 192-221.

Wigodsky's comprehensive study of *A* 8 argues for Augustan rapprochement on V' part in the alliance of Aeneas with the Greeks and the Herculean victory over Cacus. War and hostility are often necessary, says V, although the human cost is burdensome. Homer's shield of Achilles contrasts markedly with Aeneas', according to Becker; Aeneas' shield is symbolic of Rome's past and future. The theme of the shield (and its composition) concerns *Otis* who sees as main theme "the constant opposition of *virtus, consilium* and *pietas* to the forces of violence in all Roman history;" Eichholz, who favours a panoramic view with suggestive hints, scenes determined by narrative tempo rather than theme; Griffiths, who inserts elements from the Parade of Heroes in *A* 6 to yield "a selective yet satisfying inclusive epitome of the Roman past." Eden is concerned with the selection of scenes, and details, particularly 665-6 (*castae... matres*), and favours the *per annos, per dies* approach.
The Hercules-Cacus incident is treated exhaustively in Galinsky's descriptive, analytical chapter (318) and two articles. Galinsky is concerned with the symbolic bearing of the epyllion on Aeneas' career, poetic imagery, parallels between Aeneas-Turnus and Hercules-Cacus, and the relation of the episode to *A* 2 and 12. Galinsky also assesses the Hercules-Hydra event as a sermon for Aeneas' ultimate confrontation with Turnus. Gilmartin differentiates between Hercules' and Aeneas' heroism and Girod assesses the incident as a relief element, a western-style epyllion. George's monograph studies the *aition* sequence of *A* 8,1-369 as an artistic unit (Tiber, Evander, Hercules-Cacus) and measures V's examples against Callimachean use and artistry. The traveller-encounters, characteristic of Hellenistic *aitia*, are centralised around Latium and have a cumulating effect.
Binder's study of *A* 8 deals with the tripartite structural elements individually, Aeneas' entry into Roman history (1-174), the prehistory of Latium, Evander and Aeneas (306-68) and the shield (626-731). Saturnus-Aeneas-Augustus, Atlas-Hercules-Aeneas, and Saturnus-Evander-Aeneas are explored as meaningful typologies. The shield reveals new associations with Trojan legend and Augustan history. *Putnam PA* (362) analyzes the verbal construction of the book, key words and symbols. Rowland suggests that *A* 8,714-28, the imminent Golden Age, has intimations of decline. McGushin's article is concerned with Atlas-Hercules symbolism (134-42) and with the implied destiny of Aeneas and Augustus, with the endurance and incessant toil required of Trojan *pietas* and the divine will. Highet's morsel notes the omission of the description of sacrifice to Juno (81-85) and calls it another instance of V's modesty and mark of his reluctance to have Juno share the feast as discordant figure. Heubner finds a cautionary *ne plus ultra* association in the Araxes mention (*A* 8,728).

Aeneid 9

540. F. della Corte, "Commento topografico al IX dell'Eneide," *Bardon* 137-57.
541. M. A. De Cesare, "Aeneid IX; the failure of strategy," *RSC* 20 (1972) 411-22.
542. G. J. Fitzgerald, "Nisus and Euryalus: A Paradigm of Futile Behaviour and the Tragedy of Youth," *Martyn* 114-37.

543. N. Horsfall, "Numanus Remulus: Ethnography and Propaganda in Aen. IX,598f.," *Latomus* 30 (1971) 1108-16.
544. T. McLoughlin, "An unusual offer to Nisus. Aeneid IX,272-273," *PACA* 11 (1968) 55-58.
545. G. Maurach, "Der Pfeilschuss des Ascanius, zum 9. Buch der Aeneis," *Gymnasium* 75 (1968) 355-70.
546. R. P. Winnington-Ingram, *"Digna atque indigna relatu:* Observations on Aeneid IX," *PVS* 11 (1971-2) 61-74.

Nisus and Euryalus, *fortunati ambo,* occupy the limelight of scholarly attention. De Cesare shows that their old-fashioned heroism, the fight for glory and bloodlust, are futile and wasteful in the altered present. Warfare in *A* 2 is dramatised from the standpoint of the defeated; *A* 9 dramatises warfare in its most irrelevant mode. Fitzgerald and Winnington-Ingram treat the incident (a miniature tragedy in five acts) as a tragedy of youth and a basically ignominious affair. Maurach views the Nisus-Euryalus episode and Ascanius' archery as complements to earlier action and basically Vergilian. McLoughlin attaches suggestions of domestic peace to the *lectissima matrum corpora* and *captivos* (272-73). Horsfall studies Ascanius' victim and the programmatic speech (598-620); Numanus Nemulus emerges as the developed type of peasant-soldier in his most harsh and primitive aspects, a starkly original portrait of antique Italy. Della Corte defines the locale, including Ardea, Ostia (= Troia Nova) and Castel di Decimo, for the military exploits of *A* 9, the hunt of Ascanius and the peace talks.

Aeneid 10

547. H. W. Benario, "The tenth book of the Aeneid," *TAPA* 98 (1967) 23-36.
548. G. B. Conte, "Il balteo di Pallante," *RFIC* 98 (1970) 292-300.
549. J. Glenn, "Homer's God-Trusting Cyclopes," *CW* 65 (1972) 218-20.
550. G. Norcio, "Breve nota a Eneide X, 156-162," *Convivium* 1 (1963) 60-63.

Benario's article provides an analysis of *A* 10 and studies the characterization of Pallas, Lausus, and Mezentius. Conte measures the tragic associations and V's pity attaching to the Danaid myth of Pallas' swordbelt. Glenn parallels Polyphemus' impiety (*Odys.* 9,175f.) with *A* 10,689-90; both reflect the piety of the writers and both are consonant with the characters involved. Norcio interprets *A* 10,158 (*imminet Ida super*) as denoting Idaea Mater (Cybele), the ship's figurehead; Aeneas, not Pallas, is the helmsman.

Aeneid 11

551. R. D. Williams, "Aeneid 11.400-409," *CP* 61 (1966) 184-86.

Williams interprets Turnus' retort to Drances. He excludes *A* 11,404 as an inappropriate remark, but regards the Aufidus allusion (4-5) as entirely pertinent because it recalls his ancestral (Daunian) homeland where the obstreperous Aufidus (Horace, *Odes* 3,30,10) was not inclined to run backwards.

Aeneid 12

552. W. S. Anderson, "Two Passages from Book Twelve of the *Aeneid*," *UCCPh* 4 (1971) 49-65.
552a. G. Dimock, "On the end of the *Aeneid*," *RCANE* (March, 1969) 12.

553. R. Beare, "Invidious success. Some thoughts on the end of the Aeneid," *PVS* 4 (1964-65) 18-30.

554. J. Ferguson, "Book XII revisited," *PVS* 7 (1967-68) 66-77.

555. J. Fontenrose, "The gods invoked in epic oaths, Aeneid XII, 175-215," *AJP* 89 (1968) 20-38.

556. G. K. Galinsky, "Aeneas' invocation of Sol (Aeneid XII,176)," *AJP* 90 (1969) 453-58.

557. J. Hellegouarc'h, "Le récit de la mort de Turnus (Aen. XII,919-952). Analyse métrique et stylistique," *StudClas* 10 (1968) 133-39.

558. W. T. Johnson, "Aeneas and the ironies of pietas," *CJ* 60 (1965) 359-64.

559. D. A. Little, "The death of Turnus and the pessimism of the Aeneid," *AUMLA* 33 (1970) 67-76.

560. S. Lundström, "Turnus und die Wolke," *Hum. Vetensk.-Samfundet i Uppsala Arsbok* (1967-68) 21-67.

561. J. Perret, "Le serment d'Enée (Aen. XII,189-194) et les événements politiques de janvier 27," *REL* 47 bis (1970) (Mélanges Durry) 277-95.

562. A. Primmer, "Die Schluss-Szene der Aeneis," *WHB* 11 (1968) 20-26.

563. K. Quinn, "La morte di Turno," *Maia* 16 (1964) 341-49.

564. M. G. Southwell, "The Structure of Book XII of the Aeneid," *Vergilius* 10 (1964) 32-39.

565. G. Thaniel, "Turnus' fatal stone," *EMC* 15 (1971) 20-22.

566. F. I. Zeitlin, "An analysis of Aeneid, XII,176-211. The differences between the oaths of Aeneas and Latinus," *AJP* 86 (1965) 337-62.

Anderson examines the omen at the peace talks (244-56) and Aeneas' rolling eyes (939) as token of Italian irrationality in the interpretation of omens (cf. *A* 1,393-400) and as evidence of Aeneas' hesitancy. Lundström cites Turnus' recollection of *A* 10,636ff. in *A* 12,52-53: *nubes* denotes a cloud, not raiment, thereby altering *Iliad* 5,311ff. Turnus' stone, according to Thaniel, is best viewed as the weight of destiny, fruitless heroism of the old order. Ferguson treats rare usages, prolepsis, ambiguity, and word effects. Zeitlin contrasts the Trojan and Latin oaths on spiritual and human grounds, one strong in piety, the other apprehensive and pessimistic; Fontenrose answers Zeitlin by asserting that Sol cannot be equated with Apollo and that Jupiter is the common reference for both oaths. Galinsky studies oaths and prayers; Aeneas' prayer to Sol befits Latinus' ancestry and his own role as heir to Odysseus in Italy. But the final scene has evoked most discussion. *Putnam PA* charges Aeneas adversely: "The forces of violence and irrationality which swirl around Aeneas, through person and event and their accompanying symbols, lead ultimately not to his triumph over them...but rather to complete submission." *Otis* comments, somewhat less drastically: "Virgil's *humanitas* will not let Turnus or even Mezentius die without a tribute to their heroism, but he will not spare them." Williams contests the negation of Aeneas' actions: "*Est quadam prodire tenus si non datur ultra*: the Roman mission is seen to involve unpalatable actions...but it far surpassed in its ideals and conceptions anything else that the ancient world had seen." Beare explains the seeming inconsistency in Aeneas' characterization by alleging that V's glorification of success finally estranged him from his hero whose mercy diminishes after Pallas' death; Johnson assesses the killing as a failure of Aeneas' *pietas* and the victory of *furor*. Hellegouarc'h finds that metrics contribute a gravity verging on ritualistic solemnity to the final action, a sacrificial enormity with religious overtones. Little argues for V's belief in human progress combined with a sense of human frailty and the necessity for evil and concomitant suffering; Primmer responds almost identically to the final scene. Quinn, like Vance (386), conscious of Aeneas' second thoughts, finds justification for Aeneas' action in *A* 10,462ff., and 501f.; the remembrance of Pallas and Evander and the sword belt of the murdered Pallas dispel humanity at the close; Aeneas kills for vengeance and remorse.

C. CHARACTERS

General

567. E. Burck, "Das Menschenbild bei Vergil," *Das Menschenbild in der Dichtung. Sieben Essays* (ed. A. Schaefer) (München 1965) 48-82.
568. P. F. Burke, *Characterization in the Aeneid*. Diss. Stanford University, 1971. Summary in *DA* 32 (1972) 5757A-5758A.
569. M. P. Henze, "Virgile, peintre de figures," *Caesarodunum* 6 (1971) 71-81.
570. H. J. Schweizer, *Vergil und Italien. Interpretationen zu den italischen Gestalten der Aeneis* (Zürich 1964). Rev: Brisson *Latomus* 28 (1969); Eden *Gnomon* 41 (1969) 92-3; Gnilka *Gymnasium* 76 (1969) 119-21; Perret *REL* 46 (1968) 496.
571. A. Starowieyski, "De mulieribus a Vergilio in Aeneidis libris descriptis," *Meander* 21 (1966) 290-309 (Polish, with Latin résumé).

Burck (567) examines Corydon's *carmen* (*E* 2), *G* 4,2-6ff., and *A* 5,709ff. The three extracts relate to man's search for order, peace, and harmony, the established motivation for significant action. Burke's dissertation deals with methods of characterization, advancement of plot, Homeric models and other influences; Drances, Mezentius, and Amata are major concerns. Schweizer deals with methods and purposes of characterization in Italic figures (but including Evander and Mezentius); Camilla and Mezentius depict archaic heroism; Amata and Turnus are developed tragic figures; Latinus and Evander reflect the grief which follows upon commitment to a new order.
See also *Anderson; Camps; Highet; McKay; Otis; Putnam PA; Quinn.*

Achaemenides. See *Aeneid 3.*

Otis interprets the episode as a "symbol of Anchises' death"; McKay (442) suggests that Aeneas' kindness to the castaway symbolizes Augustan respect for Greek culture and his diplomatic victory over Parthia. *Highet* regards the sailor's name as unfortunate; its atmosphere is not Greece but Persia and the account has an uncomfortable resemblance to the Sinon story.

Aeneas. See Williams (393).

572. J. P. Brisson, "Le pieux Enée," *Latomus* 31 (1972) 379-412.
573. V. J. Cleary, *The function of repetition and foreshadowing in the characterization of Aeneas*. Diss. University of Pennsylvania, 1967. Summary in *DA* 28 (1967) 1414A.
574. V. J. Cleary, "Aeneas, a study in alternation," *CB* 40 (1964) 85-87.
575. E. A. Hahn, "Two notes on *Vergilius* X," *Vergilius* 11 (1965) 7-10.
576. E. L. Harrison, "Aeneas' pedigree," *CR* 22 (1972) 303-304.
577. F. Loretto, "Aeneas zwischen Liebe und Pflicht," *AU* 13:5 (1970) 27-40.
578. M. W. MacKenzie, "Who is Vergil's Aeneas? A plea to let him be himself," *Vergilius* 10 (1964) 1-6.
579. K. McLeish, "Dido, Aeneas, and the Concept of Pietas," *G&R* 19 (1972) 127-35.
580. M. Reinhold, "The unhero Aeneas," *C&M* 27 (1966) 195-207.
581. R. T. Scott, *Odysseus, Aeneas, and Abraham. Three Archetypes of Personal Identity in Western Thought*. Diss. Duke University, 1972. Summary in *DA* 33 (1972) 3020A.
582. J. R. Wilson, "Action and emotion in Aeneas," *G&R* 16 (1969) 67-75.
582a. J. W. Zarker, "Aeneas and Theseus in *Aeneid* VI," *RCANE* (March 1964) 9.

Brisson studies *pius-pietas* for insights into character. Cleary sheds light on V's technique of characterization; he regards the alternation between light and dark in the books as symbolic of the hero's ambivalence, as token of a basic character trait. *Otis* argues that Aeneas' character develops and changes contrary to Pöschl who saw Aeneas as basically the same at the end of the poem as at the start. Cleary states that *pietas* and *cedere* are Aeneas' hallmarks; the death of Turnus symbolizes the triumph of Venus over Juno. MacKenzie argues that V's Aeneas derives simply from the Aeneas of the *Iliad*, "rounded out from a minor figure into a developed character." Hahn comments on V's sympathy for the underdog (cf. *TAPA* 56 (1925) 185-212) and compassion for both sides alike; critics who inveigh against Aeneas' treatment of Turnus (and Dido) miss the fundamental message of the epic. She equates Aeneas and Turnus, in some respects, with Arjuna and Karna of the *Mahabharata* (Duckworth favoured Bhima and Duryodhana), and discounts precise parallels between Aeneas and Augustus. V, like Aeschylus, *was* interested in glorifying later events and institutions by attributing to them ancient and glamorous origins. Harrison treats *A* 1,380; 8,36f.; 7,219-30, 240-42; 6,125-6; and 6,834-5 (patrilinear terms). McLeish finds symmetry and a logical pattern in Aeneas' relationship with Dido; the hero's *pietas* is strengthened and developed through his affair with the Carthaginian queen. Meyer traces unheroic traits in the traditional Aeneas from Homer to Jean Tztetzes. Wilson argues that emotional involvements are suppressed by Aeneas' devotion to *pietas* and destiny, but the sword belt of Pallas evokes unique passion. *Highet* traces the development of Aeneas' spirit in his speeches; as the conflict moves to its climax, the hero says less and acts more.

Amata

583. J. W. Zarker, "Amata: Vergil's Other Queen," *Vergilius* 15 (1969) 2-24.

Burke (568), Schweizer (570), and others deal with the Latin queen. Zarker underlines her links with Lavinia, Aeneas, Latonus, and Turnus; certain traits recall Greek tragic heroines and Dido.

Anchises

Galinsky's study of the Trojan legend in Sicily (629) sheds light on the Trojan *pater familias*.

Anna

584. V. E. Hernández Vista, "Ana y la pasión de Dido en libro IV de la Eneida," *EClás* 10 (1966) 1-30.

Barrett (446, 447) and La Penna (460) review Anna's history, including the shadowy liaison between Aeneas and Anna as a possible factor in the Carthaginian episode; Hernández Vista regards Dido and Anna as a doublet, thereby explaining anomalies in Anna's character and role.

Antenor

E. Leon (635) adds dimension to Padua's founder.

Ascanius

Highet notes that Aeneas never addresses his son until *disce puer, virtutem ex me*

111

verumque laborem, fortunam ex aliis, instancing three leading themes of the *Aeneid.* Maurach (545) notes V's empathy in Ascanius' encounter with Numanus Remulus.

Cacus. See *Aeneid 8* and s.v. *Hercules.*

Hercules' victim exhibits character traits which accord with those of Turnus and Mark Antony according to recent scholarly assessments.

Camilla

585.   A. M. Assareto, "Dall'Etiopide all'Eneide," *Mythos. Scripta in honorem Mario Untersteiner* (Genova 1970) 51-58.
586.   A. Brill, *Der Gestalt der Camilla bei Vergil* (Heidelberg 1972).
587.   I. Lewandowski, "Italska Amazonka. Postac Kamilli w Eneidzie Wergiliusa," *Filomata* 188 (1965) 427-32.
588.   O. Schoenberger, "Camilla," *A&A* 12 (1966) 180-88.
589.   Sister Mary Ste Therese Wittenberg, "Vergil's Camilla," *CB* 42 (1966) 69-71.

Highet records Camilla's speech (*A* 11,502-6) as persuasion in spite of bluff imperatives; Turnus' reply is of a polite order (508-19). The paradoxical *virgo bellatrix* owes characteristics to Penthesileia (Arctinus, *Aethiopis*) according to Assareto. Schoenberger and Sister Mary provide sympathetic evaluations of Camilla's character. Brill's full-scale study examines Camilla's models (Harpalyke, Penthesileia, Volscian saga), her role in the Italian corps (7,803-17) and in *A* 11, through her *aristeia* and death. Schweizer (570) treats Camilla and Mezentius.

Cybele

590.   J. W. Zarker, "The role of Cybele in Vergil's Aeneid," *RCANE* (March, 1972) 16-17.

Daedalus. See *Aeneid* 6, Rutledge (372).

590a.   C. W. Barlow, "Daedalus at Cumae," *RCANE* (March, 1969) 13.

Diana. See Schweizer (570).

Highet regards Diana's biography of Camilla (*A* 11,535-94) as inept; V's justification is graceful but flimsy. Diana's narrative explains the reason for her command but V introduced it for the romantic narrative.

Dido. See *Aeneid 1, Aeneid 4.*

591.   M. C. Covi, "Dido in Vergil's Aeneid," *CJ* 60 (1964) 57-60.
592.   F. Della Corte, "Perfidus Hospes," *Renard* I, 312-21.
593.   J. Ferguson, "Women," *Phrontisterion* 5 (1967) 1-6.
594.   G. S. Duclos, "Dido as triformis Diana," *Vergilius* 15 (1969) 33-41.
595.   W. Nethercut, "Dido and Aeneas: Notes on Vergil's Art," *CO* 48 (1971) 88-90.
596.   W. R. Nethercut, "Dux Femina Facti: General Dido and the Trojan," *CB* 47 (1970) 26,30.
597.   E. Phinney, "Dido and Sychaeus," *CJ* (1965) 355-59.
598.   V. Pöschl, "Dido und Aeneas," *Festschrift Karl Vretska* (edd. Ableitinger, Gugel) (Heidelberg 1970) 148-73.

599.   K. Quinn, "Virgil's Tragic Queen," *Latin Explorations: Critical Studies in Roman Literature* (K. Quinn) (London 1963) 29-58.
600.   A. Schmitz, "Quelques aspects du personnage de Didon chez Virgile," *Conférences de la Société d'Études Latines de Bruxelles 1965-66* (Brussels 1968) 25-46.

Covi deals with Dido's *pietas*. Della Corte senses Roman imperialism in Africa behind the Aeneas-Dido encounter. Dido's *"perfidus hospes"* is a cry of despair (cf. Medea, Ariadne, Phyllis) not implying an Aeneas-Paris equation but recalling earlier tragic heroines. Ferguson finds African and Sophoclean analogues for Dido's characterization. Duclos reflects on the Dido-Diana comparison (*A* 1,498-504); Dido progresses from luminous, virginal Diana, to despondent Hecate, to Luna (*A* 6). Nethercut (596) examines *A* 1,360-6, 4,123-5 and 165ff. Schmitz's psychological study focuses on Dido's reactions. Love and marriage (so-called) engage Finney and Perret; Finney discovers Dido's *culpa* in her infidelity to Sychaeus' memory (cf. Apollonius' Hypsipyle and Medea). Pöschl treats Aeneas' complex character and his inability to communicate; Aeneas' adherence to divine orders is neither abandonment nor betrayal but the renunciation of personal happiness. Vergil favours the epic and elegiac tradition where sensual delights cannot be reconciled with human dignity. Quinn suggests that Aeneas' advance towards awareness of the magnitude of his mission, from individualistic Homeric warrior to Rome's servant, requires the sacrifice of Dido as part of the progression. "Those who think ill of Aeneas for deserting Dido are often the same people who think ill of Mark Antony for not deserting Cleopatra." The witchcraft scene (4,504-20) reinforces Dido's curse (607-27) against Aeneas and Rome, and her suicide becomes an act of *devotio*, of ritual suicide, to provoke the Punic Wars.

Diomedes

601.   W. W. De Grummond, "Virgil's Diomedes," *Phoenix* 21 (1967) 40-43.
602.   O. T. Zanco, "Diomede greco e Diomede italico," *RAL* 20 (1965) 270-82.

De Grummond defines Diomedes as a hero of epic scope, philosopher-king, idealized yet warm, dignified and courageous, a regenerated Diomedes in cherished *Saturnia regna*.

Drances. See Burke (568), Schweizer (570).

Highet studies Drances' double speech (11,343-75) and his elimination by Turnus and comments: "doubtless he (Drances) was the first to approach Aeneas after the slaying of Turnus, with eloquent phrases of congratulation." *Highet* favours Cicero as Drances' model, but with restraint.

Euryalus. See *Aeneid 9, Nisus (infra).*

603.   G. E. Duckworth, "The Significance of Nisus and Euryalus for Aeneid IX-XII," *AJP* 68 (1967) 129-50.

Evander. See *Aeneid 8.*

Binder (522) and Schweizer (570) examine Evander's role and characterization in detail. George (528) treats the *aition* of Evander and its context with precision; Heilman (531) is equally detailed and perceptive. The Atlas association for Evander (and Aeneas) is developed by McGushin (345) and Boyancé (449). *Highet* parallels

Evander's welcome to the Aeneadae with Lycus' welcome to the Argonauts (Ap. Rhod., *Argon.* 2,752-814). *Highet* detects traits of Peisistratus, Nestor's son, in Homer. The old Arcadian as *cicerone* for Aeneas at Pallanteum is pleasant parallel to Anchises as introducer of Rome's future heroes.

Helen. See *Aeneid 2*, Goold (1159), Murgia (1166).

The dispute over the authenticity of the Helen passage (2,567-88) provides noteworthy comments on her characterization.

Hercules. See *Aeneid 8* (and *Cacus*); Galinsky (318), Gilmartin (319), Zarker (397).

Galinsky's chapter on Roman Hercules (318) indicates his importance for the characterization of Aeneas and as pattern for Augustus.

Juno. See Boyancé (728), Wlosok (396), Williams (420), Gellie (453).

604.   G. Lieberg, "La dea Giunone nell'Eneide di Virgilio," *A&R* 11 (1966) 145-65.

Lieberg's discussion of the personality and actions of the vengeful goddess suggests that Juno was conceived as a political and moral force of stature, agent for Roman practices and propagandizer in the outer realms. *Highet* is less charitable: "Within the orderly system of the moral and physical universe, she is the chief source of storm and strife. She exults in evil." *Highet's* analysis of her rhetoric is immensely revealing of character. Havelock (325) is impressed with Juno's role as anti-Fate.

Jupiter. See Boyancé (728).

Jupiter's speeches and prophecies are treated with authority and insight by *Highet* and Grassmann-Fischer (322).

Latinus

605.   C. Balk, *Die Gestalt des Latinus in Vergils Aeneis* (Heidelberg 1968).

Balk's dissertation explores every facet of Latinus' characterization and associations. Smith (519) detects wisdom, righteousness, and *auctoritas* in the epic *senex*. *Highet's* study reveals a gloomy, anxiety-laden monarch, oppressed by guilt, occasionally sober and rational; at the close he resembles Priam.

Lausus

Schweizer (570), Binder (522), and Benario (547) offer detailed studies.

Mezentius. See Benario (547), Burke (568), Schweizer (570), and *Aeneid* 10.

606.   P. T. Eden, "The Etruscans in the Aeneid," *PVS* 4 (1964-65) 31-40.
607.   J. M. Glenn, *Polyphemus and Mezentius: A Study in Homeric and Vergilian Characterization.* Diss. Princeton University, 1970. Summary in *DA* 31 (1971) 4141A.
608.   J. Glenn, "Mezentius, Contemptor Deum," *Vergilius* 17 (1971) 7-8.
609.   J. Glenn, "Mezentius and Polyphemus," *AJP* 92 (1971) 129-55.
610.   J. Glenn, "The fall of Mezentius, "*Vergilius* 18 (1972) 10-15.
611.   E. W. Leach, "The blindness of Mezentius (*Aeneid* 10.762-768)," *Arethusa* 4 (1971) 83-90.
612.   F. A. Sullivan, S. J., "Mezentius. A Vergilian creation," *CP* 64 (1969) 219-25.

Eden recalls that V altered the roles of Turnus and Mezentius and made Mezentius the exiled tyrant, possibly a sacral king. Glenn examines the relationship between Polyphemus in Homer's *Odyssey* and V's Mezentius. He prefers Polyphemus as model rather than Homeric Ajax and argues that V minimized Mezentius' scorn for the gods because of the contemporary retreat from religion. Mezentius, in Glenn's view, is a creature of pathos, piety, and *gravitas*, reliant on *vis* but doomed by heaven and destiny, victim of a *theios aner*. Leach explores a simile (*A* 10,762-8) as clue to Mezentius' character; like Orion (and Polyphemus) Mezentius moves in the darkness of spiritual blindness but the final scene depicts a disillusioned Aeneas victorious over a tired *senex*. Sullivan favours Homeric and Sophoclean Ajax as model for the heroic fighter and *contemptor deum*.

Misenus. See *Aeneid 6.*

Nisus. Cf. *Euryalus, supra.*

Duckworth emphasizes the aspect of human error and consequent penalties in the Nisus-Euryalus episode and repeatedly in the final quarter of the epic. Turnus is prey to the same faults and suffers accordingly.

Numanus Remulus. See *Aeneid 9,* Schweizer (570).

Palinurus. See *Aeneid 5,* McKay (666), *Aeneid 6.*

Highet detects parallels in Horace's Archytas Ode.

Sibylla (Deiphobe). See *Aeneid 6,* McKay (668).

Sinon. See *Aeneid 2,* McKay (442).

613.   J. W. Jones, "Trojan Legend. Who is Sinon?" *CJ* 61 (1965) 122-28.

Jones argues that V's model was Odysseus (Euripides, *Philoctetes*); Paoletta (431) deals with the *ambiguitas* and novelty of the Sinon type, with parallels in Sophocles' *Philoctetes*.

Theseus. See *Aeneid 6.*

Tiberis (Thybris). See *Aeneid 7.*

Highet treats the Tiber spirit as Aeneas' third informant on how to win his wars in Italy (after Helenus and Anchises). Father Tiber plays the Sibyl's role more explicitly and helpfully.

Turnus. See *Aeneid 12,* Schweizer (570).

614.   M. von Albrecht, "Zur tragik von Vergils Turnusgestalt: Aristotelisches in der Aeneis," *Silvae. Festschrift für E. Zinn zum 60 Geburtstag.* (edd. M. von Albrecht, E. Heck) (Tübingen 1970) 1-5.
615.   M. Mueller, "Turnus and Hotspur. The political adversary in the Aeneid and Henry IV," *Phoenix* 23 (1969) 278-90.
616.   J. Perret, "La mort de Turnus," *REL* 44 (1966) 34.
617.   D. T. Stephens, "L'homme absurde," *BAGB* 31 (1972) 157-68.

The elevation of Turnus as the worthier hero in defeat has cast doubts on the poet's competence. There is sharp division over Aeneas' actions and Turnus' merits. Von Albrecht defines Turnus' *hamartema* as an Aristotelian shortcoming. His demise assumed ritual proportions with Aeneas as priest-sacrificant. Mueller examines Turnus (and Hotspur) as scapegoat and war-criminal; Aeneas cannot extend generosity to his defeated foe and so is accorded less than justice for his final act.

Venus. See Boyancé (728), Gellie (453).

Wlosok's study (396) reviews character, actions, symbolic and religious values. *Highet's* study of Venus' speeches reveals a protective guardian and mother rather than goddess of sexual love. She recalls Homer's Thetis and Odysseus' aide, Athena. Beauty, subtlety and symmetrical structure characterize her speeches.

D. THE STRUCTURE OF THE AENEID

618. O. A. W. Dilke, "Do line totals in the *Aeneid* show a preoccupation with significant numbers?" *CQ* 17 (1967) 322-26.
619. G. E. Duckworth, *Structural Patterns and Proportions in Vergil's Aeneid. A Study in Mathematical Composition* (Ann Arbor, Mich. 1962). Rev: Clarke *CR* 14 (1964) 43-45; Dalzell *Phoenix* 17 (1963) 314-16; Eden *PVS* 3 (1963-64) 48-49; Lloyd *AJP* 85 (1964) 71-77; Paratore *RCCM* 6 (1964) 326-34; Perret *RBPh* 42 (1964) 128-30; Wimmel *Gnomon* 36 (1964) 56-60; Woodcock *PACA* 6 (1963) 50-51.
620. G. E. Duckworth, "The 'Old and the New' in Vergil's Aeneid," *The Poetic Tradition* (edd. D. C. Allen, H. T. Rowell) (Baltimore 1968) 63-80.
621. J. J. Jensen, "An outline of Vergil's mathematical technique," *SO* 45 (1970) 113-17.
622. G. Stégen, "La clarté de l'ordre dans l'Enéide," *Otia* 14 (1966) 20-24.
623. W. C. Waterhouse, "Extreme and Mean Ratio in Vergil?" *Phoenix* 26 (1972) 369-76.

Duckworth's study of mathematical ratios and structural proportion has been heavily contested by reviewers and the Golden Section theory has been largely discarded as V's practice; Duckworth's structural designs have won more favour. The 'Old and the New' chapter is a concise, final account of Duckworth's ideas on structure and characterization. Dilke observes V's use of 3,7,12, and 30-line units in the epic. Jensen's capsule study of V's mathematical technique loses cogency in light of Waterhouse's rejection of Duckworth's thesis. Waterhouse, in the context of ancient mathematical thought, pronounces Duckworth's ideas improbable; data show no emphasis on Fibonacci numbers, no substantial clustering at .618, and no preference for good approximations over bad ones; they behave more like a random collection of fractions within the range considered.

E. THE TROJAN LEGEND

624. L. Alfonsi, "Creta e Virgilio," *SMEA* 5 (1968) 7-11.
625. J. K. Anderson, "The Trojan Horse again," *CJ* 66 (1970) 22-25.
626. F. Della Corte, "I giorni dell'Eneide," *Mélanges d'archéologie et d'histoire offerts à A. Piganiol* (ed. R. Chevallier) (Paris 1966) 754-60.
627. I. Dimischiotu-Popescu, "Sursele onomasticii troiene in Eneida," *Anal. Univ. Bucuresti* 19 (1970) 55-68.
628. G. Dumézil, *Mythe et épopée: l'idéologie des trois fonctions dans les épopées des peuples indo-européens* (Paris 1968) 337-47.
629. G. K. Galinsky, *Aeneas, Sicily, and Rome* (Princeton 1969). Rev: Benario *CJ* 67 (1971-72) 70-72; Bloch *Gnomon* 44 (1972) 41-7; Caputo *SE* 38 (1970) 421-24; Currie *PVS* 9 (1969-70) 113-14; Drummond *JRS* 62 (1972) 218-20; Lloyd *AJA* 93

(1972) 616-18; McKay *CW* 63 (1970) 242 and *Vergilius* 16 (1970) 44-45; Muffatti *Athenaeum* 48 (1970) 429-30; Perret *REL* 49 (1971) 39-52; van der Bruwaene *AC* (1970) 608-609.

630. V. E. Georgiev, "Troer und Etrusker. Der historischen Kern des Aeneas-Sage," *Philologus* 116 (1972) 93-97.
631. M. Grant, *Roman Myths* (New York 1971) 44-90.
632. J. Heurgon, "Les Dardaniens en Afrique," *REL* 47 (1969) 284-94.
633. J. W. Jones, "The Trojan Horse, Timeo Danos et dona ferentes," *CJ* 65 (1970) 241-47.
634. L. Lacroix, "Le légende de Philoctète en Italie méridionale," *RBPh* 43 (1965) 5-21.
635. E. Leon, "Antenor potuit," *CB* 40 (1964) 33-34.
636. G. B. Pighi, "Roma e Cartagine in Virgilio e Orazio," *RIL* 103 (1969) 741-54.
637. M. R. Scherer, *The Legends of Troy in Art and Literature* (New York 1963).
638. H. Strasburger, *Zur Sage von der Gründung Roms* (Heidelberg 1968). Rev: Bloch *Latomus* 30 (1971) 774-77.
639. W. Suerbaum, "Aeneas zwischen Troja und Rom. Zur Funktion der Genealogie und der Ethnographie in Vergils Aeneis," *Poetica* 1 (1967) 176-204.

Galinsky's important study examines the genesis of the Trojan legend in northwest Sicily and provides an analysis of the Aeneas legend in Etruria and Lavinium. Rome's claims to Trojan ancestry are examined, and the Tellus-Italia relief on the Ara Pacis Augustae is identified as Venus Erycina, the Trojan Venus imported from Sicily. Alfonsi studies the tradition of Trojan origins in Crete and assigns it to Alexandrian sources; the Trojan-Minoan conflict with the Greek-Mycenaean armament is product of V's historical imagination. The source of the Trojan Horse engages Jones who suggests that the Trojans worshipped the horse as replacement for beasts bearing gifts in more exotic traditions. Anderson suggests that the horse recalls Assyrian siege towers. Devised by Athena Hippia and disguised as an offering, it was designed to compensate for the stolen Palladium. Della Corte examines chronology and links between the Parilia enactment (21 April) and the fall of Lauretum. Georgiev treats the questionable equation, Trojans = Etruscans, with philological zeal with allusions to V's Trojan epic and its Etruscan content. Suerbaum discusses the 'return' of the Trojans to Italy; though Asiatic, and so taunted by their foes, Aeneas never appears as a Phrygian and is acceptable as a model Latin. Heurgon suggests possible African inspiration for the legend of the Trojans in the West. Aeneas, son of Aphrodite Aineias (a Sicilian tradition) and Dido in African exile (Punic myth) were combined, Pighi argues, in the Dido tragedy. Scherer's pictorial study, with connecting narrative and description, explores the Trojan legend through the ages.

F. GEOGRAPHY AND ARCHAEOLOGY

640. A. Alföldi, *Early Rome and the Latins* (Ann Arbor, Mich. 1963) 236-87.
641. G. Bendz, "Vergil in Sperlonga," *Opuscula Romana* 7 (1969).
642. P. H. von Blankenhagen, "Laocoon, Sperlonga und Vergil," *AA* (1969) 256-300.
643. R. Bloch, "Epigraphie latine et antiquités romaines," *AEHE* (1969-70) 277-80.
644. A. Booth, "Venus on the Ara Pacis," *Latomus* 25 (1966) 873-79.
645. F. Castagnoli (transl. J. M. Benario), "Lavinium and the Aeneas legend," *Vergilius* 13 (1967) 1-8.
646. F. Castagnoli, "I luoghi connessi con l'arrivo di Enea," *ArchClass* 19 (1967) 235-47.
647. J. Christern, "Der 'Jupiter tempel' in Cumae und seine umwandlung in eine Kirche," *MDAI* (RM) 73-4 (1966-67) 232-41.

117

648. J. H. D'Arms, *Romans on the Bay of Naples: A Social and Cultural Study of the Villas and their Owners from 150 B.C. to A.D. 400* (Cambridge, Mass. 1970).

649. B. Davison, "Sergestus, called Sergius," *SAN* 1 (1969-70) 12.

650. M. Delepierre, "Une scène de la prise de Troie décrite par Virgile," *MMAI* 56 (1969) 1-11.

651. F. Della Corte, *La Mappa dell'Eneide* (Firenze 1972). Rev: Rougé *Latomus* 32 (1973) 637-39.

652. J. Delz, "Die saugende Wölfin auf dem Schild des Aeneas," *MH* 23 (1966) 224-27.

653. R. Dion, "Où situer la demeure de Circe?" *BAGB* 30 (1971) 479-533.

654. R. Dion, "Rhenus bicornis (Aen. VIII,727)," *REL* 42 (1964) 469-99.

655. J. A. S. Evans, "Amsancti valles," *Vergilius* 10 (1964) 12-14.

656. G. K. Galinsky, "Venus in a relief of the Ara Pacis Augustae," *AJA* 70 (1966) 223-43.

657. M. Grant, "Illustrations of Virgil on Roman coins and medallions," *PVS* 5 (1965-66) 25.

658. R. Hampe, *Sperlonga und Vergil* (Mainz-am-Rhein 1972). Rev: Andreas *Gnomon* 45 (1973) 85-88; McKay *Phoenix* 27 (1973) 206-207; Ridgway *AJA* 77 (1973) 461; Sichtermann *Gymnasium* 80 (1973) 461-67.

659. C. G. Hardie, "The Great Antrum at Baiae," *PBSR* 37 (1969) 14-33.

660. W. R. Holloway, "The Tomb of Augustus and the Princes of Troy," *AJA* 70 (1966) 171-73.

661. D. Kienast, "Rom und die Venus vom Eryx," *Hermes* 93 (1965) 478-89.

662. H. J. Kolbe, "Lare Aeneia?" *MDAI (RM)* 77 (1970) 1-9.

663. H. Kuehner, *Latium-Land im Schatten Roms* (Köln 1967).

664. P. La Baume, "Auffindung des Poblicius-Grabsmonument in Köln," *Gymnasium* 78 (1971) 373-87.

665. L. Lacroix, "Sur les traces d'Enée en Sicile," *BFS* 42 (1964) 265-70.

666. A. G. McKay, "Aeneas' Landfalls in Hesperia," *G&R* 14 (1967) 3-11.

667. A. G. McKay, *Vergil's Italy* (Greenwich, Conn. 1970; Bath, England 1971). Rev: Galinsky, *ACR* 1 (1971) 246-47; Lloyd *Vergilius* 18 (1972) 56-57; Ogilvie *CR* 23 (1973) 41-42; Ortall *Augustinus* 17 (1972) 332; Russell *Phoenix* 25 (1971) 402-403; *TLS* (6 Aug. 1971) 948; Wellesley *JRS* 62 (1972) 220-21.

668. A. G. McKay, *Ancient Campania I: Cumae and the Phlegraean Fields* (Hamilton, Ont. 1972); *Ancient Campania II: Naples and Coastal Campania* (Hamilton, Ont. 1972). Rev: Sandy *CW* 66 (1972-73) 480-81.

669. A. G. McKay, "Vergil and Vitruvius," *Canisius College Language Methods Newsletter* 5:3 (1968) 10-15.

670. A. G. McKay, "Apollo Cumanus," *Vergilius* 19 (1973) 51-63.

671. J. D. Meerwaldt, "Vergilius' *Aeneis* VI,847 en de werkelijheidsillusie in de antieke beeldende kunst," *Hermeneus* 36 (1964) 26-42.

672. R. F. Paget, *In the Footsteps of Orpheus* (London 1967). Rev: Black *PVS* 6 (1966-67) 58-59.

673. R. F. Paget, "The Great Antrum at Baiae," *Vergilius* 13 (1967) 42-50.

674. R. F. Paget, "Portus Julius," *Vergilius* 15 (1969) 25-32.

675. B. Posti, *Die Bedeutung des Nil in der romischen Literatur* (Wien 1970).

676. Hans-Dieter Reeker, *Die Landschaft in der Aeneis* (Hildesheim 1971). Rev: Segal *Gnomon* 45 (1973) 824-26.

677. F. de Ruyt, "Paysages et folklores italiens dans l'Eneide," *JE* 36 (1963-64) 103-22.

678. A. Sadurska, *Les tables iliaques* (Warsaw 1964).

679. G. Saeflund, *The Polyphemus and Scylla Groups at Sperlonga* (Stockholm 1972). Rev: von Blankenhagen *AJA* 77 (1973) 456-60.

680. R. V. Schoder, S. J., "Ancient Cumae," *Scientific American* 209 (6 Dec. 1963) 109-18.
681. R. V. Schoder, S. J., "Vergil's Poetic Use of the Cumae Area," *CJ* 67 (1971-72) 97-109; cf. *Romanitas* 9 (1970) 187-98.
682. N. Shiel, "A 'Quotation' from the *Aeneid* on the coinage of Carausius," *PVS* 12 (1972-73) 51-53.
683. E. Simon, *Ara Pacis Augustae* (Greenwich, Conn. 1967).
684. J. P. Small, "Aeneas and Turnus on Late Etruscan Funerary Urns," *AJA* 76 (1972) 220.
685. P. Sommella, "Heroon di Enea a Lavinium. Recenti scavi a Pratica di Mare," *RPAA* 44 (1971-72) 47-74.
686. A. M. Tamassia, "Note di protostoria mantovana," *SE* 35 (1967) 361-79.
687. B. Tilly, "Some Excursions...," *Vergilius* 19 (1973) 2-19.
688. P. G. Van Wees, *Poetische Geografie in Vergilius' Aeneis* (Tilburg 1970).
689. L. Widman, "Les héros virgiliens et les inscriptions latines," *Ancient Society* 2 (1971) 162-73.
690. K. Wellesley, "Virgil's home revisited," *PVS* 3 (1963-64) 36-43.
691. K. Wellesley, "Virgil's home," *WS* 79 (1966) 330-50.

Della Corte provides a comprehensive study of the epic landscape (Troad, Antandros to Drepanum, Between Africa and Sicily, Campania, and Latium). Geographical factors, cult associations, sanctuaries, oracles are spurs to the poetic process. McKay's companion to V's works reviews Italian and Sicilian topography and archaeological finds and offers a vade mecum for readers rather than travellers with numerous quotations in English translations. McKay's Ancient Campania volumes (prepared for the Vergilian Society's Classical Summer School program in Italy) offer historical, archaeological and literary *testimonia* to Vergilian (and other) sites in Campania. Reeker's study of the *Aeneid* landscape is concerned with atmosphere, the impressionistic effects of landscape, with periplus and periegesis in Homer, Apollonius Rhodius and V, catalogues, South Italy, Sicily, Cumae, and Latium. Van Wees studies geographical names as poetic ornament, poetic alternates for customary names (e.g. Eridanus for Padus, Gnosius for Cretensis), and associational usages.

McKay's treatment of landfalls concentrates on promontories (Palinurus, Misenum, Gaieta) and includes aetiological factors and archaeological evidence. Evans reports on Lake Am(p) sanctus today (*A* 7,563-71). Paget's discovery, the Great Antrum at Baiae, an initiatory tunnel dating from the late sixth century, may have inspired V's passage through the Underworld; but Hardie (659) thinks that the tunnel was not operational in V's time. Paget's study of the Portus Julius and Schoder's illustrated accounts of Cumae are illuminating. The *immania templa* of the Cumaean acropolis engage Christern (upper terrace, probably Apolline) and McKay (lower triadic temple, recalling the Palatine Temple of Apollo).

D'Arms' study includes Vergil's *villula* on Posillipo. Tilly's eyewitness article examines the Sabine catalogue (towns, mountains, rivers, climate, and cultivation) and argues that Strabo and V drew on a common source which may be Agrippa's *Destinatio et Commentarii* (Pliny, *N.H.* 3,2,17). Castagnoli discusses recent finds along the shoreline and their relevance to Aeneas' landings, the first settlement, and cult service. Della Corte (540,651) examines topography and finds relating to *A* 7-12; Alföldi's study of Alba Longa, "Trojan" divinities in Lavinium, the Federal Sanctuary at Lavinium, Penates as Dioscuri, and the myth of the sow is a valuable complement. Sommella treats the Heroon of Aeneas at Lavinium and the Aeneas legend in Latium. Wellesley rejects Pietole-Andes as V's birthplace for Bandes and locates the farm at Montaldo. Galinsky identifies Venus Erycina on the Ara Pacis and adduces V testimony; Booth examines the same figure. Hampe ascribes the sculptural program of the recently excavated Grotto at Sperlonga to Vergil (Palinurus episode) but the thesis is strained. Grant's numismatic notice and Davidson's coin of M. Sergius Silus (109 B.C.) explore a neglected area. Bloch reviews Dumézil's study (628) which deals significantly with *A* 7-12. Delepierre discusses a Greek fourth century mirror which illustrates *A* 2,567-74. Delz (652) counters Rau on *A* 8,632 and offers a critique of the wolf. Kolbe examines the cippus inscription from Tor Tignosa (*ILLRP* 1271) and treats the Lares cult of the Roman Republic. LaBaume's grave monument portrays Aeneas, Anchises, and Ascanius. Sadurska on the Tabula Iliaca and Simon on the Ara Pacis involve V. Tamassia confirms the Etruscan regime around Mantua. Vidman studies the impact of V's names on later nomenclature.

VII. VERGIL AND HIS MILIEU

A. LIFE AND WORKS

692. L. Alfonsi, "La Grecia in Vergilio," *EEAth* 12 (1961-62) 501-14.
693. D. Armstrong, "The other Aeneid," *Arion* 7 (1967) 143-68.
694. F. Arnaldi, "La poesia di Virgilio," *Bardon* 6-18.
695. J. Bayet, "L'experience sociale de Virgile," *Mélanges de littérature latine* (Paris 1966) 281-302.
696. J. P. Brisson, *Virgile, son temps et le nôtre* (Paris 1966). Rev: Cadoni *Paideia* 22 (1967) 343-50; Clarke *CR* 17 (1967) 289-91; Duckworth *AJP* 90 (1969) 100-104; Ernout *RPh* 41 (1967) 255-58; Grimal *REA* 69 (1967) 438-42; Paratore *RCCM* 9 (1967) 132-36.
697. S. Commager (ed.), *Virgil: A Collection of Critical Essays* (Englewood Cliffs, N.J. 1966).
698. M. Conway, "The Significance of Vergil Today," *CO* 50 (1972) 1-2.
699. J. S. Coolidge, "Great things and small. The Virgilian progression," *CompLit* 17 (1965) 1-23.
700. V. D'Agostino, "Verso il 'Nuovo Virgilio'?" *Bardon* 124-36.
701. M. Delaunois, "Tendances actuelles de la recherche concernant l'oeuvre de Virgile," *Humanités chrétiennes* 14 (1971) 579-601.
702. J. Delz, "Neuere Literatur zu Vergils Aeneis," *MH* 25 (1968) 57-62.
703. P. F. Distler, *Vergil and Vergiliana* (Chicago 1966).
704. D. R. Dudley (ed.), *Virgil. Studies in Latin Literature and its Influence.* Rev: Von Albrecht *Gnomon* 42 (1970) 731-32; Borszák *Latomus* 30 (1971) 447-48; Quinn *Vergilius* 16 (1970) 40-41; *TLS* (15 May 1969) 514.
705. M. Gorrichon, "Evolution de l'art du paysage chez Virgile des Bucoliques à l'Énéide," *Caesarodunum* 2 (1968) 197-202.
706. G. Gutu, *Publius Vergilius Maro. Studiu literar* (Bucharest 1970).
707. C. G. Hardie, "Virgilius," *OCD*², 1123-8.
708. J. Higginbotham (ed.), *Greek and Latin Literature: A Comparative Study* (London 1969). Rev: Browning *JRS* 61 (1971) 299-300; Clarke *CR* 85 (1971) 75-78; Rousseau *CJ* 66 (1971) 262-63.
709. B. L. Hijmans, "Robert Graves, The White Goddess and Vergil," *Mosaic* 2:2 (1969) 58-73.
710. V. L. Johnson, "Personal quality of Vergil's art," *CB* 41 (1964) 17-23, 25-26.
711. F. Klingner, *Virgil: Bucolica, Georgica, Aeneis* (Zürich 1967). Rev: Brisson *Latomus* 27 (1968) 459-62; Delande *LEC* 36 (1968) 71; Otis *Gnomon* 41 (1969) 554-74; Verdière *RBPh* 46 (1968) 409-10.
712. S. Kresic, "L'image de Virgile au XXᵉ siècle," *EMC* 12 (1968) 41-47.
713. A. La Penna, "Neoumanesimo, neoclassicismo, neoestetismo in recenti interpretazioni tedesche di Virgilio," *Maia* 17 (1965) 340-65.

714. M. D. MacLeod, "Humour in Virgil," *PVS* 4 (1964-65) 53-67.
715. J. Oroz, "Virgil y los valores del clasicismo y del humanismo," *Helmantica* 74 (1973) 209-79.
716. B. Otis, *A Study in Civilized Poetry* (Oxford 1963). Rev: Büchner *DLZ* 86 (1965) 980-84; Duckworth *AJP* 86 (1965) 409-20; Eden *PVS* 4 (1964-65) 68-73; Hardie *JRS* 54 (1964) 246-49; La Penna *DArch* 1 (1967) 220-33; Luck *Latomus* 24 (1965) 128-32; McKay *Phoenix* 19 (1965) 330-32; MacKay *CW* 58 (1964) 21, and *Vergilius* 11 (1965) 18-21; Maguinness *Hermathena* 100 (1965) 80-81; Michel *RPh* 43 (1969) 354-55; Perret *REL* 42 (1964) 576-80; Quinn *AUMLA* 24 (1965) 290-92; Rousseau *CJ* 60 (1964) 138-39; Segal *Arion* 4 (1965) 126-49; Wilkinson *CR* 15 (1965) 182-85; Williams *CP* 60 (1965) 30-33; Wlosok *Gnomon* 42 (1970) 450-63.
717. J. Perret, *Virgile* (new edition, revised and augmented) (Paris 1965).
718. M. C. J. Putnam, "The Virgilian achievement," *Arethusa* 5 (1972) 53-70.
719. F. Robertson, "Allegorical interpretations of Virgil," *PVS* 6 (1966-67) 34-45.
719a. G. Romaniello, *La resurrezione di Virgilio* (Naples 1972).
720. H. C. Rutledge, "Classical Latin poetry: an art for our time," *The Endless Frontier: Essays on Classical Humanism* (ed. M. Morford) (Columbus, Ohio 1972) 136-68 (esp. 156ff.).
720a. A. Salvatore, *Introduzione alla lettura di Virgilio* (Naples 1965).
721. P. L. Smith, "Pathetic vignettes in Homer and Virgil," *Proc. Pacific Northwest Conference on Foreign Languages* 24 (1973) 203-208.
722. J. B. Van Sickle, "Studies of dialectical methodology in the Virgilian tradition," *MLN* 85 (1970) 884-928.
722a. K. Vretska, "Gedanken über den jungen Vergil," *Gestalt. ü. Wirklichkeit. Festgabe für Ferd. Weinhandl* (Berlin 1967) 337-47.
723. G. Williams, *Tradition and Originality in Roman Poetry* (Oxford 1968); *The Nature of Roman Poetry* (Oxford 1970) (condensed version). Rev: Anderson *Vergilius* 15 (1969) 60-62; Henry *CP* 66 (1971) 196-200; Segal *CJ* 66 (1971) 164-69.
724. R. D. Williams, *Virgil. Greece and Rome, New Surveys in the Classics* No. 1 (1967).
725. R. D. Williams, "Virgil today," *PVS* 12 (1972) 25-35.
726. A. Wlosok, "Vergil in der neueren Forschung," *Gymnasium* 80 (1973) 129-51.
727. E. Zinn, "Vergil," *LAW* (1965) 3205-12.

Otis is reflected repeatedly in this decade of scholarship. He locates *E* and *G* in the Callimachean framework; *A* is classical (or reactionary), merging neoclassical and Homeric elements. V's subjective-empathetic style, narrative continuity, symbolic structure and compositional patterns are stressed. Otis' structural and critical analyses of the poems, with due sense of Augustan outlook and ideology where apposite, are exemplary. He avoids the obtuseness and crude literalism of past critics and sidesteps the pursuit of mystical meanings and numerical correspondences. Klingner, "one of the greatest Latinists of our time" (Otis), offers brilliant observations on V stylistics and verse structure, poetic development and originality. Dudley's volume of collected essays excludes *G*. Commager's collection conveniently reprints earlier studies (Bowra, Lewis, Clausen, Otis, Parry, Knox, Brooks, Pöschl) with an introduction. Brisson's portrait of the artist, young and old, reconstructs V's life; *G* 1 (excluding 1-43) was published in 38; *E* 10 in 37 (the year of *E* publication); Maecenas ordered V to enlarge his earliest *G*; a revised edition of *G* in 26-25 replaced the *Laudes Galli* with the Aristaeus episode. Brisson's reconstruction rests heavily on the flimsy *Vitae* and piles hypothesis on hypothesis. Tanner (382), and *Camps* (308) share the historical approach; but the autonomy of literature must also be respected.

Alfonsi traces the role of Greece, myth and reality, Arcadian and spiritual landscape in V's *E, G,* and *A*. Coolidge argues that V projects his characteristic comparison of great things with small into a conception of the nature of change or evolution, to justify the processes of time from bygone Republican dispensation to new Augustan power and glory. Distler's handbook is comprehensive and useful. Pastoral gardens and extensive landscapes are studied by Gorrichon in the context of artistic conventions. Van Sickle offers structuralist interpretations of the centre of the *E*-book and extends the dialectical method from *E* 10 (Arcadia/Gallus) to *G* 4 (Arcadius magister/Orpheus) and *A* 12 (Aeneas/Pallas/Turnus). Gordon Williams offers incisive criticism and analysis of V passages; he questions the validity of modern critical studies of arrangement and structure. Deryck Williams' presidential address considers the many-sidedness of V. Robertson discusses the plausibility of historical allegories detected in *E* 1, 5, and 9 and *A* 8. Wlosok, La Penna, and Armstrong provide analyses of the present state of V studies.

B. RELIGION AND PHILOSOPHY

728. P. Boyancé, *La religion de Virgile* (Paris 1963). Rev: Granarolo *BAGB* (1964) 279-82; Luck *Latomus* 23 (1964) 851-52; Paratore *RCCM* 6 (1964) 319-26; Perret *REL* 42 (1964) 580-83; Turcan *RHR* 157 (1965) 203-206; Wagenvoort *Gnomon* 41 (1969) 276-82.
729. T. J. Haarhoff, "Vergil and the pre-Greek gods," *PVS* 6 (1966-67) 49-50.
730. W. F. Jackson Knight, *Elysion. On Ancient Greek and Roman Beliefs Concerning a Life After Death* (New York 1970).
731. G. Mincione, *L'oltretomba di Virgilio in relazione con quella di Omero e di Dante* (Pescara 1968).
732. L. J. Quintela Ferreiro, "Notas sobre el libro IV de la Eneida," *Actas* II 350-59.
733. F. Solmsen, "Greek ideas of the hereafter in Vergil's Roman epic," *PAPhS* 112 (1968) 8-14.
734. H. L. Tracy, "Auguria Divom in Vergil's works," *Vergilius* 17 (1971) 4-6.
735. E. Vanderlinden, "La foi de Virgile," *BAGB* (1964) 448-58.

Boyancé's study of V's religion considers *Vita, Dei, Fatum* (important), *Pietas, Divinitas, Sibylla,* and *Inferi.* Often highly subjective, Boyancé's remarks on belief and conceptions of deity with literary allusions are nevertheless valuable. Haarhoff shows V's profound affection for Italian divinities (di patrii, Indigetes, Romulus, Vesta). Jackson Knight's remarks on spiritualistic survival, paranormal communication, the progression of spirits from earth to a new-dimensional world (Elysium) include V. Mincione's study of the afterlife is more conventional with useful parallels from Homer and Dante. Quintela Ferreiro finds evidence for synthesis of Hellenism and Judaism in *A* 4 especially. Solmsen finds a religious orientation in V's conception of man's destiny transcending the patriotic or historical commitment. Tracy studies omens, divinations, and ominous incidents; the mysterious tones of *A* 1-6 yield to brighter colours in *A* 7-12 and the initiative in Italy is human. Vanderlinden finds three levels of awareness in V: common man's belief, reason, and faith.

736. M. R. Arundel, "Principio caelum (Aeneid VI,724-751)," *PVS* 3 (1963-64) 27-34.
737. N. I. Barbu, "Valeurs romains et idéaux humains dans le livre VI de l'Enéide," *Bardon* 19-34.
738. F. Dug Carrasco, "Los sentidos del tiempo en Virgilio," *Actas II,* 360-67.
739. G. Castelli, "Echi lucreziani nel brano della età (Verg. Georg. 1, 118-159) e nello concezione virgiliana del destino umano e del lavoro," *RSC* 17 (1969) 20-31.
740. E. Castorina, "Sull' età dell'oro in Lucrezio e Virgilio," *Studi di storio-grafia antica in memoria de Leonardo Ferrero* (Turin 1971) 99-114.

741. C. A. Forbes, "The philosophy of Vergil," *Vergilius* 10 (1964) 7-11.
742. B. Gatz, *Weltalter, goldene Zeit und sinnverwandte Vorstellungen* (Hildesheim 1967).
743. G. Gennaro, "La véritable théologie épicurienne: Lucrèce et Virgile," *Actes du viiie Congrès G. Budé*, 1968 (Paris 1969) 363-65.
744. T. Haecker, *Vergil. Schönheit. Metaphysik des Fühlens* (München 1967).
745. R. Joudoux, "La philosophie politique des 'Géorgiques' d'après le livre IV (v. 149-169)," *BAGB* (1971) 67-82.
746. J. Klein, "The Myth of Virgil's Aeneid," *Interpretation: Journal of Political Philosophy* 2:1 (1971) 10-20.
747. R. Lamacchia, "Ciceros Somnium Scipionis und das VI. Buch der Aeneis," *RhM* 107 (1964) 261-78.
748. A. Michel, "A propos de la tradition doxographique. Epicurisme et platonisme chez Virgile," *Forschungen zur römischen Literatur, Festschrift zum 60. Geburtstag von Karl Büchner* (Wiesbaden 1970) 197-205.
749. J. Oroz-Reta, "Virgile et l'Epicurisme," *Actes du viiie Congrès G. Budé, 1968* (Paris 1969) 436-47.
750. J. Perret, "L'amour romanesque chez Virgile," *Maia* 16 (1965) 3-18.
751. M. Ruch, "Le Destin dans l'Eneide: essence et réalité," *Bardon* 312-31.
752. W. Spoerri, "L'épicurisme et la cosmogonie du Silène," *Actes du viiie Congrès G. Budé, 1968* (Paris 1969) 447-56.
753. F. A. Sullivan "Virgil and the mystery of suffering," *AJP* 90 (1969) 161-77.
754. A. H. F. Thornton, "A Roman view of the universe in the first century B.C.," *Prudentia* 1 (1969) 2-13.
755. A. Traina, "Si numquam fallit imago: Reflessioni sulle *Bucoliche* e l'Epicureismo," *A&R* 10 (1965) 72-78.

Epicureanism and Lucretius, themes and concepts, recur in V's poetry. Castelli detects Lucretian reverberations in V's theodicy (*G* 1,118-59) but departures from Lucretian ataraxy for life's realities and tragic pessimism. Castorini studies the Golden Age in Lucretius and V; Gennaro studies Epicurean theology in Lucretius and V. Oroz-Reta traces Epicurean themes in V, interest in nature and scientific questions, conception of human progress, etc. Michel argues that Epicureanism was never dominant in V despite Siro's teachings; Platonic eclecticism (Carneades, Antiochus of Ascalon) affects V's view of destiny (*E*4) and his conception of beauty. Perret detects Platonic love in *E* 2 and 8 and *A* 1-4 with mystery overtones; love for the unattainable produces a sadness, not resignation, which generates important works of poetry. Arundel argues for Stoic and other Greek philosophical influences in V's conceptions of the *spiritus-mens*. Barbu treats the hierarchy of human values in *A* 6 and the law of universal necessity. According to Carrasco, V accepted the cyclical theory of time and its progressive nature. Forbes states that V was a "tireless seeker after wisdom, but he did not find all the answers in any one philosophic system or even in all the systems put together." Lamacchia finds that Cicero and V agree on human destiny; both offer Pythagorean ideas in Roman guise. Ruch deals with *fatum, fortuna*, and *casus* in the Aeneid. Sullivan accounts for heroic suffering as part of the divine plan towards the fulfillment of Aeneas' fate. Thornton discusses monotheism and polytheism in Varro, Cicero, and V.

C. ROME AND AUGUSTUS

756. P. Dionyzi, "Koncepcja apoteozy Augusta w poematach Wergiliusza (Les Apothéoses d'Auguste dans les poèmes de Virgile)," *Eos* 60 (1972) 269-83.
757. J. G. Griffiths, "The death of Cleopatra VII. A rejoinder and a postscript," *JEA* 51 (1965) 209-11.

758. A. Grisart, "Asinius Pollion commentateur de Virgile," *Athenaeum* 42 (1964) 447-88.
759. H. Malmström, *Ara Pacis and Virgil's Aeneid. A comparative study* (Malmö 1963).
760. P. M. Martin, "La propaganda augustéenne dans les Antiquités romaines de Denys d'Alicarnasse (livre I)," *REL* 49 (1971) 162-79.
761. A. Michel, "Virgile et la politique impériale; un courtisan ou un philosophe?" *Bardon* 212-45.
762. D. M. Poduska, "Ope barbarica or bellum civile" *CB* 46 (1970) 33-34, 46.
763. J. J. H. Savage, "Repartee on the Palatine Hill," *Vergilius* 16 (1970) 7-10.
764. J. J. H. Savage, "Variations on a Theme by Augustus," *TAPA* 97 (1966) 431-57.
765. J. J. H. Savage, "The *Aurea Dicta* of Augustus and the Poets," *TAPA* 99 (1968) 401-18.
766. J. J. H. Savage, "More Variations on a Theme by Augustus," *TAPA* 98 (1967) 415-30.
767. L. R. Taylor, "Republican and Augustan writers enrolled in the equestrian centuries," *TAPA* 99 (1968) 469-86.
768. D. Thompson, "Allegory and Typology in the Aeneid," *Arethusa* 3 (1970) 147-53.
769. G. Townend, *The Augustan Poets and the Permissive Society* (Abingdon-on-Thames 1972) (Fifth Jackson Knight Memorial Lecture).

Griffiths remarks on the evidence for Cleopatra's death in V and Augustan poets. Grisart deals with Pollio's essay on V's poetic language; Malmström's comparative study requires caution. Martin detects Augustan propaganda in Dionysius' Evander, Heracles, Aeneas, and Romulus. Michel argues for a mutual concern for beauty and truth in V and Augustus; V's appreciation and support was basically philosophical and entirely sincere. Michel's interpretation of *E* 1 is noteworthy. Poduska treats references to Actium in V and other Augustan writers. Savage's articles detect Vergilian allusions to Augustus' *festina lente* motto (764, 766); *G* 3,525-6, refers to V's verse offered to Augustus (763). Taylor argued that V probably became an *eques* by Augustus' intervention. Thompson (*contra* Pöschl) argues that Aeneas is a type of Augustus who completes the mission of his predecessor.

D. VERGIL AND OTHER AUGUSTAN POETS

General

770. A. Heinz, *Humor in der augusteischen Dichtung. Lachen und Lächeln bei Horaz, Properz, Tibull und Vergil* (Wien 1970).
771. R. J. Murray, "The attitude of the Augustan poets towards rex and related words," *CJ* 60 (1965) 241-46.
772. W. R. Nethercut, "Vergil's dove," *CB* 41 (1965) 65-68.
773. J. K. Newman, *Augustus and the New Poetry* (Bruxelles 1967).
774. J. K. Newman, *The Concept of Vates in Augustan Poetry* (Bruxelles 1967).
775. I. Trecsenyi-Waldapfel, "Eléments égyptiens dans la poésie latine de l'âge d'or," *Annal. Univ. Scient. Budapest de R. Eotvos nomin., Sectio Philol* 6 (1965) 3-13. See also *Williams*.

Cornelius Gallus

776. G. Barra, "Il crimen di Cornelio Gallo," *Vichiana* 5 (1968) 49-58.
777. J. P. Boucher, *Caius Cornelius Gallus* (Paris 1966).

778. G. Guadagno, "C. Cornelius Gallus praefectus fabrum nelle nuove iscrizioni dell'obelisco vaticano," *Opuscula Romana* 6 (1968) 21-26.

Horace

779. D. Ableitinger, "Die Aeneassage in Carmen Saeculare des Horaz," *WS* 6 (1972) 33-44.
780. T. V. Buttrey, "Halved Coins, The Augustan Reform, and Horace Odes 1.3," *AJA* 76 (1972) 31-48.
781. R. Gelsomino, "Leggende l'Ode des Soratte," *Helikon* 11 (1962) 553-71.
782. B. Jozefowicz, "Quo impulsu Horatiu₃ Carm. III, 4 composuerit," *Eos* 52 (1962) 309-21.
783. H. A. Khan, "Horace's Ode/to Virgil on the death of Quintilius 1, 24," *Latomus* 26 (1967) 107-17.
784. W. L. Lieberman, "Die Otium-Ode des Horaz (c. II, 16)," *Latomus* 30 (1971) 294-316.
785. L. I. Lindo, "Horace's second Epode," *CP* 63 (1968) 206-208.
786. C. W. Lockyer, "Horace's propempticon and Vergil's voyage," *CW* 61 (1967) 42-45.
787. W. Ludwig, "Horaz, c. II, 6, Eine Retractio," *WS* 4 (1970) 101-109.
788. L. A. Moritz, "Horace's Virgil," *PVS* 8 (1968-69) 13-14.
789. H. Mörland, "Die Carmina des Horaz in der *Aeneis*," *SO* 42 (1968) 102-12.
790. F. Muthmann, "Trost und Mass. Gedanken zur Ode I, 24 des Horaz," *AU* 10 (1967) 29-33.
791. E. Paratore, "Taranto nella poesia augustea," *Rassegna Pugliese* 1 (1966) 1-24.
792. A. Pieri, "L'Epodo 2 di Orazio e le *Georgiche*," *SIFC* 44 (1972) 244-66.
793. G. B. Pighi, "Roma e Cartagine in Virgilio e Orazio," *RIL* 103 (1969) 741-54.
794. K. Reckford, *Horace* (New York 1969).
795. M. Reinhold, "Horace, Carm. I, 11, 5-6," *Hermes* 97 (1969) 377-78.
796. J. J. H. Savage, "Vergil and the Pleiades," *Vergilius* 11 (1965) 1-5.
797. O. Seel, "Aneas bei Horaz," *Verschlüsselte Gegenwart* (Stuttgart 1972) 135-42.
798. H. L. Tracy, "Two Footnotes on Horace 3, 3, 37-8," *Class News & Views (EMC)* 16 (1972) 92-93.
799. J. E. G. Whitehorne, "The ambitious builder," *AUMLA* 3 (1967) 28-39.

Heinz (770) traces laughter and the comic, an elusive factor, in Augustan poetry. *Rex* and *regnum*, according to Murray, are not derogatory even in political contexts in Augustan poetry. Nethercut detects echoes of *E* 1,57-8 in Horace, Propertius and Ovid. Newman's studies are contentious but valuable. Trecsenyi-Waldapfel (775) studies the Nile and Egyptian mythology in Augustan poetry. Nilotic scenes are equally popular in wall-painting and mosaics.

The celebrated obelisk in St. Peter's Square, *monumentum aere perennius*, testifies to Gallus' public career. Barra's view, that Gallus was white-washed of treason and guilt and presented as an adventurer clashes with the evident *damnatio memoriae* on the obelisk. Dispute attaches to the locale of Forum Julium: Egypt, Rome, or Fréjus. Gallus' unquiet ghost keeps returning; Vergil and the elegists were no more immune than present-day scholars to his peculiar importance.

Ableitinger finds affinities between Horace's *Carmen Saeculare* (37-44) and *A* 6. Buttrey cites contemporary numismatic relevance for *animae dimidium meae*, divided Janus-head asses. Gelsomino's study of *Odes* 1,9 involves *G* 1,291ff., and 3,349ff. Jozefowicz finds inspiration for *Odes* 3,4 in *A* 6. Khan interprets *Odes* 1,24 with reference to V. Lieberman finds parallels and insights for the Otium Ode (2,16) in V. Lindo argues that *Epode* 2 is Horace's response to critics of V's developing *G*.

Lockyer regards *Odes* 1,3 as Horace's toast to V's success with the epic; absence of grief and protestation, normal in a propempticon, and of ship imagery, hallowed by poets, support the interpretation. Ludwig conceives *Odes* 2,16 as Horace's salute to the Corycian senex (*G* 4,125ff.). Moritz regards V as the addressee of *Odes* 4,12, a final farewell. Mörland detects *Odes* 2,17,21 in *A* 12,537ff.; *Odes* 1,26,1-3 and 3,30,10f., in *A* 9,772ff. Paratore treats Tarentum in the poems of Horace and V. Reinhold finds V inspiration for Horace *Odes* 1,11,5-6 (*mare Tyrrhenum*). *Adynta* and *palumbae* in *E* 1, according to Savage, are echoed in *Odes* 1,2. Seel examines Aeneas in Horace's poetry with Vergilian notices. Tracy notes mutual concern for *concordia ordinum* and *consensus Italiae* in both poets. Whitehorne treats the ambitious builder as commonplace in V, Horace, and Juvenal. Muthmann (790) argues that the excessive grief in *Odes* 1,24 reflects V's not Horace's immoderate sense of loss. Pieri detects allusions to *G* 2,458ff. in *Epode* 2 and *imitatio-aemulatio* of *G* 1 (close) in *Odes* 1,2,30-52.

The Elegiac Poets

800.   C. Fantazzi, "Virgilian pastoral and Roman love poetry," *AJP* 87 (1966) 171-91.

Fantazzi studies the erotic element in the *E* and discusses ties with neoteric and elegiac poetry.

Tibullus

801.   V. Buchheit, "Tibull II,5 und die Aeneis," *Philologus* 109 (1965) 104-20.
802.   K. Büchner, "Die Elegien des Lygdamus," *Hermes* 93 (1965) 65-112, 503-508.
803.   W. Gerressen, *Tibulls Elegie 2.5 und Vergils Aeneis* (Köln 1970). Rev: Kenney *CR* 22 (1972) 277.
804.   D. N. Levin, "The alleged date of Tibullus' death," *CJ* 62 (1967) 311-14.

Propertius

805.   E. Courtney, "Three poems of Propertius," *BICS* 16 (1969) 70-87.
805a.   L. C. Curran, "Propertius 4.11: Greek Heroines and Death," *CP* 63 (1968) 134-39.
806.   W. R. Nethercut, "The ironic priest: Propertius' *Roman Elegies* III,1-5: Imitations of Horace and Vergil," *AJP* 91 (1970) 385-407.
807.   V. Schmidt, "Virgile et l'apogée de la louange de Cynthie (Properce II 3,23-32)," *Mnem* 25 (1972) 402-407.
808.   H. Trankle, "Properz über Virgils Aeneis," *MH* 28 (1971) 60-63.
809.   D. W. Vessey, "Nescio quid maius," *PVS* 9 (1969-70) 53-76.

Buchheit finds echoes of *A* 8,36-65 in Tibullus 2,5,39-64 indicating that Tibullus knew the *A* after its publication (19 B. C.). Büchner identifies Lygdamus with a young nobilis, member of Messalla's circle, acquainted with V but inspired by Catullus and Gallus. Gerressen develops Buchheit (801) with an exhaustive study of Domitius Marsus' epigram (p. 111 Morel). Levin argues that Tibullus predeceased V, but Buchheit and Gerressen suggest otherwise.

Courtney suggests that Propertius 3,5 recalls *G* 2,458ff. Nethercut argues that Propertius 3,1-5, modelled on Horace's *Roman Odes*, are parodies of Horace, Ennius and V. Refutation of V's view of Augustus may therefore constitute criticism of Augustus. Schmidt finds parallels between Propertius 2,3,23-32 and *E* 4. Curran discusses reminiscences of *G*4 (and Euripides' *Alcestis*) in Propertius' Cornelia elegy. Propertius' symbolism of death challenges V's in moral complexity, vision, and ultimate ambivalence. Propertius' hopes for V concern Trankle and Vessey; Vessey remarks that Propertius 1,7 and 1,9 hail V's epic as valid and tenable because it derives from Callimachean principles.

Ovid

810. I. Cazzaniga, "Il deipnon adeipnon della Baucis Ovidiana: Ricerca di tecnica stilistica," *PP* 18 (1963) 23-35.
811. S. Doepp, *Virgilischer Einfluss im Werk Ovids*. Diss. Munich, 1968. Rev: Bardon *Latomus* 30 (1971) 1187-90; Kenney *CR* 20 (1970) 245-50; Phillips *CP* 66 (1971) 72-73.
812. W. Fauth, "Die Fama bei Vergil und Ovid," *Anregung, Zeitschrift für die Höhere Schule* 4 (1965) 232-38.
813. G. K. Galinsky, "The Cipus episode in Ovid's Metamorphoses, (15. 565-621)," *TAPA* 98 (1967) 181-91.
814. R. Gilg-Ludwig, "Die göttliche Widersacherin (Juno bei Ovid, Vergil, Seneca)," *Helikon* 6 (1966) 425-41.
815. A. W. J. Holleman, "Ovidii Metamorphoseon liber XV,622-870," *Latomus* 28 (1969) 42-60.
816. R. Hosek, "Die Auffassung der Concordia bei den Dichtern des Prinzipats," *SPFB* 16 (1967) 153-62.
817. H. H. Huxley, "Ovid's Debt to Virgil," *Canisius College Language Methods Newsletter* 5:1 (1967) 1-15; cf. *PCA* 62 (1965) 32-34.
818. H. A. Khan, "Dido and the sword of Aeneas," *CP* 63 (1968) 282-85.
819. M. Labate, "Il trionfo d'Amore in Ovidio e un passo dell'Eneide," *Maia* 23 (1971) 346-47.
820. R. Lamacchia, "Precisazioni su alcuni aspetti dell'epica ovidiana," *A&R* 14 (1969) 1-20.
821. E. W. Leach, "Georgic imagery in the Ars Amatoria," *TAPA* 95 (1964) 142-54.
822. W. Luppe, "Die Achaemenidesepisode des Ovid (Metamorphoseon XIV,154-220), Ein Beiträge zur antiken Variationskunst," *WZHalle* 6 (1966) 203-12.
823. H. Reynen, "Ewiger Frühling und goldene Zeit: Zum mythos des goldenen Zeitalters bei Ovid und Vergil," *Gymnasium* 72 (1965) 415-33.
824. C. Segal, "Ovid's Orpheus and Augustan ideology," *TAPA* 103 (1972) 473-94.
825. C. P. Segal, *Landscape in Ovid's Metamorphoses. A Study in the Transformation of a Literary Symbol* (Wiesbaden 1969).
826. G. Stégen, "Notes de lecture," *Latomus* 28 (1969) 698, 1120-21.
827. G. Stégen, "Ovide, *Ibis* 343-344," *Latomus* 26 (1967) 197.
828. B. J. Weber, *A Comparative Study of the Dido Theme in Virgil, Ovid* and *Chaucer*. Diss. Florida State University, 1970. Summary in *DA* 31 (1970) 2363A-2364A.

Segal's study of landscape treats Ovid's use of Theocritean and Vergilian scenes to contrast with violent action; shade, benevolent in V, is sinister in Ovid; Ovid's landscapes are largely symbolic quite apart from landscape painting or autopsy of the countryside. Doepp's thesis studies and catalogues verbal echoes of V in Ovid, most notably in *Met*. 13-14 where V's dignity and pathos are lacking. Fauth examines *A* 4,173-88 and Ovid *Met*. 12,39-63. Galinsky tests Ovidian *imitatio* in *Met*. 15,565-621. Gilg-Ludwig studies Juno's role in the divine company as seen by Ovid, V, and Seneca. Holleman suggests that *Met*. 15 signals Rome's error with regard to Augustus as the saviour of *E* 4. Hosek examines the concept of harmony (human relations, philosophy, music) in Ovid and V. Huxley treats larger instances of Vergilian influence. Khan adduces *Her.* 7,181-96 in connection with the exchange of arms in *A* 4. Labate confronts *Amores* 1,2,23ff., with *A* 1,291-6. Lamacchia studies *Met.* 12,623ff. for V connections. Leach finds similarity between V's arts of husbandry and Ovid's *Ars Amatoria*; Ovid parodies V's didactic technique, morals and ideals. Luppe traces deviations from *Odyssey* 9 and *A* 3 in Ovid's Achaemenides episode (*Met.* 14,154-220). V emphasizes Aeneas' *pietas* but Ovid is more concerned with the psychological traits of the castaway. Reynen examines the Golden Age in both poets. Stégen connects *Ars Amatoria* 1,26 with *A* 4,174-88; and *Ibis* 343-44 with *A* 6,94-97. Weber's thesis examines the adaptability of Dido as a legendary figure and offers a detailed analysis and comparison of V's Dido with Ovid's *Heroides* 7.

E. VARIA

829.   B. Ashmole, "A portrait of Menander, an inscribed bust in the J. Paul Getty Museum, Malibu," *AJA* 77 (1973) 61.
830.   E. Bielefeld, "Zu den Vergilbildnis des Justus van Gent für Federigo da Montefeltre," *Gymnasium* 74 (1967) 321-26.
831.   M. J. Deleprierre, "Une scène de la prise de Troie décrite par Virgile représentée sur le boitier d'un miroir grec du IVᵉ siècle av. J.-C.," *Monuments Piot* 56 (1969) 1-11.
832.   L. Fabbrini, "Il Virgilio di V. H. Poulsen, Nuovi contributi ad una geniale introduzione," *RPAA* 39 (1966-67) 117-26.
833.   L. Foucher, "Les mosaïques tunisiennes et les oeuvres des poètes latines (Virgile, Ovide, Stace)," *Conférences de la Société d'Etudes Latines de Bruxelles 1963-64, 1964-65.* Vol. I (Brussels 1965-6).
834.   G. Hafner, "Das Bildnis des L. Aemilius Paullus," *JOEAI* 48 (1966-7) 5-15.
835.   V. Poulsen, "Notes on a group of Attic portraits," *RA* (1968) (Etudes de sculpture antique offertes à Jean Charbonneaux, I) 267-78, esp. 267-74.
836.   G. M. A. Richter, *The Portraits of the Greeks.* Vol. 3 (London 1965) 224-29.
837.   R. V. Schoder, S. J., "On two portraits of Vergil," *Vergilius* 13 (1967) 8-15.
838.   O. Vessberg, "Sculptures in the Throne-Holst Collection," *BMNE* 11 (1962) 39-63.
839.   J. F. Crome, "Silio Italico studioso e cultore di Virgilio. Contributo alle indagini per la determinazione del volto di Virgilio," *Atti e Mem. dell' Accad. Virgiliana* 34 (1963) 43-51.

Vergil's portrait likeness remains disputed. The 'Menander type' has lost favour. A bronze replica of the Menander-Vergil bust in the J. Paul Getty Museum is inscribed with Menander's name. Poulsen's Vergil type appears in Justus Van Gent's portrait of the poet and, according to Bielefeld, a copy existed in the painter's time. Hafner identifies him from the Auditorium of Maecenas as L. Aemilius Paullus, not V. Poulsen's identifications of late Republican portraits by an Athenian sculptor include V., Marcellus, Augustus, Agrippa, etc. Lippold, Crome, Carpenter, and Schefold favour the Menander-Vergil portrait. Poulsen's type survives in Copenhagen (2), the Lateran Museum (2) and Leipzig. The terracotta portrait plaque in Athens, the marble bust in the Lateran, and the double-herm with the Pseudo-Seneca (Ennius?) in Copenhagen are closely related. All suggest a man in his mature years, shortly before his demise in 19 B.C. Schoder argues that the Bardo mosaic from Hadrumetum (Sousse) corresponds with the central figure of the trio in the Ara Pietatis Augustae relief. Vessberg supports the Menander-Vergil identification. Foucher's study of Tunisian mosaics includes V who enjoyed considerable popularity in African mosaic art at home and abroad, especially in Britain.

VIII. STYLE, LANGUAGE, METER

General

840.   S. Lilja, "The Treatment of Odours in the Poetry of Antiquity," *Commentationes Humanarum Litterarum* 49 (1972).
841.   D. C. Swanson, *The Names in Roman Verse. A Lexicon and Reverse Index of all Proper Names of History, Mythology and Geography found in the Classical Roman Poets* (Madison-Milwaukee 1967).
842.   F. J. Worstbrock, *Elemente einer Poetik der Aeneis. Untersuchungen zum Gattungsstil vergilianischer Epik* (Munster 1961). Rev: Buchheit *Gnomon* 36 (1964) 52-56; Camps *CR* 15 (1965) 185-86; Hanslik *DLZ* 87 (1966) 116-17; Hulley *CW* 58 (1965) 176-77; Kremers *ZRPh* 83 (1967) 91-94; La Penna *Maia* 18 (1966) 291-94; Sullivan *AJP* 87 (1966) 113-15; Westendorp Boerma *Mnem* 19 (1966) 199-200.

Lilja and Swanson offer useful reference works. Worstbrock's valuable study was neglected by reviewers when it was first published.

Style

843.   M. von Albrecht, "Zu Vergils Erzahltechnik. Beobachtungen zum Tempusgebrauch in der Aeneis," *Glotta* 48 (1970) 219-20.
844.   G. J. M. Bartelinck, *Etymologisering bij Vergilius* (Amsterdam 1965).
845.   M. Berényi-Révész, "Sur la fonction des répétitions de vers et d'expressions dans l'Enéide," *Antik Tanulmányok* 10 (1963) 181-90 (in Hungarian).
846.   J. Blansdorf, "Einige Beobachtung zum vergilischen Enjambement," *Forschungen zur römischen Literatur: Festschrift zum 60 Geburtstag von Karl Büchner* (ed. W. Wimmel) (Wiesbaden 1970) 10-13.
847.   F. Boemer, "Eine Stileigentumlichkeit Vergils. Vertauschen der Prädikate," *Hermes* 93 (1965) 130-31.
848.   C. W. Conrad, "Traditional patterns of word-order in Latin epic from Ennius to Vergil," *HSCP* 69 (1965) 195-258.
849.   A. Fontán, "Tenius ... Musa. La teoría de los *kharaktêres* en la poesía augustea," *Emerita* 32 (1964) 193-208.
850.   R. A. Hornsby, *Patterns of Action: An Interpretation of Vergil's Epic Similes* (Iowa City 1970). Rev: Bews *Phoenix* 25 (1971) 407; Miniconi *Latomus* 31 (1972) 888-92; Perret *REL* 48 (1970) 576-77; Putnam *CW* 64 (1970-71) 204; Sullivan *CP* 67 (1972) 209-13; Williams *CR* 22 (1972) 276-77.
851.   R. A. Hornsby, "The Vergilian simile as means of judgment," *CJ* 60 (1965) 337-44.
852.   G. Lieberg, "Seefahrt und Werk. Untersuchungen zu einer Metapher der Antiken, besonders der Lateinischen Literatur," *GIF* 22 (1969) 38-70.
853.   R. Lucot, "Ponctuation bucolique, accent et émotion dans l'Enéide," *REL* 43 (1965) 261-74.
854.   A. S. McDevitt, "Hysteron proteron in the Aeneid," *CQ* 17 (1967) 316-21.
855.   E. Merone, *Saggi grammaticali e stilistici latini* (Naples 1970).
856.   W. J. O'Neal, *The Form of the Simile in the Aeneid.* Diss. University of Missouri, 1970. Summary in *DA* 31 (1970) 2361A.
857.   J. Oroz-Reta, "Notas Virgilianas (en torno al empleo del adjetivo)," *Actas* 2, 382-88.
858.   A. Perutelli, "Similitudini e stile 'soggettivo' in Virgilio," *Maia* 24 (1972) 42-60.
859.   G. B. Pighi, "De re nautica vetere," *Latinitas* 14 (1966) 243-78.
860.   L. Rubio, "La lengua y el estilo de Virgilio," *Actas* 1, 355-75.

861.   A. Szantyr, "Bemerkungen zum Aufbau der Vergilischen Ekphrasis," *MH* 27 (1970) 28-40.
862.   D. West, "Multiple-correspondence similes in the Aeneid," *JRS* 59 (1969) 40-49.
· 863.   D. West, "Virgilian multiple-correspondence similes and their antecedents," *Philologus* 114 (1970) 262-75.
864.   D. A. West, "The poetry of Lucretius," *PCA* 66 (1969) 34.
See also *Anderson, Camps, Highet, Otis, Putnam PA, Putnam VP, Quinn, Wilkinson,* and *Williams.*

Hornsby's study of V's epic similes shows how they affect the structure, plot, character and imagery of the poem; they are essential, personal, technical elements of V's poetic art, relevant and vitalizing patterns of expression. Hornsby's article examines similes describing Dido for interpretation and estimation of her character and actions. Disparity between the terms of the similes and her career spell her destruction. O'Neal treats similes in phrases and clauses, and studies introductory words, form and type, to determine patterns. West's articles are important for their study of complexities of meaning and association in the similes of *A* 2 and 12. Marine metaphors are illuminated by Lieberg and Pighi. Szantyr on parataxis (ekphrasis) and Bartelinck on etymologies are important. Repetition and word-order are studied by Berényi-Révész, Conrad (important), and McDevitt (on temporal reversals and their effect). V's use of tenses is examined by von Albrecht (*A* 4) and Boemer (*A* 6,847f.; 8,3). Lucot studies 22 instances of bucolic punctuation in *A* with picturesque or emotional effects. Blansdorf comments on enjambement (*A* 1,4 and 7) and detects frequency in tirades. Fontán applies *tenuis* and ˙*gravis* to poetry and rhetoric. Nougaret's comparative study concentrates on prosody, metrics, and vocabulary. Oroz-Reta examines adjectival usages; Rubio suggests critical approaches to stylistic and linguistic analysis.

Language

865.   W. M. Clarke, *Intentional Alliteration and Rhyme in Vergil and Ovid.* Diss. The University of North Carolina, Chapel Hill, 1972. Summary in *DA* 33 (1972) 1151A.
866.   W. M. Clarke, "Intentional Rhyme in Vergil and Ovid," *TAPA* 103 (1972) 49-77.
867.   H. MacL. Currie, "Pietas-Leal-Love," *Vergilius* 18 (1972) 33.
868.   W. W. de Grummond, *Saevus: its Literary Tradition and Use in Virgil's Aeneid.* Diss. The University of North Carolina, Chapel Hill, 1968. Summary in *DA* 29 (1969) 2235A.
869.   G. Doig, "Vergil's art and the Greek language," *CJ* 64 (1968) 1-6.
870.   E. Ernout, "Composés avec in-privatif dans Virgile," *RPh* 44 (1970) 185-202.
871.   J. Fourcade, "Adjectifs pentasyllabes et hexasyllabes en -bilis chez Virgile," *Pallas* 17 (1970) 81-108.
872.   D. Gonzalo Maeso, "La onomatopeya o armonia en Virgilio," *Actas* 1,334-41.
873.   J. F. Gummere, "Petere, move," *CJ* 65 (1970) 178-79.
874.   E. Heitsche, *Epische Kunstsprache und homerische Chronologie* (Heidelberg 1968).
875.   V. J. Herrero, "Virgilio y la pronunciación del latin," *EClás* 7 (1963) 162-82.
876.   V. E. Hernández Vista, "La aliteración en Virgilio. Una definición estilística," *Actas* 2, 342-9.
877.   P. Howell, "Postis," *Philologus* 112 (1968) 132-35.
878.   R. B. Lloyd, "Superbus in the Aeneid," *AJP* 93 (1972) 125-32.

879. A. Lunelli, "Laboranti similis," *Maia* 21 (1969) 341-42.
880. S. Malosti, "Uno stemma virgiliano, l'ablativo di estensione," *Studi sulla lingua poetica latina* (ed. A. Traina) (Rome 1967) 19-101.
881. E. Mensching, "Die Interjektion heus in der Aeneis," *RhM* 113 (1970) 265-71.
882. M. Muehmelt, *Griechische Grammatik in der Vergilerklarung* (Munich 1965). Rev: Hardie *CR* 18 (1968) 64-65; Hulley *CW* 59 (1965) 91; Lasserre *Erasmus* 18 (1966) 552-54; Perret *Latomus* 24 (1965) 672; Radke *Gymnasium* 73 (1966) 326-27; Schlunk *AJP* 88 (1967) 474-76; Timpanaro *RFIC* 94 (1966) 336-41.
883. C. Moussy, "Pasco chez Virgile," *RPh* 43 (1969) 239-48.
884. L. Nougaret, *Analyse verbale comparée du De Signis et des Bucoliques. Collection d'Études latines, Série Scientifique* 30 (Paris 1966).
885. T. E. V. Pearce, "The enclosing word order in the Latin hexameter," *CQ* 16 (1966) 140-71, 298-320.
886. T. E. V. Pearce, "A pattern of word order in Latin poetry," *CQ* 18 (1968) 334-54.
887. D. W. Pye, "Latin 3rd plural perfect indicative active, its ending in verse usage," *TPhS* (1963) 1-27.
888. S. Timpanaro, "Per la storia di ilicet," *RFIC* 41 (1963) 323-37.
889. A. Traina, "Laboranti similis. Storia di un omerismo virgiliano," *Maia* 21 (1969) 71-78.
890. A. J. Vaccaro, "Adjetivación atributiva en las Eglogas," *REC* 10 (1966) 7-23.

Clarke shows that initial alliteration was intentional to accent verse-breaks; rhyming words before verse-breaks in successive verses and occupying the same metrical positions are usually concentrated; and there are occasional consecutive 'rhyme schemes.' Most instances of rhyme are allied with major sense pauses for emphasis, and syntactical agreement can account for fewer than half of the instances in *A* and *Metamorphoses*. Bartelinck and Doig examine V's use of etymology. *Pietas* as epithet connotes loyalty and love; Currie advances leal (Scottish) -love as translation. Gummere interprets the basic meaning of *petere* as 'to move.' Howell explains *postis* (*A* 2,480,493) as leaves torn off the pivot pole, not just the sockets; the pivot pole often became stiff and groaned in its sockets (cf. *A* 1,449). Lloyd's impressive article studies and defines *superbus* and offers sound comments on Turnus' failings. Lunelli and Traina treat a Homeric usage; Muehmelt's study is important. Pearce studies enclosing word order, parenthetical noun and adjective usage, ancient punctuation, and adjective separation from its noun by verb and unqualified noun, by a verb and one or more other words, and qualified nouns as clause endings.

Meter

891. R. Coleman, "Verse scansion and the analysis of Latin hexameter rhythm," *Didaskalos* 4 (1972) 192-205.
892. F. R. Dale, "A note on the trochaic caesura in the third foot," *PVS* 7 (1967-8) 53-54.
893. A. Díez Escanciano, "Métrica y figuras en Homero y en Virgilio," *Perficit* 20 (1968) 443-64.
894. G. E. Duckworth, "Variety and repetition in Vergil's hexameters," *TAPA* 95 (1964) 9-65.
895. G. E. Duckworth, "Hexameter patterns in Vergil," *PVS* 5 (1965-6) 39-49.
896. G. E. Duckworth, "Vergil's subjective style and its relation to meter," *Vergilius* 12 (1966) 1-10.
897. G. E. Duckworth, "A rare type of first foot dactyl (three words)," *AJP* 89 (1968) 437-48.

898. G. E. Duckworth, *Vergil and Classical Hexameter Poetry: A Study in Metrical Variety* (Ann Arbor, Michigan 1969). Rev: Cupaiuolo *Paideia* 25 (1970) 357-59; Hellegouarc'h *Gnomon* 44 (1972) 131-35; Liénard *AC* 39 (1970) 604-608; Perret *REL* 48 (1970) 498-500; Robinson *Vergilius* 17 (1971) 48-49; Tordeur *Latomus* 30 (1971) 862-64; Musurillo *CF* 26 (1972) 142-43.

899. H. D. Edinger, "Paulo maiora canamus," *Vergilius* 14 (1968) 28-35.

900. J. Fourcade, "Mots de structure molosse à l'initiale du vers dans les Bucoliques," *Pallas* 18 (1971) 31-53.

901. E. Frank, "The *Ictus* in the Vergilian and Silver Latin Hexameter," *RIL* 104 (1970) 327-31.

902. T. Halter, *Form und Gestalt in Vergils Aeneis. Zur Funktion sprachlicher und metrischer Stilmittel* (Zurich 1963). Rev: Buchheit *Gnomon* 36 (1964) 47-52; Hanslik *DLZ* 85 (1964) 992-95; La Penna *Maia* 18 (1966) 295-97; Liénard *Latomus* 24 (1965) 965-67; Westendorp Boerma *Mnem* 19 (1966) 201-202.

903. A. Lopez Kindler, "El hexametro y la frase gnomico en Virgilio," *Actas* 2, 375-81.

904. E. D. Kollmann, "*Et* in arsi after elidable syllables in the Vergilian hexameter," *StClas* 14 (1972) 67-84.

905. F. W. Lenz, "The incomplete verses in Vergil's Aeneid. A critical report," *Bardon* 158-74.

906. E. Liénard, "Réflexions sur l'accent latin," *Renard* 1, 551-60.

907. R. Lucot, "Rhythmes horatiens," *Pallas* 11 (1962, publ. 1964) 181-87.

908. I. A. Richmond, "On the elision of final e in certain particles used by Latin poets," *Glotta* 43 (1965) 78-103.

909. Tübingen-Seminar, "Zu elision anapästischer Worter bei Vergil und Statius," *Glotta* 50 (1972) 97-120.

910. J. Veremans, *De plaats van het verbum finitum in de latijnse dactylische hexameter. Metrisch-stilistisch onderzoek bij Ennius, Lucretius, Catullus en Vergilius* (Brussels 1963).

Duckworth's book-length study in metrical variety treats 16 metrical patterns of dactyls and spondees in the first four feet. Frequency of pattern occurrences depends on the poet's usages in emotional, subjective speeches and episodes, and in narrative, objective passages. On metrical grounds, Duckworth argues against V authorship of *Ciris* and *Dirae* but favours *Culex* and *Moretum*. *A* 10-12 differ markedly in choice and treatment of patterns and in frequency of repeated, opposite and reverse patterns found in *A* 1-9. Duckworth argues that *A* 10-12 were unrevised by V. Duckworth's thesis has been widely disputed. Edinger studies the 'singular music' of *E* 4 by examining the single syllable -*or*, its repetitions, metrical treatment and locations for tonality and climax; an important study of Vergilian assonance. Halter's exemplary work offers valuable insights. Dale argues that trochaïc caesura in successive lines is not deliberate. Coleman and Díez Escanciano offer instruction in the art of metrical analysis. Coleman analyzes *A* 1,1-7 using homodyne marks and pausal points rather than caesural marks to give structural shape to the verses. Lenz's exhaustive study of hemistichs treats 58 instances and deduces that some may be deliberate innovations, that others were left incomplete for want of inspiration, and that one may be another's contribution. Lucot examines rhythm as a factor in the introduction of rulers, divinities, important persons, etc. Liénard underscores V's originality in his use of the classic hexameter. The Tübingen group-study of anapaestic word elision and Veremans' broad research are valuable.

IX. INTERPRETATION AND TEXT CRITICISM

Opera

911. G. B. A. Fletcher, "Notes on Virgil's Eclogues, Georgics and Aeneid I to V," *Latomus* 27 (1968) 165-74.
912. G. B. A. Fletcher, "Notes on Virgil Aeneid VI to XII," *Renard* 1, 350-57.
913. H. Mörland, "Zu einigen Stellen in der Aeneis," *SO* 48 (1973) 7-23.
914. R. Verdière, "Notes de lecture," *Bardon* 378-85.

Fletcher offers critical and comparative study of Vergilian expressions. Mörland analyzes *A* 2,394; 261ff.; 114; 434ff.; and 5,840; he detects links between the Menoetes incident (*A* 5,159-83) and the Palinurus episode (5,833ff.).

Eclogues

915. A. Ernout, "Frondator: élagueur ou oiseau?" *GIF* 20 (1967) 113-14.
916. U. Schindel, "Meliboeus redux," *Hermes* 97 (1969) 472-89.
917. K. Wellesley, "Virgil's Araxes, Ecl. 1,61-66," *CP* 63 (1968) 139-41.
918. F. Capponi, "Il frondator nelle contradizioni della I ecloga vergiliana," *Latomus* 24 (1965) 581-90.
919. R. Verdière, "Commentaire sur le frondator de Virgile," *RSC* 13 (1965) 28-30.
920. V. Skanland, "Litus. The mirror of the sea. Vergil, Ecl. 2,25," *SO* 42 (1967) 93-101.
921. P. Maia de Carvalho, "A propos de Virg. Buc. II,30 (haedorumque gregem viridi compellere hibisco). Une réplique horatienne à l'idéal bucolique," *REA* 68 (1966) 278-81.
922. H. G. Mullens, "Molle atque facetum," *PVS* 8 (1968-9) 49.
923. A. Cupaiuolo, "Nota virgiliana (Buc. III,36 sqq.)," *Pontif. Ist. sup. di Scienze e Lett. S. Chiara* (Napoli) *Annali* 14 (1964) 253-59.
924. E. Ernout, "Fecere vitula (Buc. III,77)," *RPh* 37 (1963) 183-85.
925. J. F. Gummere, "Vergil used the popular form," *CJ* 64 (1969) 26.
926. B. Baldwin, "Vergil, Eclogue IV, 61, a reply," *CJ* 64 (1969) 280.
927. D. Kinzler, "Vergil, Eclogue IV, 61," *CJ* 64 (1968) 130-31.
928. H. H. Huxley, "Vergil's defective meter?" *CJ* 64 (1969) 280.
929. P. Flobert, "Sur un vers de Virgile (Buc. IV,45), la signification de sandyx," *RPh* 38 (1964) 228-41.
930. K. A. Rockwell, "Third plural perfect in -ere / erunt / erunt," *CJ* 65 (1969) 26.
931. O. Musso, "Nota a Verg. Ecl. V, 14," *Aevum* 42 (1968) 477.
932. H. Wieland, "Iubeto (zu Vergil. Ecl. 5, 15)," *MH* 23 (1966) 212-15.

Ernout (*frondator* = 'pruner,' 1,57); Schindel, *aristas* (1,69) is metonymy for *annos*; *en umquam* (1.67) registers despair; Wellesley reads *Rhenum* for *Ararim* (1,62) and *Araxen* for *Oaxen*; Capponi views *frondator* as a *rusticus* and Verdière rejects bird for man. Skanland interprets *litus* (2,25) as surf; Maia de Carvalho interprets *viridi hibisco* (2,30) as dative of direction; *viridi* suggests future promise (contrast *nigro compulerit Mercurius gregi*: *Odes* 1,24,18); Mullens discusses *disperdere* (3,27); Cupaiuolo suggests *helici* for *facili* (3,38); Ernout supports MS tradition *faciam vitula* (3,77); Flobert identifies *sandyx* (4,45) not as plant but as calcined white lead. Kinzler proposed *tulerint* for *tulerunt* (4,61); Baldwin championed *tulerunt*; Gummere and Rockwell read *tulerunt* as popular colloquial form with short 'e'; Huxley defended the metric of the line. Musso associates *descripsi*

(5,14) with Theocritus *Idyll* 7,51; Wieland favours P which omits *ut* (5,15); Tugwell, on 9,59-60, finds an echo of *Ars Poetica* 7,261. Dyer parallels 10,73-74 and *G* 2,17-19; *viridis alnus* (white alder) produces suckers (*se subicit*); Gallus' *amor* for poetry grows as offshoot in V's mind.

Georgics

933. H. H. Huxley, "Corusca dextra or corusca fulmina?," *Vergilius* 13 (1967) 51-52.
934. M. McDonald, "Acies: Virgil *Georgics* 1,395," *CP* 68 (1973) 203-205.
935. G. Doig, "Vergil, *Georgics* 1 491-2," *AJP* 86 (1965) 85-88.
936. G. Bernardi Perini, "Un problema virgiliano in Gellio (*Georg.* II,247)," *Atti Mem. Accad. Virgiliana Mantova* 37 (1969) 1-15.
937. I. C. Dodds, "Dextrae iubae," *CR* 18 (1968) 24.
938. F. Capponi, "Un irreale ornitologico," *Bardon* 92-96.
939. W. G. Arnott, "Martins and swallows," *G&R* 14 (1967) 52.
940. D. F. Shillington, "Vergil's uberrima pinus," *AClass* 10 (1967) 19-22.

Huxley argues for *corusca* (1,328) as accusative plural; McDonald translates *acies* (1,395) as 'the sharp (projected) brilliance of starlight'; Doig, on 1,491-92, suggests etymological factors, intimations of bloodshed, either the gladiatorial arena or the plain of combat as suggested by *Emathiam* and *Haemi* . . . *campos*; Dodds on 3,86 (*dextrae iubae*) points out that manes normally fall to the right; Capponi links *acalanthis* (3,338) with *alcyon* (2,328). Arnott, on 4,305-307, detects crown anemone in *rubeant* (306), a house-martin in *hirundo*. Shillington, on 4,141, associates *uberrima pinus* with substantial, healthy trees.

Aeneid

941. J. M. Pax, "Note on Aeneis I,69," *CB* 40 (1963) 31-32.
942. E. J. Kenney, "Two footnotes," *CR* 14 (1964) 13.
943. A. Ker, "Some passages from Virgil," *PCPhS* 10 (1964) 39-42.
944. G. Stégen, "Notes de lecture CLIV: Virgile, Enéide, I,395-396," *Latomus* 23 (1964) 829-30.
945. K. Quinn, "Septima aestas," *CQ* 17 (1967) 128-29.
946. F. Bliss, "Aeneid II, 347-69," *Vergilius* 10 (1964) 20-22.
947. I. Guilandri, "Nota esegetica ad Eneide 2,471-472," *Acme* 23 (1970) 149-51.
948. S. Lundström, "Ein textkritisches Problem in der Aeneis," *Eranos* 68 (1970) 95-108.
949. K. J. McKay, "Slangachtig gedrag bij Vergilius," *Hermeneus* 39 (1967) 83-85.
950. B. Munoz Sanchez, "Otra interpretación del traiectus lora de Virgilio," *EClás* 10 (1966) 169-71.
951. D. T. Raymond, "A comment on the Aeneid," *CJ* 59 (1963) 108.
952. R. Renehan, "Pseudo-Vergil's *ultrix flamma*: a problem in literary possibilities," *CP* 68 (1973) 197-202.
953. G. Stégen, "Une prétendue contradiction dans l'Enéide II, 567-88," *LEC* 35 (1967) 3-6.
954. H. L. Tracy, "Note on Aeneid 2,557," *Vergilius* 11 (1965) 54-56.
955. L. J. Quintelo Ferreiro, "Notas sobre el libro IV de la *Eneida*," *Actas* 1, 350-59.
956. D. B. Gregor, "Aeneid IV, 483," *CR* 19 (1969) 143.
957. R. Ten Kate, "Vergiliana, I & II," *Hermeneus* 36 (1965) 220-23, 279-82.
958. T. E. V. Pearce, "Virgil, Aeneid IV. 440," *CR* 18 (1968) 13-14.

959. A. Setaioli, "A proposito di Aen. IV, 504-521," *Studia Florentina A. Ronconi oblata* (Rome 1970) 393-403.
960. E. Skard, "Zu Verg. Aen. IV, 10," *SO* 41 (1966) 95-97.
961. H. Snijder, "Virgil Aeneid IV.436, quam mihi dederit(s) cumulata(m) morte remittam," *Athenaeum* 60 (1972) 417-20.
962. F. L. D. Steel & L. A. Moritz, "Infixum stridit sub pectore vulnus (Virg. Aen. IV, 689)," *PVS* 8 (1968-9) 49-51.
963. A. S. McDevitt, "A note on Aeneid V,326," *CQ* 17 (1967) 313-15.
964. T. E. V. Pearce, "Virgil, Aeneid 5.279," *CQ* 20 (1970) 154-59.
965. E. K. Borthwick, "Nicetes the Rhetorician and Vergil's *plena deo*," *Mnem* 25 (1972) 408-12.
966. L. Casson, "Sewn boats (Virgil, Aen. VI, 413-414)," *CR* 13 (1963) 257-59.
967. F. Della Corte, "The Senecan *plena deo* quotation and Servius' gloss," *Maia* 23 (1971) 102-106.
968. J. G. Garlandt, "Aeneis VI, 537-61; 625-41," *Hermeneus* 39 (1968) 176-78.
969. H. Koch, "Zum Verständnis von Vergil, Aeneis VI, 205ff.," *WS* 2 (1968) 70-73.
970. O. Seel, "Um einen Vergilvers (Aeneis, VI,468)," *Renard* 1, 677-88.
971. G. Stégen, "Le supplice de Phlégyas. Etude sur un épisode de l'Enéide," *Latomus* 26 (1967) 118-22. (Cf. 506).
972. G. Stégen, "Notes de lecture," *Latomus* 28 (1969) 1121-22.
973. P. Veyne, "Deux notes sur Virgile," *AFLA* 43 (1967) (= Etudes classiques II) 185-93.
974. K. Wellesley, "Facilis descensus Averno," *CR* 14 (1964) 235-38.
975. R. Beare, "Propiusque Periclo It Timor: *Aeneid* 8,556-7," *CQ* 19 (1969) 193-95.
976. R. Rau, "Eine Versinterpolation in Vergils Aeneis," *MH* 22 (1965) 237-38.
977. M. D. Reeve, "Seven notes," *CR* 20 (1970) 134-36.
978. H. Mörland, "Zur Aeneis (IX,772; IV,236)," *SO* 40 (1965) 72-74.
979. R. D. Williams, "Virgil, Aen. IX, 25-32," *CP* 63 (1968) 148.
980. T. Crane, "A Note on Aeneas' 'Human Sacrifice' Aeneid 10.517-20," *CW* 67 (1973) 176-77.
981. H. H. Huxley, "A note on Aeneid 10.808-10," *Vergilius* 15 (1969) 32.
982. R. D. Williams, "Virgil Aeneid XI,400-409," *CP* 61 (1966) 184-86.

Kenney recalls Williamson (*CR* 33 (1919) 30) to provide a succinct and irrefutable explanation of *sunt lacrimae rerum* (*A* 1,460). Ker treats *A* 1,573-74; 2,65-66, 486-91; 9,207-209; 6,860-66. Stégen interprets the swans' behaviour (1,395-96); Quinn reconciles 1,755-56 with 5,626; Bliss translates and annotates 2,347-69; Guilandri treats Diomedes' butchery (2,471-72); Lundström prefers *furenti* to *ruenti* (2,771); Mariner detects Greek influence in *traiectus* (passive voice) and *lora* (object) (2,273); McKay treats 2,203; Sanchez argues that *ater* relates to *pulvere* and *lora* (2,270-73), *traiectus* applies (hypallage) to Hector, *pedes tumentis* = Greek accusative; Raymond discusses 2,144 and 49; Renehan reexamines 2,587 and retains *animum explesse ultricis flammae*; Tracy interprets *litore* (2,557) as consecrated ground. Quintela Ferreiro and Ten Kate treat passages in *A* 4; Gregor (on 4,483) takes *hinc* with *monstrata* (sc. *venisse, migrasse*); Pearce translates *placidas* (4,440) as 'kindly'; Setaioli argues that 4,504-21 were inserted after completing the suicide passage; Skard associates sibilants in 4,10 with whispers; Snijder (on 4,436) reads *dederit cumulata morte*; Steel and Moritz discuss clinical details of Dido's death-throes and contrast *tacitum vulnus* (4,689,67). McDevitt prefers *ambiguumque* (5,326); Pearce favours *nexantem nodis* (5,279). Borthwick replaces *iam propiore dei* (6,51) with *nondum plena deo*; Casson (on 6,413-14) describes Charon's *cumba sutilis* as constructed of sewn planks not skins; Della Corte and Borthwick (*supra*) both treat

Seneca's *plena deo* quotation and Servius' gloss. Garlandt examines Aeneas' passage through Hades (6,537-61, 625-41); Koch interprets the Golden Bough as doubly parasitic: *loranthus europaeus*, mistletoe with yellow berries, and *viscum album*, mistletoe which retains green leaves during the winter. Seel argues that Dido's tears (6,468) are her only means of communication. Stégen comments on 6,616-20 and argues against relocation of the verses; he also explicates *aliquos* (6,664). Wellesley translates *Averno* (6,126) 'by way of Avernus'. Beare suggests that the women's fear advances from Pallanteum to the danger (8,556-57); Reeve treats 8,205-206. Mörland finds Greek etymology behind the juxtaposition *vastatorem Amycum* (9,772) and marital and sexual associations in *Lavinia arva* (4,236). Williams reads *altus* (9,30) as past participle of *alo*. Crane prefers Medicean *perfundant* (10,520) and omega group reading *sparsuros* (82); Huxley parallels 10,808-10 (*nubem belli . . . sustinet*) with Planudean Appendix, Epigram 26. Williams rejects 11,404 and Diomedes' intrusion; *vel cum* (11,406) means 'of what about when?'

X. COMPUTER STUDIES

983. N. A. Greenberg, "Vergil and the computer. Fourth foot texture in Aeneid I," *RELO* (1967) 1, 1-16.

984. N. A. Greenberg, "Scansion purement automatique de l'hexamètre dactylique," *RELO* (1967) 3, 1-30.

985. N. A. Greenberg, "Words and syllables. Four Eclogues," *RELO* (1970) 2, 5-49; 3, 131 (correction).

986. N. A. Greenberg, "The hexametrical Maze," *RELO* (1970) 4, 17-62.

987. N. A. Greenberg, "Epanastrophe in Latin Poetry," *RELO* (1972) 2,1-17.

988. N. A. Greenberg, "Line initials in the Georgics," *RELO* (1972) 4,55-58.

989. R. Lecrompe, *Virgile, Bucoliques. Index Verborum. Relevés statistiques* (Hildesheim 1971). Rev: Grimal Latomus 31 (1972) 225-27.

990. W. Martin, "A note on Herdan's theory on the recurrence of initial phonemes," *RELO* (1973) 2, 1-17.

991. W. Ott, *Metrische Analysen zu Vergil Aeneis Buch I* (Tübingen 1973).

992. W. Ott, *Metrische Analysen zu Vergil Aeneis Buch VI* (Tübingen 1973).

993. W. Ott, *Metrische Analysen zu Vergil Aeneis Buch XII* (Tübingen 1973).

994. D. W. Packard, *Vergil's Georgics:* available in computer-usable form from the American Philological Association's Repository of Greek and Latin Texts in Machine-Readable Form. (Supervisor, S. V. F. Waite, Kiewit Computation Center, Dartmouth College, Hanover, New Hampshire).

995. S. V. F. Waite, *Vergil's Eclogues* (available in computer-usable form, cf. *supra*).

996. H. J. Warwick (Minneapolis, Minn.), *Concordance to the Aeneid* (in progress).

The A.P.A. Repository of Greek and Latin Texts includes the entire Vergilian corpus. Ott's work is gradually appearing in book form and will provide metrical analyses of the separate books. The preparation of the *Aeneid* required many man-months of effort but the finished product frees scholars from exhausting drudgery and enables them to pursue projects otherwise impracticable. The A.P.A. computer works rely on Mynors' *OCT*. Warwick's forthcoming concordance will include changes in the second and third printings of Mynors' *Aeneid*. Notices of new additions to the Repository appear in *Calculi*, a bimonthly newsletter published and distributed by the Department of Classics, Dartmouth College.

Greenberg (983) deals with Jackson Knight's fourth foot texture, i.e., the distribution and arrangement of homodynamic and heterodynamic fourth feet; only about 30 per-cent of the lines in *A* 1 have a homodyned fourth foot; Greenberg offers

(984) a version of automatic scansion that is about 92 per-cent successful; and studies the texture of *E* 1, 4, 6, and 9; the formal features described may contribute to the overall aesthetic effect of the poems. Greenberg's 'maze' article illuminates how poets resemble one another, or diverge, in their metrical practices with reference to the *Eclogues, Aeneid 1, Metam.* XII, *Ars Poetica,* and *Culex.* Greenberg's study of epanastrophe (repetition of the final elements of a word or sentence as initial elements of the following word or sentence) reveals that the hexameter verse of Lucretius lacks the suppleness and flexibility which can be demonstrated qualitatively in Vergil and Ovid. Martin's paper responds to Greenberg (988) and suggests that by treating all initial letters, not merely those at the beginnings of lines, there is an unusual recurrence of form XIX, where the two X's represent the same letter and there is one intervening line. Lecrompe's study provides an alphabetic list of every word in the *Eclogues,* with poem, line, and position in line (case, tense, etc.) and a frequency count; and a statistical analysis of the frequency of nouns, adjectives, pronouns, verbs, according to declension, case, conjugation, mood, tense, etc. Ott's volumes follow a uniform format and are designed to provide materials for subsequent research and study; analysis, comparison, conclusion, and inference rest with others.

XI. VERGIL AND EARLIER WRITERS

Homer

997. M. L. Deshayes, "Virgile imitateur d'Homère," *Hum* (RES) 40 (1963-4) 25-27.

997a. R. W. Garson, "Vergil's use of sources in Aeneid XII," *Latin Teaching* 30:1 (1973) 26-27 (excerpts).

998. G. N. Knauer, *Die Aeneis und Homer. Studien zur poetischen Technik Vergils mit Listen der Homerzitate in der Aeneis* (Göttingen 1964). Rev: Buchheit *Gymnasium* 74 (1967) 470-73, and *GGA* 222 (1970) 79-94; Clarke *Gnomon* 37 (1965) 687-90; Coulter *CW* 59 (1965) 91-92; Cova *Athenaeum* 43 (1965) 472-75; Grilli *Paideia* 22 (1967) 350-54; Hardie *CR* 17 (1967) 470-73; Hovingh *Mnem* 20 (1967) 352-53; Miniconi *Latomus* 24 (1965) 667-71; Perret *REL* 43 (1965) 125-30; Reinke *CJ* 61 (1966) 276-78; Williams *CP* 62 (1967) 225-27.

999. G. N. Knauer, "Vergil's Aeneid and Homer," *GRBS* 5 (1964) 61-84.

1000. W. McLeod, "The wooden horse and Charon's bark. Inconsistency in Virgil's vivid particularization," *Phoenix* 24 (1970) 144-49.

1001. H. Nehrkorn, "A Homeric episode in Vergil's Aeneid," *AJP* 92 (1971) 566-84.

1002. J. Perret, "Du nouveau sur Homère et Virgile," *REL* 43 (1965) 125-30.

1003. R. D. Williams, "Virgil and the Odyssey," *Phoenix* 17 (1963) 266-74.

See also *Anderson, Camps, Highet, Otis, Putnam PA* and *VP; Quinn, Wilkinson, Williams.*

Knauer's monumental work studies V's use of Homeric source material, its adaptation to structure, and provides an extensive list of *loci similes* arranged from *Aeneid* to Homer and from Homer to *Aeneid* with elaborate clues to their similarities, and some schematic plans. V's rearrangement, combination, and redesigning of major Homeric episodes and characters emerge more clearly than ever before. Knauer provides an accurate *index fontium* for literary criticism, an indispensable and endlessly suggestive aid to future research into the primary relationship of V and Homer. Glenn connects Homer's Polyphemus with V's Polyphemus and Mezentius; Sullivan (612) draws parallels between Mezentius and Homeric Ajax. Nehrkorn studies echoes of *Iliad* 5,239ff., in different parts of the *Aeneid* and in various contexts; V's technique is largely reversal of the model. McLeod finds contradictory epithets for the wooden horse and Charon's boat derive from imitation of Homer (*Odyssey* 11,1-7, and 9,196-210). Williams finds Ulysses' world most apparent in *A* 1; the Roman factor is dominant in the Homeric framework although Odyssean themes are prevalent.

Homeric Cycle

1004. A. M. Assereto, "Dall' Etiopide all'Eneide," *Mythos: Scripta in hon. M. Untersteiner* (Genova 1970) 51-58.
1005. H. L. Tracy, "Vergil and the Nostoi," *Vergilius* 14 (1968) 36-40.

Assereto derives Camilla's traits from Arctinus' *Ethiopis;* Tracy treats the story pattern of the *Returns* in the *Aeneid*.

Pindar

1006. R. J. Clarke, "Two Virgilian similes and the *Herakleous katabasis*," *Phoenix* 24 (1970) 244-55.
1007. H. Lloyd-Jones, "Heracles at Eleusis, P. Oxy. 2622 and P.S.I. 1391," *Maia* 19 (1967) 206-29.

Lloyd-Jones assigns P. Oxy. 2622 to Pindar and suggests that V's descent of Hercules used this source; Clarke treats leaf and bird similes in *A* 6,309-12 and derives the leaf similes from the lost *Descent of Heracles*; the bird similes reflect similes in Apollonius Rhodius who may have derived them from Homer and the *Descent of Heracles*.

Greek Drama

1008. L. Alfonsi, "Dal teatro greco alla poesia romana," *Dioniso* 42 (1968) 5-15.
1009. G. Stégen, "L'Oreste d'Euripide dans l'Enéide," *AC* 41 (1972) 222-24.

Alfonsi finds a model for *G* 1,121ff. in Aristophanes' *Ploutos*. Stégen uses Euripides' *Orestes* 1051 to explicate *A* 4,323-24.

Greek Science

1010. J. André, "Deux notes sur les sources de Virgile, I: Virgile et Democrite," *RPh* 44 (1970) 11-17.

André cites agronomy treatises of Bolos of Mende (Pseudo-Democritus) as source for *G* 1,288, 219-26; 2,281-314, 89-102; 1,311-34 derives from an atomic philosopher; Venus' remedy for Aeneas' wound (*A* 12,382ff.) is more detailed than Homer's recipe in the *Iliad* and probably derives from a lost Greek poem.

Theocritus

1011. C. Gallavotti, "Le coppe istoriate di Teocrito e Virgilio," *PP* 21 (1966) 421-36.
1012. R. W. Garson, "Theocritean elements in Virgil's *Eclogues*," *CQ* 21 (1971) 188-203.
1013. S. Posch, *Beobachtungen zur Theokritnachwirkung bei Vergil* (Innsbruck 1969). Rev: Clarke *CR* 22 (1972) 61-62; Jenkinson *JRS* 60 (1970) 266-67; Koch *Gymnasium* 77 (1970) 252-54; Lesueur *REL* 47 (1969) 599-600; Levin *CW* 63 (1969) 58; Perret *Latomus* 28 (1969) 781-82.

1014. F. Robertson, "Virgil and Theocritus," *PVS* 10 (1970-71) 8-23.
1015. T. G. Rosenmeyer, *The Green Cabinet: Theocritus and the European Pastoral Lyric* (Berkeley 1969). Rev: Clarke *CR* 22 (1972) 120-21; Köhnken *Gnomon* 44 (1972) 750-57; Levin *CW* 64 (1970) 87; McKay *Mnem* 26 (1973) 191-92; Marinelli *Phoenix* 25 (1971) 292; Pavlovskis *CP* 66 (1971) 291-92; Van Sickle *AJP* 93 (1972) 348-54.
1016. J. P. Van Sickle, "Is Theocritus a Version of Pastoral?" *MLN* (*Comparative Literature*) 84 (1969) 942-46.
See also *Otis, Putnam VP, Williams.*

Posch provides material for a large-scale study of Vergilian *imitatio* but studies only *E* 2 and 10, the earliest and latest; he lists Vergilian passages with Theocritean correspondences and a reverse list for the entire *E*-book; *E* 4 and 6 are almost totally devoid of Theocritean echoes; *E* 2 (*Idyll* 11) is new and original; *E* 10 (*Idylls* 1 and 7). There is a Theocritean tone in the bucolic passages and a verbal dependence in more subjective passages. Posch's excursuses treat Theocritus and V on nature, and on herdsmen and their careers. Rosenmeyer examines pastoral poetry in a wider context with important remarks on Theocritus and V. Robertson studies *E* 2 for adaptations, omissions and accretions of *Idylls* 3 and 11, and finds affinities between V's poetic *lusus* and Gallus' poetic genre. Gallavotti combines philology and archaeology in his study of *Idylls* 1,27-56, *E* 3,38-39, and *G* 2,449. Garson offers a corrective to preconditioned approaches to the detection of influences. Van Sickle provides new insights into Theocritean pastoral and its relation to V's bucolics, and studies the Fourth pastoral poems of both authors.

Callimachus

1017. W. Clausen, "Callimachus and Roman Poetry," *GRBS* 5 (1964) 181-96.

Clausen's important article examines Callimachus' theory of poetry and his influence on V and other Latin poets.

Apollonius Rhodius

1018. J. D. M. Preshous, "Apollonius Rhodius and Virgíl," *PVS* 4 (1964-5) 1-17.

Preshous accents details and episodes deriving from *Argonautica* with major attention to *A* 4.

Alexandrian Scholarship

1019. P. V. Cova, *L'Omerismo alessandrinistico dell'Eneide* (Brescia 1963). Rev: Bardon *RBPh* 42 (1964) 1460; Guaita *Aevum* 37 (1963) 564-67; Miniconi *Latomus* 23 (1964) 364-66; Venini *Athenaeum* 41 (1963) 464.
1020. R. R. Schlunk, *The Homeric Scholia and the Aeneid. A contribution to the comparative study of Homer and Vergil.* Diss. University of Cincinnati, 1964. Summary in *DA* 25 (1965) 4133.
1021. R. R. Schlunk, "Vergil and the Homeric scholia. A comparative study of Aeneid XII,216-467 and Iliad IV,86-222," *AJP* 88 (1967) 33-44.

Cova and Schlunk examine V's use of Alexandrian scholia on Homer's epics; Schlunk's article examines five instances of *imitatio* in *A* 12,216-47.

Aratus and Nicander

1022. I. Cazzaniga, "Nota critico-testuali a due passi degli Scholia ai Theriaka Nicandrei I," *Maia* 16 (1964) 389-94.

1023. A. Grilli, "Virgilio e Arato (a proposito di Georg. 1. 187ss.)," *Acme* 23 (1970) 145-48.
1024. I. Gulandri, "Note esegetica ad Eneide 2.471-2," *Acme* 23 (1970) 149-51.
1025. C. Pavese, "Due noterelle greco-latine," *SIFC* 35 (1963) 117-19.

Grilli derives *G* 1,187ff., from Aratus and from commentaries on the *Phaenomena*; Pavese finds an echo of Aratus' *Phaenomena* 343 in *G* 1,304. Cazzaniga treats *A* 10,136 and Scholia on *Theriaca*, 516; Gulandri derives the Pyrrhus-serpent passage (*A* 2,471-72) from Homer and Nicander's *Theriaca*.

Early Latin Poetry

1026. H. D. Jocelyn, "Ancient Scholarship and Virgil's use of Republican Latin Literature I," *CQ* 14 (1964) 280-95; II, *CQ* 15 (1965) 126-44.
1027. D. Knecht, "Virgile et ses modèles latines," *AC* 32 (1963) 491-512.
1028. S. Stabryla, *Latin Tragedy in Virgil's Poetry* (Warsaw 1970). Rev: Calder *ACR* 1 (1971) 140; Della Corte *Maia* 24 (1972) 396-97; Eden *Gnomon* 45 (1973) 617-19; Jocelyn *Latomus* 30 (1971) 1180-85.
1029. M. M. Wigodsky, *Vergil and Early Latin Poetry* (Wiesbaden 1972).

Jocelyn makes a close study of Macrobius' *Saturnalia* (freshly available in J. Willis' Teubner edition, 1963; newly translated by P. V. Davies (Columbia 1969) and by N. Marinone (Torino 1967), and the sources of V. Wigodsky's important study of imitations includes Livius Andronicus, Naevius, Ennius (most significant), Pacuvius, Accius, Lucilius, Cicero, Catullus, and Lucretius. Stabryla's comprehensive survey of the influence of Roman tragedy on V deals with verbal, material, and structural aspects; Ennius and Accius (remarkably) are dominant; Pacuvius (although *Niptra* and *Antiopa* were popular) proved unattractive. Knecht studies V *imitatio* of Ennius, Lucretius and Catullus: word order, metrics, and vocabulary alterations are stressed. Knecht notes that wholesale reproduction of lines from the *Ciris* is not typical of V's use of earlier poetry. Foster argues that the account of Sychaeus' murder (*A* 1,343-64) was influenced by Plautus' *Mostellaria* and that *A* 4,31-33 and 291 echo Lucretian expressions.

Ennius

1030. M. von Albrecht, "Ein Pferdegleichnis bei Ennius," *Hermes* 97 (1969) 333-45.
1031. A. Bloch. "Arma virumque als heroisches Leitmotiv," *MH* 27 (1970) 206-11.
1032. S. Boscherini, "Assulae ennianae," *SIFC* 4 (1969) 128-34.
1033. D. H. Jocelyn, *The Tragedies of Ennius* (Cambridge 1967).
1034. C. D. Lanham, "Enjambement in the Annales of Ennius," *Mnem* 23 (1970) 179-87.
1035. G. Stégen, "Sur deux vers d'Ennius, Alexander," *LMV* 25 (1970) 11-12.

Von Albrecht studies the freed horse image in Ennius, *Annales* 514-18 and its appearance in V. Lanham indicates that Ennius' use of enjambement heralds the more sophisticated use of V. Jocelyn's thorough study refers frequently to V. Bloch refers *A* 9,777 to Ennius; Stégen detects *Alexander* 55-56 (Vahlens) in *A* 4,217.

Naevius and Pacuvius

1036. G. D'Anna, "Alcune osservazioni sull' Antiopa di Pacuvio," *Athenaeum* 43 (1965) 81-94.

1037.   A. Mazzarino, "Appunti sul Bellum Poenicum di Nevio, II," *Helikon* 6 (1966) 232-36.
1038.   W. Wimmel, "Vergil und das Atlantenfragment des Naevius," *WS* 4 (1970) 84-100.

D'Anna suggests a common Hellenistic source for Pacuvius' *Antiopa* and *E* 2,23-24. Mazzarino corrects a fragment of Naevius' *Bellum Punicum* and refers to *A* 4,137ff., and 1,647ff. Wimmel treats echoes of fr. 4 (*Atlantes*) in *A* 1,648 (embossed robe); the Titan-Atlantes episode may have served as caution for Carthage to refrain from war with Rome.

Cicero and Varro

1039.   L. Alfonsi, "Nota sulla Pro Marcello," *Aevum* 40 (1966) 545.
1040.   L. Alfonsi, "A proposito di Ecl. II,61,2," *Aevum* 40 (1966) 548.
1041.   L. W. Daly, "A common source in early Roman history," *AJP* 84 (1963) 68-71.
1042.   W. Madyda, "De Varrone Ciceronis et Vergilii interprete et auctore," *Eos* 56 (1966) 119-38.

Alfonsi argues that clemency in *Pro Marcello* is reflected in *A* 6,851-53 and Horace, *Carm. Saec.* 51-52. He aligns Varro, *DRR* 3,1,1f., with *E* 2,61-62. Daly suggests that *A* 7,641ff. may derive from Varro's *Antiquitates*. Madyda examines links between Varro's *De Agricultura* and V's *Georgics*.

Lucretius

1043.   G. Castelli, "Echi lucreziani nelle Ecloghe virgiliane," *RSC* 14 (1966) 313-42; 15 (1967) 14-39; 176-216.
1044.   W. J. Cleary, S. J., "The poetic influence of the *De Rerum Natura* on the Aeneid," *CB* 47 (1970) 17-21.
1045.   J. Foster, "Aeneidea: A Lucretian echo in *Aeneid* IV," *PVS* 11 (1971-2) 77-79.
1045a.   W. R. Nethercut, "Vergil's De Rerum Natura," *Ramus* 2 (1973) 41-52.
1046.   G. Vallillee, "Lucretius, Virgil and the didactic method," *EMC* 12 (1968) 8-12.

Castelli detects Epicurean cosmology in *E* 6 and examines Lucretian theme and attitudes in the *Eclogues*, overemphasizing alleged Epicurean elements. Cleary's article derives V's imagery of light and darkness from Lucretius along with a sense of time and place and an ambiguity in Venus' nature. Vallillee finds Lucretian guidance in V's use of personification, metaphor and digression. Nethercut compares V. and Lucretius on two fronts — those of imagery and of structure.

Catullus

1047.   H. Bolte, "Catullgedicht als Hinführung zu Vergil," *AU* 12:3 (1969) 5-14.
1048.   W. Clausen, "Catullus and Callimachus," *HSCP* 74 (1970) 85-94.
1049.   J. Ferguson, "Catullus and Virgil," *PVS* 11 (1971-2) 25-47.
1050.   E. L. Harrison, "Cleverness in Virgilian imitation," *CP* 65 (1970) 241-43.
1051.   G. Kilroy, "The Dido episode and the sixty-fourth poem of Catullus," *SO* 44 (1969) 48-60.
1052.   R. E. H. Westendorp Boerma, "Invloeden van Catullus op Vergilius," *Hermeneus* 40 (1969) 252-69.

Bolte treats the length of poetic books and compares Catullus' *libellus* and larger publication with V's early works. Clausen studies Catullus 64 and 65 and Vergil's borrowing of 64.39 in *A* 6.460. Ferguson shows that Catullus 64 exercised the greatest influence on V but that there are traces of all branches of Catullus' poetry; V had a limited number of favourites (ours) and his use of conversational 'Catullian' elements lightened the dignity of V's verse. Harrison treats Catullus 66,39 and *A* 6,460 as clever manipulation. Westendorp Boerma's study of Catullian influence is noteworthy.

XII. ANCIENT AUTHORS AFTER VERGIL

General

1053. G. E. Duckworth, "Five centuries of Latin hexameter poetry: Silver Age and Late Empire," *TAPA* 98 (1967) 77-150.

1054. R. E. Gaebel, *A Study of the Greek word-lists to Vergil's Aeneid appearing in Latin literary papyri.* Diss. University of Cincinnati, 1968. Summary in *DA* 29 (1968) 1523A.

1055. R. E. Gaebel, "The Greek word-lists to Vergil and Cicero," *Bull. John Rylands Library* 52 (1970) 284-325.

1056. A. Grillone, "Per la fortuna di Virgilio nel mondo greco. Lineamenti di una ricerca," *Atti dell'Accademia di Scienze, Lettere e Arti di Palermo* 28 (1967-8) 5-8.

1057. A. Grillone, "Virgilio nei papiri egiziani," *ALGP* 5-6 (1968-9) 292-93.

1058. T. Kotula, "Utraque lingua eruditi," *Renard* 2,386-92.

Duckworth's manual study of hexameter usage reflects on Vergil. Gaebel explores methods of teaching V to Greek students from ca. 215 to 600, with word lists as evidence. Grillone discusses Greek versions of *A* 1,649-51 and 702-7 in Egyptian papyri and provides guidelines for future study. Kotula discusses V and Catullus as models for North African Latin from the third century A.D.

Inscriptions

1059. R. Bloch, "Epigraphie latine et antiquitiés romaines," *Annuaire Ecole Pratique des Hautes-Etudes Section* 4 (1966-7) 199-203.

1060. H. I. Marrou, "Une inscription chrétienne de Venasque," *REL* 47 (bis) 143-50.

1061. Z. Popova, "Pour dater les Carmina epigraphica Buecheler 990, 55 et 960," *Eirene* 7 (1968) 57-66.

1062. J. W. Zarker, "A possible Vergilian parody of the Carmina Latina Epigraphica," *Helikon* 8 (1968) 392-98.

Zarker studies epigraphical echoes of the Ballista epigram, one in Germany, the other in North Africa, and concedes that the epigram is V's earliest known poetic effort.

Silver Age Pastoral

1063. A. C. Delateur, S. J., "Calpurnius Siculus and Vergil," *CO* 49 (1972) 97-98.

1063a. E. W. Leach, "Corydon Revisted: an interpretation of the political Eclogues of Calpurnius Siculus," *Ramus* 2 (1973) 53-97.

1064. R. Verdière, "La bucolique post-virgilienne," *Eos* 56 (1966) 161-85.

Silver Age Epic

1065. A. J. Gossage, "Virgil and the Flavian Epic," *Dudley* 67-93.

1066. J. H. Mozley, "Virgil and the Silver Latin epic," *PVS* 3 (1963-4) 12-26.

Gossage's study of Silius Italicus, Statius and Valerius Flaccus is instructive but underplays Statius somewhat. Mozley examines V's influence on Valerius Flaccus and Statius.

Valerius Flaccus

1067. F. Bormann, "Su alcune reminiscenze virgiliane nell'episodio delle donne de Lemno in Valerio Flacco," *Studia Florentina A. Ronconi oblata* (Rome 1970) 41-50.
1068. E. Burck, "Kampf und Tod des Cyzicus bei Valerius Flaccus," *REL* 47 (bis) 173-98.
1069. E. Courtney, "Valeriana tertia," *CR* 15 (1965) 151-55.
1070. R. W. Garson, "The Hylas episode in Valerius Flaccus' Argonautica," *CQ* 13 (1963) 260-67.
1071. R. W. Garson, "Some critical observations on Valerius Flaccus' Argonautica II," *CQ* 15 (1965) 104-20.
1072. A. Hudson-Williams, "Some Vergilian echoes in Valerius Flaccus," *Mnem* 26 (1973) 23-28.
1073. E. Nordera, "I virgilianismi in Valerio Flacco," *Contributi a tre poeti latini* (Valerio Flacco, Rutilio Namaziano, Pascoli) (ed. A. Traina) (Bologna 1969) 1-92.

Bormann finds Vergilian motifs in *Argonautica* 2,81-130; Burck compares *Argon.* 2,62-3,361 with *Aeneid* 2 and 3 (death of Anchises). Courtney charges Valerius Flaccus with failure to comprehend V's usage at some 30 junctures. Garson studies the epic catalogue in Valerius Flaccus and V and pleads for better appreciation of the former's craft. He finds V influence in the Hylas episode. Hudson-Williams enlarges the repertoire of Valerius Flaccus' borrowings from V; Nordera examines *aemulatio* and *variatio* in the *Argonautica* with reference to V.

Lucan

1074. D. B. Brennan, "Cordus and the burial of Pompey," *CP* 64 (1969) 103-104.
1075. R. T. Bruère, "The Helen episode in Aeneid 2 and Lucan," *CP* 59 (1964) 267-68.
1076. R. T. Bruère, "Some recollections of Virgil's Drances in later epic," *CP* 66 (1971) 30-33.
1077. E. Castorina, "Petronio, Lucano e Virgilio," *Bardon* 97-112.
1078. O. A. W. Dilke, "Virgil and Lucan," *PVS* 8 (1968-9) 2-12.
1079. B. M. Marti, "Cassius Scaeva and Lucan's inventio," *The Classical Tradition. Literary and Historical Studies in Honor of H. Caplan* (ed. L. Wallach) (Ithaca 1966) 239-57.
1080. M. P. O. Morford, *The Poet Lucan: Studies in Rhetorical Epic* (New York 1967).
1081. L. Paoletti, "Lucano magico e Virgilio," *A&R* 8 (1963) 11-26.
1082. W. Rutz, "Lucans Pompeius," *AU* 9 (1968) 5-22.
1083. L. Thompson and R. T. Bruère, "Lucan's use of Virgilian reminiscence," *CP* 63 (1968) 1-21.
1084. L. Thompson and R. T. Bruère, "The Vergilian Background of Lucan's Fourth Book," *CP* 65 (1970) 152-72.

Brennan finds echoes of Misenus' burial in Cordus' burial of Pompey. Bruère argues that the Helen episode was in Lucan's text of V; there are echoes in *Bellum Civile* 10,59-65, 458-60, and 462; Bruère traces Drances through Lucan, Silius Italicus and others, including Milton's description of Belial (*Paradise Lost* 2, 108-16). Castorina detaches the Petronian *Halosis Troiae* from Lucan and Nero and accents indebtedness to V. Marti detects echoes of *A* 9 in *BC* 6,140-262 with marks of independence and originality. Paoletti makes the same point in *Phars.* 6 with respect to the nekyomanteia in *A* 6. Rutz parallels the Pompey-Caesar enmity with that of Aeneas-Turnus. Thompson and Bruère ascribe deliberate allusions to V in *Pharsalia* to ironical purposes and contrast; *Pharsalia* 4 uses V as a controlling influence.

Seneca

1085. G. Mazzoli, "Ancora sul maximus poetarum," *Athenaeum* 45 (1967) 294-303.
1086. F. Morgante, "Nota anneana: L'altissimo poeta e una magnifica gnome," *GIF* 18 (1965) 288-93.
1087. A. Setaioli, "Esegesi vergiliana in Seneca," *SIFC* 37 (1965) 133-56.

Seneca's *maximus poeta* (*De Brev. Vitae* 2,2) is Vergil, according to Mazzoli and Morgante, and aligns with *G* 3,66f. Setaioli examines more than 100 citations of V in Seneca's writings, many of them relating to Stoic philosophy and the Stoic sage represented by Aeneas. Seneca uses V's verses freely for philosophical purposes sometimes with strictures on the poet's terminology.

Columella

1088. E. de Saint-Denis, "Réhabilitons Columelle poète," *GIF* 21 (1969) 121-36.
1089. E. de Saint-Denis, "Columelle, miroir de Virgile," *Bardon* 328-43.

Saint-Denis pleads for more sympathetic study of Columella whose deep indebtedness to V does not impair his own artistry and style. He also uses Columella to explicate *G* 1,56 (*frondator*), 2,9-37, and 3,40-42.

Manilius

1090. B. Effe, "Labor improbus. Ein Grundgedanke der Georgica in der Sicht des Manilius," *Gymnasium* 78 (1971) 393-99.

Silius Italicus

1091. M. von Albrecht, "Die Punica und Vergils Aeneis," *Silius Italicus. Freiheit und Gebundenheit römischer Epik* (Amsterdam 1964) 166-84.

Statius

1092. J. F. Burgess, "Pietas in Virgil and Statius," *PVS* 11 (1971-2) 48-61.
1093. B. Kytzler, "Imitatio und Aemulatio in der Thebais des Statius," *Hermes* 97 (1969) 209-32.
1094. B. Kytzler, "Der Bittgang der argivischen Frauen (Statius. *Theb.* X, 49-83)," *AU* 11 (1968) 50-61.

Pliny the Younger

1095. L. Winniczuk, "Quid C. Plinius Secundus de poetice senserit," *Meander* 23 (1968) 306-18.

Tacitus

1096. L. Alfonsi, "Note all'Agricola di Tacito," *Aevum* 37 (1963) 340-41.

1097.   R. T. S. Baxter, *Virgil's influence on Tacitus*. Diss. Stanford University, 1968. Summary in *DA* 29 (1969) 2233A.
1098.   R. T. S. Baxter, "Virgil's influence on Tacitus in Book 3 of the Histories," *CP* 66 (1971) 93-107.
1099.   R. T. S. Baxter, "Virgil's influence on Tacitus in Book 1 and 2 of the Annals," *CP* 67 (1972) 246-49.
1100.   H. W. Benario, "Vergil and Tacitus," *CJ* 63 (1967) 24-27.
1101.   H. W. Benario, "Tacitus, Germ. VI,3," *CW* 60 (1967) 270.
1102.   H. W. Benario, "Priam and Galba," *CW* 65 (1972) 146-47.
1103.   P. Colaclides, "On a textual problem in the Agricola of Tacitus," *Hermes* 100 (1972) 125-26.
1104.   M. Marcovich, "Tanta moles," *PP* 134 (1970) 135.
1105.   J. Soubiran, "Thèmes et rhythmes d'épopée dans les Annales de Tacite," *Pallas* 12 (1964) 55-79.
1106.   R. Verdière, "De la tisane de Britannicus au berceau de l'enfant de la IV [e] Bucolique virgilienne," *RSC* 12 (1964) 113-24.

Baxter's dissertation and articles detect V influence in words and phrases. Logical correspondence invests *Annals* 1-2 with evocative power. His analysis of three climactic passages in *Histories* 3 discovers numerous V reminiscences grouped in too significant a fashion to be fortuitous. Benario finds affinity between views of Augustus in V and Tacitus; the historian emerges as bard of V's dream perverted. Benario also finds parallels between the deaths of Priam and Galba and finds textual support for *Germ.* 6,3 in *A* 10,885. Alfonsi argues that *Agricola* 12,6 recalls *A* 6,847-48. Colaclides suggests that *A* 10,276-84 informs *Agricola* 33,4. Marcovich finds reverberations of *A* 1,33 in *Annals* 1,11,1; 1,4,3; 12,66,1; *Histories* 2,16,1; 2,74,2. Soubiran senses a poetic character in Tacitus' account of Germanicus' campaigns (*Annals* 1) in expression, metre, and phraseology, and recollections of V, Ovid, and Lucan. Verdière aligns Britannicus' medical potion with the cradle of the Messianic Eclogue. Octavia's malady (like Britannicus' epilepsy) requires medication, and the cradle adornments signal the birth of her daughter Julia.

Juvenal

1107.   D. Joly, "Juvenal et les Géorgiques," *Renard* 290-308.
1108.   D. A. Kidd, "Juvenal I, 149 and X, 106-107," *CQ* 14 (1964) 103-108.
1109.   J. R. C. Martyn, "Juvenal II, 78-81 and Virgil's plague," *CP* 65 (1970) 49-50.
1110.   D. Singleton, "Juvenal VI,1-20, and some ancient attitudes to the Golden Age," *G&R* 19 (1972) 151-65.

Joly detects Juvenal's fondness for V's *Georgics* in terms, proper names, verse-endings, metaphors, and images; *G* 2 prompted a more relaxed attitude in Juvenal. Kidd finds echoes of *A* 2,460-67 in *Satires* 1,149 and 10,106-107. Martyn treats a deliberate echo of *G* 3 (the plague) in *Satires* 2,78-81. A comprehensive study of V's influence on Juvenal (and Petronius) is needed.

Martial

1111.   P. Veyne, "Martial, Virgile et quelques epitaphes," *REA* 66 (1964) 48-52.

Aulus Gellius

1112.   B. Baldwin, "Aulus Gellius on Vergil," *Vergilius* 19 (1973) 22-27.

1112a. P. K. Marshall, "Some second century criticism of Virgil," *RCANE* (March, 1964) 8.
1113. G. Bernardi Perini, "Un problema virgiliano in Gellio: sensu torquebitur amator," *Atti e Mem. Accad. Virgiliana Mantova* 37 (1969) 1-15.

Noctes Atticae accords V praise and castigation. Baldwin's article reveals that V's use and abuse of Greek models was a favourite topic of argument; Vergilian style (colour terms), euphony, distinctive use of common words, textual criticism and antiquarian lore are other matters of interest. Gellius gives us some notion of the contents of the *Vergiliomastix* volumes according to Baldwin. Bernardi Perini supports *amaror* (*NA* 1,21,4) in *G* 2,247.

Ausonius

1114. M. Bonaria, "Appunti per la storia della tradizione vergiliana nel IV secolo," *Bardon* 35-40.
1115. W. Görler, "Vergilzitate in Ausonius' Mosella," *Hermes* 97 (1969) 94-114.

Bonaria is concerned with V influence on Ausonius of Trier and on Proba's cento. Görler argues that *G* 2 (*Laudes Italiae*) and *A* 6 were most influential on Ausonius. The Mosel valley recalls the Elysian fields, the pleasure domes of Baiae, and the idealised countryside.

Claudian

1116. L. Bracelis, "La influencia literaria de Virgilio sobre C. Claudiano: Imitación formal del contenido," *REC* 11 (1967) 65-105.
1117. L. Bracelis, "El mundo de Virgilio y el de Claudiano comparados; Virgilio e Claudiano, poetas áulicos," *REC* 9 (1965)

Minucius Felix

1118. P. Courcelle, "Virgile et l'immanence divine chez Minucius Felix," *Mullus. Festchrift für Th. Klauser* (Münster 1964) 34-42.

Sortes Vergilianae

1119. Y. De Kisch, "Les *Sortes Vergilianae* dans l'Histoire Auguste," *Mél. Arch. Hist.* 82 (1970) 321-62.

Curtius Rufus

1120. R. Balzer, *Der Einfluss Vergils auf Curtius Rufus* (Munich 1971).

Commodianus

1121. L. Callebat, "Tradition et innovation dans la poésie de Commodien", *Pallas* 8 (1966) 85-94.

Christian Writers

1122. L. Alfonsi, "L'ecphrasis embrogiana del libro delle api virgiliano," *VCHR* (1965) 2,129-38.
1123. M. R. Cacioli, "Adattamenti semantici e sintattici nel Centone virgiliano di Proba," *SFIC* 41 (1969) 118-246.

1124. A. Cameron, "Echoes of Vergil in St. Jerome's Life of St. Hilarion," *CP* 63 (1968) 55-56.

1125. A. Ceresa-Gastaldo, "La tradizione virgiliana nell'esegesi biblica di Cassiodoro," *RSC* 16 (1968) 304-309.

1126. Sister Charles, "The classical Latin quotations in the Letters of St. Ambrose," *G&R* 15 (1968) 186-97.

1127. G. Davis, "Strategics of lament and consolation in Fortunatus' De Geleuintha," *Agon* 1 (1967) 118-34.

1128. I. Del Ton, "Hexaemeron S. Ambrosii Vergilium sapit," *Latinitas* 18 (1970) 27-31.

1129. J. Fontaine, "Trois variations de Prudence sur le thème du paradis," *Forschungen zur römischen Literatur. Festschrift zum 60 Geburtstag von Karl Büchner* (ed. W. Wimmel) (Wiesbaden 1970) 96-115.

1130. R. Godel, "Reminiscences des poètes profanes dans les Lettres de Saint-Jérome," *MH* 21 (1964) 65-70.

1131. H. Hagendahl, "Zu Augustins Beurteilung von Rom," *WS* 79 (1966) 509-16.

1132. H. Hagendahl, *Augustine and the Latin Classics. Vol. I: Testimonia; Vol. II: Augustine's Attitude* (Göteborg 1967).

1133. A. Hudson-Williams, "Virgil and the Christian Latin Poets," *PVS* 6 (1966-7) 11-21.

1134. W. R. Jones, "Vergil as magister in Fulgentius," *Classical, Mediaeval, and Renaissance Studies in Honor of B. L. Ullman* (ed. C. Henderson, Jr.) (Rome 1964) 1,273-75.

1135. J. O'Meara, "Augustine the artist and the Aeneid," *Mélanges offerts à Chr. Mohrmann* (edd. Engels, Hoppen-Brouwers, Vermeulen) (Uttrecht 1963) 252-61.

1136. J. O'Meara, "Virgil and Saint Augustine," *Strenas Augustinus Copanaga oblatas* (ed. Oroz Reta) (Madrid 1968) 2,307-26.

1137. A. Quacquarelli, "Una difesa retorica di Tertulliano. L'auxesis di Virgilio Aeneis IV,174 a favore dei cristiani," *Oikoumene. Studi paleocristiani in onore de Concilio Ecumenico Vaticano II* (Catania 1964) 159-74.

1138. M. L. Ricci, "Motivi ed espressioni biblici nel centone virgiliano De Ecclesia," *SIFC* 35 (1963) 161-85.

1139. G. Richard, "L'Apport de Virgile à la création épique de Prudence dans le Peristephanon liber," *Caesarodunum* 3 (1969) 187-93.

1140. L. C. Stokes, *Fulgentius and the Expositio Virgilianae Continentiae.* Diss. Tufts University, 1969. Summary in *DA* 31 (1970) 1781A.

1141. L. C. Stokes, "Fulgentius: Expositio Virgilianae Continentiae," *CF* 26 (1972) 27-63.

1142. B. R. Voss, "Vernachlässigte Zeugnisse klassischer Literatur bei Augustin und Hieronymus," *Lemmata. Donum natalicium W. Ehlers...oblatum* (Munich 1968) 300-11.

1143. L. G. Whitbread, "Fulgentius and dangerous doctrine," *Latomus* 30 (1971) 1157-61.

1144. D. S. Wiesen, "Virgil, Minucius Felix and the Bible," *Hermes* 99 (1971) 70-91.

Alfonsi examines St. Ambrose's paraphrase of *G* 4 in *Hexaemeron* 5; Del Ton detects other borrowings. Cacioli's study of Proba examines her Vergilian cento on Old Testament stories and the Life of Christ. Sister Charles limits St. Ambrose's classical library to Sallust, Vergil, and Cicero. Fortunatus (Venantius) links *G* 2,416-7 and *Isaiah* 5,2 in *Carmen* 5,2,37-40. Hagendahl's work is essential for future study of influences; his article detects differences between both writers. Hudson-Williams is enlightening on V's reappearance in Juvencus, Paulinus, Avitus, and Prudentius. Davis associates Fortunatus' laments with tragic heroines of elegy, epyllion, and epic;

V's pastoral *eros* is superimposed as passport to apotheosis and Christian paradise. Jones perceives V as schoolmaster in Fulgentius' *De Continentia Vergiliana*. O'Meara traces St. Augustine's obsession against sex as a Vergilian legacy. Ricci studies Mavortius' cento. Stokes provides an annotated prose translation of Fulgentius' *Exposition of Vergil's Content*, the first Christian allegory of the *Aeneid*. Voss treats echoes in St. Augustine, *Epist.* 14.

XIII. ANCIENT LIVES

1145. C. Hardie (ed.), *Vitae Vergilianae antiquae: Vita Donati, Vita Servii, Vita Probiana, Vita Focae, S. Hieronymi excerpta* (Oxford 1965).
1146. G. Brugnoli, "Magus e figulus," *Maia* 19 (1967) 387-88.
1147. G. Brugnoli and R. Scarcia, "Osservazioni sulla Vita Probiana di Virgilio," *StudUrb* 39 (1965) 18-46.
1148. G. Brugnoli, "La Vita Vergiliana di Foce fonte della Vita Probiana," *Philologus* 108 (1964) 148-52.
1149. G. Marconi, "Il testamento di Virgilio," *Studi Latini* (Rome 1972) 143-205.
1150. G. Nenci, "Ps. Probus, Vita Verg. 4," *RCCM* 9 (1967) 230-33.
1151. R. Scarcia, "Osservazioni critiche," *RCCM* 6 (1964) 287-302.
1152. C. J. Vooys, "Bathyllus ontmaskerd," *Hermeneus* 35 (1963) 53-54.

Hardie's magisterial edition of the Lives surpasses any earlier attempts. Brugnoli regards *figulus* (Donatus, *Vita Verg.* 1) as interpolation, and assigns the Vita Probiana a 6th-century date, deriving from Donatus through Focas. Marconi reconsiders statements in the Donatus Life concerning V's death and will in response to Scarcia, *RCCM* 5 (1963) 303-21. Scarcia treats Seneca's remarks on V's poetry-readings and traces similarities between the Lives of Persius and V.

XIV. ANCIENT COMMENTATORS

1153. A. F. Stocker, A. H. Travis, with H. T. Smith, G. B. Waldrop, and R. T. Bruère, *Servianorum in Vergilii carmina Commentariorum editionis Harvardianae Vol. III, quod in Aeneidos libros III-V explanationes continet* (Oxford 1965). Rev: Elder *CW* 59 (1966) 282; Ernout *RPh* 40 (1966) 366-67; Knecht *AC* 35 (1966) 297-99; Mountford *CR* 17 (1967) 286-89; Préaux *RBPh* 44 (1966) 595-98; Williams *CJ* 62 (1967) 234-36.
1154. J. J. Brewer, *An analysis of the Berne scholia and their relation to Philargyrius, The Servian commentaries, and other exegesis of Vergil's Eclogues.* Diss. University of Virginia, 1973. Summary in *DA* 34 (1973) 1877A.
1155. C. O. Brink, "Limaturae," *RhM* 115 (1972) 28-42.
1156. W. Clausen, "Adnotatiunculae in Servium," *HSCP* 71 (1966) 57-58.
1157. C. Daicoviciu, "Coniuratus Dacas," *Acta Musei Napocensis* (Cluj) 2 (1965) 649-50.
1158. H. Fuchs, "Servius über Lucilius und Vergil," *Hermes* 93 (1965) 256.
1159. G. P. Goold, "Servius and the Helen Episode," *HSCP* 74 (1970) 101-68.
1160. H. Haffter, "Zum Pentheus des Pacuvius," *WS* 79 (1966) 290-93.
1161. J. Le Gall, "Rites de fondation," Studi sulla città antica (*Atti Conv. sulla città etrusca e italica*) (ed. G. Mansuelli) (Bologna 1970) 59-65.
1162. H. L. Levy, "Servius in his classroom," *CJ* 67 (1971-72) 167-74.
1163. N. Marinone, "Per la cronologia di Servio," *AAT* 104 (1969-70) 181-211.
1164. C. E. Murgia, *Relations of the manuscripts of Servius' Commentary on the Aeneid.* Diss. Harvard University, 1966. Summary in *HSCP* 71 (1966) 331-33.
1165. C. E. Murgia, "Critical notes on the text of Servius' commentary on Aeneid III-V," *HSCP* 72 (1967) 311-50.

1166. C. E. Murgia, "More on the Helen episode," *CSCA* 4 (1971) 203-17.

1167. C. E. Murgia, *Prolegomena to Servius 5: The Manuscripts. CPCS* 11 (1974).

1168. H. T. Rowell, "The ancient evidence of the Helen episode in Aeneid II," *The Classical Tradition. Literary and Historical Studies in Honor of H. Caplan* (ed. L. Wallach) (Ithaca 1966) 210-21.

1169. G. Polara, "Servio ad Aen. XI, 33 e il significato attivo della parola alumnus," *AFLN* 11 (1964-5) 69-107.

1170. A. L. Prosdocimi, "Un nome del Tevere, Serra (ad Aen. VIII, 63)," *PP* 23 (1968) 45-48.

1171. S. Timpanaro, "Note e interpreti virgiliani antichi," *RFIC* 95 (1967) 428-45.

1172. M. L. West, "An epic fragment in Servius," *CR* 14 (1964) 242.

1173. R. D. Williams, "Servius, commentator and guide," *PVS* 6 (1966-7) 50-56.

1174. I. Zicàri, "Pisaurum-Pensaurum. Nota a Serv. ad. Aen. VI, 825," *Soliv* 12 (1964) 55-59.

1175. A. Cameron, "A fragment of a lost commentary on Virgil," *Philologus* 109 (1965) 157-59.

1176. D. G. Brearley, *Sedulius Scottus' commentary on Donatus.* Diss. University of Toronto, 1967. Summary in *DA* 28 (1968) 5033A.

1177. R. A. Osebold, *Aelius Donatus' introduction to Virgil's Eclogues and its relationship to the introduction by Servius.* Diss. The Johns Hopkins University, 1968. Summary in *DA* 29 (1968) 1524A-1525A.

1178. R. Scarcia, "Gli antibucolica di Numitorio," *RCCM* 11 (1969) 169-89.

1179. W. O. Schmitt, "Zum (alt)preussischen Donatus des Wilhelm von Modena," *Helikon* 6 (1966) 484-92.

1180. P. V. Davies (tr.), *Macrobius: The Saturnalia* (New York 1969).

1181. E. Tuerk, "Les Saturnales de Macrobe, source de Servius Danielis," *REL* 41 (1963) 327-49.

1182. J. Willis, "Macrobius," *Altertum* 12 (1966) 155-61.

1183. L. Castano, "Il commento di Probo alle Georgiche di Virgilio nel codice posseduto dal Poliziano," *Helikon* 9-10 (1969-70) 524-73.

1184. E. Chirila, "Un pasaj din Scholia Bernensia despre daci (ad Georg. II, 497)," *Acta Musei Napocensis* (Cluj) I (1964) 465-67.

1185. E. Fraenkel, "Aeneis VI,242," *MH* 20 (1963) 234-36.

The Harvard Servius now offers two volumes: Volume II (*Aeneid* 1, 2), published in 1946, and Volume III (edited by A. F. Stocker and A. H. Travis), published in 1965. Both are serviceable, lucid, and altogether valuable. Murgia's forthcoming *Prolegomena to Servius V — The Manuscripts*, presents the basis of selection and evaluation of codices to be cited in Volume V (*Aeneid* 9-12) of the Editio Harvardiana of the Servian commentaries. Volume I will contain the *Eclogues* and *Georgics*; Volume IV, *Aeneid* 6-8; and Volume VI, *Epilegomena* and *Index.* Brewer studies Scholia Bernensia on *E.*, an anonymous adaptation in form and content of Philargyrius' *Explanationes* containing traditional interpretations along with allegorical treatments. Brink emends Servius *ad Aen.* 6,160 to include *quia* of Isidore, *Et.* 6,8,3. Clausen provides five critical notes on Servius. Servius' biography of V quotes *A* 2,567-88 and states that they 'are known to have been removed' by Tucca and Varius. Servius auctus quotes them but offers no comment thus indicating that scholia were wanting. Rowell conjectures that Servius' discussion and the actual lines derive from Donatus' commentary. Bruère argues that they were in Lucan's text of Vergil (1075); *Highet* compromises (326): "Vergil wrote the lines, and somehow showed in his manuscript that he was not satisfied with them and had not definitely made them a part of the poem" (pp. 166-67). Camps, Austin, Stégen, and Duckworth, side with Rowell and Williams; Goold's brilliant article, enlarged by Murgia, argues that the characteristics (Golden Section, Vergilian metrics, effective use of rhetoric and drama, both Ennius and Euripides), indicate a Neronian author. Varius never saw the passage and it was never included in the canonical text; Servius must have found it in an older commentary. Hafter argues that Servius *ad Aen.* 4,469 was not drawing on Pacuvius' *Pentheus*. Levy discusses Servius' paedagogical approach to V by providing classroom notes. Marinone offers a chronology of Servius' birth (ca. 370-80) and commentary on V (ca. 430-435). Murgia's study of Servian manuscripts and critical notes on Harvard Servius III are essential. Prosdicimi on Servius, *ad Aen.* 8, 63, discusses Serra as an ancient name for the Tiber. Timpanaro treats Servius Danielis *ad Aen.* 8,361. West derives Servius *ad Aen.* 12,691 from an Alexander epic. Williams urges caution with Servius' commentary, but praises his erudition and general good sense. Cameron detects evidence of a lost commentary, of Servius' period, in MS *Glasguensis* 113, referring to Cloelia. Brearley edits Sedulius Scottus' commentary on Donatus. Osebold argues that Servius' version of Donatus' introduction to the *Eclogues* merely reflects Donatus in the altered version. Scarcia's account of Numitorius' entertaining *Antibucolica* (cf. Donatus, *Vita Verg.* 43) highlights V's hypocritical melancholy, fortune's favourite in shepherd's guise, and examines Donatus, *Vita Verg.* 6-7 on the problematical *toga virilis*. Davis' translation of Macrobius draws useful comments on quotations from V. Jocelyn's notes (1026) on Macrobius, *Saturnalia* 6 and the scholia relating to V's parallels with earlier authors merit close attention. Tuerk detects the influence of Macrobius in Servius Danielis. Willis, who provided the Teubner text, praises Macrobius for his sensitivity to poetry and his abilities as commentator. Fraenkel regards *A* 6,242 as an interpolation accepted as genuine by Priscian.

XV. MANUSCRIPTS

1186. G. Baligan, "Inediti versi di Virgilio (?)," *Convivium* (Bologna) 36 (1968) 355-61.

1187. A. Carandini, "Per riprendere lo studio del Codex Romanus di Virgilio," *Problemi attuali di scienza e cultura* 105 (1968) 329-48.

1188. C. P. Finlayson, "Florius infortunatus," *Scriptorium* 16 (1962) 378-80.

1189. M. Geymonat, "Due frammenti virgiliani ritrovati in Egitto," *Helikon* 4 (1964) 343-47.

1190. M. Geymonat, "Lezioni e varianti virgiliani," *SCO* 14 (1965) 86-99.

1191. M. Geymonat, "I codici G e V di Virgilio," *MIL* 29 (1966) 289-438. Rev: Granarolo *Latomus* 30 (1971) 470-72.

1192. J. Jimenez Delgado, "Primera edición illustrada de Virgilio," *Helmantica* 23 (1972) 471-91.

1193. R. Merkelbach, "Palinurus," *ZeitPap* 9 (1972) 83.

1194. C. D. Oliver, *The Illustrations of the Roman Vergil.* Diss. Catholic University of America, 1971. Summary in *DA* 33 (1972) 678A.

1195. T. B. Stevenson, *The Miniatures of the Vatican Virgil* (*Vat. Lat.* 3225) Diss. New York University, 1970. Summary in *DA* 31 (1970) 1710A.

1196. J. de Wit, *Die Miniaturen des Vergilius Vaticanus* (Amsterdam 1959). Rev: Buchthal *ArtBull* 45 (1963) 372-75.

Mynors (2) and Geymonat (1) include summaries of the major and minor codices, including ninth and thirteenth century material. Pack (*The Greek and Latin Literary Texts from Graeco-Roman Egypt* (Ann Arbor 1965) includes Vergilian fragments in his collection (2935-2952). Geymonat examines Pap. Rainer Lat. 24 (*A* 5,671-4; 683-4) and Pap. Lat. 2 (Nat. Libr. Strasburg) on *E* 7,17-34. His critical notes on the 5th century-palimpsests G and V establish their importance for editors. Carandini's study of Codex Romanus is enlarged by Cornelia Oliver's study of the coloured miniatures with scenes from *E, G* and *A*. The Eclogue miniatures seem to derive from a roll. Naive and inept, the drawings can be dated ca. 500, but derive from works of the

Constantinian era. De Wit and Stevenson treat the miniatures of the Vatican Vergil. Stevenson relates the codex paintings to the Quedlenburg Itala fragments and the cycle of nave mosaics in Santa Maria Maggiore, Rome. Stevenson conjectures that the work was commissioned by a patrician family of the late fourth or early fifth century in metropolitan Rome. Baligan examines a seven-line verse fragment (Codex Bononiensis 401³, f. 52V, 15th century) and assigns its it to a conjectural Vergilian epic on Octavian (cf. *G* 3,46-48). Finlayson identifies Florius Infortunatus, 15th-century scribe of the Edinburgh University MS 195, as Franciscus Florius Florentinus of Tours.

XVI. VERGIL AND LATER AGES

Middle Ages

1197. R. Argenio, "Gli autori congeniali al Petrarca nelle Epistole metriche," *Convivium* (Bologna) 33 (1965) 449-64.
1198. M. S. Batts, "The origins of numerical symbolism and numerical patterns in Medieval German literature," *Traditio* 20 (1964) 462-71.
1199. A. C. Cutler, "Octavian and the Sibyl in Christian hands," *Vergilius* 11 (1965) 22-32.
1200. A. David, "Gawain and Aeneas," *English Studies* 49 (1968) 402-409.
1201. M. L. Dittrich, *Die Eneide Heinrichs von Veldeke, I: Quellenkritischer Vergleich Roman d'Eneas und Vergils Aeneis* (Wiesbaden 1966).
1202. J. J. Duggan, "Virgilian inspiration in the *Roman d'Enéas* and the Chanson de Roland," *Univ. South. Calif. Studies Comp. Lit.* 1 (1968) 9-23.
1203. J. B. Friedman, "Eurydice, Heurodis, and the noon-day demon," *Speculum* 41 (1966) 22-29.
1204. J. Gajda, "De Bello Troiano et de Aeneae casibus in Carminibus quae dicuntur Buranis descriptis," (Polish, with Latin résumé) *Eos* 53 (1963) 373-90.
1205. J. Gardner, "Fulgentius' *Expositio Vergilianae Continentiae* and the plan of the Beowulf; another approach to the poem's style and structure," *Papers on Lang. & Lit.* 6 (1970) 227-62.
1206. L. K. R. R. Gros, "Robert Henryson's *Orpheus and Eurydice* and the Orpheus traditions," *Speculum* 41 (1966) 643-55.
1207. T. B. Haber, *A Comparative Study of the Beowulf and the Aeneid* (New York 1968).
1208. J. Hellegouarc'h, "Un poète latin de XIIᵉ siècle, Gautier de Lille, dit Gautier de Chatillon," *BAGB* 26 (1967) 95-115.
1209. E. Kaminkova, "Un imitateur adroit d'Horace et de Virgile au moyen age," (in Czech) *ZJFK* 11 (1969) 87-89.
1210. H. C. R. Lawrie, "A new look at the marvellous in Eneas, and its influence," *Romania* 91 (1970) 48-74.
1211. H. C. R. Lawrie, "Eneas and the Lancelot of Chrétien de Troyes," *MAev* 37 (1968) 142-56.
1212. T. A. McVeigh, S. J., *The allegory of the poets: a study of classical tradition in mediaeval interpretation of Virgil.* Diss. Fordham University, 1964. Summary in *DA* 25 (1964) 1894.
1213. E. Paratore, "L'Orlando Innamorato del'Eneide," *Il Boiardo e la critica contemporanea* (1970) 347-75.
1214. B. M. Peebles, "The Ad Maronis mausoleum. Petrarch's Virgil and two fifteenth century manuscripts," *Classical, Medieval, and Renaissance Studies in Honor of B. L. Ullman* (ed. C. Henderson Jr.) (Rome 1964) 2,169-98.
1215. G. Petricchi, "Virgilio e la poetica di Tasso," *GIF* 2 (1971) 1-12.
1216. R. Petullà, "Il Roman d'Eneas e l'Eneide," *RIL* 102 (1968) 409-31.

1217.   F. J. E. Raby, "Amor and amicitia. A medieval poem," *Speculum* 40 (1965) 599-610.
1218.   R. J. Rowland, "Aeneas as a hero in twelfth-century Ireland," *Vergilius* 16 (1970) 29-32.
1219.   J. Schwartz, "Survivances littéraires païennes dans le Pasteur d'Hermas," *RBi* 72 (1965) 240-47.
1220.   J. W. Wittig, "The Aeneas-Dido allusion in Chrétien's *Erec et Enide*," *CompLit* 22 (1970) 237-53.

Argenio treats V's influence on Petrarch; Batts derives mediaeval German use of the Golden Section from V. Cutler treats the theme of the Sibyl, Octavian and prophetic Vergil during the Middle Ages. Davis treats mediaeval use of Troy and Aeneas as paradigms. Duggan finds that the *Roman d'Enéas* retains the vacillating hero, extended comparison and catalogues; the *Chanson de Roland* is an oral, traditional poem with no such features. Friedman discusses use of V by the 13th-century author of Sir Orfeo. Gardner detects Fulgentius' scheme (*arma* = fortitude; *virum* = wisdom; *primus* = fame, glory) in the structure of *Beowulf*. Henryson's *Orpheus*, 'the last mythological poem of the Middle Ages', has Vergilian traits according to Gros. Hellegouarc'h discusses Gautier de Lille's *Alexandréide* as an imitation of V. Lawrie argues that Chrétien de Troyes shows better assimilation of V and Ovid in his romantic hero Lancelot. McVeigh argues that mediaeval allegorical interpretations of V's *Aeneid* originated in Stoic and Neoplatonic commentaries on Homer. Peebles provides an important study of the Pauline tradition relating to V's tomb in Naples. Raby analyzes the 12th century poem often attributed to Abelard for Vergilian echoes (*E* 8,44-46). Rowland pleads that Aeneas' 12th century Irish transformation is designedly more humane and more heroic than V's Trojan. Chrétien's *Erec et Enide* 5196-99 reveals thematic contents of the Old French Aeneas and allegorical versions of the poet's work.

Dante

1221.   J. B. Berrigan, "Vinculum Pacis: Vergil and Dante," *CB* 43 (1966-7) 49-53.
1222.   D. Consoli, *Significato del Virgilio dantesco* (Florence 1967). Rev: Goffis *Paideia* 22 (1967) 297-300.
1223.   R. Hollander, "Dante's use of Aeneid I in Inferno I and II," *CompLit* 20 (1968) 142-56.
1224.   W. J. Kennedy, "Irony, Allegoresis, and Allegory in Virgil, Ovid, and Dante," *Arcadia* 7 (1972) 115-34.
1225.   H. Kuss, "Vergil und Dante. Vergleichende Interpretation der Darstellungen von Dido und Francesca im Lateinunterricht," *AU* 12 (1969) 15-29.
1226.   T. P. Logan, *The characterization of Ulysses in Homer, Vergil, and Dante. A study in sources and analogues.* Annual Report Dante Society 82 (1964).
1227.   R. Montano, "Dante and Virgil," *Yale Review* 60 (1971) 550-61.
1228.   E. Pasoli, "Colei che s'uccise amorosa, e ruppe fede al cener di Sicheo," *Annuario del Liceo-Ginnasio Scipione Maffei di Verona...* (Verona 1965) 37-58.
1228a. B. Reynolds, "The Aeneid in Dante's eyes," *PVS* 5 (1965-6) 1-13.
1229.   E. Skassis, "Dantes kai Vergilios," *EEAth* 16 (1965-6) 434-37.
1230.   P. Somville, "Didon et Bérénice," *LEC* (1971) 79-90.
1231.   A. Vallone, "Interpretazione del Virgilio dantesco," *L'Alighieri* 10 (1968) 14-40.
1232.   J. H. Whitfield, "Virgil into Dante," *Dudley* 94-118.
1233.   J. H. Whitfield, "Dante e Virgilio," *P&I* 7 (1965) 3-16.

Berrigan finds rapport between V and Dante in their troubled times. Consoli offers a balanced assessment of V's influence on Dante as man, poet, and symbol. Hollander analyses five passages in the *Inferno* reflecting *A* 1,157-86. Kuss treats Dante as *aemulator* of V. Montano explores relationships; Pasoli studies Dido in Dante and variant versions. Reynolds senses Dante's maturing understanding of the *Aeneid*. V, according to Skassis, is Dante's model for style and motifs, but Dante creates a new poetic art. Somville compares Dido and Berenice. Vallone highlights problems of comparative criticism. Whitfield argues that Dante's V is not the historical poet but Dante's medium as the New Vergil; V differs often in statement and poetic tone from Dante's figure.

Chaucer

1234. C. Brookhouse, "Chaucer's impossibilities," *MAev* 34 (1965) 40-42.
1235. W. S. Wilson, "Exegetical grammar in the *House of Fame*," *English Lang. Notes* 1 (1964) 244-48.
1236. J. Wimsatt, "The sources of Chaucer's Seys and Alcyone," *MAev* 36 (1967) 231-41.
1237. M. Winterbottom, "The style of Aethelweard," *MAev* 36 (1967) 109-118.

Brookhouse suggests that Chaucer's *adynata* may derive from *E* 1,60-64, or 8,52-4. Wilson assesses Chaucer's version of the *Aeneid* in the *House of Fame* as deliberate comedy. Wimsatt promotes V and Statius as influences on Chaucer's *Seys and Alcyone*.

The Renaissance

1238. D. C. Allen, *Mysteriously Meant. The Rediscovery of Pagan Symbolism and Allegorical Interpretation in the Renaissance* (Baltimore 1969).
1239. G. Cambier, "Le Laocoon de Sadoleto," *LM* 16-17 (1968) 2-8.
1240. F. Della Corte, "Cinquettando al mattin dare il buon giorno," *Maia* 16 (1964) 3-5.
1241. G. E. Duckworth, "Mephaeus Vegius and Vergil's Aeneid. A metrical comparison," *CP* 64 (1969) 1-6.
1242. M. Feo, "Dal pius agricola al villano empio e bestiale," *Maia* 20 (1968) 98-136, 206-23.
1243. K. W. Gransden, "The pastoral alternative," *Arethusa* 3 (1970) 103-21.
1244. R. Hapgood, "The Judge in the Firie Tower; another Virgilian passage in *The Spanish Tragedy*," *Notes and Queries* 13 (1966) 287-88.
1245. M. T. Herrick, "Hyrcanian tigers in Renaissance tragedy," *The Classical Tradition. Literary and Historical Studies in Honor of H. Caplan* (ed. L. Wallach) (Ithaca 1966) 559-71.
1246. B. L. Hijman, Jr., "Aeneia Virtus: Vegio's *Supplementum* to the *Aeneid*," *CJ* 67 (1971-2) 144-55.
1247. E. Leube, *Fortuna in Karthago: Die Aeneas-Dido-Mythe Vergils in den romanischen Literaturen von 14. bis zum 16. Jahrhundert* (Heidelberg 1969). Rev: Cleary *CW* 64 (1970) 93; Halk *CR* 22 (1972) 62-64.
1248. H. Levin, *The Myth of the Golden Age in the Renaissance* (Bloomington 1969).
1249. W. S. Maguinness, "Maffeo Vegio continuatore dell'Eneide," *Aevum* 42 (1968) 478-85.
1250. M. J. Murrin, *Mantuan (Baptista Mantuanus, 1448-1516) and the English Eclogue.* Diss. Yale University, 1965. Summary in *DA* 26 (1965) 2188-9.
1251. H. M. Richmond, "Rural lyricism, a Renaissance mutation of the pastoral," *CompLit* 16 (1964) 193-210.

Allen studies 'undermeanings' in V's works and their survival. Cambier provides text and translation of Jacopo Sadoleto's *Laocoon*. Della Corte detects V's influence (*A* 8,455-56) in Michelangelo's poetry. Duckworth's metrical comparison of Mephaeus Vegius' *Thirteenth Aeneid* shows resemblances to V, to Republican and later poets, including Ovid. Hijman's study of Vegio deals with poetic structure and heroic characterization. Maguinness' study echoes his Virgil Society lecture (London 1957). Feo argues that Annibale Caro's version of *A* 7,772-82 evidences class discrimination between labourer and shepherd. Gransden accounts for classical influences in Renaissance pastoral. Hapgood detects *A* 6,548-74 in Kyd's *Spanish Tragedy*. Herrick traces Hyrcanian tigers (*A* 4,365-7) in 16th century English and Italian tragedies. Leube investigates versions of the Dido and Aeneas story by vernacular writers in France, Italy, and the Iberian peninsula from ca. 1300 to ca. 1600; malevolent Fortuna, absent in V's Fourth *Aeneid*, plays a malevolent role in the tradition. Levin's comprehensive study examines V's influence on the conception of the Golden Age of Lorenzo the Magnificent, Pope Leo X, Francis I, and Elizabeth Regina. Murrin treats an important influence on English pastoral. Richmond discusses pastoral from Ronsard to Milton within the Vergilian tradition.

Sixteenth to Eighteenth Centuries

1252. P. A. Bates, "Shakespeare's sonnets and pastoral poetry," *Shakespeare Jahrbuch* (Weimar) 103 (1967) 81-96.

1253. H. Berger, Jr., "Archaism, vision and revision: studies in Virgil, Plato, and Milton," *Centennial Review* 11 (1967) 24-52.

1254. J. H. Betts, "Classical allusions in Shakespeare's Henry V with special reference to Virgil," *G&R* 15 (1968) 147-63.

1255. M. D. Bristol, "Structural patterns in two Elizabethan pastorals," *Studies in English Lit., 1500-1900* 10 (1970) 33-48.

1256. R. A. Brower, "Form and defect of form in eighteenth century poetry: A memorandum," *College English* 29 (1968) 535-41.

1257. J. Bull, "Business calls from the Plains," *Delta* 50 (1972) 22-35.

1258. J. Chalker, *The English Georgic: A Study in the Development of a Form* (Baltimore 1969).

1259. R. M. Cummings, "Two Sixteenth Century Notices of Numerical Composition in Virgil's Aeneid," *Notes and Queries* 16 (1969) 26-27.

1260. H. MacL. Curry, "Johnson and the Classics," *New Rambler* B 17 (1965) 13-27.

1261. S. L. Curry, "The literary criticism of William Warburton," *English Studies* 48 (1967) 398-408.

1262. M. di Cesare, "Paradise Lost and Epic Tradition," *Milton Studies* 1 (1969) 31-50.

1263. G. E. Duckworth, "Milton's hexameter patterns — Vergilian or Ovidian?" *AJP* 93 (1972) 52-60.

1264. A. V. Ettin, *Style and Ethics in the Pastoral Eclogues of Vergil and Spencer*. Diss. University of Washington, 1972. Summary in *DA* 33 (1972) 1140A.

1265. J. Freehafer, "Dryden's Indian Emperour," *Explicator* 27 (1968) 24.

1266. A. E. Friedmann, *The Description of Landscape in Spenser's Faerie Queen. A Study of Rhetorical Tradition.* Diss. Columbia University, 1965. Summary in *DA* 26 (1966) 6039.

1267. J. Fuchs, *Pope's Poetry and the Augustan Tradition of Horace and Vergil*. Diss. University of California (Irvine), 1971. Summary in *DA* 33 (1972) 2932A.

1268. K. W. Gransden, "Paradise Lost and the Aeneid," *Essays in Criticism* 17 (1967) 281-303.

1269. T. W. Harrison, "English Virgil. The Aeneid in the XVIII Century,"

Philologica Pragensia 10 (1967) 1-11, 80-91.

1270. R. G. Hunter, "Cleopatra and the Oestre Junonicque," *Shakespeare Studies* 5 (1969) 236-39.

1270a. H. H. Huxley, "Aeneid VI and the English poets," *Proc. Pacific Northwest Conference on Foreign Languages* 24 (1973) 212-16.

1271. D. R. Johnson, *Plowshares, Politics and Poetry: The Georgic Tradition from Dryden to Thomson.* Diss. University of Wisconsin, 1972. Summary in *DA* 33 (1973) 6314A.

1272. M. L. Kelsall, "What god, what mortal? The Aeneid and English mock-heroic," *Arion* 8 (1969) 359-79.

1273. C. Laga, "Didon et Hermione. Une contribution à l'étude des sources de Racine," *Alfa* (Marilia) 2 (1962) 21-42.

1274. F. N. Lee, "*Dido, Queen of Carthage* and *The Tempest*," *Notes and Queries* 11 (1964) 147-49.

1275. J. C. Maxwell, "A Virgilian echo in Spenser," *Notes and Queries* 14 (1967) 458.

1276. E. Miner, "The Death of Innocence in Marvell's Nymph Complaining for the Death of the Faun," *Modern Philology* 65 (1967) 9-16.

1277. P. J. Minichino, *Vergil in Spenser's Faerie Queen.* Diss. Columbia University, 1971. Summary in *DA* 32 (1971) 3262A.

1278. J. F. Nash, *John Gay and the Georgic Tradition.* Diss. University of Virginia, 1971. Summary in *DA* 32 (1972) 4626A.

1279. R. M. Ogilvie, "Two notes on Dryden's Absolom and Achitophel," *Notes and Queries* 17 (1970) 415-16.

1280. R. G. Peterson, "Larger manners and events: Sallust and Virgil in Absolom and Achitophel," *PMLA* 82: 2 (1967) 236-44.

1281. D. H. Rawlinson, "Pope and Addison on Classical Greatness," *Wascana Review* 2 (1967) 69-74.

1282. M. Reinhold, "The naming of Pygmalion's animated statue," *CJ* 66 (1971) 316-19.

1283. F. M. Rener, "Friedrich Spee and Virgil's Fourth Georgic," *CompLit* 24 (1972) 118-35.

1284. P. Rogers, "Defoe and Virgil: The Georgic element in *A Tour Thro' Great Britain*," *English Miscellany* 22 (1971) 93-106.

1285. W. E. Rudat, *Pope's Mind at Work: Virgil and the Road to the Lock.* Diss. University of California, 1972. Summary in *DA* 32 (1972) 7002A.

1286. J. E. Seaman, "The chivalric cast of Milton's epic hero," *English Studies* 49 (1968) 97-107.

1287. M. Starowieyeski, "Parodies de Virgile," (Polish, with Latin résumé) *Meander* 23 (1968) 91-100.

1288. S. R. Swaminathan, "Virgil, Dryden and Yeats," *Notes and Queries* 19 (1972) 328-30.

1289. J. W. Velz, *Shakespeare and the Classical Tradition: A Critical Guide to Commentary, 1660-1960* (Minneapolis 1968).

1290. J. Welcher, "The opening of *Religio Laici* and its Virgilian associations," *Studies in Eng. Lit. 1500-1900* 8 (1968) 391-96.

1291. S. P. Zitner, "Spenser's diction and classical precedent," *PhQ* 45 (1966) 360-71.

Bates associates *E* 2 with Shakespeare's *Sonnets* relating to Mr. W. H., the Dark Lady, and the rival poet by concentrating on common or similar lines, images, and ideas. Bates' intriguing article points to similarities in expression, comparable imagery, and common ideas between V's works and Shakespeare's *Henry the Fifth*. Berger provides a comparison of V's *Aeneid* and *Paradise Lost* indicating that both share a movement from 'the extensive and external stresses of early historical experience to the intensive and internal stresses of later historical experience.' Bristol shows that Spenser's *Shepheardes Calendar* and Drayton's *Shepheard's Garland* both imitate V's reciprocal pairing in the *Eclogues* with each pair of poems receding from a central point; Spenser's structural approach is ironic, Drayton's is mythic. Brower cautions critics against exalting secondary contrivances while ignoring obvious formal weaknesses. Dryden's *Aeneid* suffers from a superimposed, repetitive form, distracting sound devices, and heightened rhetoric which obfuscates V's essential concerns. Bull notes that Gay's *Rural Sports* (1713) followed the pragmatic, realistic tradition of the *Georgics* with conflict between town and country traditions: a revised version (1720) excised the satire against the aristocracy. Chalker deals with late 17th and early 18th century Georgics and their debt to Vergil: "Virgil expressed, in unusual combination, attitudes which had a particular potency for the period." Cummings cites 16th century remarks on numerology in V and Spenser. Currie comments on Johnson's Latinist temperament but preference for the *Odyssey* over the *Aeneid*. Warburton's 18th century criticism of *A* 4 and 6, according to Curry, favours the historical method; *A* 6 is an enigmatic representation of initiation into the Eleusinian mysteries. Di Cesare argues that V's traditional catalogues transcend the conventional by juxtaposing the warlike and the humane; the conflict between arms and the man, a dramatic and psychological duel, is part of the double perspective (of V and Milton) left unresolved at the close. Duckworth finds both Vergilian and Ovidian patterns in Milton. Ettin argues that V and Spenser are ethical poets with the same values and purposes; Vergil's *Eclogues* have a programmatic character picturing the actual and the ideal, with a sense of values that save and destroy humanity; all-consuming love for V is destructive. V's reader is the central character becoming gradually aware of the values and qualities required for the recovery of the Golden Age. Friedmann finds Vergilian and Ovidian imitations of landscape in Spenser. Fuchs examines Pope's Pastorals and Georgics (*Essay on Criticism, Windsor Forest*) and mock epics. Gransden describes Milton's imitation of Vergilian structure, language and syntax, and manipulation of time. Hapgood finds echoes of *A* 6,548-74 in Kyd's *Spanish Tragedy*. Harrison shows that the 18th century rejected the political and moral aspects of V and favoured his sublimity, love of nature, and pathos; the age was ill-disposed to absolute monarchy and condemned Augustus as tyrant. Hunter treats indebtedness of Shakespeare and Rabelais to V's gadfly (*G.* 3,146-53). Johnson studies the influence of the *Georgics* on Pope's contemporaries and James Thomson's *The Seasons*. Kelsall senses hostility to V's divine machinery in Neo-Classical mock epic. Laga traces Racine's Hermione to Dido. Lee argues that Marlowe's Dido and Vergil's *Aeneid* probably influenced Shakespeare's *The Tempest:* Alonso's landing (II,1) and the 'insubstantial pageant' of Prospero's speech in Act IV. Martz argues that *Paradise Regained* converts V's *Georgics* into a channel for religious meditation; classical didactic poetry and Christian meditations on the Gospels are merged. Miner finds echoes of Silvia's pet deer (*A* 7,475-509) in Marvell's *Nymph Complaining*. Minichino treats Spenser, "England's Vergil," serious, grand, and restrained, as imitator of Vergil. Nash's study treats Gay's *Rural Sports* and *Trivia*, his mock-heroic. Ogilvie traces *Absolom and Achitophel* 272 to *A* 4,402-7. Rawlinson compares representative passages from Pope's and Addison's analyses of Homer and Vergil. Reinhold's study includes Galatea (V's flirt in the *Eclogues*, first adapted by de Cordonnier in 1741) and Elise (introduced by Johan Jakob Bodmer in 1747), deriving perhaps from Vergil's Elissa; G. B. Shaw chose Eliza for his flower-girl 'Galatea' in *Pygmalion*. Rener studies Spee's (1591-1635) imitation of V's *Georgics,* especially *G* 4. Syntactical peculiarities in Milton reminiscent of V are Richardson's concern. Rogers finds influence of the *Georgics* in Defoe's *Tour* with elegiac undertones. Rudat compares the Baron's amorous assault on Belinda in Pope's *Rape of the Lock* with Arruns' pursuit of Camilla (*A* 11), and discovers rape imagery in her death. Seaman

156

finds heroic virtue in Milton's Christ rather than in Adam or Satan. Starowieyski examines parodies of the *Aeneid* by Blumauer (18th century) and Chtomski (19th century). Swaminathan detects echoes of Dryden's *Alexander's Feast* and of Vergil in Yeats' *Two Songs from a Play*. Welcher shows verbal dependence in *Religio Laici* on *A* 6,268-72 in the opening image. Zitner accounts for Spenser's epic diction.

Nineteenth Century

1292.　N. Carini, *Virgilio nell'opera filologica di Giacomo Leopardi* (Assisi 1964).
1293.　O. Chadwick, "Tennyson and Virgil," *Tennyson Research Bulletin* 3 (1968)
1294.　M. L. D'Avanzo, "Immortality's Winds and Fields of Sleep: A Virgilian Elysium," *Wordsworth Circle* 3 (1972) 168-71.
1295.　M. L. D'Avanzo, "Keats' and Vergil's underworlds: source and meaning in Book II of *Endymion*," *Keats-Shelley Journal* 16 (1967) 61-72.
1296.　G. Hennecke, *Stefan Georges Beziehung zur antiken Literatur und Mythologie. Die Bedeutung antiker Motivik und der Werke des Horaz und Vergil für die Ausgestaltung des locus amoenus in den Hirten- und Preisgedichten Stefan Georges* (Köln 1964).
1297.　H. H. Huxley, "C. S. Calverley's *Carmen Saeculare* and F. W. Farrar's *Eric*," *Notes and Queries* 19 (1972) 265-66.
1298.　A. D. Kahn, "Byron's single difference with Homer and Virgil — the definition of the epic in *Don Juan*," *Arcadia* 5 (1970) 143-62.
1299.　M. Mommsen, "Hölderlins Lösung von Schiller. Zu Hölderlins Gedichten *An Herkules* und Die Eichbaüme und der Übersetzungen aus Ovid, Vergil und Euripides," *Jahrbuch des Deutschen Schiller-Gesellschaft* 9 (1965) 203-44.
1300.　B. O'Hehir, "Vergil's first Georgic and Denham's Cooper's Hill," *PhQ* 42 (1963) 542-47.
1301.　R. Oroz, "Andrés Bello, imitador de las bucolicas de Virgilio," *BFC* 17 (1965) 237-59.
1302.　W. J. B. Owen, "A Virgilian reminiscence in 'The Excursion'," *Notes and Queries* 11 (1964) 177-78.

Chadwick finds accord between V and Tennyson in their patriotic sentiments and their doubts about prevailing religion, even their despair. D'Avanzo studies Wordsworth's Immortality Ode for Vergilian parallels on the soul's process of regeneration. Owen traces *A* 9,433-37 in Wordsworth's *The Excursion* (Book 6, 100-102). D'Avanzo detects many similarities between *A* 6 and Keats' *Endymion*. Both Aeneas and Endymion achieve 'partial fulfilment of visionary experience.' Huxley comments on Calverley's parody of the *Aeneid* and Farrar's double indebtedness to V and to Calverley. Kahn's paper deals with the First Canto of *Don Juan* (Dido and Aeneas, 147-50). O'Hehir underlines Swift's structural debt to V's *Georgics*. Hennecke's study of Stefan George's debt to V is exhaustive. Mommsen reviews Hölderlin's translations of V. Oroz examines the classical background of Bello's *Egloga* (1806-8), Neo-Classical poetry in the Spanish-American bucolic tradition.

Twentieth Century

1303.　G. T. Gordon, "Lake Island of Innisfree: a classical allusion in Evelyn Waugh's *The Loved One*," *Evelyn Waugh Newsletter* 5 (1971) 1-2.
1304.　G. Munson, "The classicism of Robert Frost," *Modern Age* 8 (1964) 291-305.
1305.　H. C. Rutledge, "Eliot and Vergil. Parallels in the sixth *Aeneid* and *Four Quartets*," *Vergilius* 12 (1966) 11-20.
1306.　T. Slate, "Edgar Rice Burroughs and the heroic epic," *Riverside Quarterly*

3 (1968) 118-23.
1307. H. W. Stubbs, "Virgil and H. G. Wells: Prophets of a New Age," *PVS* 9 (1969-70) 34-53.

Gordon shows that Evelyn Waugh caricatured V's Charon and Hades in *The Loved One*. Munson treats V as Robert Frost's model (with Horace and 'the old Greeks'). Rutledge suggests resemblances between Eliot's *Four Quartets* and *Aeneid* 6. Slate sees parallels between Burrough's fiction and the prototypal epics of Homer and V. Stubbs examines V's tendency to the apocalyptic, beginning with the Messianic *Eclogue* and discovers common traits between the tender Roman visionary and the robust moralizing science writer.

Translators

1308. B. S. Adams, *Dryden's Translation of Vergil and its Eighteenth Century Successors*. Diss. Michigan State University, 1970. Summary in *DA* 32 (1971) 417A.
1309. A. de Bernart, "Una rara traduzione dell'Eneide dedicata ad un patrizio leccese," *StudSal* 16 (1963) 334-37.
1310. E. Bernstein, "Thomas Murner's Latin: Some Notes on the First German Aeneid," *CF* 26 (1972) 72-82.
1311. M. Boddy, "The Irrenavigable, Innavigable, Irremeable, Irregressive Styx," *Notes and Queries* 16 (1969) 253-55.
1312. D. F. C. Coldwell (ed.), *Virgil's Aeneid translated into Scottish verse by Gavin Douglas* (Edinburgh 1964). Rev: Austin *MAev* 35 (1966) 154-57.
1313. G. N. Crosland, "Notes on an unpublished manuscript by Robert Heath (FL. 1650)," *Notes and Queries* 19 (1972) 19-20.
1314. J. M. Dryoff, *Approaches to the study of Richard Stanyhurst's translation of Virgil's Aeneid*. Diss. Boston University, 1971. Summary in *DA* 33 (1972) 1678A.
1315. R. Fitzgerald (ed.), *The Aeneid of Virgil, translated by John Dryden* (New York 1965). Rev: Clarke *CR* 20 (1970) 99.
1316. R. Fitzgerald, "Dryden's Aeneid," *Arion* 2:3 (1963) 17-31.
1317. R. Godenne, "Etienne Jodelle, traducteur de Virgile," *BiblH&R* 31 (1969) 195-204.
1318. E. S. Leedham Green, "Four unpublished translations of Arthur Hugh Clough," *Review of English Studies* 23:90 (1972) 179-87.
1319. Q. G. Johnson, *Gavin Douglas as poet-translator: Eneados and Aeneid IV*. Diss. University of Orgeon, 1967. Summary in *DA* 29 (1968) 230A.
1320. W. I. McLachian, "Translation and critical judgment: a comparative study of Ezra Pound and Gavin Douglas," *Diliman Review* 14 (1966) 166-91.
1321. R. T. Meyer, "The Middle-English version of the Aeneid," *Tennessee Stud. Lit.* 11 (1966) 97-109.
1322. U. Mueller, "Vergils Aeneis in den Ubersetzung von Friedrich Schiller und Rudolf Alexander Schröder," *Jahrb. der Dt. Schillerges.* 14 (1970) 347-65.
1323. E. G. Quinn, *A critical edition of Thomas Phaer's translation of The nine fyrst bookes of the Eneidos*. Diss. New York University, 1963. Summary in *DA* 25 (1964) 455.
1324. H. Raue, *Französische Vergilübersetzungen in der zweiten Hälfte des 16. Jahrhunderts* (Köln 1966). Rev: Desmed *Latomus* 27 (1968) 684-87; Ernout *RPh* 42 (1968) 187.

1325. F. H. Ridley (ed.), *The Aeneid of Henry Howard, Earl of Surrey* (Berkeley 1963). Rev: Austin *CR* 15 (1965) 292-94; Simon *Latomus* 23 (1964) 137.

1326. F. H. Sandbach, "Some translators of Virgil," *PVS* 10 (1970-71) 24-36.

1327. Sir Charles Sedley (tr.), *The 1692 Fourth Book of Virgil, Review of English Studies* 15 (1964) 364-80.

1328. "Ruffe raffe roaring. A sixteenth century Virgil," *Arion* 7 (1968) 296-97.

1329. P. S. Starkey, *Douglas's Eneados: Virgil in 'Scottis'*. Diss. City University of New York, 1971. Summary in *DA* 32 (1972) 4635A.

1330. W. T. Zyla, "A Ukrainian version of the Aeneid: Ivan Kotljarev'skyj's Enejida," *CJ* 67 (1972) 193-97.

Adams studies Dryden's influence on 18th century translators: William Benson, Joseph Trapp, Christopher Pitt, Joseph Warton, James Beresford, and William Sotheby. Fitzgerald's introduction and article are freshly critical and appreciative of Dryden's effort. Boddy compares English translations of *A* 6,425. Coldwell's edition of Gavin Douglas' translation of the epic reawakened interest in the Scottish version. Johnson concentrates on *A* 4; Starkey provides a critical study of the text, with comments on Douglas' intentions, techniques, and personal involvement; Douglas' version recreates V's epic in contemporary Scottish terms. Lewis praises Douglas' sensitivity to V's imagery as basic to the movement of the epic. McLachian discounts accuracy as a value-criterion in translation in favour of relevance to the translator's time; Ezra Pound's *Translations from the Chinese* and Gavin Douglas' *Eneados* are prime examples. Dyroff studies Stanyhurst's translation of the epic with reference to Elizabethan Vergilianism and Tudor methodology in translation: Henry Howard and Thomas Phaer (and Dryden) are included in his study of this experimental, avant garde version. *Arion's* editors reprinted Stanyhurst's version of *A* 8,416-39. Green studies Clough's versions of *E* 1 (omitting 11-45) and of *A* 8,319-32. Meyers treats free alterations of the original in Middle-English versions of the epic; Irish tradition provided new incidents, sentiment, and similes. Quinn's critical edition of Phaer's translation of *A* 1-9 includes a comparative study of 16th century versions and praises Phaer for metrical flexibility and rhetorical mastery. Ridley provides a new edition of Henry Howard's version of the epic. The editors of *Review of English Studies* offer Sir Charles Sedley's translation of the Fourth *Aeneid*. Sandbach's comprehensive lecture touches on Phaer, Vicars, Dryden, deplores 19th century translations and praises Dickinson (1961), Humphries (1951) and C. Day Lewis for their versions. Crosland describes an unpublished 17th century translation in heroic couplets in the Williams Andrews Clark Library. Godenne provides a comparative study of du Bellay's version of the Fourth *Aeneid* and Jodelle's tragedy *Didon se sacrifiant*. Raue's study of French translations from 1550-1600 is important for comparative study with English, Italian, and other versions. Bernstein discusses Thomas Murner, the Franciscan monk, who provided the first *Aeneid* in German with remarkably few errors. Mueller treats Schiller and Schroeder as translators. Bernart studies Giuseppe Maria Candido's translation of 1769. Zyla commends Kotljarews'kyj's poetical travesty of the epic which transforms classical heroes into Ukrainian Cossacks set amid colorful portrayals of Ukrainian life.

Vergil and European Art

1331. J. J. G. Alexander, "A Virgil illuminated by Marco Joppo," *BurlingtonMag* 111 (1969) 514-17.

1332. M. Ayrton, "The path to Daedulus," *Dudley* 176-201.
1333. R. A. Brower, "Visual and verbal translation of myth: Neptune in Virgil, Rubens, Dryden," *Daedalus* 101:1 (1972) 155-82.
1334. A. G. McKay, "Virgilian landscape into art: Poussin, Claude and Turner," *Dudley* 139-60.
1335. M. P. O. Morford, "Bruegel and the first Georgic," *G&R* 13 (1966) 50-53.
1336. J. Rowlands, "Simone Martini and Petrarch: a Virgilian episode," *Apollo* 81 (1965) 264-69.
1337. G. de Tervarent, *Présence de Virgile dans l'art* (Brussels 1967). Rev: Bardon *RBPh* 47 (1969) 107-109; Courcelle *JS* (1968) 62-63.
1338. G. de Tervarent, "Rendons à Virgile . . . ," *JS* (1969) 243-46.
1339. B. H. Wiles, "Two Parmigianino drawings from the Aeneid," *MusStud* 1 (1966) 96-111.

Ayrton's interesting essay provides background for his contemporary interpretations of the Daedalus myth which were inspired by the Sixth *Aeneid* and by visits to Cumae. Ayrton's works include prose, verse, painting, and, most notably, sculpture. Brower studies a 'Parallel Betwixt Poetry and Painting' using *A* 1,135, *quos ego . . .* as a poet's experience of nature, subsequently translated into a spectacular English version and a great painting. McKay examines Vergilian associations in the paintings of Poussin, Claude, and Turner. Claude, particularly, found in V's epic the spur to his greatest period after 1669. Morford associates the *Georgics* with Bruegel's *The Fall of Icarus*. De Tarvarent's studies are instructive and important.

Music and Opera

1340. D. Cairns, "Berlioz's epic opera," *Listener* 76 (1966) 364.
1341. D. Cairns, "Berlioz and Virgil: a consideration of 'Les Troyens' as a Virgilian opera," *Royal Musical Assoc. Proc.* 95 (1968-9) 97-110.
1342. J. R. Elliott, Jr., "Virgil Shakespeareanised: Berlioz and the Trojans," *TLS* (9, 10, 69) 1160-61.
1343. I. Kemp, "Love and War (The Trojans)," *Listener* 82 (1969) 428.
1344. J. W. Klein, "Berlioz's sublime epic," *Opera* 20 (1969) 753-58.

The centennial celebrations in honour of Hector Berlioz aroused fresh interest in the composer's magnificent *Les Troyens*. Cairns, Elliott, Kemp, and Klein study the opera's indebtedness to V's epic with skill and finesse. They suggest new lines of inquiry into the influence of V's works on opera (and music) from the beginnings.

Vergil Societies

The Virgil Society (England) holds meetings four to five times annually in London to hear the Presidential address and papers on Vergilian topics. The lithographed *Proceedings* with addresses and book reviews are published annually and are distributed to members of the Society. The Society organized a conference on the Teaching of Virgil in May, 1968. For further details refer to the Hon. Secretary, F. Robertson, Faculty of Letters, The University, Whiteknights Park, Reading. Professor R. Deryck Williams, Reading University, is President.

The Vergilian Society Inc., with 1600 members, is the American counterpart of the British society. It holds meetings twice annually: the Annual Meeting in December in conjunction with the APA-AIA conventions, and a regional meeting in conjunction with the Annual Meeting of the Classical Association of the Middle West and South. The Society's publication, *Vergilius*, edited by Professor Janice M. Benario, Department of Foreign Languages, Georgia State University, Atlanta, appears once annually and contains articles on Vergilian topics, relevant historical and archaeological matters, Vergilian bibliography, and book reviews. The annual report of the Secretary and the report of the Managing Director of the Classical Summer School at Cumae are also included. The Society's overseas programs for students and teachers of Vergil, ancient history, art, and archaeology are offered annually with scholarship aid at the Villa Vergiliana at Cumae, and in Campania, Sicily, Rome, Latium and Etruria. Recent programs have included study tours of Northern Italy, Greece and the Islands, Cyprus and Turkey. Charles T. Murphy's *A Candid History of the Vergilian Society and the Villa Vergiliana at Cumae* (*Vergilius, Supplement I*, 1971) provides a brief and entertaining report of the Society's experience at Cumae. For further details refer to the Treasurer, Charles P. Twichell, Choate School, Wallingford, Connecticut 06492. Professor Alexander G. McKay, McMaster University, is President.

McMaster University,   *Alexander G. McKay*
Hamilton, Canada

A Bibliographical Handlist
on Vergil's *Aeneid*

Jane Ellen Heffner
with Mason Hammond and M.C.J. Putnam

from Volume 60, pp. 377-388

A BIBLIOGRAPHICAL HANDLIST ON VERGIL'S *AENEID*

for Teachers and Students in Secondary Schools

by

Jane Ellen Heffner

with Mason Hammond and M. C. J. Putnam

TABLE OF CONTENTS

INTRODUCTION

This bibliographical handlist has been prepared with the aim of broadening the study of the *Aeneid* in the high school Latin curriculum. As masterpiece of Latin literature, the *Aeneid* should be studied not as an isolated work, but as an epic poem in relation to its literary, religious, and historical features. By suggesting both collateral reading for students in high school and works of reference helpful for the teacher, the author aims to enhance their understanding of the poem. Only with a wider background can students begin to attain the proper comprehension of the diverse elements in the poem, its significance in literature, and its reflection of Roman civilization. Similarly teachers are provided with a handy reference for meaningful classwork.

The books included in the bibliography are ones which a high school library might well purchase or which, being available in inexpensive paperbacks, could be bought by students or teachers themselves. In a few cases, significant books have been listed though they are not in print, in the hope that they may be available to teachers in nearby libraries.

Two or three suggested readings have been given under each topic. The principles of selections are: suitability for the students or teachers, cost of the books, assumed budget for the school library, and availability of the books. For each book, there is the necessary bibliographical information and a brief critique. The capital letters (S) and (T) indicate whether the book is suggested for Students or Teachers respectively.

This handlist was originally prepared in the spring of 1964, when the author was a candidate for the Master of Arts in Teaching at Harvard University. It has been revised for publication by Professor Mason Hammond of Harvard University and Professor Michael C. J. Putnam of Brown University. Bibliographical information and book prices have been checked so far as feasible in *Books in Print* for 1966; since prices are rising and since books are likely to go out of print, the information cannot be guaranteed as fully accurate.

In the comments, the author's name has been spelled "Vergil"; the practice of the titles as between this and "Virgil" has been followed.

[Reprints of this *Handlist* may be ordered from the Editorial Office at 50c. © 1967 by The Classical Association of the Atlantic States, Inc.—The Editor is grateful to the author, and to Professors Hammond and Putnam. for this valued addition to *CW*'s bibliographies. He wishes also to thank Margaret Mayo, Doris Ormsby, Howard Busch, and James Dramis of his Rutgers Vergil seminar for helpful suggestions.]

I. EDITIONS

A. VERGIL'S WORKS

No text editions with critical apparatus, e.g. that of F. Hirtzel in the *Oxford Classical Texts* series or that of W. Janell (Teubner), are given. The following editions with commentaries will be of help to the teacher; they are probably too full for the student.

Conington, J., and Nettleship, H. *P. Vergili Maronis Opera: The Works of Virgil, with a Commentary.* 3 vols.: vol. I: *Eclogues* and *Georgics* (1898; ed. 5 by Haverfield, F.); vol. II: *Aeneid I-VI* (1884; ed. 4); vol. III: *Aeneid VII-XII* (1883). Photostat reprint published by Georg Olms, Hildesheim, Germany, 1964. Price about $60.00. (T)

Page, T. E. *P. Vergili Maronis Bucolica et Georgica* and *The Aeneid of Virgil.* New York:

St. Martin's Press; London: Macmillan. (Classical Series.) 3 vols.: vol. I: *Aeneid I-VI* (1894); vol. II: *Aeneid VII-XII* (1900); vol. III: *Bucolica et Georgica* (1898). All three volumes have been reprinted frequently. Price for each volume, $3.25. (T)

> This is the best edition for literary criticism.

Papillon, T. L., and Haigh, A. E. *P. Vergili Maronis Opera: Vergil, with an Introduction and Notes.* Oxford: Clarendon Press, 1892. 2 vols.: vol. I: *Introduction and Test;* vol. II: *Notes.* Out of print. (T)

> The notes are brief and not as useful as Page's.

(Loeb Classical Library.) *Virgil,* text and English translation by Fairclough, H. Rushton. Cambridge, Mass.: Harvard University Press. 2 vols.: I: *Eclogues, Georgics,* and *Aeneid I-VI;* vol. II: *Aeneid VII-XII* and *Appendix Vergiliana.* (#63-64 in Loeb Series; ed. 1, 1916; rev. ed., 1935 [and later reprints].) $4.00 each. (T)

> The translation serves as a commentary for difficult passages.

B. INDIVIDUAL BOOKS OF THE *AENEID*

Editions of individual books with commentaries are either briefly annotated school texts or learned editions with full commentaries. The few suggested here contain along with the text helpful and complete, yet concise, notes. In these notes stylistic and metrical features as well as religious, philosophical, and related topics are annotated. The introduction to each edition discusses the important elements of the particular book. For details on other editions, the annual list of "Textbooks in Greek and Latin" in the *Classical World* should be consulted.

Book 2: Austin, R. G. *P. Verg. Mar. Aen. Lib. Secundus.* Oxford: Clarendon Press, 1964. Pp. 311. $4.00. (T)

> In his prefatory remarks the editor focuses on the narrative structure of the book, Vergil's use of the various traditions of the fall of Troy, and his art of characterization. The *index nominum, index verborum,* and *index rerum* are helpful.

Book 3: Williams, R. D. *P. Verg. Mar. Aen. Lib. Tertius.* Oxford: Clarendon Press, 1962. Pp. 220. $3.40. (T)

> The introduction discusses the role of Book III in the poem; Aeneas, Anchises and the Roman mission; sources of Book III; the treatment of subject matter; and problems of the book in relation to the rest of the poem. Bibliography and index.

Book 4: Austin, R. G. *P. Verg. Mar. Aen. Lib. Quartus.* Oxford: Clarendon Press, 1955. Pp. 212. $3.40. (T)

> The introduction includes a careful analysis of Dido's and Aeneas' actions and the drama of the book. There is an appendix with Ovid's *Heroides* VII: *Dido Aeneae;* also an *index verborum* and *index nominum et rerum.* (T)

Book 5: Williams, R. D. *P. Verg. Mar. Aen. Lib. Quintus.* Oxford: Clarendon Press, 1960. Pp. 219. $3.20. (T)

> The introduction contains a discussion of the purpose of the book, a description of funeral games, and a study of the character of Aeneas and the nature of his mission. Bibliography and index. (T)

Book 6: Fletcher, (Sir) Frank. *Aeneid VI.* Oxford: Clarendon Press, 1941. Pp. 111. $2.00. (T)

> This book is suggested for the advanced student. The introduction and commentary emphasize a stylistic approach to the poem. (T)

Book 12: Maguinness, W. S. *Virgil: Aeneid Book XII.* London: Methuen; New York: St. Martin's Press, 1953. Pp. 150. $1.50; with vocabulary, $2.00. (T)

> An edition for schools.

II. TRANSLATIONS

There are several translations into English of the *Eclogues* and the *Georgics* and many of the *Aeneid.* The following, most of which are in major series of paperbacks, are readily available for the students. Teachers, of course, may prefer some other. Reference should be made to the annual list of "Inexpensive Books for Teaching the Classics" in the *Classical World* for information on new translations.

A. *ECLOGUES*

Lewis, C. Day. *The Eclogues of Virgil.* London: Cape, 1963. Pp. 46. $2.25. Verse. Paperback ed. with *Georgics* and facing Latin texts: New York: Doubleday, Anchor Books (A390), 1964. Pp. 233. $1.25. (S)

> Day Lewis uses for this attractive translation a meter with six stresses to the line except for the four eclogues with singing matches, which are set to folk songs. In his own inimitable way, he communicates the poetic feeling and varying moods of the *Eclogues.*

Johnson, Geoffrey. *The Pastorals of Vergil: A Verse Translation of the Eclogues.* Lawrence, Kan.: University of Kansas Press, 1960. Pp. 61. $3.00. (S)

> This translation is smooth and accurate; there is a helpful introduction by L. R. Lind.

Rieu, E. V. *Virgil, the Pastoral Poems.* Baltimore: Penguin Books (Penguin L8), 1949 (and later reprints). Pp. 152. $0.95. Prose. (S)

> Latin text on one side of page, prose translation on facing page; informative introduction as well as a brief essay on each eclogue; there is a glossary of proper names. A good, accurate translation.

B. *GEORGICS*

Bovie, Smith Palmer. *Virgil's Georgics.* Chicago: University of Chicago Press, (Phoenix P 221), 1956. Pp. 311. $1.75. (pb). Verse. (S)

> An excellent introductory essay discusses his-

torical background, Vergil and the Hesiodic tradition, and the *Georgics* as a work of art. In the fine translation, Bovie has preserved the vigorous spirit which Vergil infused into his prosaic subject, life and labor on the land. By accurately imitating Vergil's use of personification, he vitalizes nature.

Lewis, C. Day. *The Georgics of Virgil*. London: Cape, 1940. Pp. 96. $2.25. Verse, with facing Latin text. Also in paperback with *Eclogues:* New York: Doubleday, Anchor Books (A390), 1964. Pp. 233. $1.25 (see above under A). (S)

Day Lewis conveys the spirit of the *Georgics* and Vergil's love of nature. He well understands the tradition of didactic verse and Vergil's profound reverence for religion.

C. *AENEID*

Copley, Frank O. *Vergil: The Aeneid*. Indianapolis & New York, Bobbs-Merrill (Library of Liberal Arts 212), 1965. Pp. 320. $1.95 (pb). Also cloth, $6.50. Verse. (S)

Brooks Otis, in a brief introduction (pp. vii-xxi), summarizes the conclusions of his *Virgil: A Study in Civilized Poetry* (see VII). Copley's translation is line for line with the original, in a free iambic pentameter verse. Despite occasional colloquialisms, it has life and movement. At the end is a useful Glossary of Proper Names (pp. 293-320).

Humphries, Rolfe. *The Aeneid of Virgil*. New York: Charles Scribner's Sons (SL6), 1951. Pp. 381. $1.65 (pb); $4.50 (cloth). Verse. (S)

The introduction contains a discussion of the purpose of the poem and the character of Aeneas. The appendix includes information on Vergil's life and time and the cast of characters. In this popular translation, Humphries has successfully copied Vergil's variation of theme and tone and his heroic style. The translator's occasional anachronisms and ungrammatical forms constitute the only disagreeable aspects.

Knight, W. F. Jackson. *Virgil: the Aeneid*. Baltimore: Penguin Books (Penguin L51), 1936 (and later reprints). Pp. 361. $0.95. Prose. (S)

Although this is a prose translation, it is equal in tone and spirit to the verse renditions. Knight preserves Vergilian moods and dramatic effects; also, Vergil's impressive glorification of Rome is presented in full force. At the end are a glossary of names, a two-page map of the voyage of Aeneas, and a genealogical chart of the royal houses of Troy and Greece.

Lewis, C. Day. *The Aeneid of Virgil*. New York: Doubleday, Anchor Books (A20), 1953. Pp. 320. $0.95 (pb); $3.75 (cloth). Verse. Reprint of ed. in cloth by Oxford University Press, 1952. (S)

Day Lewis recaptures the general tone of the original in all its variations. The heightening of intensity remains as do the stylistic effects. The only negative criticism is his use of colloquial and trite expressions. The reader may find the version too modern.

Lind, L. R. *Vergil's Aeneid*. Bloomington, Ind.: University of Indiana Press (Midland Books MB45), 1963. Pp. 301. $1.95 (pb); $5.75 (cloth). Verse. (S)

The accurate reproduction of the emotions of the individual and of the various moods of the poem are the outstanding features of this translation of the *Aeneid*. There are an introduction on Vergil and the meaning of the *Aeneid;* a map of Aeneas' route; an appendix with a discussion of the life and work of Vergil; a bibliography; notes on the text and translation; and a glossary of proper names.

III. DISCUSSION OF V's LIFE AND WORKS

A. ANCIENT LIVES AND COMMENTARIES

A number of ancient lives of Vergil have been preserved and handed down through the generations. Teachers may be interested in securing texts to read or to extract for classroom use. The following editions will be of help.

Hardie, Colin, ed. *Vitae Vergilianae Antiquae*. (Oxford Classical Texts.) 1954. Pp. 64. $1.70. (T)

This selection of *Lives* (Latin only) was originally published with Ellis, Robinson: *Appendix Vergiliana* (1907). Since the *Appendix* has now been re-edited by Clausen, W. V., and others (OCT. 1966. Pp. 185. $2.90), the *Vitae* are now available independently.

Nettleship, H., ed. *Ancient Lives of Vergil*. Oxford: Clarendon Press, 1897. Pp. 70. Out of print. (T)

This, though out of print, is the only discussion in English of the principal *Lives*.

Vergil's works, particularly the *Aeneid*, became a school-book almost at once; among the quotations from authors scratched on the walls of Pompeii before 79 A.D., fifty-six, by far the largest number, are from the *Aeneid*. In consequence, Vergil's works early became matter for learned annotation and comment. The earliest preserved, and best known, commentary is that by Servius on all the works, of the mid fourth century A.D. He drew heavily on his teacher Aelius Donatus. His commentary, in turn, was expanded in a form known from its first modern publisher (1600) as *Servius Danielis*. The commentary of Servius has preserved much valuable material both on Vergil and his works and generally on Greek and Roman subjects; it is therefore often cited both in longer commentaries on Vergil and in other works on the classics. Unfortunately the standard edition by Thilo and Hagen (3 vols., vol. III in 2 parts, 1881-1902) and a still incomplete edition begun at Harvard University (vols. II & III on *Aen*. I-V; American Philological Association, 1946 & 1965) are probably not readily available to teachers. Nor is there any English translation or convenient discussion.

About 400 A.D. a certain Macrobius composed in seven books his *Saturnalia*. This purports to report discussions among a group of friends during the holidays of the feast of Saturn in December. They use the works of Vergil as the basis for discursive comments on philological, historical, and antiquarian lore. In particular many comparisons are drawn between passages from Vergil and ones from earlier poets, notably Homer and Ennius. Unfortunately, again, there is no English translation and the latest Teubner edition of the text (2 vols., 1963) is not readily available for teachers.

B. MODERN BOOKS

The discussion of Vergil in the following two histories of Roman literature which are in print are helpful for both students and teachers.

Duff, J. W. *A Literary History of Rome from the Origins to the Close of the Golden Age.* New York: Barnes & Noble (Up41), 1964. Pp. 543. $2.95 (pb); $8.75 (cloth). Paperback reprints of ed. 3, 1959, by A. M. Duff, which reproduced ed. 2, 1910, with further notes and bibliography to 1959 at the end. (S)

Ch. I of Pt. III (pp. 316-352) gives a good general introduction to Vergil. There is a brief description of Vergil's life and a discussion of the contents of each of his works. A consideration of its literary genre and outstanding features follows. This discussion gives a good interpretation of the *Eclogues,* the *Georgics,* and the *Aeneid,* which reveals their relationship to each other and the development in Vergil's thought and poetic style. Furthermore, Duff traces Vergil's debt to his Greek predecessors. There is a great emphasis on Vergil's love of nature. On the negative side, Duff is a Victorian critic.

Duff devotes a special chapter to "Minor Poems Attributed to Vergil" (ch. II of Pt. III, pp. 353-362). These are the poems ascribed to his early career and grouped under the title *Appendix Vergiliana,* for which see under Hardie above in A and the text and translation in the Loeb ed. (see I A), vol. II, pp. 367-541. Scholars of the early twentieth century tended to accept these as largely Vergil's work; see under Prescott below. But modern scholars are sceptical about his authorship of most of the pieces. However, these poems, or the bulk of them, are sufficiently contemporary with Vergil to illustrate his literary milieu. Duff's work will be referred to hereafter simply as Duff.

Rose, Herbert Jennings. *A Handbook of Latin Literature.* New York: Dutton & Co., (D67), 1960. Pp. 557. $2.15 (pb); $6.95 (cloth). Paperback reprint of ed. 3, 1954 (from ed. 1, 1936), with front page of addenda and corrigenda; the bibliography at the end has not been brought up-to-date from 1936. (S)

On pp. 233-264 of ch. 9: "Vergil and Augustan Poetry," Rose deals with Vergil, although more briefly than Duff; nevertheless, this section is as useful in its own way. Rose begins with a brief description of Vergil's life, based on the ancient *Lives* (see under A above). There follows a discussion of each of his works according to a definite pattern: a detailed review of the contents of the work, other pertinent information, and an indication of Vergil's borrowings from his Greek predecessors. Rose summarizes each book of the *Aeneid* and discusses such points as Vergil's desire to destroy the poem, his sensitivity, and his hatred of war. By this emphasis on the content of the poems,

Rose offers a helpful background to the students who have a quick acquaintance with Vergil's works.

The following two excellent books are still in print and will be referred to frequently hereafter; special discussion of relevant portions will be given under appropriate headings:

Mackail, J. W. *Virgil and His Meaning to the World of Today.* New York: Cooper Square Publishers, 1963. Pp. 159. $2.95 (cloth). Reprint of 1922 ed., New York: Longmans, Green, & Co., in *Our Debt to Greece and Rome* series. (S)

Mackail, in a full account of Vergil's life (ch. IV, pp. 29-44), examines his education, literary companions, character, and even his physical appearance. Vergil's personality is presented as revealed in the ancient biographies and in the poet's own works. In two following chapters (chs. V & VI, pp. 45-71), Mackail gives a general impression of the *Eclogues* and of the *Georgics,* without a detailed discussion. Chs. VII-X (pp. 72-119) discuss the *Aeneid.* Mackail presents the prominent characteristics of each of Vergil's works without too detailed discussion. Thus students even without a background in classics can easily get a general impression of them. The chief criticism of Mackail's presentation, aside from its brief and general character, is that he assumes that the *Georgics* and *Aeneid* were written as propaganda for the Augustan principate. This work will be referred to hereafter simply as Mackail.

Prescott, Henry W. *The Development of Virgil's Art.* London: Russell & Russell, 1963. Pp. 481. $8.50. Reprint of 1927 ed., University of Chicago Press. (T)

Prescott, in his second chapter on Vergil's life (pp. 18-75), uses the poems of the *Appendix Vergiliana* to reconstruct his early career, as did other writers of the early twentieth century, such as Edward Kennard Rand and Tenney Frank. Modern criticism denies to Vergil all save at most two or three of the minor poems in this collection; see under Duff above. The following two chapters on the *Eclogues* and *Georgics* excellently summarize their contents. Prescott emphasizes in these Vergil's debt to his Greek models and shows the relationship of each eclogue to the various idylls of Theocritus and of the *Georgics* to Hesiod's *Works and Days.* Yet for both works he claims for Vergil originality, which the ancients defined as variation in a traditional convention of poetic style and themes. The bulk of the book (pp. 138-481) gives a careful, sound, and useful evaluation of the *Aeneid* as "The National Epic." Because of the detail of the treatment and the author's assumption of familiarity with Vergil's works, this book is not suitable for students but would be most helpful for teachers. Hereafter it will be referred to as Prescott.

See also the books by Knight, Pöschl, Otis, Commager, and Duckworth, for which bibliographical detail and comment are given under VII: Style and Language.

IV. MANUSCRIPTS

A. THE ANCIENT BOOK

Kenyon, Frederick G. *Books and Readers in Ancient Greece and Rome.* Oxford: Clarendon

Press, ed. 2, 1951 (from ed. 1, 1932). Pp. 136. Apparently out of print as of 1966. (T)

This book describes the methods of book production from earliest times until the fourth century A.D. when papyrus was replaced by vellum. It also relates the origins and growth of the habit of reading in Greece and Rome. The importance of the ancient library is revealed throughout the discussion. This is a very worth-while book for information both on the publication of a poem like the *Aeneid* and on its popularity among a certain group of readers. It includes an appendix with illustrative passages from Latin authors who discussed book publication, an index, and illustrations of book and writing materials. Furthermore, the author's approach is clear and comprehensive.

B. MANUSCRIPTS IN GENERAL

Diringer, David. *The Hand-Produced Book.* New York: Philosophical Library, 1953 (and later reprints). Pp. 603. Apparently out of print as of 1966. (T)

Diringer, like Kenyon, discusses in a few chapters the production of ancient books, both Greek and Latin. He also reviews the historical fate of manuscripts, i.e., the preservation of significant works, the destruction of other manuscripts, and the occasional dramatic recovery of old texts. He includes the important role of the libraries in the survival of manuscripts. This is a valuable account, but is recommended only for the very interested teacher.

Hall, Frederick W. *A Companion to Classical Texts.* New York: Frederick Ungar Publishing Company, 1965. Pp. 363. $6.00. Reprint of 1913 ed., Oxford: Clarendon Press. (T)

In this book the history of classical texts or manuscripts from the age of Charlemagne to the Italian Renaissance is given along with examples and rules of revision and emendation in these periods. Hall also describes the production of the ancient book and texts of Greek and Latin writers. This book is suitable only for the teacher who is interested in the study of manuscripts.

C. MANUSCRIPTS OF VERGIL

There are no recent specific discussions of the manuscripts of Vergil. Reference should be made to the prefaces of the following standard editions:

Conington & Nettleship (see I A). (T)

The introduction discusses the more important surviving manuscripts of Vergil (pp. cx-cxi). Moreover, the editors explain the way in which certain ancient commentators aided in the survival of the Vergilian text. The Bodleian manuscripts are described on pp. cxii-cxv. This short sketch is helpful but not essential.

Papillon & Haigh (see I A). (T)

Papillon & Haigh's edition presents a clear account in which the text tradition of various manuscripts and the use of ancient commentators for the determination of the text itself are explained (pp. xxiv-xxix). In the history of textual criticism during certain periods (pp. xxxvi-xliv), the editors indicate where and by whom Vergilian and other

texts were corrected and revised; in addition, they discuss the fate of the various manuscripts.

Knight, W. F. Jackson. *Roman Vergil.* New York: Hillary House Publishers, ed. 2, 1946 (from ed. 1, 1944). Pp. 348. $7.00. (T)

Knight succinctly treats the manuscript tradition of Vergil's works (ch. VI, pp. 282-298); however, he describes the chief manuscripts in greater detail than do the editors mentioned above. He presents the many difficulties in constituting Vergil's text: the apparent gaps, the transposition of passages, lines, and words, and the authenticity of the lines. He considers the textual criticism of Vergil as a "pleasant puzzle." Hereafter this book will be referred to as Knight.

V. RELIGION AND PHILOSOPHY

Rose, Herbert Jennings. *Religion in Greece and Rome.* New York: Harper (Torch Books, TB 55), 1959 (and later reprints). Pp. 312. $1.95. Reprint of ed. 1, 1959. Orig. eds.: *Ancient Greek Religion, Ancient Roman Religion;* Hutchinson University Library, 1947, 1949. Available from Hillary House Publ., New York, $3.00 each. (S)

Since the *Aeneid* is infused with the religious piety of the poet and thus shows many religious features, it can be fully appreciated only by the help of a knowledge of Roman religion. Rose's book provides this necessary background. This publication combines two separate books by the author: *Ancient Greek Religion* and *Ancient Roman Religion,* without any change in content or organization. In compact size, the book offers the advantage of allowing one to investigate the relationships of the two ancient civilizations. For the more immediate purpose, it is an excellent study of all aspects of Roman religion, including the gods of the Roman state and their meaning, religious festivals and rites, and institutions. Moreover, it offers the background for a more complete understanding of the *Aeneid* by the inclusion of material which is expressly alluded to in the poem. The author also attempts to define the meaning of *pietas,* an abstract quality which is an essential aspect of Roman religion and one of the themes of the *Aeneid.*

Not only the content, but also the clear and straightforward style, make this book suitable for high school students as well as for teachers.

Bailey, Cyril. *Religion in Virgil.* Oxford: Clarendon Press, 1935. Pp. 337. Out of print; Barnes & Noble, New York, announce a reprint for July 1967. $7.00. (T)

This handbook, in which every aspect of religion in Vergil's poems is considered in detail, is invaluable for the teacher. Bailey explains the ritual of sacrifice and prayer as well as burial rites with direct references to Vergil's poetry. In this all-embracing commentary, he studies the festival celebrations, various meanings of the significant words *fatum* and *fortuna,* the worship of the emperor and of different gods, and the Underworld, with a detailed description of Vergil's Hades. Throughout the book the author analyzes the religious context of the main passages of the poem, and at the conclusion he synthesizes Vergil's attitude to religious ideas and cults. Fully to appreciate this book requires some preliminary knowledge of Roman religion; with such a background, its study of Vergil's religious devotion will be found fascinating.

Highbarger, Ernest Leslie. *The Gates of Dreams: An Archaeological Examination of Vergil's Aeneid VI.893-899,* Baltimore: Johns Hopkins University Press, 1940, reprint 1963. Pp. 149; diagrams. Apparently out of print in 1966. (T)

Highbarger's book, though not essential, greatly elucidates Book VI in the two chapters on Vergil's concept of the Underworld and Aeneas' visit to it (chs. VII and VIII, pp. 68-114). By his diagram of Aeneas' journey through Hades, Highbarger facilitates the teacher's explanation of this very significant but difficult part of the poem. A student interested in the philosophical and religious ideas presented in the *Aeneid,* such as the transmigration of the soul and the meaning of the Underworld, will find this book worth-while.

Knight, W. F. Jackson. *Vergil: Epic and Anthropology* (ed. Christie, John D.). Oxford: Blackwell, 1967. 55 shillings; will probably become available in the U.S. (T)

This book republishes two earlier books by Knight, of which the second, *Cumaean Gates: A Reference of the Sixth Aeneid to Initiation Patterns* (Oxford: Blackwell, 1936. Pp. 190, ill.), discusses the legendary and anthropological sources for Book VI.

VI. HISTORY AND ARCHAEOLOGY

The number of textbooks available on Roman history is great. The following books have been listed for the reasons stated:

Dudley, Donald R. *The Civilization of Rome.* New York: Mentor (MT472), 1960. Paperback original. Pp. 256; 29 illustrations of monuments, coins, and culture on 16 plates. $0.75. (S)

This brief history covers from the founding of Rome to the fall of the Empire and treats social, economic, and cultural aspects as well as political. The author provides a general impression of the different periods of Roman history through his broad approach and a solid background specifically for the historical references in the *Aeneid,* especially those found in the prophecies, and for the literary activity of the Augustan Age. As a handbook for reading the *Aeneid,* this history is very adequate. The explanations are clear enough so that the student who is unfamiliar with Roman history can comprehend the information. The author's constant comparisons to other epochs of history are beneficial for the student, as are his literary references from important Roman authors and his dependence on ancient sources. However, the limited space for such a long and momentous period of history has resulted in the author's failure to give much interpretation. Another disappointing feature of the book, the omission of subdivisions within chapters, handicaps the student in finding particular information and following trends. However, despite some weak-

nesses, this is the best cheap book on Roman history.

Scullard, H. H. *From the Gracchi to Nero: A History of the Roman World from 133 B.C. to A.D. 68.* New York: Barnes & Noble (UP45), 1965. Pp. 460. $3.50 (pb). Reprint of ed. 2, New York: Barnes & Noble, 1963. Cloth $5.75. Ed. 2 (from ed. 1, 1959) publ. in London by Methuen is a paperback reprint of ed. 1 publ. in New York by Praeger (now out of print). (T)

Scullard covers the significant last one hundred years of the Republic, the creation of the Principate and the early years of the Empire. He features some points which Dudley's book lacks: a neat and clear organization, a determined effort at interpretation, and a logical emphasis on trends. The explanation of the downfall of the Republic is penetrating and well-supported, as is the discussion of the political foundation of the Principate. Furthermore, Scullard includes many of the prominent features of Dudley's book, such as the concentration on the various dimensions of history. However, although the teacher will find the book extremely good, the following drawbacks hinder recommending it for students: the limited period of history covered (133 B.C. - 68 A.D.), the difficult style, and a treatment too full for students. On the other hand, in the excellent notes of the conclusion, the reader who is interested in a more extensive background is referred to valuable primary and secondary sources.

Cochrane, Charles Norris. *Christianity and Classical Culture.* New York: Oxford University Press (Galaxy 7), 1957 (and reprints). Pp. 253. $2.45. Reprint of cloth corrected ed., 1944 (from ed. 1, 1940), $7.00. (T)

Although this book deals primarily with the third century A.D., the second chapter (Pt. I, pp. 27-73) briefly provides a keen and valuable analysis of Vergil's philosophy of history as it is presented in the *Aeneid.* The author's explanation of the prophecies in Books I, VI, and VIII in which the destiny of Rome is set forth reveals one of the profound messages of the poem. Cochrane views Vergil's perception of Rome's present and future role in the civilization of the west as the spreading of peace over the Mediterranean world and its political and cultural unification. Despite a difficult style and an unsystematic presentation of ideas, this chapter affords stimulating reading.

Although this handlist normally includes only books or chapters in books, the following article in a scientific journal may be mentioned because of its great relevance to the *Aeneid:*

Schoder, Raymond V., S.J. "Ancient Cumae," *Scientific American,* vol. 209, no. 12 (Dec. 1963), pp. 109-121. $0.60. (if obtainable). (T)

This article relates the history of the city of Cumae from the pre-Roman period to the Middle Ages; more specifically, from the eleventh century B.C. to the thirteenth century A.D. The author naturally takes an archaeological approach; as well, he gives emphasis to the economic life of the city. The article is valuable because of the discussion of Vergil's treatment of Cumae in the *Aeneid*. In this section, Aeneas' trip to Cumae and the importance of his visit to the Sibyl's grotto are considered. Moreover, Schoder describes the various sites in the city, and, on the basis of the accuracy of Vergil's descriptions, he deduces that the poet has been present at these sites. Beautiful photographs display the places of interest, including those described in the *Aeneid:* the Sibyl's cavern and the temple of Apollo. The significant background given for Book VI and the excellent pictures render this study very useful for the teacher.

Tilly, Bertha. *Vergil's Latium*. Oxford: Blackwell, 1947. Pp. 123; ill. Available from Hillary House Publ., New York, $3.00. (T)

A useful discussion of the sites in Latium (the modern Roman Camagna) which Vergil mentions in the *Aeneid*.

Knight: *Vergil: Epic and Anthropology* (see V). (T)

The first of Knight's two books here republished is *Vergil's Troy: Essays on the Second Book of the Aeneid* (Oxford: Blackwell, 1932. Pp. 158), which gives the literary, anthropological, and archaeological background of *Aeneid*, Book II. See also the second book: *Cumaean Gates,* noted above under V.

See also Highbarger above under V. (T)

VII. STYLE AND LANGUAGE

The language of Vergil is studied only incidentally in the various discussions of Vergil's style by the writers listed below. For more detailed information on language, reference should be made to scholarly articles in classical journals. However, the books suggested here contain both general and specific discussions of Vergil's style.

Mackail (see III B). (S)

The summary of the *Aeneid* in ch. VIII (pp. 86-99) reveals both the great skill in the construction of the poem and its unity of design. In the discussion of style and diction (ch. XII, pp. 142-150), Mackail reviews the development of the hexameter to its most complete form as shaped by Vergil. On the whole he gives little indication of Vergil's style. This is one of the few books in print which affords high school students some understanding of the different levels of meaning in the poem. However, the author is often too vague and general, and fails to convey his ideas to the reader, especially to the beginner. The book is mentioned here because it is not as specific or advanced as the other books.

Prescott (see III B). (T)

Prescott's discussion of the *Aeneid* (pp. 246-262) concentrates on Vergil's stylistic techniques. He emphasizes the distinctive features of each book, such as the narrative account of the eye witness in Books II and III, the drama of Book IV, the central position of Book VI, and the artistic symmetry and variety of Books VII-XII. This is the most comprehensive book available for a study of the *Aeneid*, and, accordingly, can almost be considered a general reference book. It contributes material on other topics in the study of the *Aeneid* which are not categorized in this handlist, e.g. the characters, the role of Aeneas, and his humanity. The attitude of the poet is revealed throughout the commentary. Although Prescott states in the preface that he has written the book for use by his school students as well as by those in college, he often assumes too broad a background in classical literature for the school student. Yet the book is highly recommended in its entirety for the teacher and in many parts for the student.

Knight (see IV C). (T)

Ch. V (pp. 180-281), entitled "Language, Verse, and Style," provides a close analysis of Vergil's style, by which Knight means the combination of meter, rhythm, and language. He discusses these three aspects at great length. He first analyzes the conflict ("heterodyne") and coincidence ("homodyne") of word accent and verse stress in Vergil's hexameter (see VIII). Then he illustrates how Vergil achieved variety by different metrical devices within several verses composing a single unit of expression. Finally he talks about the Latin language. He goes on to show the influence of previous writers on Vergil's hexameter and on his literary techniques. Although the book is difficult reading, it is worth-while for the teacher for the general impression of Vergil's poetry which it conveys.

Otis, Brooks. *Virgil: A Study in Civilized Poetry*. Oxford: Clarendon Press, 1963. Pp. 436. $7.20. Appendix with bibliography. (T)

This scholarly work is a careful attempt to discover how Vergil recreated the heroic-epic age (of Homer) in an urban civilization. For Otis, this means penetrating the secret of the *Aeneid*. The author has a thesis which he aims to prove throughout this discussion of Vergil's three works; namely, that the poet combined ancient form and content with a novel narrative style and novel method of symbolism for his own contemporary purpose to reveal the Roman-Augustan ideal. The result, according to Otis, was the creation of an original, unique work of art, a truly Roman poem, the *Aeneid*. The book focuses on the subjective style of Vergil and his psychologically continuous narrative. Vergil's original structure of symbols and his sympathetic-empathetic attitudes are emphasized, for it is these features which are instrumental in conveying the Augustan theme. In three long chapters on the *Aeneid* (chs. III, VI, VII), Otis examines the poem to prove his thesis which he supports with abundant specific material. He also discusses the *Eclogues* and *Georgics* in detail (chs. IV, V), in order to present the origin of Vergil's ideas and techniques and to show their gradual development and later elaboration in the *Aeneid*. This is a different, exciting interpretation of the *Aeneid*, even though it raises possible points of disagreement. The book has been thoughtfully arranged. Moreover, the author by continually referring to his thesis, never allows the reader to forget his aim. The book is a fundamental work for the teacher, but too academic for the student.

Pöschl, Viktor. *The Art of Vergil: Image and Symbol in the Aeneid* (trans. by Gerda Seligson). Ann Arbor, Mich.: University of Michigan Press,

1962. Pp. 216. $3.95. (T) (Trans. from German ed. of 1950.)

Pöschl's subject is indicated in the subtitle of the book: "Image and Symbol in the *Aeneid*." His emphasis is on the extent to which the basic themes of the poem and the personalities of the main characters: Aeneas, Dido, and Turnus, are expressed through the imagery. Vergil's use of language as a vehicle of fine expression is interpreted by Pöschl at all its levels. He constantly refers to Homer and compares the writings of the two poets. In the final part of the book, he discusses the ways by which Vergil created the varying moods of the poem. This profound and detailed examination of Vergil's language, the only such study presently available in book form in English, gives the teacher great insight into the *Aeneid* and thus helps the presentation of the poem to a class. It is a thought-provoking book, even if the teacher does not agree with the interpretations set forth.

Putnam, Michael C. J. *The Poetry of the Aeneid: Four Studies in Imaginative Unity and Design*. Cambridge, Mass.: Harvard University Press, 1965. Pp. 238. $5.50. (T)

In this study of Vergil's literary style, the author examines in detail the symbolic images of four books of the poem (Books II, V, VIII, and XII), with the aim of revealing the unifying theme of these individual parts. Putnam also stresses similarities in word and thought to other passages and episodes in the poem. By this approach, he provides interesting insights into the meaning of the poem. Furthermore, his method of citing references and including whole passages in the original contributes to a clearer understanding of the poem. Thus this discussion encourages new modes of thought and suggests parallels elsewhere in Vergil, even if the reader finds it at times forced and too "imagistic."

Commager, Steele. *Virgil: A Collection of Critical Essays*. Englewood, N.J.: Prentice-Hall (Spectrum Book S-TC62; in "Twentieth Century Views"), 1966. Pp. 186. $1.95 (pb). Also cloth, $3.95. (T)

This collection of twelve articles by different authors, all previously published in learned journals, brings together significant reinterpretations of various aspects of Vergil's thought and art. Teachers will find its insights stimulating and might well suggest articles to intelligent students.

Duckworth, George E. *Structural Patterns and Proportions in Vergil's Aeneid: A Study in Mathematical Composition*. Ann Arbor, Mich.: University of Michigan Press, 1962. Pp. 268. $7.50. (T)

This book, with its elaborate mathematical argument and detailed and diagrammed analyses, is at best for a busy teacher's summer reading. Duckworth argues that Vergil, both in his overall plan of the *Aeneid* and in lesser episodes, adapted the number of lines in various portions to a numerical ratio known variously as the Golden Section, the Divine Proportion, or the Golden Mean ratio; that is, the numbers of lines in two parts of any whole are such that the larger number of lines is to the smaller as the total number is to the larger. His opening two chapters describe major patterns of organization in all three of Vergil's works; the third analyzes the *Eclogues* and the *Georgics* according to his ratio; and the remaining two apply the ratio to episodes in the *Aeneid*. Despite the careful work devoted by Duckworth to his analyses, critics have not been convinced that Vergil composed with so conscious a numerical scheme in mind as this.

VIII. METER

For information on meter, the students must rely on brief descriptions in the Vergil textbooks. Several more advanced and technical books are suggested for the teacher. The books by Halporn and Hardie, as their titles suggest, contain material on all Greek as well as Latin meters and include comparisons of the two; Raven's new book, on the other hand, is devoted to Latin meters; he has written a parallel one on Greek meters (1962).

A. TECHNICAL

Halporn, James W., Ostwald, Martin, & Rosenmeyer, Thomas G. *The Meters of Greek and Latin Poetry*. Indianapolis & New York: Bobbs-Merrill (Library of Liberal Arts 126), 1963. Pp. 137. $1.75 (pb); also cloth, $3.50. (T)

This compact handbook contains short, clear descriptions of all the Greek and Latin meters. The explanation of Greek hexameter and Latin hexameter with illustrative examples from Homer and Vergil respectively is helpful (pp. 10-12, 67-71). The book briefly sets forth the development of the Latin hexameter from Ennius to Catullus to Vergil, who established its final form. This good reference book for all meters includes at the end a glossary of technical terms, a list of meters, and indices of Greek and Latin authors cited.

Hardie, William Ross. *Res Metrica: An Introduction to the Study of Greek and Roman Versification*. Oxford: Clarendon Press, 1920. Pp. 275. Out of print. (T)

Hardie presents general notions of rhythm and meter. However, this book would be beneficial only for the teacher who has sufficient familiarity with meter to understand the more complex aspects of scansion and the comparison of Greek and Latin meters, which are the main features of the book. Ch. 1 (pp. 1-29) is devoted to a thorough discussion of the hexameter. The book contains a glossary of some metrical terms and a chronological table.

Raven, D. S. *Latin Metre: An Introduction*. London: Faber and Faber, 1965. Pp. 182. Available from Humanities Press, New York, $6.00. (T)

Raven's is a comparatively simple book on Latin meter. His three introductory chapters present the basic elements of Latin meter as well as its relation to the Greek models. In the subsequent chapters the author describes in clear detail each meter with its various forms. In the extensive chapter on the hexameter, emphasis is placed on the major aspects of this meter, its historical development, and its use by Vergil with examples from his work. This work on meter fulfills many of the requirements for a book on the topic. The author imparts an understanding of the rhythmical flow of Latin meter; additionally, he draws his examples from works with which the reader would be familiar. He manages to avoid awesome technical terms, and he places in brackets more difficult and detailed material which is not necessary for the student, nor in many cases for the teacher. The book is essential for the teacher, and might well be useful for students.

B. GENERAL

Mackail (see III B). (S)

Mackail devotes a brief concluding chapter (ch. XII, pp. 142-150) to "The Virgilian Hexameter," in which he gives general impressions of its effect but no metrical details.

Knight (see IV C). (T)

Knight's view of the importance of word accent in Vergil's meter has been mentioned in the outline of his book (above, under VII). His discussion (ch. V, pp. 180-281) incorporates his earlier study of *Accentual Symmetry in Vergil* (Oxford: Blackwell, 1939; reprint 1950. Pp. 107. Available from Hillary House Publ., New York, $1.50).

Wilkinson, L. P. *Golden Latin Artistry.* Cambridge and New York: Cambridge University Press, 1963. Pp. 283. $10.50. (T)

This urbane and readable study of the use of sound, rhythm, and sentence structure in Latin prose and verse has a brief discussion of hexameter rhythm on pp. 127-132.

Beare, William. *Latin Verse and European Song.* London: Methuen, 1957. Pp. 296. Available from Hillary House Publ., New York, $7.50. (T)

Beare considers the development of Latin verse in relation to that of other Indo-European languages and argues that the earliest meter (Saturnian) was in part accentual. In his chapter on classical meters (ch. XIV, pp. 169-176), however, he criticizes Knight's view that word accent was important in Vergil's hexameters, and holds that the shift to Greek quantitative rhythms minimized the importance of word accent in Latin verse except at the popular level, whence it emerged into literary poetry in the later Empire and in Christian hymnology. He concludes with a brief consideration of mediaeval Latin verse.

IX. PREDECESSORS AND INFLUENCE

A. VERGIL AND EARLIER WRITERS

There is no adequate short discussion for the student of Vergil's relation to his predecessors. However, the following suggestions may be helpful:

Mackail (see III B). (S)

Mackail's brief ch. III (pp. 22-28) on "Virgil's Predecessors" gives a general impression of his indebtedness to them but no specific detail.

Duff (see III B). (S)

Duff's book is to be recommended for its outstanding consideration of Latin writers and its presentation of the development of Latin literature.

Duff accomplishes this task by emphasis on significant works of literature and by comparisons of individual writers. The introduction to each chapter, in which the writer is placed in his political, social, and literary setting, is an additional positive feature. The book, one of the foremost literary histories of Rome, is essential for every high school library.

Knight (see IV C). (T)

Knight emphasizes Vergil's ability to integrate, i.e. his use of poetic devices, of traditions, and of legends in a novel way to create a peculiarly individual and fresh work. The author gives many illustrations of Vergil's adaptations, derivations, etc. from his Greek and Roman predecessors: Homer, Apollonius, Ennius, Catullus. He stresses Vergil's choice of forms and expressions on the basis of their imaginative value. Though the book is heavy reading, it is valuable for insight into Vergil's relation to his predecessors.

Otis (see VII). (T)

The *Aeneid*, like Vergil's other works, is a combination of inheritance and the poet's own contribution. Yet Otis feels that the neoteric and Hellenistic heritage was small. He acknowledges that Vergil used Homer; i.e., Homer gave him form, something of style, and a great deal of content. But the essential ideal, the Augustan theme, and its presentation belong to Vergil's creativity alone. This thesis, which attributes true originality to the poet, is in disagreement with most Vergilian critics, especially Knight.

Prescott (see III B). (T)

Prescott says in his preface that he hopes to show the "development of Latin poetry and Vergil's relation to earlier epic" with the intention of revealing Vergil's artistic aims, principles, and originality. Prescott succeeds fully in achieving this aim. An opening chapter (pp. 1-17) on "Literary Heritage" analyzes the different theories and ideas of Greek and Latin writers of epic preceding Vergil and presents a perceptive view of the development of Latin poetry in the first century B.C. In a later chapter (pp. 169-245) on "The Epic Tradition," the author discusses Vergil's debt to Homer and the Hellenistic writers in content and style. In both chapters, he indicates Vergil's dependence on these various models, his variation from them, and hence his creativity.

B. VERGIL'S LATER INFLUENCE

The influence of Vergil's epic was felt in Rome immediately, e.g. by Ovid in his *Heroides* and *Metamorphoses.* The *Aeneid* set the standard towards which later Latin epic writers strove without success. The influence continued during the Middle Ages and on modern western vernacular literature. Consideration thereof will therefore enable the teacher to relate the study of the *Aeneid* to work being done by students in English and other modern languages. It is, however, difficult to suggest accessible books on this subject.

Mackail (see III B). (S)

The Series *Our Debt to Greece and Rome* (republished by Cooper Square Publishers, New York) was intended to show the influence of classical authors and disciplines on modern literature; Mackail, however, devotes specifically to this only ch. XI (pp. 120-141): "Mediaeval and Modern World."

Highet, Gilbert. *The Classical Tradition: Greek and Roman Influences on Western Literature.* Oxford University Press (Galaxy GB5), 1949. Pp. 763. $2.95 (pb). Also cloth, $10.00. (T)

Since the treatment here is by periods rather than by authors, it is necessary to consult the index under "Vergil" for references to discussions of his influence. While these are not in themselves detailed or profound, the notes afford useful bibliographical guidance to fuller discussions.

Eliot, T(homas) S(terns). "What is a Classic?," pp. 52-74, and "Virgil and the Christian World," pp. 135-148, of *On Poetry and Poets.* New York: Farrar, Straus & Giroux (Noonday Press 214), 1961 (and later reprints). Pp. 308. $1.95 (pb). From cloth ed., 1957, $4.50. (S)

The first essay, a Presidential Address in 1944 to the Virgil Society of England (publ. Faber & Faber, 1945), establishes the *Aeneid* as a classic against whose characteristics may be measured the strengths and weaknesses of classics in later western literatures. The second, a B.B.C. broadcast of 1951 publ. in *The Listener,* first discusses the Fourth *Eclogue* as interpreted by the Christians as a Messianic prophecy and then treats the general characteristics which recommended Vergil, and particularly the *Aeneid,* to Christian thought.

Bowra, C(ecil) M(aurice). *From Virgil to Milton.* New York: St. Martin's (& London: Macmillan), 1945 (and later reprints). Pp. 247. (Papermac 24), $2.95 (pb). Also in cloth $5.00. (T)

The first chapter attempts to define "What is an Epic?" The second (pp. 33-85) discusses "Virgil and the Ideal of Rome." Three further chapters treat the Portuguese Camoes, the Italian Tasso, and the English Milton. Thus this study places Vergil in the tradition of the great epics of western Europe.

For more general books:

Thomson, J(ames) A(lexander). Three of his books have been republished by Collier (now affiliated with Macmillan, New York) as pbs. at $0.95 each. All were first published by Allen & Unwin, London: *The Classical Background of English Literature.* 1948. Pp. 272. *Classical Influences on English Poetry.* 1951. Pp. 271. *Classical Influences on English Prose.* 1956. Pp. 303.

X. MYTHOLOGY

Of the great number of books available on mythology such as the older Bulfinch, *Mythology* (pb) and Graves, *Greek Myths* (in 2 vols.), the following are selected for the indicated reasons.

Hamilton, Edith. *Mythology.* New York: New American Library (Mentor MP520), 1963. Pp. 335. $0.60 (pb); also available in cloth from Little Brown Co., Boston, 1942. $5.95; and Grossett and Dunlop, New York (University Library UL93), 1963, $1.95. (pb) (S)

Hamilton's account of mythology has become a standard text in high schools. It contains a brief account of the major myths in a clear style, adapted for grades 7-9 and allowing any student to comprehend them easily. The arrangement is orderly, based on the importance or rank of the gods. However, although Miss Hamilton's book elucidates the myths in the *Aeneid,* it is not stimulating and is too elementary to challenge the able high school student.

Macpherson, Jay. *Four Ages of Man: the Classical Myths.* New York: St. Martin's Press, 1962. Pp. 205; ill., maps. $4.50. Special school edition of text only, $1.25. (S)

This gives a full, well-integrated coverage of the numerous myths. They are admirably arranged in a logical sequence which reflects their chronological development and which is divided into four major phases: the creation and coming of the gods; pastoral life and ordering of the seasons; the adventures and labors of the heroes; war, tragic tales, and transition to historical events. Furthermore, the author discusses in the introduction the different interpretations of myths. The book also has a modern, interesting style which will keep the reader deeply engrossed. An outstanding feature for the study of Vergil is the author's inclusion of the complete story of Troy. By interweaving its various major and minor parts, the author provides a short, but good background for the *Aeneid.* In addition, the literary sources of the myths, both Greek and Latin, are provided in the notes. A descriptive and pronouncing index, family trees, a mythology-history chart as well as fine illustrations of the gods further enhance the usefulness of this book.

Rose, Herbert Jennings. *A Handbook of Greek Mythology including its Extension to Rome.* New York: E. P. Dutton (D41), 1959; (reprint of ed. 6, 1958, from ed. 1, 1928). Pp. 363. $1.55 (pb). Also cloth, $6.95. (S)

A comprehensive and systematic account of Greek myths with informative interpretations. In his discussion of the different versions of the Trojan War, both in the *Iliad* and for what is known of the post-Homeric accounts, Rose describes the role of Aeneas in the War. He also summarizes the connection of the Trojan myth and Aeneas with the founding of Rome. He carries the Roman legendary period through Romulus and concludes with a treatment of the Italic gods and their gradual assimilation to the Greek gods and cults. There are thorough notes at the end of each chapter and a full bibliography. Rose provides sufficient material for three levels of readers: student, teacher, and scholar; thus his book is most suitable for school use. Unfortunately, his style is at times prosaic and heavy.

XI. ATLASES

Grundy, G. B., ed. *Murray's Classical Atlas for Schools* (also entitled *Small Classical Atlas).* London: John Murray, 1954. (Reprint of ed. 2, 1917, from ed. 1, 1904). Available (as *Small Class. Atlas)* from Dufour Editions Inc., Chester Springs, Pa. 29425, $6.00. (S)

Index of places is followed by 14 maps in color, many of which are 2 pages in folio. The best available larger atlas in English.

Scullard, H. H., & Van der Hayden, A. A. M., eds. *Atlas of the Classical World*. London & New York: Nelson, 1960. Pp. 222. $18.00. (S)

This book combines the cultural history of Greece and Rome with many photographs and maps. Students may find the text and beautiful illustrations exciting. The essays are also good. Nelson likewise publishes a less adequate abbreviation: *Shorter Atlas of the Classical World* (1962. Pp. 239. $3.95), which is also available in paperback, New York: Dutton (D195), $2.95. (S)

Thomson, J. Oliver. *Everyman's Classical Atlas*. New York: E. P. Dutton & Co., 1961. Pp. 125; ill. $5.00. (S)

The introduction contains an essay on the development of ancient geographical knowledge and theory, and notes on some battlefields. There are sketch maps, maps in color, an index and 32 photographs. This is an excellent atlas for individual use, though the maps are small.

XII. WORKS OF REFERENCE

Among older classical dictionaries, those by William Smith in various editions and forms are still useful, particularly for mythology but also for history and geography. Many older school libraries will contain a copy. The Nettleship-Sandys translation of Seyffert's *Dictionary of Classical Antiquities* (1891) does not give complete coverage. The three following classical dictionaries are in print:

Harper's Dictionary of Classical Literature and Antiquities (ed. Peck, Harry T.). New York: Cooper Square Publishers, 1963 (reprint of the standard 1896 ed.). Pp. 1700. $25.00; special price for schools and libraries, $19.95. (S)

1500 illustrations and over 10,000 entries.

New Century Classical Handbook (ed. Avery, Catherine B.). New York: Appleton-Century-Crofts, Inc., 1962. Pp. 1162. $17.95. (S)

6000 entries in alphabetical order. This dictionary is modern and up-to-date; briefer than the following one, but useful, especially for mythology.

Oxford Classical Dictionary (ed. Cary, M., and others). Oxford: Clarendon Press, 1949. Pp. 971. $14.50. (S)

This is the most scholarly, moderate-sized dictionary in English. It is particularly good on history, literature, and antiquities, less so on mythology. A thoroughly revised second ed. is in press as of spring, 1967.

The following miscellaneous reference books may be mentioned for their value to both students and teachers:

Harvey, Paul. *The Oxford Companion to Classical Literature*. London: Oxford University Press, 1959 (revised from ed. 1, 1937). Pp. 468; 6 plates, 7 maps. $4.50. (S)

Information on the literatures of Greece and Rome and their influence on modern European literature.

Sandys, (Sir) J. E. *A Companion to Latin Studies*. New York: Hafner, 1963 (reprint of ed. 3, 1921, Cambridge Univ. Press; reprinted in 1935). Pp. 879. $17.50. (S)

These short discussions by scholars on various aspects of Latin studies, though now old, are still helpful for interested students.

Wetmore, Monroe Nichols. *Index Verborum Vergilianus*. Reprint by Hildesheim; Georg Olms, (and Darmstadt: Wissenschaftliche Buchgesellschaft), 1961 (from ed. 2: New Haven: Yale Univ. Press, 1930; reprint of ed. 1, 1911). Pp. 554. DM 62 (about $15.50). (T)

A complete word index both to the generally accepted works of Vergil *(Eclogues, Georgics,* and *Aeneid)* and to the *Appendix Vergiliana* (see III A). This index provides guidance for the close textual study of the poems and a means of identifying passages. Thus it aids in effective teaching.

XIII. BIBLIOGRAPHY

If a more extensive study of the poem is desired or necessary, of excellent bibliographies which include additional books the following will be found helpful:

Duckworth, George E. *Recent Work on Vergil: A Bibliographical Survey, 1940-1956* (reprint from *Classical World,* vol. 51 [1958], and *Recent Work on Vergil, 1957-1963* (reprint from *Classical World,* vol. 57 [Feb. 1964]). (T)

The Vergilian Society has reprinted these two very thorough bibliographies on works on Vergil for the years 1940-1963, originally published in *Classical World.* Teachers and students interested in pursuing works on specific topics or the individual poems will find useful leads in these. Copies may be purchased for $0.75 each ($0.50 for members of the Vergilian Society; see XIV), either from the Editorial Office, *Classical World,* Rutgers, The State University, Newark, N.J. 07102; or from Mr. Howard T. Easton, Secretary, The Vergilian Society, 12 Pleasant View Dr., Exeter, N.H. 03833.

Glover, T. R. "The Literature of the Augustan Age." Ch. XVI of the *Cambridge Ancient History,* vol. X. New York: Cambridge Univ. Press, 1954. $17.50. (T)

Bibliography for Vergil on pp. 955-956.

Lind (see II C). (S)

This translation contains a good "Reading List for Vergil" (pp. 268-270). (S)

Commager (see VII). (S)

Brief bibliography on pp. 185-186.

Nairn, J. A. *Classical Hand-List.* Oxford: Blackwell, ed. 3, 1953 (revised and enlarged from ed. 2). Pp. 164. Reprinted, 1960. (T)

Vergil bibliography on pp. 69-71; history of Latin literature on pp. 75-77.

Histories of classical literature, such as Duff

and Rose, contain recommendations of books, as do school texts and the various more complete editions.

XIV. THE VERGILIAN SOCIETY

The Vergilian Society is open for membership both to Latin teachers and to others interested in classical studies. While its main emphasis is on the study of Vergil, it also aims to encourage the general study of the classics both in schools and in other areas of education. To further this aim, the Society has various activities. Notably, it publishes an annual magazine, *Vergilius*, which contains scholarly articles, and reports and notices of interest to members of the Society. The current copy is free each year for members; additional copies and back issues are $0.50 for members and $0.75 for non-members. They may be purchased with prepayment through the Secretary. The Society also conducts a series of four two-week summer sessions for teachers and students at its Villa Vergiliana in Cumae, near Naples. These include lectures and visits to Campanian sites and museums. A six weeks tour of the Naples area, Sicily, and Rome and its environs is also a major part of the summer program. Scholarship help is available for these sessions. Annual membership dues for 1966-67 are $2.00, but after October 1967, dues will be raised to $3.50. To apply for membership or to obtain further information, enquiries may be addressed to Mr. Howard T. Easton, 12 Pleasant View Drive, Exeter, N.H., 03833.

XV. GENERAL INFORMATION

A. *CLASSICAL WORLD*

Classical World publishes an annual list of "Textbooks in Greek and Latin" and a list of "Inexpensive Books for Teaching the Classics." — It also compiles a list of "Audio-Visual Materials for the Teaching of the Classics." The magazine should be consulted for these helpful lists as well as for its book reviews.

B. *AMERICAN CLASSICAL LEAGUE*

The American Classical League, Miami University, Oxford, Ohio, is primarily concerned with aids to teachers. Its Service Bureau publishes a list of visual aids for teaching Latin. The list may be obtained free of charge by writing the League, while the aids suggested may be purchased at a minimal cost. Furthermore, the League publishes a periodical, the *Classical Outlook*, which includes items of current interest.

C. *FOLKWAYS RECORDS*

This record company has produced a series of records with readings from Greek and Latin writers. On record #FL9969, entitled "Selections from Vergil," John F. C. Richards reads the *Aeneid*, Books I, II, IV, and VI in Latin. There is an accompanying Latin text and English translation. The cost is $5.95. For purchase of the record or more information, write Folkways Records, 121 West 47 St., New York, N.Y. 10036.